Andrew Kippis

A Narrative of the Voyages Round the World

Performed by Captain James Cook, with an account of his life during the previous

and intervening periods

Andrew Kippis

A Narrative of the Voyages Round the World
Performed by Captain James Cook, with an account of his life during the previous and intervening periods

ISBN/EAN: 9783744775069

Printed in Europe, USA, Canada, Australia, Japan

Cover: Foto ©Andreas Hilbeck / pixelio.de

More available books at **www.hansebooks.com**

A NARRATIVE

OF THE

VOYAGES ROUND THE WORLD

PERFORMED BY

CAPTAIN JAMES COOK.

WITH AN

ACCOUNT OF HIS LIFE

DURING THE PREVIOUS AND INTERVENING PERIODS.

BY A. KIPPIS, D.D., F.R.S. AND S.A

COMPLETE IN ONE VOLUME.

NEW YORK:
DERBY & JACKSON.
1860.

W. H. Tinson, Stereotyper. Geo. Russell, & Co., Printers.

PREFACE.

ALTHOUGH I have often appeared before the public as a writer, I never did it with so much diffidence and anxiety as on the present occasion. This arises from the peculiar nature of the work in which I have now engaged. A Narrative of the Life and Actions of Captain Cook must principally consist of the voyages and discoveries he has made, and the difficulties and dangers to which he was exposed. The private incidents concerning him, though collected with the utmost diligence, can never compare, either in number or importance, with his public transactions. His public transactions are the things that mark the man, that display his mind and his character; and therefore, they are grand objects to which the attention of his biographer must be directed. However, the right conduct of this business is a point of no small difficulty and embarrassment. The question will frequently arise, How far the detail should be extended? There is a danger, on the one hand, of being carried to an undue length, and of enlarging, more than is needful, on facts which may be though already sufficiently known; and, on the other hand, of giving such a jejune account, and such a slight enumeration of important events, as shall disappoint the wishes and expectations of the reader. Of the two extremes, the last seems to be that which should most be avoided; for unless what Captain Cook performed, and what he encountered, be related somewhat at large, his Life and Actions would be imperfectly represented to the world. The proper medium appears to be, to bring forward the things in which he was personally concerned, and to pass slightly over other matters. Even here it is scarcely possible, nor would it be desirable, to avoid the introduction of **some of the** most striking circumstances which relate **to the new countries and** inhabitants **that were** visited by **our great navigator, since these constitute a part of the** knowledge and benefit derived from his undertakings. **Whether I have been so happy as to** preserve the due medium, I presume not to determine. I have been anxious to do it, without always being able fully to satisfy my own mind that I have succeeded; on which account I shall not be surprised if different opinions should be formed on the subject. In that case, all that I can offer in my own defence will be, that I have acted to the best of my judgment. At any rate, I flatter myself with the hope of having presented to the public a work not wholly uninteresting or unentertaining. Those who are best acquainted with Captain Cook's expeditions, may be pleased with reviewing them in a more compendious form, and with having his actions placed in a closer point of view, in consequence of their being divested of the minute nautical, and other details, which were essentially necessary in the voyages at large. As to those persons, if there be any, who have hitherto obtained but an imperfect knowledge of what was done and discovered by this illustrious man, they will not be offended with the length of the following narrative.

In various respects, new information will be found in the present performance; and other things, which were less perfectly known before, are set in a clearer, and fuller light. This, I trust, will appear in the first, third, fifth, and seventh chapters. It may be observed, likewise, that the fresh matter now communicated is of the most authentic kind, and derived from the most respectable sources. My obligations of this nature are, indeed, very great, and call for my warmest gratitude. The dates and facts relative to Captain Cook's different promotions are taken from the books of the Admiralty, by the direction of the noble lord who is at the head of that Board, and the favour of Mr. Stephens. I embrace with pleasure this opportunity of mentioning that, in the course of my life, I have experienced, in several instances, Lord Howe's condescending and favourable attention. To Mr. Stephens I am indebted for other communications besides those which concern the times of Captain Cook's preferments, and for his general readiness in forwarding the design of the present work. The Earl of Sandwich, the great patron of our navigator, and the principal mover in his mighty undertakings, has honoured me with some important information concerning him, especially with regard to the circumstances which preceded his last voyage. To Sir Hugh Palliser's zeal for the memory of his friend, I stand particularly obliged. From a long communication, with which he was so good as to favour me, I have derived very material intelligence, as will appear in the course of the narrative, and especially in the first chapter. In the same chapter are some facts which I received from Admiral Graves, through the hands of the Rev. Dr. Douglas, now Bishop of Carlisle, (whose admirable Introduction to the Voyage to the Pacific Ocean must be of the most essential service to every writer of the Life of Captain Cook.) The Captain's amiable and worthy Widow, who is held in just esteem by all his friends, has given me an account of several domestic circumstances. I should be deficient in gratitude, were I here to omit the name of Mr. Samwell: for, though what is inserted from him in this work has already been laid before the public, it should be remembered, that through the interposition of our common friend, the Rev. Mr. Gregory, it was originally written for my use, and freely consigned to my disposal; and that it **was** at my particular instance and request that it was separately printed. My obligations to other gentlemen will be mentioned in their proper places.

But my acknowledgments are, above all, due to Sir Joseph Banks, President of the Royal Society, for the interest he has taken in the present publication. It was in consequence of his advice, that it was given to the world in the form which it now bears; and his assistance has been invariable through every part of the undertaking. To him the inspection of the whole has been submitted; and to him it is owing, that the work is, in many respects, far more complete than it would otherwise have been. The exertions of zeal and friendship I have been so happy as to experience from him in writing the account of Captain Cook, have corresponded with that ardour which Sir Joseph Banks is always ready to display in promoting whatever he judges to **be subservient to the cause of science and literature.**

CONTENTS.

CHAPTER I.
Account of Captain Cook previous to his First Voyage round the World, ... 9

CHAPTER II.
Narrative of Captain Cook's First Voyage round the World, during the years 1768, 1769, 1770 and 1771, ... 17

CHAPTER III.
Account of Captain Cook during the period between his First and Second Voyage, ... 152

CHAPTER IV.
Narrative of Captain Cook's Second Voyage round the World, during the years 1772, 1773, 1774 and 1775, ... 158

CHAPTER V.
Account of Captain Cook during the period between his Second and Third Voyage, ... 257

CHAPTER VI.
Narrative of Captain Cook's Third Voyage, to the period of his Death, during the years 1776, 1777, 1778 and 1779, ... 272

CHAPTER VII.
Character of Captain Cook—Effects of his Voyages—Testimonies of Applause—Commemorations of his Services—Regard paid to his family—Conclusion, ... 394

THE
AUTHENTIC AND COMPLETE NARRATIVE
OF
CAPT. COOK'S VOYAGES ROUND THE WORLD.

CHAPTER I.

ACCOUNT OF CAPTAIN COOK, PREVIOUS TO HIS FIRST VOYAGE ROUND THE WORLD.

CAPTAIN JAMES COOK had no claims to distinction on account of the lustre of his birth, or the dignity of his ancestors. His father, James Cook, who, from his dialect, is supposed to have been a Northumbrian, was in the humble station of a servant in husbandry, and married a woman of the same rank with himself, whose christian name was Grace. Both of them were noted in their neighbourhood for their honesty, sobriety, and diligence. They first lived at a village called Morton, and then removed to Marton, another village in the North-riding of Yorkshire, situated in the high road from Gisborough, in Cleveland, to Stockton upon Tees, in the county of Durham, at the distance of six miles from each of these towns. At Marton, Captain Cook was born, on the 27th of October, 1728 ;* and agreeably to the custom of

---
* The mud house in which Captain Cook drew his first breath is pulled down, and no vestiges of it are now remaining.

the vicar of the parish, whose practice it was to baptize infants soon after their birth, he was baptized on the 3d of November following. He was one of nine children, all of whom are now dead, excepting a daughter, who married a fisherman at Redcar. The first rudiments of young Cook's education were received by him at Marton, where he was taught to read by Dame Walker, the schoolmistress of the village. When he was eight years of age, his father, in consequence of the character he had obtained for industry, frugality, and skill in husbandry, had a little promotion bestowed upon him, which was that of being appointed head servant or hind,* to a farm belonging to the late Thomas Skottow, Esq., called Airy Holme, near Great Ayton. To this place, therefore, he removed with his family;† and his son James, at Mr. Skottow's expense, was put to a day-school, in Ayton, where he was instructed in writing, and in a few of the first rules of arithmetic.

Before he was thirteen years of age, he was bound an apprentice to Mr. William Sanderson, a haberdasher, or shop-keeper, at Straiths, a considerable fishing town, about ten miles north of Whitby. This employment, however, was very unsuitable to young Cook's disposition. The sea was the object of his inclination; and his passion for it could not avoid being strengthened by the situation of the town in which he was placed; and the manner of life of the persons with whom he must frequently converse. Some disagreement having happened between him and his master, he obtained his discharge, and soon after bound himself for seven years to Messrs. John and Henry Walker, of Whitby, Quakers by religious profession, and principal owners of the ship Free-love, and of another vessel, both of which were constantly employed in the coal trade. The greatest part of his ap-

---

* This is the name which, in that part of the country, is giving to the head servant, or bailiff of a farm.

† Mr. Cook, senior, spent the close of his life with his daughter, at Redcar, and is supposed to have been about eighty-five years of age when he died.

prenticeship was spent on board the Free-love. After he was out of his time, he continued to serve in the coal and other branches of trade (though chiefly in the former) in the capacity of a common sailor, till at length, he was raised to be mate of one of Mr. John Walker's ships. During this period it is not recollected that he exhibited anything very peculiar, either in his abilities or his conduct; though there can be no doubt but that he had gained a considerable degree of knowledge in the practical part of navigation, and that his attentive and sagacious mind was laying up a store of observations, which would be useful to him in future life.

In the spring of the year 1755, when hostilities broke out between England and France, and there was a hot press for seamen, Mr. Cook happened to be in the river Thames with the ship to which he belonged. At first he concealed himself to avoid being pressed; but reflecting that it might be difficult, notwithstanding all his vigilance, to elude discovery or escape pursuit, he determined, upon further consideration, to enter voluntarily into his majesty's service, and to take his future fortune in the royal navy. Perhaps he had some presage in his own mind, that by his activity and exertions he might rise considerably above his present situation. Accordingly he went on to a rendezvous at Wapping, and entered with an officer of the Eagle man of war, a ship of sixty guns, at that time commanded by Captain Hamer. To this ship Captain (afterwards Sir Hugh) Palliser was appointed, in the month of October, 1755; and when he took the command, found in her James Cook, whom he soon distinguished to be an able, active, and diligent seaman. All the officers spoke highly in his favor, and the captain was so well pleased with his behaviour, that he gave him every encouragement which lay in his power.

In the course of some time Captain Palliser received a letter from Mr. Osbaldeston, then member of Parliament for Scarborough, acquainting him that several neighbours of his had solicited him to write in favour of one Cook, on board the captain's ship. They had heard that Captain Palliser had taken notice of him, and they requested, if he thought Cook deserving of it, that he would point out in what manner Mr. Osbaldeston might best contribute his assistance towards forwarding the young man's promotion. The captain, in his reply, did justice to Cook's merit; but, as he had been only a short time in the navy, informed Mr. Osbaldeston that he could not be promoted as a commission officer. A master's warrant, Captain Palliser added, might perhaps be procured for Mr. Cook, by which he would be raised to a station that he was well qualified to discharge with ability and credit.

Such a warrant he obtained on the 10th of May, 1759, for the Grampus sloop; but the proper master having unexpectedly returned to her, the appointment did not take place. Four days after, he was made master of the Garland; when upon inquiry it was found that he could not join her, as the ship had already sailed. On the next day, the 15th of May, he was appointed to the Mercury. These quick and successive appointments show that his interest was strong, and that the intention to serve him was real and effectual.

The destination of the Mercury was to North America, where she joined the fleet under the command of Sir Charles Saunders, which, in conjunction with the land forces under General Wolfe, was engaged in the famous siege of Quebec. During that siege a difficult and dangerous service was necessary to be performed. This was to take the soundings in the channel of the river St. Lawrence, between the island of Orleans and the north shore, directly in the front of the French fortified camp at Montmorency and Beauport, in order to enable the admiral to place ships against the enemy's batteries, and to cover our army on a general attack, which the heroic Wolfe intended to make on the camp. Captain Palliser, in consequence of his acquaintance with Mr. Cook's sagacity and resolution, recommended him to the service; and he performed it in the most complete manner. In this business he was employed during the night-time for several nights together. At length he was discovered by the enemy, who collected a great number of Indians and canoes, in a wood near the water-side, which were launched in the night for the purpose of surrounding him, and cutting him off. On this occasion he had a very narrow escape. He was obliged to run for it, and pushed on shore on the island of Orleans, near the guard of the English hospital. Some of the Indians entered at the stern of the boat as Mr. Cook leaped out at the bow; and the boat, which was a barge belonging to one of the ships of war, was carried away in triumph. However, he furnished the admiral with as correct and complete a draft of the channel and soundings as could have been made after our countrymen were in possession of Quebec. Sir Hugh Palliser has good reason to believe that before this time Mr. Cook had scarcely ever used a pencil, and that he knew nothing of drawing. But such was his capacity that he speedily made himself master of every object to which he applied his attention.

Another important service was performed by Mr. Cook while the fleet continued in the river of St. Lawrence. The navigation of that river is exceedingly difficult and hazardous. It was particularly so to the English, who were then in a great measure strangers to this part of North America, and who had no chart, on the correctness of which they could depend. It was, therefore, ordered by the admiral, that Mr. Cook should be employed to survey those parts of the river, below Quebec, which navigators had experienced to be attended with peculiar difficulty and danger; and he executed the business with the same diligence and skill of which he had already afforded so happy a specimen. When he had finished the undertaking, his chart of the river St. Lawrence was published, with soundings and directions for sailing in that river. Of the accuracy and utility of this chart, it is sufficient to say, that it hath never since been found necessary to publish any other. One which has appeared in France, is only a copy of our author's on a reduced scale.

After the expedition to Quebec, Mr. Cook, by warrant from Lord Colvill, was appointed, on the 22d of September, 1759, master of the Northumberland man of war, the ship in which his lordship staid, in the following winter, as commodore, with the command of a squadron at Halifax. In this station Mr. Cook's behaviour did not fail to gain him the esteem and friendship of his commander. During the leisure which the season of winter afforded him, he employed his time in the acquisition of such knowledge as eminently qualified him for the future service. It was at Halifax that he first read Euclid, and applied himself to the study of astronomy and other branches of science. The books of which he had the assistance were few in number: but his industry enabled him to supply many defects, and to make a progress far superior to what could be expected from the advantages he enjoyed.

While Mr. Cook was master of the Northumberland under Lord Colvill, that ship came to Newfoundland, in September, 1762, to assist in the recapture of the island from the French, by the forces under the command of Lieutenant-colonel Amherst. When the island was recovered, the English fleet staid some days at Placentia, in order to put it in a more complete state of defence. During this time Mr. Cook manifested a diligence in surveying the harbor and heights of the place, which arrested the notice of Captain (now Admiral) Graves, commander of the Antelope, and governor of Newfoundland. The governor was hence induced to ask Cook a variety of questions, from the answers to which he was led to entertain a very favourable opinion of his abilities. This opinion was increased, the more he saw of Mr. Cook's conduct; who, wherever they went, continued to display the most unremitting attention to every object that related to the knowledge of the coast, and was calculated to facilitate the practice of navigation. The esteem which Captain

Graves had conceived for him, was confirmed by the testimonies to his character, that were given by all the officers under whom he served.

In the latter end of 1762, Mr. Cook returned to England; and, on 21st of December, in the same year, married, at Barking, in Essex, Miss Elizabeth Batts, an amiable and deserving woman, who was justly entitled to and enjoyed his tenderest regard and affection. But his station in life, and the high duties to which he was called, did not permit him to partake of matrimonial felicity, without many and very long interruptions.

Early in the year 1763, after the peace with France and Spain was concluded, it was determined that Captain Graves should go out again, as governor of Newfoundland. As the country was **very** valuable in a commercial view, and had been an object of great contention between the English and the French, the captain obtained an establishment for the survey of its coasts; which, however, he procured with some difficulty, because the matter was not sufficiently understood by Government at home. In considering the execution of the plan, Mr. Cook appeared to Captain Graves to be a proper person for the purpose; and proposals were made to him, to which, notwithstanding his recent marriage, he readily and prudently acceded. Accordingly, he went out with the captain as surveyor; and was first employed to survey Miquelon and St. Pierre, which had been ceded by the treaty to the French; who, by order of administration, were to take possession of them at a certain period, even though the English commander should not happen to be arrived in the country. When Captain Graves had reached that part of world, he found there the governor, who had been sent from France, (Mons. D'Aujac,) with all the settlers and his own family, on board a frigate and some transports. It was contrived, however, to keep them in that disagreeable situation for a whole month, which was the time taken by Mr. Cook to complete his survey. When the business was finished, the French were put into possession of the two islands, and left in the quiet enjoyment of them, with every profession of civility.

At the end of the season Mr. Cook returned to England, but did not long continue at home. In the beginning of the year 1764, his old and constant friend and patron, Sir Hugh Palliser, was appointed governor and commodore of Newfoundland and Labrador; upon which occasion, he was glad to take Mr. Cook with him, in the same capacity that he had sustained under Captain Graves. Indeed, no man could have been found, who was better qualified for finishing the design which had been begun in the preceding year. The charts of the coasts, in that part of North America, were very erroneous; and it was highly necessary to the trade and navigation of his majesty's subjects, that new ones should be formed which would be more correct and useful. Accordingly, under the orders of Commodore Palliser, Mr. Cook was appointed on the 18th of April, 1764, marine surveyor of Newfoundland and Labrador; and he had a vessel, the Grenville schooner, to attend him for that purpose. How well he executed his commission, is know to every man acquainted with navigation. The charts, which he afterwards published of the different surveys he had made, reflected great credit on his abilities and character, and the utility of them is universally acknowledged. It is understood, that, so far as Newfoundland is concerned, they were of considerable service to the king's ministers in settling the terms of the last peace. Mr. Cook explored the inland parts of this island in a much completer manner than had ever been done before. By penetrating further into the middle of the country than any man had hitherto attempted, he discovered several large lakes, which are indicated upon the general chart. In these services, Mr. Cook appears to have been employed, with the intervals of occasionally returning to England for the winter season, till the year 1767, which was the last time that he went out upon his station of marine surveyor of Newfoundland. It must not be omitted, that while he occupied this post, he had an opportunity of exhibiting to the Royal Society a proof of his progress in the study of astronomy. A short paper was written by him, and inserted in the fifty-seventh volume of the Philosophical Transactions, entitled, "An Observation of an Eclipse of the Sun at the Island of Newfoundland, August 5, 1766, with the Longitude of the Place of Observation deduced from it." The observation was made at one of the Burgeo Islands, near Cape Ray, in latitude 47° 36' 19", on the southwest extremity of Newfoundland, Mr. Cook's paper having been communicated by Dr. Bevis to Mr. Witchell, the latter gentleman compared it with an observation at Oxford, by the Rev. Mr. Hornsby, on the same eclipse, and thence computed the difference of longitude respecting the places of observation, making due allowance for the effect of parallax, and the prolate spheroidal figure of the earth. It appears from the Transactions, that our navigator had already obtained the character of being an able mathematician.

CHAPTER II.

NARRATIVE OF CAPTAIN COOK'S FIRST VOYAGE AROUND THE WORLD.

There is scarcely anything from which the natural curiosity of man receives a higher gratification, than from the accounts of distant countries and nations. Nor is it curiosity alone that is gratified by such accounts; for the sphere of human knowlege is hereby enlarged, and various objects are brought into view, an acquaintance with which greatly contributes to the improvement of life and the benefit of the world. With regard to information of this kind, the moderns have eminently the advantage over the ancients. The ancients could neither pursue their inquiries with the same accuracy, nor carry them on to the same extent. Travelling by land was much more inconvenient and dangerous than it hath been in later times; and, as navigation was principally confined to coasting, it must necessarily have been circumscribed within very narrow limits.

The invention of the compass, seconded by the ardent and enterprising spirit of several able men, was followed by wonderful discoveries. Vasco di Gamo doubled the cape of Good Hope; and a new way being thus found out to the East Indies, the countries in that part of the earth became more accurately and extensively known. Another world was discovered by Columbus; and, at length, Magalhaens accomplished the arduous and hitherto unattempted task of sailing round the globe. At different periods, he was succeeded by other circumnavigators, of whom it is no part of the present narrative to give an account.

The spirit of discovery, which was so vigorous during the latter end of the fifteenth, and through the whole of the sixteenth century, began, soon after the commencement of the seventeenth century, to decline. Great navigations were only occasionally undertaken, and more from the immediate views of avarice or war, than from any noble and generous principles. But of late years they have been revived, with the enlarged and benevolent design of promoting the happiness of the human species.

A beginning of this kind was made in the reign of George the Second, during which two voyages were performed; the first under the command of Captain Middleton, and the next under the direction of Captains Smith and More, in order to discover a north-west passage, through Hudson's Bay. It was reserved, however, for the glory of the present reign to carry the spirit of discovery to its height, and to conduct it on the noblest principles; not for the purpose of covetousness or ambition; nor to plunder or destroy the inhabitants of newly-explored countries;

but to improve their condition, to instruct them in the arts of life, and to extend the boundaries of science.

No sooner was peace restored in 1763, than these laudable designs engaged his majesty's patronage; and two voyages round the world had been undertaken, before Mr. Cook set out on his first command. The conductors of these voyages were the Captains Byron, Wallis, and Carteret,* by whom several discoveries were made, which contributed in no small degree to increase the knowledge of geography and navigation. Nevertheless, as the purpose for which they were sent out appears to have had a principal reference to a particular object in the South Atlantic, the direct track they were obliged to hold, on their way homeward by the East Indies, prevented them from doing so much as might otherwise have been expected towards giving the world a complete view of that immense expanse of ocean which the South Pacific comprehends.

Before Captain Wallis and Captain Carteret had returned to Great Britain, another voyage was resolved upon, for which the improvement of astronomical science afforded the immediate occasion. It having been calculated by astronomers, that a transit of Venus over the Sun's disk would happen in 1769, it was judged, that the best place for observing it would be in some part of the South Sea, either at the Marquesas, or at one of those islands which Tasman had called Amsterdam, Rotterdam, and Middleburg, and which are now better known under the appellation of the Friendly Islands. This being a matter of eminent consequence in astronomy, and which excited the attention of foreign nations as well as of our own, the affair was taken up by the Royal Society, with the zeal which has always been displayed by that learned body for the advancement of every

---

* The Captains Wallis and Carteret went out together upon the same expedition; but the vessels they commanded having actually parted company, they proceeded and returned by a different route. Hence their voyages are distinctly related by Dr. Hawkesworth.

branch of philosophical science. Accordingly, a long memorial was addressed to his majesty, dated February the 15th, 1768, representing the great importance of the object, together with the regard which had been paid to it by the principal courts of Europe; and entreating, among other things, that a vessel might be ordered, at the expense of government, for the conveyance of suitable persons, to make the observation of the transit of Venus, at one of the places before mentioned. This memorial having been laid before the king by the Earl of Shelburne, (now the Marquis of Lansdown), one of the principal secretaries of state, his majesty graciously signified his pleasure to the lords commissioners of the Admiralty, that they should provide a ship for carrying over such observers as the Royal Society should judge proper to send to the South Seas, and, on the 3d of April, Mr. Stephens informed the society that a bark had been taken up for the purpose.

The gentleman who had originally been fixed upon to take the direction of the expedition, was Alexander Dalrymple, Esq., an eminent member of the Royal Society, and who, besides possessing an accurate knowledge of astronomy, had distinguished himself by his inquiries into the geography of the Southern Oceans, and by the collections he had published of several voyages to those parts of the world. Mr. Dalrymple being sensible of the difficulty, or rather of the impossibility, of carrying a ship through unknown seas, the crew of which were not subject to the military discipline of his majesty's navy, he made it the condition of his going, that he should have a brevet commission as captain of the vessel, in the same manner as such a commission had been granted to Dr. Halley, in his voyage of discovery. To this demand, Sir Edward Hawke, who was then at the head of the Admiralty, and who possessed more of the spirit of his profession than either of education or science, absolutely refused to accede. He said at the board, that his conscience would not allow him to trust any **ship** of his majesty's to a person who had not regularly been bred a seaman. On being further pressed upon the subject, Sir Edward declared, that he would suffer his right hand to be cut off before he would sign any such commission. In this he was, in some degree, justified by the mutinous behaviour of Halley's crew, who refused to acknowledge the legal authority of their commander, and involved him in a dispute which was attended with pernicious consequences. Dr. Dalrymple, on the other hand, was equally steady in requiring a compliance, with the terms he had proposed. Such was the state of things when Mr. Stephens, secretary to the Admiralty, whose discrimination of the numerous characters with which by his station he is conversant, reflects as much credit on his understanding, as his upright and able conduct does on the office he has filled for so many years, and under so many administrations, with honour to himself and advantage to the public, observed to the board, that since Sir Edward Hawke, and Mr. Dalrymple were equally inflexible, no method remained but that of finding out another person capable of the service. He knew, he said, a Mr. Cook, who had been employed as marine surveyor of Newfoundland, who had been regularly educated in the navy, in which he was a master, and whom he judged to be fully qualified for the direction of the present undertaking. Mr. Stephens, at the same time, recommended it to the board, to take the opinion of Sir Hugh Palliser, who had lately been governor of Newfoundland, and was intimately acquainted with Cook's character. Sir Hugh rejoiced in the opportunity of serving his friend. He strengthened Mr. Stephens's recommendation to the utmost of his power; and added many things in Mr. Cook's favor, arising from the particular knowledge which he had of his abilities and merit. Accordingly, Mr. Cook was appointed to the command of the expedition by the lords of the Admiralty; and, on this occasion, he was promoted to the rank of a lieutenant in the royal navy; his commission bearing date on the 25th of May, 1768.

When the appointment had taken place, the first object was to provide a vessel adapted to the purposes of the voyage. This business was committed to Sir Hugh Palliser; who took Lieutenant Cook to his assistance, and they examined together a great number of the ships, which then lay in the river Thames. At length they fixed upon one of three hundred and seventy tons, to which was given the name of the Endeavour.

While preparations were making for Lieutenant Cook's expedition, Captain Wallis returned from his voyage round the world. The Earl of Morton, president of the Royal Society, had recommended it to this gentleman, on his going out, to fix upon a proper place for observing the transit of Venus. He kept, accordingly, the object in view; and having discovered, in the course of his enterprise, an island called by him George's Island, but which hath since been found to bear the name of Otaheite, he judged that Port Royal harbour in this, island, would afford an eligible situation for the purpose. Having, immediately on his return to England, signified his opinion to the Earl of Morton, the captain's idea was adopted by the society, and an answer conformable to it was sent to the commissioners of the Admiralty, who had applied for directions to what place the observers should be sent.

Mr. Charles Green, a gentleman who had long been assistant to Dr. Bradley at the royal observatory at Greenwich, was united with Lieutenant Cook in conducting the astronomical part of the voyage: and, soon after their appointment, they received ample instructions, from the council of the Royal Society, with regard to the method of carrying on their inquiries. The lieutenant was also accompanied by Joseph Banks, Esq., (now Sir Joseph Banks, Bart.) and Dr. Solander, who, in the prime of life, and the first of them at great expense to himself, quitted all the gratifications of polished society, and engaged in a very tedious, fatiguing, and hazardous navigation, with the laudable views of acquiring knowledge in general, of promoting natural knowledge in particular, and of contributing something to the improvement and the happiness of the rude inhabitants of the earth.

Though it was the principal, it was not the sole object of Lieutenant Cook's voyage, to observe the transit of Venus. A more accurate examination of the Pacific Ocean was committed to him, although in subserviency to his main design ; and, when his chief business was accomplished, he was directed to proceed in making further discoveries in the great Southern Seas.

The complement of Lieutenant Cook's ship consisted of eighty-four persons, besides the commander. Her victualling was for eighteen months ; and there were put on board of her, ten carriage and ten swivel guns, together with an ample store of ammunition and other necessaries.

On the 25th of May, 1768, Lieutenant Cook was appointed by the lords of the Admiralty to the command of the Endeavour, in consequence of which he went on board on the 27th, and took charge of the ship. She then lay in the basin in Deptford-yard, where she continued to lie till she was completely fitted for sea. On the 30th of July she sailed down the river, and on the 13th of August anchored in Plymouth Sound. The wind becoming fair on the 26th of that month, our navigators got under sail, and on the 13th of September anchored in Funchal Road, in the Island of Madeira.

While Lieutenant Cook and his company were in this island, they were treated with the utmost kindness and liberality by Mr. Cheap, the English consul there, and one of the most considerable merchants in the town of Funchal. He insisted upon their taking possession of his house, and furnished them with every possible accommodation during their stay at Madeira. They received, likewise, great marks of attention and civility from Dr. Thomas Heberden, the principal physician of the island, and brother to the excellent and learned Dr. William Heberden, of London. Dr. Thomas Heberden afforded all the assistance in his power to Mr. Banks and Dr. Solander, in their botanical inquiries.

It was not solely from the English that the lieutenant and his friends experienced a kind reception. The fathers of the Franciscan convent displayed a liberality of sentiment towards them which might not have been expected from Portuguese friars; and, in a visit which they paid to a convent of nuns, the ladies expressed a particular pleasure in seeing them. At this visit the good nuns gave an amusing proof of the progress they had made in the cultivation of their understandings. Having heard that there were great philosophers among the English gentlemen, they asked them a variety of questions; one of which was, when it would thunder; and another, whether a spring of fresh water, which was much wanted, was any where to be found within the walls of the convent. Eminent as our philosophers were, they were puzzled by these questions.

Lieutenant Cook, having laid in a fresh stock of beef, water, and wine, set sail from the island of Madeira, in the night of the 18th of September, and proceeded on his voyage. By the 7th of November, several articles of the ship's provisions began to fall short; for which reason, the lieutenant determined to put into Rio de Janeiro. This place he preferred to any other port in Brazil or to Falkland's Islands, because he could there be better supplied with what he wanted, and had no doubt of meeting with a friendly reception.

During the run between Madeira and Rio Janeiro, Lieutenant Cook and the gentlemen in the Endeavour, had an opportunity of determining a philosophical question. On the evening of the 29th of October, they observed that luminous appearance of the sea which hath so often been mentioned by navigators, and which has been ascribed to such a variety of causes. Flashes of light appeared to be emitted, exactly resembling those of lightning, though without being so considerable, and such was the frequency of them, that sometimes eight or ten were visible almost at the same moment. It was the opinion of Mr. Cook and the other gentlemen, that these flashes proceeded from some luminous animal; and their opinion was confirmed by experiment.

At Rio de Janeiro, in the port of which Lieutenant Cook came to an anchor on the 13th of November, he did not meet with the polite reception that, perhaps, he had too sanguinely expected. His stay was spent in continual altercations with the viceroy, who appeared not a little jealous of the designs of the English: nor were all the attempts of the lieutenant, to set the matter right, capable of producing any effect. The viceroy was by no means distinguished either by his knowledge or his love of science; and the grand object of Mr. Cook's expedition was quite beyond his comprehension. When he was told, that the English were bound to the southward, by the order of his Britannic majesty, to observe a transit of the planet Venus over the Sun, an astronomical phenomenon of great importance to navigation, he could form no other conception of the matter, than that it was the passing of the North Star through the South Pole.

During the whole of the contest with the viceroy, Lieutenant Cook behaved with equal spirit and discretion. A supply of water and other necessaries could not be refused him, and these were gotten on board by the 1st of December. On that day the lieutenant sent to the viceroy for a pilot to carry the Endeavour to sea; but the wind preventing the ship from getting out, she was obliged to continue some time longer in the harbour. A Spanish packet having arrived at Rio de Janeiro on the 2d of December, with despatches from Buenos Ayres for Spain, the commander, Don Antonia de Monte Negro y Valasco, offered, with great politeness, to convey the letters of the English to Europe. This favour Lieutenant Cook accepted, and gave Don Antonia a packet for the secretary of the Admiralty, containing copies of all the papers that had passed between himself and the viceroy. He left, also, duplicates with the viceroy, that he might forward them, if he thought proper, to Lisbon.

On the 5th of December, it being a dead calm, our navigators weighed anchor, and towed down the Bay; but, to their great astonishment, two shots were fired at them when they had gotten abreast of Santa Cruz, the principal fortification of the harbour. Lieutenant Cook immediately cast anchor, and sent to the fort to demand the reason of this conduct; the answer to which was, that the commandant had received no order from the viceroy to let the ship pass; and that, without **such an** order, no vessel was ever suffered to go below the fort. It now became necessary to send to the viceroy, to inquire why the order had not been given; and his behaviour appeared the more extraordinary, as notice had been transmitted to him of the departure of the English, and he had thought proper to write a polite letter to Mr. Cook, wishing him a good voyage. The lieutenant's messenger soon returned with the information that the order had been written several days, and that its not having been sent had arisen from some unaccountable negligence. It was not till the 7th of December that the Endeavour got under sail.

In the account which Lieutenant Cook has given of Rio de Janeiro, and the country round it, one circumstance is recorded, which cannot be otherwise than very painful to humanity. It is the horrid expense of life at which the gold mines are wrought. No less than forty thousand negroes are annually imported for this purpose, on the king of Portugal's account; and the English were credibly informed, that, in the year 1766, this number fell so short, that twenty thousand more were drafted from the town of Rio.

From Rio de Janeiro, Lieutenant Cook pursued his voyage, and, on the 14th of January, 1769, entered the Strait of Le Maire, at which time the tide drove the ship out with so much violence, and raised such a sea off Cape St. Diego, that she frequently pitched so that the bowsprit was under water. On the next day the lieutenant anchored ; first before a small cove, which was understood to be Port Maurice, and afterwards in the Bay of Good Success. While the Endeavour was in this station, happened the memorable adventure of Mr. Banks, Dr. Solander, Mr. Monkhouse the surgeon, and Mr. Green the astronomer, together with their attendants and servants, and two seamen, in ascending a mountain to search for plants. In this expedition, they were all of them exposed to the utmost extremity of danger and cold ; Dr. Solander was seized with a torpor which had nearly proved fatal to his life ; and two black servants actually died. When the gentlemen had, at length, on the second day of their adventure, gotten back to the ship, they congratulated each other on their safety, with a joy that can only be felt by those who have experienced equal perils ; and Mr. Cook was relieved from a very painful anxiety. It was a dreadful testimony of the severity of the climate, that this event took place when it was the midst of summer in that part of the world, and at the close of a day, the beginning of which was as mild and warm as the month of May usually is in England.

In the passage through the Strait of Le Maire, Lieutenant Cook and his ingenious associates had an opportunity of gaining a considerable degree of acquaintance with the inhabitants of the adjoining country. Here it was that they saw human nature in its lowest form. The natives appeared to be the most destitute and forlorn, as well as the most stupid, of the children of men. Their lives are spent in wandering about the dreary wastes that surround them ; and their dwellings are no other than wretched hovels of sticks and grass, which not only admit the wind, but the snow and the rain. They are almost naked ; and so devoid are they of every convenience which is furnished by the rudest art, that they have not so much as an implement to dress their food. Nevertheless, they seemed to have no wish for acquiring more than they possessed ; nor did any thing that was offered them by the English appear acceptable but beads, as an ornamental superfluity of life. A conclusion is hence drawn by Dr. Hawkesworth, that these people may be upon a level with ourselves, in respect to the happiness they enjoy. This, however, is a position which ought not hastily to be admitted. It is, indeed, a beautiful circumstance, in the order of Divine Providence, that the rudest inhabitants of the earth, and those who are situated in the most unfavourable climates, should not be sensible of their disadvantages. But still it must be allowed, that their happiness is greatly inferior, both in kind and degree, to that intellectual, social, and moral felicity, which is capable of being attained in a highly cultivated state of society.

In voyages to the South Pacific Ocean, the determination of the best passage from the Atlantic is a point of peculiar importance. It is well known what prodigious difficulties were experienced in this respect by former navigators. The doubling of of Cape Horn, in particular, was so much dreaded, that in the general opinion it was far more eligible to pass through the Strait of Magellan. Lieutenant Cook hath fully ascertained the erroneousness of this opinion. He was but three-and-thirty days in coming round the land of Terra del Fuego, from the east entrance of the Strait of Le Maire, till he had advanced about twelve degrees to the westward, and three and a half to the northward of the Strait of Magellan; and during this time, the ship scarcely received any damage. Whereas, if he had come in the Pacific Ocean by that passage, he would not have been able to accomplish it in less than three months; besides which, his people would have been fatigued, and the anchors, cables, sails, and rigging of the vessel much injured. By the course he pursued, none of these inconveniences were suffered. In short, Lieutenant Cook, by his own example in doubling Cape Horn, by his accurate ascertainment of the latitude and longitude of the places he came to, and by his instructions to future voyagers, performed the most essential services to this part of navigation.

It was on the 26th of January that the Endeavour took her departure from Cape Horn; and it appeared, that from that time to the 1st of March, during a run of six hundred and sixty leagues, there was no current which affected the ship. Hence it was highly probable that our navigators had been near no land of any considerable extent, currents being always found when land is not remote.

In the prosecution of Lieutenant Cook's voyage from Cape Horn to Otaheite, several islands were discovered; to which the names were given of Lagoon Island, Thrumb Cap, Bow Island, the Groups, Bird Island, and Chain Island. It appeared that most of these islands were inhabited; and the verdure, and groves of palm-trees, which were visible upon some of them, gave them the aspect of a terrestrial paradise to men who, excepting the dreary hills of Terra del Fuego, had seen nothing for a long time but sky and water.

On the 11th of April the Endeavour arrived in sight of Otaheite, and on the 13th she came to an anchor in Port Royal Bay, which is called *Matavia* by the natives. As the stay of the English in the island was not likely to be very short, and much depended on the manner in which traffic should be carried on with the inhabitants, Lieutenant Cook, with great good sense and humanity, drew up a set of regulations for the behaviour of his people, and gave it in command, that they should punctually be observed.*

---

* The rules were as follows: "1. To endeavour, by every fair means, to cultivate a **friendship with** the natives; and to treat them with all imaginable humanity. 2. A proper person or persons, will be appointed to trade with the natives for all manner of provisions, fruit and other productions of the earth; and no officer or seaman, or other person belonging to the ship, excepting such as are so appointed, shall trade, or offer to trade, for any sort of provisions, fruit, or other productions of the earth, unless they have leave so to do. 3. Every person employed on shore on any duty whatsoever, is strictly to attend to the same; and if by any neglect he loseth any of his arms, or working tools, or suffers them to be stolen, the full value thereof will be charged against his

One of the first things that occupied the lieutenant's attention, after his arrival at Otaheite, was to prepare for the execution of his grand commission. For this purpose, as, in an excursion to the westward, he had not found any more convenient harbour than that in which the Endeavour lay, he determined to go on shore and fix upon some spot, commanded by the guns of the ship, where he might throw up a small fort for defence, and get every thing ready for making the astronomical observation. Accordingly, he took a party of men, and landed; being accompanied by Mr. Banks, Dr. Solander, and Mr. Green. They soon fixed upon a place very proper for their design, and which was at a considerable distance from any habitation of the natives. While the gentlemen were marking out the ground which they intended to occupy, and seeing a small tent erected, that belonged to Mr. Banks, a great number of the people of the country gathered gradually around them, but with no hostile appearance; as there was not among the Indians a single weapon of any kind. Mr. Cook, however, intimated that none of them were to come within the line he had drawn, excepting one, who appeared to be a chief, and Owhaw, a native who had attached himself to the English, both in Captain Wallis's expedition and in the present voyage. The lieutenant endeavoured to make these two persons understand that the ground which had been marked out was only wanted to sleep upon for a certain number of nights, and that then it would be quitted. Whether his meaning was comprehended or not, he could not certainly determine; but the people behaved with a deference and respect that could scarcely have been expected, and which were highly

pay, according to the custom of the navy in such cases, and he shall receive such further punishment as the nature of the offence may deserve. 4. The same penalty will be inflicted on every person who is found to embezzle, trade, or offer to trade, with any part of the ship's stores, of what nature soever. 5. No sort of iron, or any thing that is made of iron, or any sort of cloth, or other useful or necessary articles, are to be given in exchange for any thing but provision

"J. Cook."

pleasing. They sat down without the circle, peaceably and uninterruptedly attending to the progress of the business, which was upwards of two hours in completing.

This matter being finished, and Mr. Cook having appointed thirteen marines and a petty officer to guard the tent, he and the gentlemen with him set out upon a little excursion into the woods of the country. They had not, however, gone far, before they were brought back by a very disagreeable event. One of the Indians, who remained about the tent after the lieutenant and his friends had left it, watched an opportunity of taking the sentry unawares, and snatched away his musket. Upon this, the petty officer who commanded the party, and who was a midshipman, ordered the marines to fire. With equal want of consideration, and, perhaps, with equal inhumanity, the men immediately discharged their pieces among the thickest of the flying crowd, who consisted of more than a hundred. It being observed that the thief did not fall, he was pursued, and shot dead. From subsequent information, it happily appeared, that none of the natives besides were either killed or wounded.

Lieutenant Cook, who was highly displeased with the conduct of the petty officer, used every method in his power to dispel the terrors and apprehensions of the Indians, but not immediately with effect. The next morning but few of the inhabitants were seen upon the beach, and not one of them came off to the ship. What added particularly to the regret of the English was, that even Owhaw, who had hitherto been so constant in his attachment, and who the day before had been remarkably active in endeavouring to renew the peace which had been broken, did not now make his appearance. In the evening, however, when the lieutenant went on shore with only a boat's crew and some of the gentlemen, between thirty and forty of the natives gathered around them, and trafficked with them, in a friendly manner, for cocoa-nuts and other fruit.

On the 17th, Mr. Cook and Mr. Green set **up a tent** on shore, and spent the night there, in order to observe an eclipse of the first satellite of Jupiter; but they met with a disappointment, in consequence of the weather becoming cloudy. The next day the lieutenant, with as many of his people as could possibly be spared from the ship, began to erect the fort. While the English were employed in this business, many of the Indians were so far from hindering, that they voluntarily assisted them, and with great alacrity brought the pickets and fascines from the wood where they had been cut. Indeed, so scrupulous had Mr. Cook been of invading their property, that every stake which was used was purchased, and not a tree was cut down till their consent had first been obtained.

On the 26th, the lieutenant mounted six swivel guns upon the fort; on which occasion he saw, with concern, that the natives were alarmed and terrified. Some fishermen, who lived upon the point, removed to a greater distance; and Owhaw informed the English, by signs, of his expectation that in four days they would fire their great guns.

The lieutenant, on the succeeding day, gave a striking proof of his regard for justice, and of his care to preserve the inhabitants from injury and violence, by the punishment he inflicted on the butcher of the Endeavour, who was accused of having threatened, or attempted the life of a woman that was the wife of Tubourai Tomaida, a chief remarkable for his attachment to our navigators. The butcher wanted to purchase of her a stone hatchet for a nail. To this bargain she absolutely refused to accede; upon which the fellow catched up the hatchet, and threw down the nail; threatening, at the same time, that if she made any resistance, he would cut her throat with a reaping hook which he had in his hand. The charge was so fully proved in the presence of Mr. Banks, and the butcher had so little to say in exculpation of himself, that not the least doubt remained of his guilt. The affair being reported by Mr. Banks to Lieutenant Cook, he took an opportunity when the chief and his women and others of the natives, were on board the ship, to call up the offender, and after recapitulating the accusation and the proof of it, to give orders for his immediate punishment. While the butcher was stripped, and tied up to the rigging, the Indians preserved a fixed attention, and waited for the event in silent suspense. But as soon as the first stroke was inflicted, such was the humanity of these people, that they interfered with great agitation, and earnestly entreated that the rest of the punishment might be remitted. To this, however, the lieutenant, for various reasons, could not grant his consent, and when they found that their intercessions were ineffectual, they manifested their compassion by tears.

On the first of May the observatory was set up, and the astronomical quadrant, together with some other instruments, was taken on shore. When, on the next morning, Mr. Cook and Mr. Green landed for the purpose of fixing the quadrant in a situation for use, to their inexpressible surprise and concern it **was** not to be found. It had been deposited in a tent reserved for the lieutenant's use, where no one had slept : it had never been taken out of the packing-case, and the whole was of considerable weight ; none of the other instruments were missing, and a sentinel had been posted the whole night within five yards of the tent. These circumstances induced a suspicion that the robbery might have been committed by some of our own people, who, having seen a deal box, and not knowing the contents, might imagine that it contained nails, or other articles for traffic with the natives. The most diligent search, therefore, **was** made, and a large reward was offered for the finding of the quadrant, but with no degree of success. In this exigency, Mr. Banks was of eminent service. As this gentleman had more influence over the Indians than any other person on board the Endeavour, and as there could now be little doubt of the quadrant's having been conveyed away by some of the natives, he determined to go in search of it into the woods : and it was recovered in consequence of his judicious and spirited exertions. The pleasure with which it was brought back was equal to the importance of the event; for the grand object of the voyage could not otherwise have been accomplished.

Another embarrassment, though not of so serious a nature, was occasioned on the very same day, by one of our officers having inadvertently taken into custody Tootahah, a chief who had connected himself in the most friendly manner with the English. Lieutenant Cook, who had given express orders that none of the Indians should be confined, and who, therefore, was equally surprised and concerned at this transaction, instantly set Tootahah at liberty. So strongly had this Indian been possessed with the notion that it was intended to put him to death, that he could not be persuaded to the contrary till he was led out of the fort. His joy at his deliverance was so great, that it displayed itself in a liberality which our people were very unwilling to partake of, from a consciousness that on this occasion they had no claim to the reception of favours. The impression, however, of the confinement of the chief operated with such force upon the minds of the natives, that few of them appeared: and the market was so ill supplied, that the English were in want of necessaries. At length, by the prudent exertions of Lieutenant Cook, Mr. Banks, and Dr. Solander, the friendship of Tootahah was completely recovered, and the reconciliation worked upon the Indians like a charm; for it was no sooner known that he had gone voluntarily on board the Endeavour, than bread-fruit, cocoa-nuts and other provisions were brought to the fort in great plenty.

The lieutenant and the rest of the gentlemen had hitherto, with a laudable discretion, bartered only beads for the articles of food now mentioned. But the market becoming slack, they were obliged for the first time, on the 8th of May, to bring out their nails; and such was the effect of this new commodity, that one of the smallest size, which was about four inches long, procured twenty cocoa-nuts, and bread fruit in proportion.

It was not till the 10th of the month that our voyagers learned that the Indian name of the island was OTAHEITE, by which name it hath since been always distinguished.

On Sunday, the 14th, an instance was exhibited of the inattention of the natives to our modes of religion. The lieutenant had directed that divine service should be performed at the fort; and he was desirous that some of the principal Indians should be present. Mr. Banks secured the attendance of Tubourai Tomaide and his wife Tomio, hoping that it would give occasion to some inquiries on their part, and to some instruction in return. During the whole service, they very attentively observed Mr. Banks' behaviour, and stood, sat, or kneeled as they saw him do; and they appeared to be sensible that it was a serious and important employment in which the English were engaged. But when the worship was ended, neither of them asked any questions, nor would they receive any explanations which were attempted to be given of what had been performed.

As the day approached for executing the grand purpose of the voyage, Lieutenant Cook determined, in consequence of some hints which he had received from the Earl of Morton, to send out two parties to observe the Transit of Venus from other situations. By this means, he hoped that the success of the observation would be secured, if there should happen to be any failure at Otaheite. Accordingly, on Thursday, the first of June, he despatched Mr. Gore in the longboat to Eimeo, a neighbouring island, together with Mr. Monkhouse and Mr. Sporing, a gentleman belonging to Mr. Banks. They were furnished by Mr. Green with proper instruments. Mr. Banks himself chose to go upon this expedition, in which he was accompanied by Tubourai Tomaide and Tomio, and by others of the natives. Early the next morning the lieutenant sent Mr. Hicks, in the pinnace, with Mr. Clark and Mr. Pickersgill, and Mr. Saunders, one of the midshipmen, ordering them to fix upon some convenient spot to the eastward, at a distance from the principal observatory, where they also might employ the instruments they were provided with for observing the transit.

The anxiety for such weather as would be favourable to the success of the experiment, was powerfully felt by all parties concerned. They could not sleep in peace the preceding night; but their apprehensions were happily removed by the sun's rising, on the morning of the 3d of June, without a cloud. The weather continued with equal clearness through the whole of the day, so that the observation was successfully made in every quarter. At the fort, where Lieutenant Cook, Mr. Green, and Dr. Solander were stationed, the whole passage of the planet Venus over the sun's disk was observed with great advantage. The magnifying power of Dr. Solander's telescope was superior to that of those which belonged to the lieutenant and to Mr. Green. They all saw an atmosphere or dusky cloud round the body of the planet, which much disturbed the times of the contact, and especially of the internal ones; and in their accounts of these times, they differed from each other in a greater degree than might have been expected. According to Mr. Green—

	Morning.
	h. min. sec.
The first external contact, or first appearance of Venus on the sun was	9 25 42
The first internal contact, or total immersion, was	9 44 4
The second internal contact, or beginning of the immersion, was	3 14 8
The second external contact, or total immersion, was	3 32 10

The latitude of the observatory was found to be 17° 29′ 15″; and the longitude 149° 32′ 30″ west of Greenwich.

A more particular account of this great astronomical event, the providing for the accurate observations of which reflects so much honour on his majesty's munificent patronage of science, may be seen in the sixty-first volume of the Philosophical Transactions.

The pleasure which Lieutenant Cook and his friends derived, from having thus successfully accomplished the first grand object of the voyage, was not a little abated by the conduct of some of the ship's company; who, while the attention of the officers was engrossed by the transit of Venus, broke into one of the storerooms, and stole a quantity of spike-nails, amounting to no less than a hundred weight. This was an evil of a public and serious nature; for these nails, if injudiciously circulated among the Indians, would be productive of irreparable injury to the English, by reducing the value of iron, their staple commodity. One of the thieves, from whom only seven nails were recovered, was detected; but, though the punishment of two dozen lashes was inflicted upon him, he would not impeach any of his accomplices.

Upon account of the absence of the two parties who had been sent out to observe the transit, the king's birth-day was celebrated on the 5th, instead of the 4th of June; and the festivity of the day must have been greatly heightened by the happy success with which his majesty's liberality had been crowned.

On the 12th, Lieutenant Cook was again reduced to the necessity of exercising the severity of discipline. Complaint having been made to him, by certain of the natives, that two of the seamen had taken from them several bows and arrows, and some strings of platted hair, and the charge being fully supported, he punished each of the criminals with two dozen of lashes.

On the same day it was discovered that Otaheite, like other countries in a certain period of society, has its bards and its minstrels. Mr. Banks, in his morning's walk, had met with a number of natives, who appeared, upon inquiry, to be travelling musicians; and, having learned where they were to be at night, all the gentlemen of the Endeavour repaired to the place. The band consisted of two flutes, and three drums; and the drummers accompanied the music with their voices. To the surprise of the English gentlemen, they found that themselves were generally the subject of the song, which was unpremeditated. These minstrels were continually going about from place to place; and they were rewarded by the master of the house and the audience with such things as they wanted.

The repeated thefts which were committed by the inhabitants of Otaheite brought our voyagers into frequent difficulties, and it required all the wisdom of Lieutenant Cook to conduct himself in a proper manner. His sentiments on the subject displayed the liberality of his mind. He thought it of consequence to put an end, if possible, to thievish practices at once, by doing something that should engage the natives in general to prevent them, from a regard to their common interest. Strict orders had been given by him that they should not be fired upon, even when they were detected in attempting to steal any of the English property. For this the lieutenant had many reasons. The common sentinels were in no degree fit to be entrusted with a power of life and death; neither did Mr. Cook think that the thefts committed by the Otaheitans deserved so severe a punishment. They were not born under the law of England; nor was it one of the conditions under which they claimed the benefits of civil society, that their lives should be forfeited unless they abstained from theft. As the lieutenant was not willing that the natives should be exposed to fire-arms loaded with shot, neither did he approve of firing only with powder, which, if repeatedly found to be harmless, would at length be despised. At a time when a considerable robbery had been committed, an accident furnished him with what he hoped would be a happy expedient for preventing future attempts of the same kind. Above twenty of the sailing canoes of the inhabitants came in with a supply of fish. Upon these Lieutenant Cook immediately seized, and, having brought them into the river behind the fort, gave notice that unless the things which had been stolen were returned, the canoes should be burnt. This menace, without designing to put it into execution, he ventured to publish, from a full conviction that, as restitution was thus made a common cause, the stolen goods would all of them speedily be brought back. In this, however, he was mistaken. An iron coal-rake, indeed, was restored; upon which great solicitation was made for the release of the canoes; but he still insisted on his original condition. When the next day came, he was much surprised to find that nothing further had been returned; and, as the people were in the utmost distress for the fish, which would in a short time be spoiled, he was reduced to the disagreeable alternative, either of releasing the canoes, contrary to what he had solemnly and publicly declared, or of detaining them, to the great damage of those who were innocent. As a temporary expedient, he permitted the natives to take the fish, but still detained the canoes. So far was this measure from being attended with advantage, that it was productive of new confusion and injury; for as it was not easy at once to distinguish to what particular persons the several lots of fish belonged, the canoes were plundered by those who had no right to any part of the cargo. At length, most pressing instances being still made for the restoration of the canoes, and Lieutenant Cook having reason to believe, either that the things for which he detained them were not in the island, or that those who suffered by their detention were absolutely incapable of prevailing upon the thieves to relinquish their booty, he determined, though not immediately, to comply with the solicitations of the natives. Our commander was, however, not a little mortified at the ill success of his project.

About the same time, another accident occurred, which, notwithstanding all the caution of our principal voyagers, was very near embroiling them with the Indians. The lieutenant having sent a boat on shore to get ballast for the ship, the officer, not immediately finding stones suitable to the purpose, began to pull down some part of an inclosure in which the inhabitants had deposited the bones of their dead. This action a number of the natives violently opposed, and a messenger came down to the tents to acquaint the gentlemen that no such thing would be suffered. Mr. Banks directly repaired to the place, and soon put an amicable end to the contest, by sending the boat's crew to the river, where a sufficient quantity of stones might be gathered without a possibility of giving offence. These Indians appeared to be much more alarmed at any injury which they apprehended to be done to the dead than to the living. This was the only measure in which they ventured to oppose the English; and the only insult that was ever offered to any individual belonging to the Endeavour was upon a similar occasion. It should undoubtedly be the concern of all voyagers to abstain from wantonly offending the religious prejudices of the people among whom they come.

To extend the knowledge of navigation and the sphere of discovery, objects which we need not say that Lieutenant Cook kept always steadily in view, he set out, in the pinnace, on the twenty-sixth of June, accompanied by Mr. Banks, to make the circuit of the island; during which the lieutenant and his companions were thrown into great alarm, by the apprehended loss of the boat. By this expedition Mr. Cook obtained an acquaintance with the several districts of Otaheite, the chiefs, who presided over them, and a variety of curious circumstances respecting the manners and customs of the inhabitants. On the first of July he got back to the fort at Matavai, having found the circuit of the island, including the two peninsulas of which it consisted, to be about thirty leagues.

The circumnavigation of Otaheite was followed by an expedition of Mr. Banks to trace the river up the valley from which it issues, and examine how far its banks were inhabited. During this excursion he discerned many traces of subterraneous fire. The stones, like those of Madeira, displayed evident tokens of having been burnt, and the very clay upon the hills had the same appearance.

Another valuable employment of Mr. Banks was the planting of a great quantity of the seeds of water-melons, oranges, lemons, limes, and other plants and trees, which he had collected at Rio de Janeiro. For these he prepared ground on each side of the fort, and selected as many varieties of soil as could be found. He gave, also, liberally of these seeds to the natives, and planted many of them in the woods.

Lieutenant Cook now began to prepare for his departure. On the 7th of July the carpenters were employed in taking down the gates and palisadoes of the fortification ; and it was continued to be dismantled during the two following days. Our commander and the rest of the gentlemen were in hopes that they should quit Otaheite without giving or receiving any further offence ; but in this respect they were unfortunately disappointed. The lieutenant had prudently overlooked a dispute of a smaller nature between a couple of foreign seamen and some of the Indians, when he was immediately involved in a quarrel, which he greatly regretted, and which yet, it was totally out of his power to avoid. In the middle of the night, between the 8th and 9th, Clement Webb and Samuel Gibson, two of the marines, went privately from the fort. As they were not to be found in the morning, Mr. Cook was apprehensive that they intended to stay behind ; but, being unwilling to endanger the harmony and goodwill which at present subsisted between our people and the natives, he determined to wait a day for the chance of the men's return. As, to the great concern of the lieutenant, the marines were not come back on the morning of the tenth, inquiry was made after them of the Indians, who acknowledged that each of them had taken a wife, and had resolved to become inhabitants of the country. After some deliberation, two of the natives undertook to conduct such persons to the place of the deserters' retreat, as Mr. Cook should think proper to send ; and, accordingly, he despatched with the guides a petty officer and the corporal of the marines. As it was of the utmost importance to recover the men, and to do it speedily, it was intimated to several of the chiefs who were in the fort with the women, among whom were Tubourai Tomaide, Tomio, and Oberea, that they would not be permitted to leave it till the fugitives were returned; and the lieutenant had the pleasure of observing, that they received the intimation with very little indications of alarm, and with assurances that his people should be secured and sent back as soon as possible. While this transaction took place at the fort, our commander sent Mr. Hicks in the pinnace to fetch Tootahah on board the ship. Mr. Cook had reason to expect, if the Indian guides proved faithful, that the deserters, and those who went in search of them, would return before the evening. Being disappointed, his suspicions increased, and thinking it not safe, when the night approached, to let the persons whom he had detained as hostages continue at the fort, he ordered Tubourai Tomaide, Oberea, and some others, to be taken on board the Endeavour; a circumstance which excited so general an alarm, that several of them, and especially the women, expressed their apprehensions with great emotion and many tears. Webb, about nine o'clock, was brought back by some of the natives, who declared that Gibson, and the petty officer and corporal, would not be restored till Tootahah should be set at liberty. Lieutenant Cook now found that the tables were turned upon him; but, having proceeded too far to retreat, he immediately despatched Mr. Hicks in the long boat, with a strong party of men, to rescue the prisoners. Tootahah was, at the same time, informed that it behoved him to send some of his people with them, for the purpose of affording them effectual assistance. With this injunction he readily complied, and the prisoners were restored without the least opposition. On the next day they were brought back to the ship, upon which the chiefs were released from their confinement. Thus ended an affair which had given the lieutenant a great deal of trouble and concern. It appears, however, that the measure which he pursued was the result of an absolute necessity; since it was only by the seizure of the chiefs that he recovered his men. Love was the seducer of the two marines. So strong was the attachment which they had formed to a couple of girls, that it was their design to conceal themselves till the ship had sailed, and to take up their residence in the island.

Tupia was one of the natives who had so particularly devoted himself to the English, that he had scarcely ever been absent from them during the whole of their stay at Otaheite. He had been Oberea's first minister, while she was in the height of her power; and he was also chief priest of the country. To his knowledge of the religious principles and ceremonies of the Indians, he added great experience in navigation, and a particular acquaintance with the number and situation of the neighbouring islands. This man had often expressed a desire to go with our navigators, and when they were ready to depart, he came on board with a boy about thirteen years of age, and entreated that he might be permitted to proceed with them on their voyage. To have such a person in the Endeavour was desirable on many accounts; and, therefore, Lieutenant Cook gladly acceded to his proposal.

On the 13th of July the English weighed anchor; and as soon as the ship was under sail, the Indians on board took their leaves, and wept with a decent and silent sorrow, in which there was something very striking and tender. Tupia sustained himself in this scene with a truly admirable firmness and resolution; for though he wept, the effort he made to conceal his tears, concurred with them to do him honor.

The stay of our voyagers at Otaheite was three months, the greater part of which time was spent in the most cordial friendship with the inhabitants and a perpetual reciprocation of good offices. That any differences should happen was greatly regretted on the part of Lieutenant Cook and his friends, who were studious to avoid them as much as possible. The principal causes of them resulted from the peculiar situation and circumstances of the English and the Indians, and especially from the disposition of the latter to theft. The effects of this disposition could not always be submitted to or prevented. It was happy, however, that there was only a single instance in which the differences that arose were attended with any fatal consequence; and by **that accident** the lieutenant was instructed to take the most effectual measures for the future prevention of similar events. He had nothing so much at heart, as that in no case the intercourse of his people with the natives should be productive of bloodshed.

The traffic with the inhabitants for provisions and refreshments, which was chiefly under the management of Mr. Banks, was carried on with as much order as in any well-regulated market in Europe. Axes, hatchets, spikes, large nails, looking-glasses, knives and beads, were found to be the best articles to deal in; and for some of these, everything which the inhabitants possessed might be procured. They were, indeed, fond of fine linen cloth, whether white or printed; but an axe worth half a crown would fetch more than a piece of cloth of the value of twenty shillings.

It would deviate from the plan of this narrative to enter into a minute account of the nature, productions, inhabitants, customs, and manners of the countries which were discovered or visited by **Mr. Cook;** or to give a particular detail of every nautical, geographical, and astronomical observation. It will be sufficient here to take notice, that our commander did not depart from Otaheite without accumulating a store of information and instruction for the enlargement of knowledge, and the benefit of navigation.

While the Endeavour proceeded on her voyage under an easy sail, Tupia informed Lieutenant Cook, that at four of the neighbouring islands, which he distinguished by names of Huaheine, Ulietea, Otaha, and Bolabola, hogs, fowls, and other refreshments, which had latterly been sparingly supplied at Otaheite, might be procured in great plenty. The lieutenant, however, was desirous of first examining an island that lay to the northward, and was called Tethuroa. Accordingly, he came near it; but having found it to be only a small, low island, and being told, at the same time, that it had no settled inhabitants, he determined to drop any further examination of it, and to go in search of Huaheine and Ulietea, which were described to be well peopled, and as large as Otaheite.

On the 15th of July, the weather being hazy, with light breezes and calms succeeding each other, so that no land could be seen, and little way was made, Tupia afforded an amusing proof that, in the exercise of his priestly character, he knew how to unite some degree of art with his superstition. He often prayed for a wind to his god Tane, and as often boasted of his success; this, indeed, he took a most effectual method to secure; for he never began his address to his divinity till he perceived the breeze to be so near, that he knew it must approach the ship before his supplications could well be brought to a conclusion.

The Endeavour, on the 16th, being close in with the northwest part of Huaheine, some canoes soon came off, in one of which was the king of the island and his wife. At first the people seemed afraid; but upon seeing Tupia, their apprehensions were in part dispersed, and at length, in consequence of frequent and earnestly-repeated assurances of friendship, their majesties, and several others, ventured on board the ship. Their astonishment at everything which was shown them was very great; and yet their curiosity did not extend to any objects but what were particularly pointed out to their notice. When they had become more familiar, Mr. Cook was given to understand that the king was called Oree, and that he proposed, as a mark of amity, their making an exchange of their names. To this our commander readily consented; and during the remainder of their being together, the lieutenant was Oree, and his majesty was Cookee. In the afternoon, the Endeavour having come to an anchor in a small, but excellent, harbour on the west side of the island, the name of which was Owharre, Mr. Cook, accompanied by Mr. Banks, Dr. Solander, Mr. Monkhouse, Tupia, and the natives who had been on board ever since the morning, immediately went on shore. The English gentlemen repeated their excursions on the two following days, in the course of which they found that the people of Huaheine had a very near resemblance to those of Otaheite, in person, dress, language, and every other circumstance, and that the productions of the country were exactly similar.

In trafficking with our people, the inhabitants of Huaheine displayed a caution and hesitation which rendered the dealing with them slow and tedious. On the 19th, therefore, the English were obliged to bring out some hatchets, which it was at first hoped there would be no occasion for, in an island that had never before been visited by any European. These procured three very large hogs; and as it was proposed to sail in the afternoon, Oree and several others came on board to **take their leave**. To the king, Mr. Cook gave a small pewter plate, on which was stamped this inscription: "His Britannic Majesty's ship Endeavour, Lieutenant James Cook, commander, 16th July, 1769, **Hua**heine." Among other presents made to Oree, were some medals or counters, resembling the coin of England, and struck in the **year** 1761; all of which, and particularly the plate, he promised carefully and inviolably to preserve. This the lieutenant thought to be as lasting a testimony as any he could well provide, that the English had first discovered the island, and having dismissed his visitors, who were highly pleased with the treatment they had met with, he sailed for Ulietea, in a good harbour of which he anchored next day.

Tupia had expressed his apprehensions that our navigators, if they landed upon the island, would be exposed to the attacks of the men of Bolabola, whom he represented as having lately conquered it, and of whom he entertained a very formidable idea. This, however, did not deter Mr. Cook, Mr. Banks, Dr. Solander, and the other gentlemen, from going immediately on shore

Tupia, who was of the party, introduced them, by performing some ceremonies which he had practised before at Huaheine. After this, the lieutenant hoisted an English jack, and in the name of his Britannic majesty, took possession of Ulietea, and the three neighbouring islands, Huaheine, Otaha, and Bolabola, all of which were in sight.

On the 21st, the master was despatched in the long-boat, to examine the coast of the south part of the island; and one of the mates was sent in the yawl, to sound the harbour where the Endeavour lay. At the same time, Lieutenant Cook went himself in the pinnace, to survey that part of Ulietea which lies to the north. Mr. Banks, likewise, and the gentlemen, again went on shore, and employed themselves in trading with the natives, and in examining the productions and curiosities of the country; but they saw nothing worthy of notice, excepting some human jaw-bones, which, like scalps among the Indians of North America, were trophies of war, and had probably been hung up by the warriors of Bolabola, as a memorial of their conquest.

The weather being hazy on the 22d and 23d, with strong gales, the lieutenant did not venture to put to sea; but on 24th, though the wind continued to be variable, he got under sail, and plied to the northward within the reef, purposing to go out at a wider opening than that by which he had entered the harbour. However, in doing this, he was in imminent danger of striking on the rock. The master, who by his order had kept continually sounding in the chains, suddenly called out "two fathom." Though our commander knew that the ship drew at least fourteen feet, and consequently that the shoal could not possibly be under her keel, he was nevertheless justly alarmed. Happily, the master was either mistaken or the Endeavour went along the edge of a coral rock, many of which, in the neighborhood of these islands, are as steep as a wall.

After a tedious navigation of some days, during which several small islands, were seen, and the long-boat landed at Otaha,

Lieutenant Cook returned to Ulietea, but to a different part of it from that which he had visited before. In a harbor belonging to the west side of the island, he came to an anchor on the 1st of August. This measure was necessary, in order to stop a leak which the ship had sprung in the powder-room, and to take the more ballast, as she was found too light to carry sail upon a wind. The place where the Endeavour was secured was conveniently situated for the lieutenant's purpose of obtaining ballast and water.

Mr. Banks, Dr. Solander, and the gentlemen who went on shore this day, spent their time much to their satisfaction. The reception they met was respectful in the highest degree, and the behaviour of the Indians to the English indicated a fear of them, mixed with a confidence that they had no propensity to commit any kind of injury. In an intercourse which the lieutenant and his friends carried on for several days, with the inhabitants of this part of the island, it appeared that the terrors which Tupia had expressed of the Bolabola conquerors were wholly groundless. Even Opoony, the formidable king of Bolabola, treated our navigators with respect. Being at Ulietea on the 5th of August, he sent Mr. Cook a present of three hogs, some fowls, and several pieces of cloth of uncommon length, together with a considerable quantity of plantains, cocoa-nuts, and other refreshments. This present was accompanied with a message, that, on the next day, he intended to pay our commander a visit. Accordingly, on the 6th, the lieutenant and the rest of the gentlemen all staid at home, in expectation of this important visitor, who did not, however, make his appearance, but sent three very pretty girls as his messengers, to demand something in return for his present. In the afternoon, as the great king would not go to the English, the English determined to go to the great king. From the account which had been given of him, as lord of the Bolabola men, who were the conquerors of Ulietea, and the terror of all the other islands, Lieutenant Cook and his companions expected to see a young and vigorous chief with an intelligent countenance and the marks of an enterprising spirit; instead of which, they found a feeble wretch, withered and decrepit, half blind with age, and so sluggish and stupid, that he scarcely appeared to be possessed even of a common degree of understanding. Otaha being the principal place of Opoony's residence, he went with our navigators to that island on the next day; and they were in hopes of deriving some advantage from his influence, in obtaining such provisions as they wanted. In this respect, however, they were disappointed; for, though they had presented him with an axe, as an inducement to him to encourage his subjects in dealing with them, they were obliged to leave him without having procured a single article.

The time which the carpenters had taken up in stopping the leak of the ship, having detained our voyagers longer at Ulietea than they would otherwise have staid, Lieutenant Cook determined to give up the design of going on shore at Bolabola, especially as it appeared to be difficult of access. The principal islands, about which the English had now spent somewhat more than three weeks, were six in number: Ulietea, Otaha, Bolabola, Huaheine, Tubai, and Maurua. As they lie contiguous to each other, the lieutenant gave them the general appellation of the Society Islands; but did not think proper to distinguish them separately by any other names than those by which they were called by the natives.

On the 9th of August, the leak of the vessel having been stopped, and the fresh stock that had been purchased being brought on board, our commander took the opportunity of a breeze which sprung up at east, and sailed out of the harbour. As he was sailing away, Tupia strongly urged him to fire a shot towards Bolabola; and though that island was at seven leagues distance, the lieutenant obliged him by complying with his request. Tupia's views probably were, to display a mark of his resentment, and to show the power of his new allies.

Our voyagers pursued their course, without meeting with any event worthy of notice, till the 13th, when land was discovered, bearing south east, and which Tupia informed them to be an island called Oheteroa. On the next day, Mr. Cook sent Mr. Gore, one of his lieutenants, in the pinnace, with orders that he should endeavour to get on shore, and learn from the natives whether there was anchorage in a bay then in sight, and what land lay further to the southward. Mr. Gore was accompanied in this expedition by Mr. Banks, Dr. Solander, and Tupia, who used every method, but in vain, to conciliate the minds of the inhabitants, and to engage them in a friendly intercourse. As, upon making the circuit of the island, neither harbour nor anchorage could be found upon it, and, at the same time, the disposition of the people was so hostile that landing would be rendered impracticable without bloodshed, Mr. Cook determined, with equal wisdom and humanity, not to attempt it, having no motive that could justify the risk of life.

From Tupia our navigators learned that there were various islands lying at different distances, and in different directions from Oheteroa, between the south and the northwest, and that to the northeast there was an island called Manua, Bird Island. This he represented as being at the distance of three days' sail; but he seemed most desirous that Lieutenant Cook should proceed to the westward, and described several islands in that situation, which he said he had visited. It appeared, from his description of them, that these were probably Buscawen and Keppel's Islands, which were discovered by Captain Wallis. The furthest island that Tupia knew of to the southward, lay, he said, at the distance of about two days' sail from Oheteroa, and was called Moutou. But he added, that his father had informed him of there being islands still more to the south. Upon the whole, our commander determined to stand southward, in search of a continent, and to lose no time in attempting to discover any other islands, than such as he might happen to fall in with during his course.

On the 15th of August our voyagers sailed from Oheteroa, and on the 25th of the same month was celebrated the anniversary of their departure from England. The comet was seen on the 30th. It was a little above the horizon, in the eastern part of the heavens, at one in the morning; and at about half an hour after four it passed the meridian, and its tail subtended an angle of forty-two degrees. Tupia, who was among others that observed the comet, instantly cried out, that as soon as it should be seen by the people of Bolabola, they would attack the inhabitants of Ulietea, who would be obliged to endeavour to preserve their lives by fleeing with the utmost precipitation to the mountains.

On the 6th of October land was discovered, which appeared to be large. When, on the next day, it was more distinctly visible, it assumed a still larger appearance, and displayed four or five ranges of hills, rising one over the other, above all which was a chain of mountains of an enormous height. This land naturally became the subject of much eager conversation; and the general opinion of the gentlemen on board the Endeavour was, that they had found the *Terra australis incognita*. In fact it was a part of New Zealand, where the first adventures the English met with were very unpleasant, on account of the hostile disposition of the inhabitants.

Lieutenant Cook having anchored on the 8th, in a bay at the entrance of a small river, went on shore in the evening, with the pinnace and yawl, accompanied by Mr. Banks and Dr. Solander, and attended with a party of men. Being desirous of conversing with some natives whom he had observed on the opposite side of the river from that on which he had landed, he ordered the yawl in, to carry himself and his companions over, and left the pinnace at the entrance. When they came near the place where the Indians were assembled, the latter all ran away; and the gentlemen, having left four boys to take care of the yawl, walked up to several huts which were about two or three hundred yards from the water side. They had not gone very far, when four men, armed with long lances, rushed out of the woods, and running up to attack the boat, would certainly have cut her off, if they had not been discovered by the people in the pinnace, who called to the boys to drop down the stream. The boys instantly obeyed ; but being closely pursued by the natives, the cockswain of the pinnace, to whom the charge of the boats was committed, fired a musket over their heads. At this they stopped and looked around them ; but their alarm speedily subsiding, they brandished their lances in a threatening manner, and in a few minutes renewed the pursuit. The firing of a second musket **over their heads** did not draw from them any kind of notice. At last, one of them having lifted up his spear to dart it at the boat, another piece was fired, by which he was shot dead. At the fall of their associate, the three remaining Indians stood for a while motionless, and seemed petrified with astonishment. No sooner had they recovered themselves, than they went back, dragging after them the dead body, which, however, they were obliged to leave, that it might not retard their flight. Lieutenant Cook and his friends, who had straggled to a little distance from each other, were drawn together upon the report of the first musket, and returned speedily to the boat, in which, having crossed the river, they soon beheld the Indian lying dead upon the ground. After their return to the ship, they could hear the people on shore talking with great earnestness, and in a very loud tone of voice.

Notwithstanding this disaster, the lieutenant, being desirous of establishing an intercourse with the natives, ordered, on the following day, three boats to be manned with seamen and marines, and proceeded towards the shore, accompanied by Mr. Banks, Dr. Solander, the other gentlemen, and Tupia. About fifty of the inhabitants seemed to wait for their landing, having seated themselves upon the ground, on the opposite side of the river. This being regarded as a sign of fear, Mr Cook, with only

Mr. Banks, Dr. Solander, and Tupia, advanced towards them; but they had not gone many paces before all the Indians started up, and every man produced either a long pike, or a small weapon of green talk. Though Tupia called to them in the language of Otaheite, they only answered by flourishing their weapons, and making signs for the gentlemen to depart. On a musket's being fired wide of them, they desisted from their threats; and our commander, who had prudently retreated till the marines could be landed, again advanced towards them, with Mr. Banks, Dr. Solander, and Tupia, to whom were now added Mr. Green and Mr. Monkhouse. Tupia was a second time directed to speak to them, and it was perceived with great pleasure that he was perfectly understood, his and their language being the same, excepting only in a diversity of dialect. He informed them that our voyagers only wanted provision and water, in exchange for iron, the properties of which he explained as far as he was able. Though the natives seemed willing to trade, Tupia was sensible, during the course of his conversation with them, that their intentions were unfriendly; and of this he repeatedly warned the English gentlemen. At length twenty or thirty of the Indians were induced to cross the river, upon which presents were made them of iron and beads. On these they appeared to set little value, and particularly on the iron, not having the least conception of its use, so that nothing was obtained in return excepting a few feathers. Their arms, indeed, they offered to exchange for those of our voyagers, and this being refused, they made various attempts to snatch them out of their hands. Tupia was now instructed to acquaint the Indians that our gentlemen would be obliged to kill them, if they proceeded to any further violence; notwithstanding which, one of them, while Mr. Green happened to turn about, seized his hanger, and retired to a little distance, with a shout of exultation. The others, at the same time, began to be extremely insolent, and more of the natives were seen coming to join them from the opposite side of the river. It being, therefore, necessary to repress them, Mr. Banks fired, with small shot, at the distance of about fifteen yards, upon the man who had taken the hanger Though he was struck, he did not return the hanger, but continued to wave it round his head, while he slowly made his retreat. Mr. Monkhouse then fired at him with ball, and he instantly dropped. So far, however, were the Indians from being sufficiently terrified, that the main body of them, who, upon the first discharge had retired to a rock in the middle of the river, began to return, and it was with no small difficulty that Mr. Monkhouse secured the hanger. The whole number of them continuing to advance, three of the English party discharged their pieces at them, loaded only with small shot, upon which they swam back for the shore, and it appeared, upon their landing, that two or three of them were wounded. While they retired slowly up the country, Lieutenant Cook and his companions re-embarked in their boats.

As the lieutenant had unhappily experienced that nothing at this place could be done with these people, and found that the water in the river was salt, he proceeded in the boats round the head of the bay, in search of fresh water. Beside this, he had formed a design of surprising some of the natives, and taking them on board, that, by kind treatment and presents, he might obtain their friendship, and render them the instruments of establishing for him an amicable intercourse with their countrymen. While, upon account of a dangerous surf which every where beat upon the shore, the boats were prevented from landing, our commander saw two canoes coming in from the sea; one under sail, and the other worked with paddles. This he thought to be a favourable opportunity for executing his purpose. Accordingly, the boats were disposed in such a manner as appeared most likely to be successful in intercepting the canoes. Notwithstanding this, the Indians in the canoe which was paddled, exerted themselves with so much vigour at the first apprehension of danger, that they escaped to the nearest land The other canoe sailed on without discerning the English, till she was in the midst of them ; but no sooner had she discovered them, than the people on board struck their sail, and plied their paddles so briskly, as to outrun the boat by which they were pursued. Being within hearing, Tupia called to them to come alongside, with assurances that they should not in any degree be hurt or injured. They trusted, however, more to their own paddles, than to Tupia's promises, and continued to flee from our navigators with all their power. Mr. Cook, as the least exceptionable expedient of accomplishing his design, ordered a musket to be fired over their heads. This, he hoped, would either make them surrender or leap into the water, but it produced a contrary effect. The Indians, who were seven in number, immediately formed a resolution not to fly, but to fight. When, therefore, the boat came up, they began to attack with their paddles, and with stones and other offensive weapons ; and they carried it on with so much vigour and violence, that the English thought themselves obliged to fire upon them in their own defence ; the consequence of which was, that four were unhappily killed. The other three, who were boys, the eldest about nineteen, and the youngest about eleven, instantly leaped into the water, and endeavoured to make their escape ; but being with some difficulty overpowered by our people, they were brought into the boat.

It is impossible to reflect upon this part of Lieutenant Cook's conduct with any degree of satisfaction. He, himself, upon a calm review, did not approve of it ; and he was sensible that it would be censured by the feelings of every reader of humanity It is probable that his mind was so far irritated by the disagreeable preceding events of this unfortunate day, and by the unexpected violence of the Indians in the canoe, as to lose somewhat of that self-possession by which his character in general was eminently distinguished. Candour, however, requires that I should relate what he hath offered in extenuation, not in defence of the transaction, and this shall be done in his own words. "These people certainly did not deserve death for not choosing to confide in my promises, or not consenting to come on board my boat, even if they had apprehended no danger. But the nature of my service required that I should obtain a knowledge of their country, which I could no otherwise effect than by forcing my way into it in a hostile manner, or gaining admission through the confidence and good will of the people. I had already tried the power of presents without effect; and I was now prompted, by my desire to avoid further hostilities, to get some of them on board, as the only method left of convincing them that we intended them no harm, and had it in our power to contribute to their gratification and convenience. Thus far my intentions certainly were not criminal; and though in the contest, which I had not the least reason to expect, our victory might have been complete without so great an expense of life, yet in such situations, when the command to fire has been given, no man can restrain its excess, or prescribe its effect."

Our voyagers were successful in conciliating the minds of the three boys, to which Tupia particularly contributed. When their fears were allayed, and their cheerfulness returned, they sang a song with a degree of taste that surprised the English gentlemen. The tune, like those of our psalms, was solemn and slow, containing many notes and semitones.

Some further attempts were made to establish an intercourse with the natives, and Mr. Cook and his friends, on the 10th, went on shore for this purpose; but being unsuccessful in their endeavours, they resolved to re-embark, lest their stay should embroil them in another quarrel, and cost more of the Indians their lives. On the next day, the lieutenant weighed anchor, and stood away from this unfortunate and inhospitable place. As it had not afforded a single article that was wanted, excepting wood, he gave it the name of Poverty Bay. By the inhabitants it is called Taoneroa, or Long-sand. I shall not regularly pursue the course of our commander round New Zealand. In this course he spent nearly six months, and made large additions to the knowledge of navigation and geography. By making almost the whole circuit of New Zealand, he ascertained it to be two islands, with a strength of evidence which no prejudice could gainsay or resist. He obtained, likewise, a full acquaintance with the inhabitants of the different parts of the country, with regard to whom it was clearly proved that they are eaters of human flesh. Omitting a number of minute circumstances, I shall only select a few things which mark Mr. Cook's personal conduct, and relate to his intercourse with the natives.

The good usage the three boys had met with, and the friendly and generous manner in which they were dismissed to their own homes, had some effect in softening the dispositions of the neighbouring Indians. Several of them who had come on board while the ship lay becalmed in the afternoon, manifested every sign of friendship, and cordially invited the English to go back to their old bay, or to a cove which was not quite so far off. But Lieutenant Cook chose rather to prosecute his discoveries, having reason to hope that he should find a better harbour than any he had yet seen.

While the ship was hauling round to the south end of a small island, which the lieutenant had named Portland, from its very great resemblance to Portland in the British Channel, she suddenly fell into shoal water and broken ground. The soundings were never twice the same, jumping at once from seven fathom to eleven. However, they were always seven fathom or more; and in a short time the Endeavour got clear of danger, and again sailed in deep water. While the ship was in apparent distress, the inhabitants of the island, who in vast numbers sat on its white cliffs, and could not avoid perceiving some appearance of confusion on board and some irregularity in the working of the vessel, were desirous of taking advantage of her critical situation

3*

Accordingly five canoes, full of men, and well armed, were put off with the utmost expedition; and they came so near and showed so hostile a disposition, by shouting, brandishing their lances, and using threatening gestures, that the lieutenant was in pain for his small boat, which was still employed in sounding. By a musket, which he ordered to be fired over them, they were rather provoked than intimidated. The firing of a four pounder, loaded with grapeshot, though purposely discharged wide of them, produced a better effect. Upon the report of the piece, the Indians all rose up and shouted, but instead of continuing the chase, they collected themselves together, and, after a short consultation, went quietly away.

On the 14th of October, Lieutenant Cook having hoisted out his pinnace and long-boat to search for water, just as they were about to set off, several boats, full of New Zealand people, were seen coming from the shore. After some time, five of these boats, having on board between eighty and ninety men, made towards the ship, and four more followed at no great distance as if to sustain the attack. When the first five had gotten within about a hundred yards of the Endeavour, they began to sing their war-song, and brandishing their pikes, prepared for an engagement. As the lieutenant was extremely desirous of avoiding the unhappy necessity of using fire-arms against the natives, Tupia was ordered to acquaint them that our voyagers had weapons which, like thunder, would destroy them in a moment; that they would immediately convince them of their power, by directing their effect so that they should not be hurt; but that, if they persisted in any hostile attempt, they would be exposed to the direct attack of these formidable weapons. A four pounder, loaded with grape-shot, was then fired wide of them; and this expedient was fortunately attended with success. The report, the flash, and above all, the shot, which spread very far in the water, terrified the Indians to such a degree that they began to paddle away with all their might. At the instance, however, of Tupia, the people of one of the boats were induced to lay aside their arms, and to come under the stern of the Endeavour, in consequence of which they received a variety of presents.

On the next day a circumstance occurred, which showed how ready one of the inhabitants of New Zealand was to take an advantage of our navigators. In a large, armed canoe, which came boldly alongside of the ship, was a man who had a black skin thrown over him somewhat like that of a bear. Mr. Cook, being desirous of knowing to what animal it originally belonged, offered the Indian for it a piece of red baize. With this bargain he seemed to be greatly pleased, immediately pulling off the skin and holding it up in the boat. He would not, however, part with it till he had the cloth in his possession; and as there could be no transfer of property, if equal caution should be exercised on both sides, the lieutenant ordered the baize to be delivered into his hands. Upon this, instead of sending up the skin, he began, with amazing coolness, to pack up both that and the cloth, which he had received as the purchase of it, in a basket; nor did he pay the least regard to Mr. Cook's demand or remonstrances, but soon after put off from the English vessel. Our commander was too generous to revenge this insult by any act of severity.

During the course of a traffic which was carrying on for some fish, little Tayeto, Tupia's boy, was placed among others over the ship's side, to hand up what was purchased. While he was thus employed, one of the New-Zealanders, watching his opportunity, suddenly seized him, and dragged him into a canoe. Two of the natives then held him down in the forepart of it, and the others, with great activity, paddled her off with all possible celerity. An action so violent rendered it indispensably necessary that the marines, who were in arms upon the deck, should be ordered to fire. Though the shot was directed to that part of the canoe which was furthest from the boy, and somewhat wide of her, it being thought favourable rather to miss the rowers than to run the hazard of hurting Tayeto, it happened that one man dropped. This occasioned the Indians to quit their hold of the youth, who instantly leaped into the water, and swam towards the ship. In the meanwhile, the largest of the canoes pulled round and followed him; and till some muskets and a great gun were fired at her, did not desist from the pursuit. The ship being brought to, a boat was lowered, and the poor boy was taken up unhurt. Some of the gentlemen, who, with their glasses traced the canoes to shore, agreed in asserting that they saw three men carried up the beach, who appeared to to be either dead, or wholly disabled by their wounds.

While, on the 18th, the Endeavour lay abreast of a peninsula within Portland Island, called Terakako, two of the natives, who were judged to be chiefs, placed an extraordinary degree of confidence in Mr. Cook. They were so well pleased with the kindness which had been shown them in a visit to the ship, that they determined not to go on shore till the next morning. This was a circumstance by no means agreeable to the lieutenant, and he remonstrated against it; but as they persisted in their resolution, he agreed to comply with it, provided their servants also were taken on board, and their canoe hoisted into the ship. The countenance of one of these two chiefs was the most open and ingenuous that our commander had ever seen, so that he soon gave up every suspicion of his entertaining any sinister design. When the guests were put on shore the next morning, they expressed some surprise at seeing themselves so far from their habitations.

On Monday, the 23d, while the ship was in Tegadoo Bay, Lieutenant Cook went on shore to examine the watering-place, and found everything agreeable to his wishes. The boat landed in the cove without the least surf; the water was excellent, and conveniently situated; there was plenty of wood close to the high-water mark, and the disposition of the people was as favourable in all respects as could be desired. Early the next morning, our commander sent Lieutenant Gore to superintend the cutting of wood and filling of water, with a sufficient number of men for both purposes, and all the marines as a guard. Soon after, he went on shore himself, and continued there during the whole day. Mr. Banks and Dr. Solander, who had landed on the same day, found in their walks several things worthy of notice. As they were advancing in some of the valleys, the hills on each side of which were very steep, they were suddenly struck with the sight of an extraordinary natural curiosity. It was a rock perforated through its whole substance, so as to form a rude but stupendous arch or cavern, opening directly to the sea. This aperture was seventy-five feet long, twenty-seven broad, and five-and-forty feet high, commanding a view of the bay and the hills on the other side, which were seen through it, and opening at once upon the view, produced an effect far superior to any of the contrivances of art.

When, on the 28th, the gentlemen of the Endeavour went on shore, upon an island which lies to the left hand of the entrance of Tolaga Bay, they saw there the largest canoe they had yet met with; her length being sixty-eight feet and a half, her breadth five feet, and her height three feet six inches. In the same island was a larger house than any they had hitherto seen; but it was in an unfinished state, and full of chips.

While the ship was in Hicks's Bay, the inhabitants of the adjoining coast were found to be very hostile. This gave much uneasiness to our navigators, and was, indeed, contrary to their expectation; for they had hoped that the report of their power and clemency had spread to a greater extent. At day-break, on the 1st of November, they counted no less than five-and-forty canoes that were coming from the shore towards the Endeavour; and these were followed by several more, from another place. Some of the Indians traded fairly; but others of them took what was handed down to them without making any return, and added derision to fraud. The insolence of one of them was very remarkable. Some linen hanging over the ship's side to dry, this man, without any ceremony, untied it, and put it up in his bundle. Being immediately called to, and required to return it, instead of doing so, he let his canoe drop astern, and laughed at the English. A musket, which was fired over his head, did not put a stop to his mirth. From a second musket, which was loaded with small shot, he shrunk a little, when the shot struck him upon his back; but he regarded it no more than one of our men would have done the stroke of a rattan, and continued with great composure to pack up the linen which he had stolen. All the canoes now dropped astern, and set up their song of defiance, which lasted till they were at about four hundred yards' distance from the ship. As they did not appear to have a design of attacking our voyagers, Lieutenant Cook was unwilling to do them any hurt; and yet he thought that their going off in a bravado might have a bad effect, when it should be reported on shore. To convince them, therefore, that they were still in his power, though far beyond the reach of any missile weapon with which they were acquainted, he ordered a four-pounder to be fired in such a manner as to pass near them. As the shot happened to strike the water, and to rise several times at a great distance beyond the canoes, the Indians were so much terrified, that, without once looking behind them, they paddled away as fast as they were able.

In standing westward from a small island called Mowtohora, the Endeavour suddenly shoaled her water from seventeen to ten fathom. As the lieutenant knew that she was not far off from some small islands and rocks, which had been seen before it was dark, and which he had intended to have passed that evening, he thought it more prudent to tack, and to spend the night under Mowtohora, where he was certain that there was no danger. It was happy for himself, and for all our voyagers, that he formed this resolution. In the morning they discovered, ahead of them, several rocks, some of which were level with the surface of the water, and some below it, and the striking against which could not, in the hour of darkness, have been avoided. In passing between these rocks and the main, the ship had only from ten to seven fathom water.

While Mr. Cook was near an island which he called the Mayor, the inhabitants of the neighbouring coast displayed many instances of hostility, and in their traffic with our navigators, committed various acts of fraud and robbery. As the lieutenant intended to continue in the place five or six days, in order to make an observation of the transit of Mercury, it was absolutely necessary, for the prevention of future mischief, to convince these people that the English were not to be illtreated with impunity. Accordingly, some small shot were fired at a thief of uncommon insolence, and a musket-ball was discharged through the bottom of his boat. Upon this it was paddled to about a hundred yards distance ; and to the surprise of Mr. Cook and his friends, the Indians in the other canoes took not the least notice of their wounded companion, though he bled very much, but returned to the ship, and continued to trade with the most perfect indifference and unconcern. For a considerable time they dealt fairly. At last, however, one of them thought fit to move off with two different pieces of cloth which had been given for the same weapon. When he had gotten to such a distance that he thought himself secure of his prizes, a musket was fired after him, which fortunately struck the boat just at the water's edge, and made two holes in her side. This excited such an alarm, that not only the people who were shot at, but all the rest of the canoes, made off with the utmost expedition. As the last proof of superiority, our commander ordered a round shot to be fired over them, and not a boat stopped till they got to land.

After an early breakfast on the 9th of November, Lieutenant

Cook went on shore, with Mr. Green, and proper instruments, to observe the transit of Mercury. Mr. Banks and Dr. Solander were of the party. The weather had for some time been very thick, with much rain; but this day proved so favourable, that not a cloud intervened during the whole transit. The observation of the ingress was made by Mr. Green alone, Mr. Cook being employed in taking the sun's altitude, to ascertain the time.

While the gentlemen were thus engaged on shore, they were alarmed by the firing of a great gun from the ship, and on their return, received the following account of the transaction from Mr. Gore, the second lieutenant, who had been left commanding officer on board. During the carrying on of a trade with some small canoes, two very large ones came up, full of men. In one of the canoes were forty-seven persons, all of whom were armed with pikes, stones, and darts, and assumed the appearance of a hostile intention. However, after a little time, they began to traffic, some of them offering their arms, and one of them a square piece of cloth, which makes a part of their dress, called *haabow*. Mr. Gore having agreed for it, sent down the price, which was a piece of British cloth, and expected his purchase. But as soon as the Indian had gotten Mr. Gore's cloth in his possession, he refused to part with his own, and put off his canoe. Upon being threatened for his fraud, he and his companions began to sing their war song in defiance, and shook their paddles. Though their insolence did not proceed to an attack, and only defied Mr. Gore to take any remedy in his power, he was so provoked, that he levelled a musket loaded with ball at the offender, while he was holding the cloth in his hand, and shot him dead. When the Indian fell, all the canoes put off to some distance, but continued to keep together in such a manner, that it was apprehended they might still meditate an attack. To secure, therefore, a safe passage for the boat of the Endeavour, which was wanted on shore, a round shot was fired with so much effect over their heads, as made them all flee with the utmost precipitation. It was a matter of regret to Lieutenant Cook that Mr. Gore had not, in the case of the offending Indian, tried the experiment of a few small shot, which had been successful in former instances of robbery.

On Friday, the 10th, our commander, accompanied by Mr. Banks and the other gentlemen, went with two boats to examine a large river that empties itself into the head of Mercury Bay. As the situation they were now in abounded with conveniences, the lieutenant has taken care to point them out, for the benefit of future navigators. If any occasion should ever render it necessary for a ship either to winter here, or to stay for a considerable length of time, tents might be built on a high point or peninsula in this place, upon ground sufficiently spacious for the purpose: and they might easily be made impregnable to the whole force of the country. Indeed the most skilful engineer in Europe could not choose a situation better adapted to enable a small number to defend themselves against a greater. Among other accommodations which the Endeavour's company met with in Mercury Bay, they derived an agreeable refreshment from some oyster beds, which they had fortunately discovered. The oysters, which were as good as ever came from Colchester, and about the same size, were so plentiful, that not the boat only, but the ship itself, might have been loaded in one tide.

On Wednesday, the 15th, Lieutenant Cook sailed out of Mercury Bay. This name had been given to it on account of the observation which had there been made of the transit of that planet over the sun. The river where oysters had been so plentifully found, he called Oyster River. There is another river, at the head of the bay, which is the best and safest place for a ship that wants to stay any length of time. From the number of mangroves about it, the lieutenant named it Mangrove River. In several parts of Mercury Bay our voyagers saw thrown upon the shore great quantities of iron sand, which is brought down by every little rivulet of fresh water that finds its way from the country. This is a demonstration that there is ore of that metal not far inland; and yet none of the inhabitants of New Zealand, who had yet been seen, knew the use of iron, or set upon it the least degree of value. They had all of them preferred the most worthless and useless trifle, not only to a nail, but to any tool of that metal. Before the Endeavour left the bay, the ship's name and that of the commander were cut upon one of the trees near the watering-place, together with the date of the year and month when our navigators were there. Besides this, Mr. Cook, after displaying the English colours, took formal possession of the place in the name of his Britannic Majesty, King George the Third.

In the range from Mercury Bay, several canoes, on the 18th, put off from different places, and advanced towards the Endeavour. When two of them, in which their might be about sixty men, came within the reach of the human voice, the Indians sung their war song; but seeing that little notice was taken of them, they threw a few stones at the English, and then rowed off towards the shore. In a short time, however, they returned, as if with a fixed resolution to provoke our voyagers to a battle, animating themselves by their song, as they had done before. Tupia, without any directions from the gentlemen of the Endeavour, began to expostulate with the natives, and told them that our people had weapons which could destroy them in a moment. Their answer to this expostulation was, in their own language, "Come on shore, and we will kill you all." "Well," replied Tupia, "but why should you molest us while we are at sea? As we do not wish to fight, we shall not accept your challenge to come on shore; and here there is no pretence for a quarrel, the sea being no more your property than the ship." This eloquence, which greatly surprised Lieutenant Cook and his friends, as they had not suggested to Tupia any of the arguments he made use of, produced no effect **upon** the minds of the Indians, who soon renewed their attack. The oratory of a musket, which was fired through one of their boats, quelled their courage, and sent them instantly away.

While our commander was in the Bay of Islands, he had a favourable opportunity of examining the interior part of the country and its produce. At daybreak, therefore, on the 20th of the month, he set out in the pinnace and long-boat, accompanied by Mr. Banks, Dr. Solander, and Tupia, and found the inlet, at which they entered, end in a river, about nine miles above the ship. Up this river, to which was given the name of the Thames, they proceeded till near noon, when they were fourteen miles within its entrance. As the gentlemen then found the face of the country to continue nearly the same, without any alteration in the course of the stream, and had no hope of tracing it to its source, they landed on the west side, to take a view of the lofty trees which everywhere adorned its banks. The trees were of a kind which they had seen before, both in Poverty Bay, and Hawke's Bay, though only at a distance. They had not walked a hundred yards into the woods, when they met with one of the trees, which at the height of six feet above the ground, was nineteen feet eight inches in the girt. Lieutenant Cook, having a quadrant with him, measured its height from the root to the first branch, and found it to be eighty-nine feet. It was as straight as an arrow, and tapered but very little, in proportion to its height; so that, in the lieutenant's judgment, there must have been three hundred and fifty-six feet of solid timber in it, exclusive of the branches. As the party advanced, they saw many other trees, which were still larger. A young one they cut down, the wood of which was heavy and solid, not fit for masts, but such as would make the finest plank in the world. The carpenter of the ship, who was with the party, said that the timber resembled that of the pitch-pine, which is lightened by tapping. If it should appear that some such method would be successful in lightening these trees, they would then furnish masts superior to any country in Europe. As the wood was swampy, the gentlemen could not range far ; but they found many stout trees of other kinds, with which they were totally unacquainted, and specimens of which they brought away.

On the 22d another instance occurred in which the commanding officer left on board did not know how to exercise his power with the good sense and moderation of Mr. Cook. While some of the natives were in the ship below with Mr. Banks, a young man, who was upon the deck, stole a half-minute glass, and was detected just as he was carrying it off. Mr. Hicks, in his indignation against the offender, was pleased to order that he should be punished, by giving him twelve lashes with a cat-o'nine tails. When the other Indians who were on board saw him seized for the purpose, they attempted to rescue him, and being resisted, they called for their arms, which were handed from the canoes. At the same time, the people of one of the canoes attempted to come up the side of the Endeavour. The tumult having called up Mr. Banks and Tupia, the natives ran to the latter, and solicited his interposition. All, however, which he could do, as Mr. Hicks continued inexorable, was to assure them that nothing was intended against the life of their companion, and that it was necessary that he should suffer some punishment for his offence With this explanation they appeared to be satisfied ; and when the punishment had been inflicted, an old man among the spectators, who was supposed to be the criminal's father, gave him a severe beating, and sent him down into his canoe. Notwithstanding this, the Indians were far from being reconciled to the treatment which their countryman had received. Their cheerful confidence was gone ; and though they promised, at their departure, to return with some fish, the English saw them no more.

On the 29th of November, Lieutenant Cook, Mr. Banks, Dr. Solander, and others with them, were in a situation somewhat critical and alarming. Having landed upon an island in the neighbourhood of Cape Bret, they were in a few minutes surrounded by two or three hundred people. Though the Indians were all armed, they came on in so confused and straggling a manner, that it did not appear that any injury was intened by them; and the English gentlemen were determined that hostilities should not begin on their part. At first the natives continued quiet; but their weapons were held ready to strike, and they seemed to be rather irresolute than peaceable. While the lieutenant and his friends remained in a state of suspense, another party of Indians came up; and the boldness of the whole body being increased by the augmentation of their number, they began the dance and song, which are the preludes to a battle. An attempt that was made by a number of them to seize the two boats which had brought our voyagers to land, appeared to be the signal for a general attack. It now became necessary for Mr. Cook to exert himself with vigour. Accordingly, he discharged his musket, which was loaded with small shot, at once at the forwardest of the assailants, and Mr. Banks, and two of our men, fired immediately afterwards. Though this made the natives fall back in some confusion, nevertheless, one of the chiefs, who was at the distance of about twenty yards, had the courage to rally them, and calling loudly to his companions, led them on to the charge. Dr. Solander instantly disharged his piece at this champion, who, upon feeling the shot, stopped short, and then ran away with the rest of his countrymen. Still, however, they did not disperse, but got upon rising ground, and seemed only to want some leader of resolution to renew their assault. As they were now gotten beyond the reach of small shot, the English fired with ball, none of which taking effect, the Indians continued together in a body. While our people were in this doubtful situation, which lasted about a quarter of an hour, the ship, from which a much greater number of natives were seen than could be discovered on shore, brought her broadside to bear, and entirely dispersed them by firing a few shots over their heads. In this skirmish only two of them were hurt with the small shot, and not a single life was lost; a case which would not have happened if Lieutenant Cook had not restrained his men, who, either from fear or the love of mischief, showed as much impatience to destroy the Indians as a sportsman to kill his game. Such was the difference between the disposition of the common seamen and marines, and that of their humane and judicious commander.

On the same day Mr. Cook displayed a very exemplary act of discipline. Some of the ship's people, who, when the natives were to be punished for a fraud, assumed the inexorable justice of a Lycurgus, thought fit to break into one of their plantations, and to dig up a quantity of potatoes. For this the lieutenant ordered each of them to receive twelve lashes, after which two of them were discharged. But the third, in a singular strain of morality, insisted upon it, that it was no crime in an Englishman to plunder an Indian plantation. The method taken by our commander to refute his casuistry, was to send him back to his confinement, and not permit him to be released till he had been punished with six lashes more.

The Endeavour, on the 5th of December, was in the most imminent hazard of being wrecked. At four o'clock in the morning of that day, our voyagers weighed, with a light breeze; but it being variable with frequent calms, they made little way. From that time till the afternoon, they kept turning out of the bay, and about ten at night were suddenly becalmed, so that the ship could neither wear nor exactly keep her station. The tide or current setting strong, she drove towards land so fast, that before any measures could be taken for her security, she was within a cable's length of the breakers. Though our people had thirteen fathom water, the ground was so foul that they did not dare to drop their anchor. In this crisis, the pinnace being immediately hoisted out to take the ship in tow, and the men, sensible of their danger, exerting themselves to the utmost, a faint breeze sprang up off the land, and our navigators perceived, with unspeakable joy, that the vessel made headway. So near was she to the shore, that Tupia, who was ignorant of the hair's breadth escape the company had experienced, was at this very time conversing with the Indians upon the beach, whose voices were distinctly heard, notwithstanding the roar of the breakers. Mr. Cook and his friends now thought that all danger was over: but about an hour afterwards, just as the man in the chains had cried "seventeen fathom," the ship struck. The shock threw them into the utmost consternation; and almost instantly the man in the chains cried out "five fathom." By this time, the rock on which the ship had struck being to the windward, she went off without having received the least damage; and the water very soon deepening to twenty fathom, she again sailed in security.

The inhabitants in the Bay of Islands were found to be far more numerous than in any other part of New Zealand which Lieutenant Cook had hitherto visited. It did not appear that they were united under one head; and, though their towns were fortified, they seemed to live together in perfect amity.

The Endeavour, on the 9th of December, lying becalmed in Doubtless Bay, an opportunity was taken to inquire of the natives concerning their country; and our navigators learned from them, by the help of Tupia, that at the distance of three days' rowing in their canoes, at a place called Moore-Whennua, the land would take a short turn to the southward, and thence extend no more to the west. This place the English gentlemen concluded to be the land discovered by Tasman, and which had been named by him Cape Maria Van Diemen. The lieutenant, finding the inhabitants so intelligent, inquired further, if they knew of any country besides their own. To this they answered, that they had never visited any other; but that their ancestors had told them, that there was a country of great extent to the northwest by north, or north-northwest, called Ulimaroa, to which some people had sailed in a very large canoe; and that only a part of them had returned, who, reported, that, after a passage of a month, they had seen a country where the people eat hogs.

On the 30th December our navigators saw the land, which they judged to be Cape Maria Van Diemen, and which corresponded with the account that had been given of it by the Indians. The next day, from the appearance of Mount Camel, they had a demonstration that, where they now were, the breadth of New Zealand could not be more than two or three miles from sea to sea. During this part of the navigation, two particulars occurred which are very remarkable. In latitude 35° S. and in the midst of summer, Lieutenant Cook met with a gale of wind, which, from its strength and continuance, was such as he had scarcely ever been in before; and he was three weeks in getting ten leagues to the westward, and five weeks in getting fifty leagues; for at this time, being the 1st of January, 1770, it was so long since he had passed Cape Bret. While the gale lasted, our voyagers were happily at a considerable distance from the land; since, otherwise, it was highly probable that they would never have returned to relate their adventures.

The shore at Queen Charlotte's Sound, where the English had arrived on the 14th of January, seemed to form several bays, into one of which the lieutenant proposed to carry the ship, which was now become very foul, in order to careen her, to repair some defects, and to obtain a recruit of wood and water. At day-break the next morning, he stood in for an inlet, and at eight got within the entrance. At nine o'clock, there being little wind, and what there was being variable, the Endeavour was carried by the tide or current within two cables' length of the northwest shore, where she had fifty-four fathom water. By the help of the boats she was gotten clear; and about two, our people anchored in a very safe and convenient cove. Soon after, Mr. Cook, with most of the gentlemen, landed upon the coast, where they found a fine stream of excellent water, and wood in the greatest plenty. Indeed the land, in this part of the country, was one forest of vast extent. As the gentlemen had brought the seine with them, it was hauled once or twice; and with such success, that different sorts of fish were caught, amounting nearly to three hundred weight. The equal distribution of these among the ship's company, furnished them with a very agreeable refreshment.

When Lieutenant Cook, Mr. Banks, Dr. Solander, Tupia, and some others, landed on the 16th, they met with an Indian family, among whom they found horrid and indisputable proofs of the custom of eating human flesh. Not to resume so disagreeable a subject, it may here be observed, once for all, that evidences of the same custom appeared on various occasions.

On the next day a delightful object engaged the attention of our voyagers. The ship lying at the distance of somewhat less than a quarter of a mile from the shore, they were awakened by the singing of an incredible number of birds, who seemed to strain their throats in emulation of each other. This wild melody was infinitely superior to any they had ever heard of the same kind, and seemed to be like small bells, most exquisitely tuned. It is probable, that the distance, and the water between, might be of no small advantage to the sound. Upon inquiry, the gentlemen were informed that the birds here always began to sing about two hours after midnight; and that continuing their music till sunrise, they were silent the rest of the day. In this last respect, they resemble the nightingales of our own country.

On the 18th, Lieutenant Cook went out in the pinnace, to take a view of the bay in which the ship was now at anchor; and found it to be of great extent, consisting of numberless small harbours and coves, in every direction. The Lieutenant confined his excursion to the western side, and the coast where he landed being an impenetrable forest, nothing could be seen worthy of notice. As our commander and his friends were returning, they saw a single man in a canoe, fishing; rowing up to

4

him, to their great surprise, he took not the least notice of them; and even when they were alongside of him, continued to follow his occupation, without adverting to them any more than if they had been invisible. This behaviour was not, however, the result either of sullenness or stupidity; for upon being requested to draw up his net, that it might be examined, he readily complied. He showed, likewise, to our people, his mode of fishing, which was simple and ingenious.

When, on the 19th, the armourer's forge was set up, and all hands on board were busy in careening, and in other necessary operations about the vessel, some Indians, who had brought plenty of fish, exchanged them for nails, of which they had now begun to perceive the use and value. This may be considered as one instance in which they were enlightened and benefited by their intercourse with our navigators.

While, on the 22d, Mr. Banks and Dr. Solander employed themselves in botanizing near the beach, our commander, taking a seaman with him, ascended one of the hills of the country. Upon reaching its summit, he found the view of the inlet, the head of which he had a little before in vain attempted to discover in the pinnace, intercepted by hills still higher than that on which he stood, and which were rendered inaccessible by impenetrable woods. He was, however, amply rewarded for his labour; for he saw the sea on the eastern side of the country, and a passage leading from it to that on the west, a little to the eastward of the entrance of the inlet where the ship lay. The main land, which was on the southeast side of this inlet, appeared to be a narrow ridge of very high hills, and to form part of the southwest side of the strait. On the opposite side, the land trended away east as far as the eye could reach; and to the southeast there was discerned an opening to the sea, which washed the eastern coast. The lieutenant saw, also, on the east side of the inlet, some islands which he had before taken to be part of the main land. In returning to the ship, he examined the harbours and coves, that lie behind the islands which he had seen from the hills. The next day was employed by him in further surveys and discoveries.

During a visit to the Indians, on the 24th, Tupia being of the party, they were observed to be continually talking of guns and shooting people. For this subject of their conversation the English gentlemen could not at all account. But, after perplexing themselves with various conjectures, they at length learned, that on the 21st, one of our officers, under the pretence of going out to fish, had rowed up to a hippah, or village, on the coast. When he had done so, two or three canoes coming off towards his boat, his fears suggested that an attack was intended, in consequence of which three muskets were fired, one with small shot, and two with ball, at the Indians, who retired with the utmost precipitation. It is highly probable, that they had come out with friendly intentions, for such intentions were expressed by their behaviour, both before and afterwards. This action of the officer exhibited a fresh instance how little some of the people under Lieutenant Cook had imbibed of the wise, discreet, and humane spirit of their commander.

On the morning of the 26th, the lieutenant went again out in the boat, with Mr. Banks and Dr. Solander, and entered one of the bays which lie on the east side of the inlet, in order to obtain another sight of the strait which passed between the eastern and western seas. Having landed for this purpose at a convenient place, they climbed a hill of very considerable height, from which they had a full view of the strait, with the land on the opposite shore, which they judged to be about four leagues distant. As it was hazy in the horizon, they could not see far to the southeast; but Mr. Cook saw enough to determine him to search the passage with the ship, as soon as he should put to sea. The gentlemen found on the top of the hill a parcel of loose stones, with which they erected a pyramid, and left in it some musket balls, small shot, beads, and such other things which they hap pened to have about them, as were likely to stand the test of time. These, not being of Indian workmanship, would convince any European, who should come to the place and pull it down, that natives of Europe had been there before. After this, the lieutenant and his friends went to a town of which the Indians had informed them, and which, like one they had already seen, was built upon a small island or rock, so difficult of access, that they gratified their curiosity at the risk of their lives. Here, as had been the case in former visits to the inhabitants of that part of the country near which the ship now lay, they were received with open arms, carried through the whole of the place, and shown all that it contained. The town consisted of between eighty and a hundred houses, and had only one fighting stage. Mr. Cook, Mr. Banks, and Dr. Solander, happened to have with them a few nails and ribands, and some paper, with which the people were so highly gratified, that when the gentlemen went away, they filled the English boat with dried fish, of which it appeared that they had laid up large quantities.

A report was spread, that one of the men that had been so rashly fired upon by the officer who had visited the hippah, under the pretence of fishing, was dead of his wounds. But, on the 29th, the lieutenant had the great consolation of discovering that this report was groundless. On the same day he went again on shore, upon the western point of the inlet, and from a hill of considerable height, had a view of the coast to the northwest. The farthest land he could see in that quarter was an island at the distance of about ten leagues, lying not far from the main. Between this island and the place where he stood, he discovered, close under the shore, several other islands, forming many bays in which there appeared to be good anchorage for shipping. After he had set off the different points for his survey, he erected another pile of stones, in which he left a piece of silver coin, with some musket-balls and beads, and a fragment of an old pendant flying at the top.

On the 30th January, the ceremony was performed of giving name to the inlet where our voyagers now lay, and of erecting a memorial of the visit which they had made to this place. The carpenter having prepared two posts for the purpose, our commander ordered them to be inscribed with the ship's name and the dates of the year and the month. One of these he set up at the watering-place, hoisting the union-flag upon the top of it; and the other he carried over to the island that lies nearest the sea, and which is called by the natives Motuara. He went first, accompanied by Mr. Monkhouse and Tupia, to the neighbouring village, or hippah, where he met with an old man who had maintained a friendly intercourse with the English. To this old man, and several Indians besides, the lieutenant, by means of Tupia, explained his design, which, he informed them was to erect a mark upon the island, in order to show to any other ship which should happen to come thither, that our navigators had been there before. To this the inhabitants readily consented, and promised that they never would pull it down. He then gave something to every one present, and to the old man a silver three-pence, and some spike-nails, with the king's broad arrow cut deep upon them. These were things which Mr. Cook thought were the most likely to be long preserved. After this he conveyed the post to the highest part of the island; and having fixed it firmly in the ground, hoisted upon it the union-flag, and honoured the inlet with the name of Queen Charlotte's Sound. At the same time, he took formal possession of this and the adjacent country, in the name and for the use of his majesty King George the Third. The ceremony was concluded by the gentlemen's drinking a bottle of wine to her majesty's health, and the bottle being given to the old man, who had attended them up the hill, he was highly delighted with his present.

A philosopher, perhaps, might inquire on what ground Lieutenant Cook could take formal possession of this part of New

Zealand, in the name and *for the use* of the King of Great Britain, when the country was already inhabited, and of course belonged to those by whom it was occupied, and whose ancestors might have resided in it for many preceding ages. To this the best answer seems to be, that the lieutenant, in the ceremony performed by him, had no reference to the original inhabitants, or any intention to deprive them of their natural rights, but only to preclude the claims of future European navigators, who, under the auspices and for the benefit of their respective states or kingdoms, might form pretensions to which they were not entitled by prior discovery.

On the 31st, our voyagers having completed their wooding and filled their water casks, Mr. Cook sent out two parties, one to cut and make brooms and another to catch fish. In the evening there was a strong gale from the northwest, with such a heavy rain, that the little wild musicians on shore suspended their song, which till now had been constantly heard during the night, with a pleasure that it was impossible to lose without regret. The gale, on the 1st of February, increased to a storm, with heavy gusts from the high land, one of which broke the hawser, that had been fastened to the shore, and induced the necessity of letting go another anchor. Though, towards midnight, the gale became more moderate, the rain continued with so much violence that the brook which supplied the ship with water, overflowed its banks; in consequence of which ten small casks, that had been filled the day before, were carried away, and notwithstanding the most diligent search for them, could not be recovered.

The Endeavour, on Monday, the 5th, got under sail; but the wind soon failing, our commander was obliged again to come to anchor, a little above Motuara. As he was desirous of making still farther inquiries whether any memory of Tasman had been preserved in New Zealand, he directed Tupia to ask of the old man before mentioned, who had come on board to take his leave of the English gentlemen, whether he had ever heard that such a vessel as theirs had before visited the country. To this he replied in the negative; but said that his ancestors had told him, that there once had arrived a small vessel from a distant land, called Ulimaroa, in which were four men, who upon their reaching the shore were all killed. On being asked where this country lay, he pointed to the northward. Of Ulimaroa, Lieutenant Cook had heard something before, from the people about the Bay of Islands, who said that it had been visited by their ancestors. Tupia had also some confused traditionary notions, concerning it; but no certain conclusion could be drawn either from his account or that of the old Indian.

Soon after the ship came to anchor the second time, Mr. Banks and Dr. Solander, who had gone on shore to see if any gleanings of natural knowledge remained, fell in, by accident with the most agreeable Indian family they had yet seen, and which afforded them a better opportunity of remarking the personal subordination among the natives than had before offered. The whole behaviour of this family was affable, obliging, and unsuspicious. It was matter of sincere regret to the two gentlemen, that they had not sooner met with these people, as a better acquaintance with the manners and disposition of the inhabitants of the country might hence have been obtained in a day, than had been acquired during the whole stay of the English upon the coast.

When, on the 6th of February, Lieutenant Cook had gotten out of the sound, he stood over to the eastward, in order to get the strait well open before the tide of the ebb approached. At seven in the evening, two small islands, which lie off Cape Koamaroo, at the southeast head of Queen Charlotte's Sound, bore east, at the distance of about four miles. It was nearly calm, and the tide of ebb setting out, the Endeavour, in a very short time, was carried by the rapidity of the stream close upon one of the islands, which was a rock rising almost perpendicularly out of the sea. The danger increased every moment, and there was but one expedient to prevent the ship's being dashed to pieces, the success of which a few moments would determine. She was now within a little more than a cable's length of the rock, and had above seventy-five fathom water. But, upon dropping an anchor, and veering above one hundred and fifty fathom of cable, she was happily brought up. This however would not have saved our navigators, if the tide, which set south by east, had not, upon meeting with the island, changed its direction to southeast, and carried them beyond the first point. In this situation they were not above two cables' length from the rocks; and here they remained in the strength of the tide, which set to the south east, after the rate of at least five miles an hour, from a little after seven till midnight, when the tide abated, and the vessel began to heave. By three in the morning, a light breeze at northwest having sprung up, our voyagers sailed for the eastern shore; though they made but little way, in consequence of the tide being against them. The wind, however, having afterwards freshened, and come to the north and northeast, with this, and the tide of ebb, they were in a short time hurried through the narrowest part of the strait, and then stood away for the southernmost land they had in prospect. There appeared, over this **land** a mountain of stupendous height, which was covered with snow. The narrowest part of the strait, through which the Endeavour had been driven with such rapidity, lies between Cape Tierawitte, on the coast of Eaheinomauwe, and Cape Koamaroo; the distance between which our commander judged to be four or five leagues. Notwithstanding the difficulties arising from this tide, now its strength is known, the strait may be passed without danger.

Some of the officers started a notion, that Eaheinmauwe was not an island, and that the land might stretch away to the southeast, from between Cape Turnagain and Cape Palliser, there being a space of between twelve and fifteen leagues which had not yet been seen. Though Lieutenant Cook, from what he had observed the first time he discovered the strait, and from many other concurrent circumstances, had the strongest conviction that they were mistaken, he, nevertheless, resolved to leave no possibility of doubt with respect to an object of so much importance. For this purpose he gave such a direction to navigation of the ship, as would most effectually tend to determine the matter. After a course of two days he called the officers upon deck, and asked them whether they were not now satisfied that Eaheinomauwe was an island. To this question they readily answered in the affirmative; and all doubts being removed, the lieutenant proceeded to further researches.

During Mr. Cook's long and minute examination of the coast of New Zealand, he gave names to the bays, capes, promontories, islands and rivers, and other places which were seen or visited by him; excepting in those cases where their original appellations were learned from the natives. The names he fixed upon were either derived from certain characteristic or adventitious circumstances, or were conferred in honour of his friends and acquaintance, chiefly those of the naval line. Such of the readers of the present work as desire to be particularly informed concerning them, will naturally have recourse to the indications of them in the several maps on which they are described.

The ascertaining of New Zealand to be an island did not conclude Lieutenant Cook's examination of the nature, situation, and extent of the country. After this, he completed his circumnavigation, by ranging from Cape Turnagain southward along the eastern coast of Poenammoo, round Cape South, and back to the western entrance of the strait he had passed, and which was very properly named Cook's Strait. This range, which commenced on the 9th of February, I shall not minutely and regularly pursue; but content myself, as in the former course, with mentioning such circumstances as are more directly adapted to my immediate design.

In the afternoon of the 14th, when Mr. Banks was out in the

boat a-shooting, our voyagers saw, with their glasses, four double canoes put off from the shore towards him, having on board fifty-seven men. The lieutenant, being alarmed for the safety of his friend, immediately ordered signals to be made for his return; but he was prevented from seeing them by the situation of the sun with regard to the ship. However, it was soon with pleasure observed that his boat was in motion; and he was taken on board before the Indians, who perhaps had not discerned him, came up. Their attention seemed to be wholly fixed upon the ship. They came within about a stone's cast of her, and then stopped, gazing at the English with a look of vacant astonishment. Tupia in vain exerted his eloquence to prevail upon them to make a nearer approach. After surveying our navigators some time, they left them, and made towards the shore. The gentlemen could not help remarking, on this occasion, the different dispositions and behaviour of the different inhabitants of the country, at the first sight of the Endeavour. The people now seen kept aloof with a mixture of timidity and wonder; others had immediately commenced hostilities; the man who was found fishing alone in his canoe appeared to regard our voyagers as totally unworthy of notice; and some had come on board almost without invitation, and with an air of perfect confidence and good will. From the conduct of the last visiters, Lieutenant Cook gave the land from which they had put off, and which had the appearance of an island, the name of Lookers-on.

When an island, which lies about five leagues from the coast of Tovy-Poenammoo, and which was named Banks' Island, was first discovered in the direction of south by west, some persons on board were of opinion that they saw land bearing south-south-east, and southeast by east. Our commander, who was himself upon the deck at the time, told them, that in his judgment it was no more than a cloud, which, as the sun rose, would dissipate and vanish. Being, however, determined to leave no subject for disputation which experiment could remove, he ordered the ship to steer in the direction which the supposed country was said to bear. Having gone in this direction eight-and-twenty miles, without discovering any signs of land, the Endeavour resumed her intended course to the southward, it being the particular view of the lieutenant to ascertain whether Poenammoo was an island or a continent.

In passing some rocks on the 9th of March, in the night, it appeared in the morning that the ship had been in the most imminent danger. Her escape was indeed critical in the highest degree. To these rocks, therefore, which, from their situation, are so well adapted to catch unwary strangers, Mr. Cook gave the name of the Traps. On the same day he reached a point of land which he called the South Cape, and which he supposed, as proved in fact to be the case, the southern extremity of the country.

In sailing, on Wednesday the 14th, the Endeavour passed a narrow opening in the land, where there seemed to be a very safe and convenient harbour, formed by an island, which lay eastward in the middle of the opening. On the land, behind the opening, are mountains, the summits of which were covered with snow, that appeared to have recently fallen. Indeed our voyagers, for two days past, had found the weather extremely cold. On each side the entrance of the opening, the land rises almost perpendicularly from the sea to a stupendous height. For this reason Lieutenant Cook did not choose to carry the ship into the harbour. He was sensible that no wind could blow there but right in or right out; and he did not think it by any means advisable to put into a place whence he could not have gotten out, but with a wind which, experience had taught him, did not blow more than one day in a month. Sagacious as this determination of our commander was, it did not give universal satisfaction. He acted in it contrary to the opinion of some persons on board, who expressed in strong terms their desire of coming to harbour; not sufficiently considering that present convenience ought not to be purchased at the expense of incurring great future disadvantages.

By the 27th of March, Mr. Cook had circumnavigated the whole country of Tovy-Poenammoo, and arrived within sight of the island formerly mentioned, which lies at the distance of nine leagues from the entrance of Queen Charlotte's Sound. Having at this time thirty tons of empty water-casks on board, it was necessary to fill them before he finally proceeded on his voyage. For this purpose he hauled round the island, and entered a bay, situated between that and Queen Charlotte's Sound, and to which the name was given of Admiralty Bay.

The business of wooding and watering having been completed on the 30th, and the ship being ready for the sea, the point now to be determined was, what route should be pursued in returning home, that would be of most advantage to the public service. Upon this subject the lieutenant thought proper to take the opinion of his officers. He had himself a strong desire to return by Cape Horn, because that would have enabled him to determine whether there is or is not a southern continent. But against this scheme it was a sufficient objection, that our navigators must have kept in a high southern latitude, in the very depth of winter, and in a vessel which was not thought to be in a condition fit for the undertaking. The same reason was urged with still greater force, against their proceeding directly for the Cape of Good Hope, because no discovery of moment could be expected in that route. It was, therefore, resolved that they should return by the East Indies, and that with this view, they should steer westward, till they should fall in with the east coast of New Holland, and then follow the direction of that coast to the northward, till they should arrive at its northern extremity. If that should be found impracticable, it was farther resolved, that they should endeavour to fall in with the land, or islands, said to have been discovered by Quiros.

In the six months which Lieutenant Cook had spent in the

examination of New Zealand, he made very large additions to the knowledge of geography and navigation. That country was first discovered in the year 1642, by Abel Jansen Tasman, a Dutch navigator. He traversed the eastern coast from latitude 34° 43' and entered the strait now called Cook's Strait; but being attacked by the natives soon after he came to an anchor, in the place which he named Murderer's Bay, he never went on shore. Nevertheless, he assumed a kind of claim to the country by calling it Staaten Land, or the Land of the States, in honour of the States-General. It is now usually distinguished in maps and charts by the name of New Zealand. The whole of the country, excepting that part of the coast which was seen by Tasman from on board his ship, continued from his time to the voyage of the Endeavour, altogether unknown. By many persons it has been supposed to constitute a part of a southern continent; but it was now ascertained by Mr. Cook to consist of two large islands, divided from each other by a strait or passage, which is about four or five leagues broad. These islands are situated between the latitudes of 35° and 48° south, and between the longitudes of 181° and 194° west; a matter which Mr. Green determined with uncommon exactness, from innumerable observations of the sun and moon, and one of the transits of Mercury. The northernmost of these islands is called by the natives Eaheinomauwe, and the southernmost Tovy, or Tavai Poenammoo. It is not, however certain, whether the whole southern island, or only part of it, is comprehended under the latter name.

Tovy-Poenammoo is principally a mountainous, and to all appearance a barren country. The only inhabitants, and signs of inhabitants, that were discovered upon all the islands, were the people whom our voyagers saw in Queen Charlotte's Sound, some that came off to them under the snowy mountains, and several fires that were discerned to the west of Cape Saunders Eaheinomauwe has a much better appearance. Though it is not only hilly, but mountainous, even the hills and mountains are covered with wood, and every valley has a rivulet of water. The soil in these valleys, and in the plains, many of which are not overgrown with wood, is in general light, but fertile. It was the opinion of Mr. Banks and Dr. Solander, as well as of the other gentlemen on board, that all kinds of European grain, plants, and fruit, would flourish here in the utmost luxuriance. There is reason to conclude, from the vegetables which our navigators found in Eaheinomauwe, that the winters are milder than those in England; and the summer was experienced not to be hotter, though it was more equally warm. If this country, therefore, should be settled by people from Europe, they might, with a little industry, very soon be supplied, in great abundance, not merely with the necessaries, but even with the luxuries of life.

In Eaheinomauwe there are no quadrupeds but dogs and rats; at least, no other were seen by our voyagers, and the rats are so scarce, that they wholly escaped the notice of many on board. Of birds, the species are not numerous; and of these no one kind, excepting perhaps the gannet, is exactly the same with those of Europe. Insects are not in greater plenty than birds. The sea makes abundant recompense for this scarcity of animals upon the land. Every creek swarms with fish, which are not only wholesome, but equally delicious with those in our part of the world. The Endeavour seldom anchored in any station, or with a light gale passed any place, that did not afford enough, with a hook and line, to serve the whole ship's company. If the seine was made use of, it seldom failed of producing a still more ample supply. The highest luxury of this kind, with which the English were gratified, was the lobster, or sea cray-fish. Among the vegetable productions of the country, the trees claim a principal place; there being forests of vast extent, full of the straightest, the cleanest, and the largest timber Mr. Cook and his friends had ever seen. Mr. Banks and Dr. Solander were gratified by the novelty, if not by the variety of the plants.

Out of about four hundred species, there were not many which had hitherto been described by botanists. There is one plant that serves the natives instead of hemp and flax, and which excels all that are applied to the same purposes in other countries.

If the settling of New Zealand should ever **be** deemed an object deserving the attention of Great Britan, our commander thought that the best place for establishing a colony, would either be on the banks of the Thames, or in the territory adjoining to the Bay of Islands. Each of these places possesses the advantage of an excellent harbour. By means of the river, settlements might be extended, and a communication established with the inland parts of the country. Vessels might likewise be built of the fine timber which is everywhere to be met with, at very little trouble and expense.

But I am in danger of forgetting myself, and of running into a detail which may be thought rather to exceed the intentions of the present narrative. It is difficult to restrain the pen, when such a variety of curious and entertaining matter lies before it; and I must entreat the indulgence of my readers while I mention two or three farther particulars. One circumstance peculiarly worthy of notice, is the perfect and uninterrupted health of the inhabitants of New Zealand. In all the visits made to their towns, where old and young, men and women, crowded about our voyagers, they never observed a single person who appeared to have any bodily complaint; nor among the numbers that were seen naked, was once perceived the slightest eruption upon the skin, or the least mark which indicated that such an eruption had formerly existed. Another proof of the health of these people, is the facility with which the wounds they at any time receive are healed. In the man who had been shot with a musket-ball throught the fleshy part of his arm, the wound seemed to be so well digested, and in so fair a way of being perfectly healed, that if Mr. Cook had not known that no application had been made to it, he declared that he should certainly have inquired, with a very interested curiosity, after the vulnerary herbs and surgical art of the country. An additional evidence of human nature's being untainted with disease in New **Zealand, is** the great number of old men with whom it abounds. Many of them, by the loss of their hair and teeth, appeared to be very ancient, and yet none of them were decrepit. Although they were not equal to the young in muscular strength, they did not come in the least behind them with regard to cheerfulness and vivacity. Water, as far as our navigators could discover, is the universal and only liquor of the New Zealanders. It is greatly to be wished that their happiness in this respect may never be destroyed by such a connexion with the European nations, as shall introduce that fondness for spirituous liquors which **hath been so** fatal to the Indians of North America.

From the observations which Lieutenant Cook and his friends made on the people of New Zealand, and **from** the similitude which was discerned between them and the inhabitants of the South Sea Islands, a strong proof arose that both of them had one common origin ; and this proof was rendered indubitable by the conformity of their language. When Tupia addressed himself to the natives of Eaheinomauwe and Poenammoo, he was perfectly understood. Indeed, it did not appear that the language of Otaheite differed more from that of New Zealand, than the language of the two islands into which it is divided, did from each other.

Hitherto the navigation of Lieutenant Cook had been unfavourable to the notion of a southern continent ; having swept away at least three-fourths of the positions upon which that notion had been founded. The track of the Endeavour had demonstrated that the land seen by Tasman, Juan Fernaudes, Hermite, the commander of a Dutch squadron, Quiros, and Roggewein, was not, as they had supposed, part of such a continent. It had also totally destroyed the theoretical arguments

LANDING OF CAPT. COOK FROM THE "ENDEAVOUR," AT NEW HOLLAND. PAGE 69.

in favour of a southern continent, which had been drawn from the necessity of it to preserve an equilibrium between the two hemispheres. As, however, Mr. Cook's discoveries, so far as he had already proceeded, extended only to the northward of forty degrees, south latitude, he could not, therefore, give an opinion concerning what land might lie farther to the southward. This was a matter, therefore, which he earnestly wished to be examined; and to him was, at length, reserved the honor, as we shall hereafter see, of putting a final end to the question.

On Saturday, the 31st of March, our commander sailed from Cape Farewell, in New Zealand, and pursued his voyage to the westward. New Holland, or as it is now called, New South Wales, came in sight on the 19th of April; and on the 28th of that month the ship anchored in Botany Bay. On the preceding day, in consequence of its falling calm when the vessel was not more than a mile and a half from the shore, and within some breakers, our navigators had been in a very disagreeable situation; but happily a light breeze had sprung from the land, and carried them out of danger.

In the afternoon the boats were manned, and Lieutenant Cook and his friends, having Tupia of their party, set out from the Endeavour. They intended to land where they had seen some Indians, and began to hope that, as these Indians had paid no regard to the ship when she came into the bay, they would be as inattentive to the advances of the English towards the shore. In this, however, the gentlemen were disappointed, for as soon as they approached the rocks, two of the men came down upon them to dispute their landing, and the rest ran away. These champions, who were armed with lances about ten feet long, called to our navigators in a very loud tone, and in a harsh dissonant language, of which even Tupia did not understand a single word. At the same time, they brandished their weapons, and seemed resolved to defend their coast to the utmost, though they were but two to forty. The lieutenant, who could not but admire their courage, and who was unwilling that hostilities should commence with such inequality of force on their side, ordered his boat to lie upon her oars. He and the other gentlemen then parleyed with them by signs, and, to obtain their good will, he threw them nails, beads, and several trifles besides, with which they appeared to be well pleased. After this our commander endeavoured to make them understand that he wanted water, and attempted to convince them, by all the methods in his power, that he had no injurious design against them. Being willing to interpret the waving of their hands as an invitation to proceed, the boat put in to the shore; but no sooner was this perceived, than it was opposed by the two Indians, one of whom seemed to be a youth about nineteen or twenty years old, and the other a man of middle age. The only resource now left for Mr. Cook, was to fire a musket between them, which being done, **the** youngest of them brought a bundle of lances on the rock, but, recollecting himself in an instant, he snatched them up again in great haste. A stone was thrown at the English, upon which the lieutenant ordered a musket to be fired with small shot. This struck the eldest upon the legs, and he immediately ran to one of the houses, which was at about a hundred yards' distance. Mr. Cook, who now hoped that the contest was over, instantly landed with his party; but they had scarcely quitted the boat when the Indian returned, having only left the rock to fetch a shield or target for his defence. As soon as he came up, he and his comrade threw each of them a lance in the midst of our people, but happily without hurting a single person. At the firing of a third musket, one of the two men darted another lance, and then both of them ran away. After this the gentlemen repaired to the huts, and threw into the house where the children were, some beads, ribands, pieces of cloth, and other presents. These they hoped would procure them the good will of the inhabitants. When, however, the lieutenant and his companions returned the next day, they had the mortification of finding that the beads and ribands which they had left the night before, had not been removed from their places, and that not an Indian was to be seen.

Several of the natives of the country came in sight on the 30th, but they could not be engaged to begin an intercourse with our people. They approached within a certain distance of them, and, after shouting several times, went back into the woods. Having done this once more, Mr. Cook followed them himself, alone and unarmed, a considerable way along the shore, but without prevailing upon them to stop.

On the first of May, he resolved to make an excursion into the country. Accordingly, our commander, Mr. Banks, Dr. Solander, and seven others, all of them properly accoutred for the expedition, set out, and repaired first to the huts near the watering place, whither some of the Indians continued every day to resort. Though the little presents which had been left there before had not yet been taken away, our gentlemen added others of still greater value, consisting of cloth, beads, combs, and looking-glasses. After this they went up into the country, the face of which is finely diversified by wood and lawn. The soil they found to be either swamp or light sand.*

In cultivating the ground, there would be no obstruction from the trees, which are tall, straight, and without underwood, and stand at a sufficient distance from each other. Between the trees, the land is abundantly covered with grass. Our voyagers saw many houses of the inhabitants, but met with only one of the people, who ran away as soon as he discovered the English. At every place where they went they left presents, hoping that at length they might procure the confidence and good will of the Indians. They perceived some traces of animals; and the trees over their heads abounded with birds of various kinds, among

---

* In a part of the country that was afterwards examined, the soil was found to be much richer; being a deep black mould, which the lieutenant thought very fit for the production of grain of any kind.

which were many of exquisite beauty. Loriquets and cockatoos, in particular, were so numerous, that they flew in flocks of several scores together.

While the lieutenant and his friends were on this excursion, Mr. Gore, who had been sent out in the morning to dredge for oysters, having performed that service, dismissed his boat, and taking a midshipman with him, set out to join the waterers by land. In his way, he fell in with a body of two-and-twenty Indians, who followed him, and were often at no greater distance than that of twenty yards. When he perceived them so near, he stopped and faced about, upon which they likewise stopped; and when he went on again they continued their pursuit. But though they were all armed with lances, they did not attack Mr. Gore; so that he and the midshipman got in safety to the watering-place. When the natives came in sight of the main body of the English, they halted at about the distance of a quarter of a mile, and stood still. By this Mr. Monkhouse and two or three of the waterers were encouraged to march up to them; but seeing the Indians keep their ground, they were seized with a sudden fear, which is not uncommon to the rash and foolhardy, and made a hasty retreat. This step increased the danger which it was intended to avoid. Four of the Indians immediately ran forward and discharged their lances at the fugitives, with such force that they went beyond them. Our people recovering their spirits, stopped to collect the lances, upon which the natives, in their turn, began to retire. At this time Mr. Cook came up, with Mr. Banks, Dr. Solander, and Tupia; and being desirous of convincing the Indians that they were neither afraid of them, nor designed to do them any injury, they advanced towards them, endeavouring by signs of expostulation and entreaty, to engage them to an intercourse, but without effect.

From the boldness which the natives discovered on the first landing of our voyagers, and the terror that afterwards seized them at the sight of the English, it appears that they were sufficiently intimidated by our fire-arms. There was not, indeed, the least reason to believe that any of them had been much hurt by the small shot which had been fired at them when they attacked our people on their coming out of the boat. Nevertheless, they had probably seen, from their lurking-places, the effects which the muskets had upon birds. Tupia, who was become a good marksman, frequently strayed abroad to shoot parrots; and while he was thus employed, he once met with nine Indians, who, as soon as they perceived that he saw them, ran from him in great alarm and confusion.

While, on the 3d of May, Mr. Banks was gathering plants near the watering-place, Lieutenant Cook went with Dr. Solander and Mr. Monkhouse to the head of the bay, for the purpose of examining that part of the country, and of making further attempts to form some connections with the natives. In this excursion they acquired additional knowledge concerning the nature of the soil, and its capacities for cultivation, but had no success in their endeavours to engage the inhabitants in coming to a friendly intercourse. Several parties that were sent into the country on the next day, with the same view, were equally unsuccessful. In the afternoon our commander himself, with a number of attendants, made an excursion to the north shore, which he found to be without wood, and to resemble in some degree, our moors in England. The surface of the ground was, however, covered with a thin brush of plants, rising to about the height of the knee. Near the coast the hills are low, but there are others behind them, which gradually ascend to a considerable distance, and are intersected with marshes and morasses. Among the articles of fish which at different times were caught, were large stingrays. One of them, when his entrails were taken out, weighed three hundred and thirty-six pounds.

It was upon account of the great quantity of plants which Mr. Banks and Dr. Solander collected in this place, that Lieutenant Cook was induced to give it the name of Botany Bay. It is situated in the latitude of 34° south, and in the longitude of 208° 37' west; and affords a capacious, safe, and convenient shelter for shipping. The Endeavour anchored near the south shore, about a mile within the entrance, for the convenience of sailing with a southerly wind, and because the lieutenant thought it the best situation for watering. But afterwards he found a very fine stream on the north shore, where was a sandy cove, in which a ship might lie almost land-locked, and procure wood and water in the greatest abundance. Though wood is everywhere plentiful, our commander saw only two species of it that could be considered as timber. Not only the inhabitants who were first discovered, but all who afterwards came in sight, were entirely naked. Of their mode of life, our voyagers could know but little, as not the least connection could be formed with them; but it did not appear that they were numerous, or that they lived in societies. They seemed, like other animals, to be scattered about along the coast, and in the woods. Not a single article was touched by them of all that were left at their huts, or at the places which they frequented: so little sense had they of those small conveniences and ornaments, which are generally very alluring to the uncivilized tribes of the globe. During Mr. Cook's stay at this place, he caused the English colours to be displayed every day on shore, and took care that the ship's name, and the date of the year, should be inscribed upon one of the trees near the watering-place.

At day-break, on Sunday the 6th of May, our navigators sailed from Botany Bay; and as they proceeded on their voyage, the lieutenant gave the names that are indicated upon the map to the bays, capes, points, and remarkable hills which successively appeared in sight. On the 14th, as the Endeavour advanced to the northward, being then in latitude 30° 22' south, and longitude 206° 39' west, the land gradually increased in height, so that it may be called a hilly country. Between this latitude and Botany Bay, it exhibits a pleasing variety of ridges, hills, valleys, and plains, all clothed with wood, of the same appearance with that which has been mentioned before. The land near the shore is in general low and sandy, excepting the points, which are rocky, and over many of which are high hills, that, at their first rising out of the water, have the semblance of islands. On the next day, the vessel being about a league from the shore, our voyagers discovered smoke in many places, and having recourse to their glasses, they saw about twenty of the natives, who had each of them a large bundle upon his back. The bundles our people conjectured to be palm leaves for covering the houses of the Indians, and continued to observe them above an hour, during which they walked upon the beach, and up a path that led over a hill of gentle ascent. It was remarkable, that not one of them was seen to stop and look towards the Endeavour. They marched along without the least apparent emotion either of curiosity or surprise, though it was impossible that they should not have discerned the ship, by some casual glance, as they went along the shore, and though she must have been the most stupendous and unaccountable object they had ever beheld.

While, on the 17th, our navigators were in a bay, to which Lieutenant Cook had given the name of Moreton's Bay, and at a place where the land was not at that time visible, some on board, having observed that the sea looked paler than usual, were of opinion that the bottom of the bay opened into a river. The lieutenant was sensible that there was no real ground for this supposition. As the Endeavour had here thirty-four fathom water, and a fine sandy bottom, these circumstances alone were sufficient to produce the change which had been noticed in the colour of the sea. Nor was it by any means necessary to suppose a river, in order to account for the land at the bottom of the bay not being visible. If the land there was as low as it had been experienced to be in a hundred other parts of the coast, it would be impossible to see it from the station of the ship. Our commander would, however, have brought the matter to the test of experiment, if the wind had been favourable to such a purpose. Should any future navigator be disposed to determine the question, whether there is or is not a river in this place, Mr. Cook has taken care to leave the best directions for finding its situation.

On the 22d, as our voyagers were pursuing their course from Harvey's Bay, they discovered with their glasses that the land was covered with palm-nut trees, which they had not seen from the time of their leaving the islands within the tropic. They saw also two men walking along the shore, who paid them as little attention as they had met with on former occasions. At eight o'clock in the evening of this day, the ship came to an anchor in five fathom, with a fine sandy bottom. Early in the morning of the next day, the lieutenant, accompanied by Mr. Banks, Dr. Solander, the other gentlemen, Tupia, and a party of men, went on shore, in order to examine the country. The wind blew fresh, and the weather was so cold, that, being at a considerable distance from land, they took their cloaks as a necessary equipment for the voyage. When they landed, they found a channel leading into a large lagoon. Both the channel and the lagoon were examined by our commander with his usual accuracy. There is in the place a small river of fresh water, and room for a few ships to lie in great security. Near the lagoon grows the true mangrove, such as exists in the West India islands, and the first of the kind that had been yet met with by our navigators. Among the shoals and sand banks of the coast, they saw many large birds, and some in particular of the same kind which they had seen in Botany Bay. These they judged to be pelicans, but they were so shy as never to come within reach of a musket. On the shore was found a species of the bustard, one of which was shot, that was equal in size to a turkey, weighing seventeen pounds and a half. All the gentlemen agreed that this was the best bird they had eaten since they left England ; and in honour of it they called the inlet Bustard Bay. Upon the mud banks, and under the mangroves, were innumerable oysters of various kinds, and among others the hammer oyster, with a large proportion of small pearl oysters. If in deeper water there should be equal plenty of such oysters at their full growth, Mr. Cook was of opinion that a pearl fishery might be established here to very great advantage.

The people who were left on board the ship asserted that, while the gentlemen were in the woods, about twenty of the natives came down to the beach, abreast of the Endeavour, and, after having looked at her for some time, went away. Not a single Indian was seen by the gentlemen themselves, though they found various proofs, in smoke, fires, and the fragments of recent meals, that the country was inhabited. The place seemed to be much trodden, and yet not a house, or the remains of a house, could be discerned. Hence, the lieutenant and his friends were disposed to believe that the people were destitute of dwellings, as well as of clothes ; and that, like the other commoners of nature, they spent their nights in the open air. Tupia himself was struck with their apparently unhappy condition, and shaking his head with an air of superiority and compassion, said that they were " taata enos," poor wretches.

On the 25th, our voyagers, at the distance of one mile from the land, were abreast of a point, which Mr. Cook found to lie directly under the tropic of Capricorn ; and for this reason he called it Cape Capricorn. In the night of the next day, when the ship had anchored at a place which was distant four leagues from Cape Capricorn, the tide rose and fell near seven feet ; and the flood set to the westward, and the ebb to the eastward. This circumstance was just the reverse of what had been experienced when the Endeavour was at anchor to the eastward of Bustard Bay.

While our people were under sail, on the 26th, and were surrounded with islands, which lay at different distances from the main land, they suddenly fell into three fathom of water. Upon this the lieutenant anchored, and sent away the master to sound a channel, which lay between the northernmost island and the main. Though the channel appeared to have a considerable breadth, our commander suspected it to be shallow, and such was in fact the case. The master reported, at his return, that he had only two fathom and a half in many places; and where the vessel lay at anchor, she had only sixteen feet, which was not two feet more than she drew. Mr. Banks, who, while the master was sounding the channel, tried to fish from the cabin window with hook and line, was successful in catching two sorts of crabs, both of them such as our navigators had not seen before. One of them was adorned with a most beautiful blue, in every respect equal to the ultramarine. With this blue all his claws and joints were deeply tinged; while the under part of him was white, and so exquisitely polished, that in colour and brightness it bore an exact resemblance to the white of old china. The other crab was also marked, though somewhat more sparingly, with the ultramarine on his joints and his toes, and on his back were three brown spots of a singular appearance.

Early the next morning, Lieutenant Cook, having found the passage between the islands, sailed to the northward, and, on the evening of the succeeding day, anchored at about two miles distance from the main. At this time a great number of islands, lying a long way without the ship, were in sight. On the 29th the lieutenant sent away the master with two boats to sound the entrance of an inlet, which lay to the west, and into which he intended to go with the vessel, that he might wait a few days for the moon's increase, and have an opportunity of examining the country. As the tide was observed to ebb and flow considerably, when the Endeavour had anchored within the inlet, our commander judged it to be a river, that might run pretty far up into land. Thinking that this might afford a commodious situation for laying the ship ashore, and cleaning her bottom, he landed with the master, in search of a proper place for the purpose. He was accompanied in the excursion by Mr. Banks and Dr. Solander; and they found walking exceedingly troublesome, in consequence of the ground's being covered with a kind of grass, the seeds of which were very sharp and bearded. Whenever these seeds stuck into their clothes, which happened at every step, they worked forward by means of the beard, till they got at the flesh. Another disagreeable circumstance was, that the gentlemen were incessantly tormented with the stings of a cloud of mosquitoes. They soon met with several places were the ship might conveniently be laid ashore, but were much disappointed in not being able to find any fresh water. In proceeding up the country they found gum trees, the gum upon which existed only in very small quantities. Gum trees of a similar kind, and as little productive, had occurred in other parts of the coast of New South Wales. Upon the branches of the trees were ants' nests, made of clay, as big as a bushel. The ants themselves, by which the nests were inhabited, were small, and their bodies white. Upon another species of the gum tree, was found a small black ant, which perforated all the twigs, and, having worked out the pith, occupied the pipe in which it had been contained. Notwithstanding this, the parts in which these insects, to an amazing number, had formed a lodgment, bore leaves and flowers, and appeared to be entirely in a flourishing state. Butterflies were found in such multitudes, that the account of them seems almost to be incredible. The air was so crowded with them, for the space of three or four acres, that millions might be seen in every direction; and the branches and twigs of the trees were at the same time covered with others that were not upon the wing. A small fish of a singular kind was likewise met with in this place. Its size was about that of a minnow, and it had two very strong breast-fins. It was found in places which were quite dry, and where it might be supposed that it had been left by the tide; and yet it did not appear to have become languid from that circumstance: for when it was approached, it leaped away as nimbly as a frog. Indeed it did not seem to prefer water to land.

Though the curiosity of Mr. Cook and his friends was gratified by the sight of these various objects, they were disappointed in the attainment of their main purpose, the discovery of fresh water; and a second excursion, which was made by them on the afternoon of the same day, was equally unsuccessful. The failure of the lieutenant's hopes determined him to make but a short stay in the place. Having, however, observed from an eminence, that the inlet penetrated a considerable way into the country, he formed a resolution of tracing it in the morning. Accordingly, at sunrise, on Wednesday, the 30th of May, **he went on** shore, and took a view of the coast and the islands that lie off it, with their bearings. For this purpose he had with him, an azimuth compass; but he found that the needle differed very considerably in its position, even to thirty degrees; the variation being in some places more, in others less. Once the needle varied from itself no less than two points in the distance of fourteen feet. Mr. Cook having taken up some of the loose stones which lay upon the ground, applied them to the needle, but they produced no effect; whence he concluded that **in the hills** there was iron ore, traces of which he had re**marked both** here and in the neighbouring parts. After he had made his observations upon the hill he proceeded with Dr. Solander up the inlet. He set out with the first of the flood, and had advanced above eight leagues, long before it was high water. The breadth of the inlet, thus far, was from two to five miles, upon a direction southwest by south; but here it opened every way, and formed a large lake, which to the northwest communicated with the sea. Our commander not only saw the sea in this direction, but found the tide of flood coming strongly in from that point. He observed also an arm of this lake extending to the eastward. Hence he thought it not improbable, that it might communicate with the sea in the bottom of the bay, which lies to the westward of the Cape that on the chart is designated by the name of Cape Townshend. On the south side of the lake is a ridge of hills which the lieutenant was desirous of climbing. As however it was high water, and the day was far spent; and as the weather, in particular, was dark and rainy, he was afraid of being bewildered among the shoals in the night, and therefore was obliged to give up his inclination and to make the best of his way to the ship. Two people only were seen by him, who followed the boat along the shore a good way at some distance; but he could not prudently wait for them, as the tide run strongly in his favour. Several fires in one direction, and smoke in another, exhibited farther proofs of the country's being in a certain degree inhabited.

While Mr. Cook, with Dr. Solander, was tracing the inlet, Mr. Banks and a party with him engaged in a separate excursion, in which they had not proceeded far within land, before their course was obstructed by a swamp covered with mangroves. This however they determined to pass, and having done it with great difficulty, they came up to a place where there had been four small fires, near to which lay some shells and bones of fish that had been roasted. Heaps of grass were also found lying together, on which four or five people appeared to have slept. Mr. Gore, in another place, observed the track of a large animal. Some bustards were likewise seen, but not any other bird, excepting a few beautiful loriquets of the same kind with those which had been noticed in Botany Bay. The country in general, in this part of New South Wales, appeared sandy and barren, and destitute of the accommodations which could fit it for being possessed by settled inhabitants. From the ill-success that attended the searching for fresh water, Lieutenant Cook called the inlet in which the ship lay, Thirsty Sound. No refreshment of any other sort was here procured by our voyagers.

Our commander, not having a single inducement to stay

longer in this place, weighed anchor in the morning of the 31st and put to sea. In the prosecution of the voyage, when the Endeavour was close under Cape Upstart, the variation of the needle, at sun-set, on the 4th of June, was 9° east, and at sunrise the next day it was no more than 5° 35'. Hence the lieutenant concluded, that it had been influenced by iron ore, or by some other magnetical matter contained under the surface of the earth. In the afternoon of the 7th, our navigators saw upon one of the islands what had the appearance of cocoa-nut trees; and as a few nuts would at this time have been very acceptable, Mr. Cook sent Lieutenant Hicks ashore, to see if he could procure any refreshment. He was accompanied by Mr. Banks and Dr. Solander; and in the evening the gentlemen returned, with an account that what had been taken for cocoa-nut trees were a small kind of cabbage-palm, and that excepting about fourteen or fifteen plants, nothing could be obtained which was worth bringing away. On the 8th, when the Endeavour was in the midst of a cluster of small islands, our voyagers discerned with their glasses upon one of the nearest of these islands, about thirty of the natives, men, women and children, all standing together, and looking with great attention at the ship. This was the first instance of curiosity that had been observed among the people of the country. The present Indian spectators were entirely naked. Their hair was short, and their complexion the same with that of such of the inhabitants as had been seen before.

In navigating the coast of New South Wales, where the sea in all parts conceals shoals, which suddenly project from the shore and rocks that rise abruptly like a pyramid from the bottom, our commander had hitherto conducted his vessel in safety, for an extent of two-and-twenty degrees of latitude, being more than one thousand three hundred miles. But, on the 10th of June, as he was pursuing his course from a bay to which he had given the name of Trinity Bay, the Endeavour fell into a situation as critical and dangerous as any that is recorded in the history of navigation; a history which abounds with perilous adventures and almost miraculous escapes. Our voyagers were now near the latitude assigned to the islands that were discovered by Quiros, and which without sufficient reason, some geographers have thought proper to join to this land. The ship had the advantage of a fine breeze, and a clear moonlight night; and in standing off from six till near nine o'clock, she had deepened her water from fourteen to twenty-one fathom. But while our navigators where at supper, it suddenly shoaled, and they fell into twelve, ten, and eight fathom, within the compass of a few minutes. Mr. Cook immediately ordered every man to his station, and all was ready to put about and come to an anchor, when deep water being met with again at the next cast of the lead, it was concluded that the vessel had gone over the tail of the shoals which had been seen at sun-set, and that the danger was now over. This idea of security was confirmed by the water's continuing to deepen to twenty and twenty-one fathom, so that the gentlemen left the deck in great tranquillity, and went to bed. However, a little before eleven, the water shoaled at once from twenty to seventeen fathom, and before the lead could be cast again, the ship struck, and remained immovable, excepting so far as she was influenced by the heaving of the surge, that beat her against the crags of the rock upon which she lay. A few moments brought every person upon deck, with countenances suited to the horrors of the situation. As our people knew from the breeze which they had in the evening that they could not be very near the shore, there was too much reason to conclude that they were upon a rock of coral, which, on account of the sharpness of its points, and the roughness of its surface, is more fatal than any other. On examining the depth of water round the ship, it was speedily discovered, that the misfortune of our voyagers was equal to their apprehensions. The vessel had been lifted over a ledge of the rock, and lay in a hollow within it, in some places of which hollow there were from three to four fathom, and in others not so many feet of water to complete the scene of distress, it appeared, from the light of the moon, that the sheathing boards from the bottom of the ship were floating away all around her, and at last her false keel; so That every moment was making way for the whole company's being swallowed up by the rushing in of the sea. There was now no chance but to lighten her, and the opportunity had unhappily been lost of doing it to the best advantage; for as the Endeavour had gone ashore just at high water, and by this time it had considerably fallen, she would, when lightened, be but in the same situation as at first. The only alleviation of this circumstance was, that as the tide ebbed, the vessel settled to the rocks, and was not beaten against them with so much violence. Our people had, indeed some hope from the next tide, though it was doubtful whether the ship would hold together so long, especially as the rock kept grating part of her bottom with such force as to be heard in the fore store-room. No effort, however, was remitted from despair of success. That no time might be lost, the water was immediately started in the hold, and pumped up; six guns being all that were upon the deck, a quantity of iron and stone ballast, casks, hoop-staves, oil jars, decayed stores, and a variety of things besides, were thrown overboard with the utmost expedition. Every one exerted himself, not only without murmuring and discontent, but even with an alacrity which almost approached to cheerfulness. So sensible, at the same time, were the men, of the awfulness of their situation, that not an oath was heard among them, the detestable habit of profane swearing being instantly subdued by the dread of incurring guilt when a speedy death was in view.

While Lieutenant Cook and all the people about him were thus employed, the opening of the morning of the 11th of June presented them with a fuller prospect of their danger. The land was seen by them at about eight leagues' distance, without any island in the intermediate space, upon which, if the ship had gone to pieces, they might have been set ashore by the boats, and carried thence by different turns to the main. Gradually, however, the wind died away, and, early in the forenoon, it became a dead calm; a circumstance this, peculiarly happy in the order of Divine Providence; for if it had blown hard, the vessel must inevitably have been destroyed. High water being expected at eleven in the morning, and everything being made ready to heave her off if she should float, to the inexpressible surprise and concern of our navigators, so much did the day tide fall short of that of the night, that though they had lightened the ship nearly fifty ton, she did not float by a foot and a half. Hence it became necessary to lighten her still more, and every thing was thrown overboard that could possibly be spared. Hitherto the Endeavour had not admitted much water; but as the tide fell, it rushed in so fast, that she could scarcely be kept free, though two pumps were incessantly worked. There were now no hopes but from the tide at midnight, to prepare for taking the advantage of which the most vigorous efforts were exerted. About five o'clock in the afternoon the tide began to rise, but, at the same time, the leak increased to a most alarming degree. Two more pumps, therefore, were manned, one of which unhappily would not work; three pumps, however, were kept going, and at nine o'clock the ship righted. Nevertheless, the leak had gained so considerably upon her, that it was imagined that she must go to the bottom as soon as she ceased to be supported by the rock. It was, indeed, a dreadful circumstance to our commander and his people, that they were obliged to anticipate the floating of the vessel, not as an earnest of their deliverance, but as an event which probably would precipitate their destruction. They knew that their boats were not capable of carrying the whole of them on shore, and that when the dreadful crisis should arrive, all command and subordination being at an end, a contest for preference might be expected, which would increase even the horrors of shipwreck, and turn their rage against each other. Some of them were sensible that if they should escape to the main land, they were likely to suffer more upon the whole, than those who would be left on board to perish in the waves. The latter would only be exposed to instant death; whereas the former, when they got on shore, would have no lasting or effectual defence against the natives, in a part of the country where even nets and fire-arms could scarcely furnish them with food. But supposing that they should find the means of subsistence, how horrible must be their state, to be condemned to languish out the remainder of their lives in a desolate wilderness, without the possession or hope of domestic comfort; and to be cut off from all commerce with mankind, excepting that of the naked savages, who prowl the desert, and who perhaps are some of the most rude and uncivilized inhabitants of the earth!

The dreadful moment which was to determine the fate of our voyagers now drew on; and every one saw, in the countenances of his companions, the picture of his own sensations. Not, however, giving way to despair, the lieutenan tordered the capstan and windlass to be manned with as many hands as could be spared from the pumps, and the ship having floated about twenty minutes after ten o'clock, the grand effort was made, and she **was** heaved into deep water. It was no small consolation to **find,** that she **did** not now admit of more water than she had done when **upon the rock.** By the gaining, indeed, of the leak upon the pumps, three feet and nine inches of water were in the hold; notwithstanding which, the men did not relinquish their labour. Thus they held the water as it were at bay: but having endured excessive fatigue of body, and agitation of mind, for more than twenty-four hours, and all this being attended with little hope of final success, they began at **length** to flag. None of them could work at the pump above five or six minutes together, after which, being totally exhausted, they threw themselves down upon the deck, though a stream of water, between three and four inches deep, was running over it from the pumps. When those who succeeded them had worked their time, and in their turn were exhausted, they threw themselves down in the same manner, and the others started up again, to renew their labour. While thus they were employed in relieving each other, an accident was very nearly putting an immediate end to all their efforts. The planking, which lines the ship's bottom is called the ceiling, between which and the outside planking there is a space of about eighteen inches. From this ceiling only, the man who had hitherto attended the well had taken the depth of the water, and had given the measure accordingly. But, upon his being relieved, the person who came in his room reckoned the depth to the outside planking, which had the appearance of the leak's having gained upon the pumps eighteen inches in a few minutes. The mistake, however, was soon detected; and the accident, which in its commencement was very formidable to them, became, in fact, highly advantageous. Such was the joy which every man felt, at finding his situation better than his fears had suggested, that it operated with wonderful energy, and seemed to possess him with a strong persuasion that scarcely any real danger remained. New confidence and new hope inspired fresh vigor; and the efforts of the men were exerted with so much alacrity and spirit, that before eight o'clock in the morning the pumps had gained considerably upon the leak. All the conversation now turned upon carrying the ship into some harbour, as a thing not to be doubted; and as hands could be spared from the pumps, they were employed in getting up the anchors. It being found impossible to save the little bower anchor, it was cut away at a whole cable, and the cable of the stream anchor was lost among the rocks; but, in the situation of our people, these were trifles that scarcely attracted their notice. The fore-topmast and fore-yard were next erected, and there being a breeze from the sea, the Endeavour, at eleven o'clock, got once more under sail, and stood for the land.

Notwithstanding these favourable circumstances, our voyagers were still very far from being in a state of safety. It was not possible long to continue the labour by which the pumps had been made to gain upon the leak; and as the exact place of it could not be discovered, there was no hope of stopping it within. At this crisis, Mr. Monkhouse, one of the midshipmen, came to Lieutenant Cook, and proposed an expedient he had once seen used on board a merchant ship, which had sprung a leak that admitted more than four feet of water in an hour, and which by this means had been safely brought from Virginia to London. To Mr. Monkhouse, therefore the care of the expedient, which is called fothering the ship, was, with proper assistance, committed, and his method of proceeding was as follows. He took a lower studding sail, and having mixed together a large quantity of oakum and wool, he stitched it down as tightly as possible, in handsful upon the sail, and spread over it the dung of the sheep of the vessel and other filth. The sail being thus prepared, it was hauled under the ship's bottom by ropes, which kept it extended. When it came under the leak, the suction that carried in the water, carried in with it the oakum and wool from the surface of the sail. In other parts the water was not sufficiently agitated to wash off the oakum and the wool. The success of the expedient was answerable to the warmest expectations; for hereby the leak was so far reduced, that, instead of gaining upon three pumps, it was easily kept under with one. Here was such a new source of confidence and comfort, that our people could scarcely have expressed more joy if they had been already in port. It had lately been the utmost object of their hope, to run the ship ashore in some harbour, either of an island or the main, and to build a vessel from her materials, to carry them to the East Indies. Nothing, however, was now thought of but to range along the coast in search of a convenient place to repair the damage the Endeavour had sustained, and then to prosecute the voyage upon the same plan as if no impediment had happened. In justice and gratitude to the ship's company, and the gentlemen on board, Mr. Cook has recorded that although in the midst of their distress all of them seemed to have a just sense of their danger, no man gave way to passionate exclamations, or frantic gestures. "Every one appeared to have the perfect possession of his mind, and every one exerted himself to the utmost, with a quiet and patient perseverance, equally distant from the tumultuous violence of terror, and the gloomy inactivity of despair." Though the lieutenant hath said nothing of himself, it is well known that his own composure, fortitude, and activity, were equal to the greatness of the occasion.

To complete the history of this wonderful preservation, it is necessary to bring forward a circumstance which could not be discovered till the ship was laid down to be repaired. It was then found, that one of her holes, which was large enough to have sunk our navigators, if they had had eight pumps instead of four, and had been able to keep them incessantly going, was in a great measure filled up by a fragment of the rock upon which the Endeavour had struck. To this singular event, therefore, it was owing, that the water did not pour in with a violence which must speedily have involved the Endeavour and all her company in inevitable destruction.

Hitherto none of the names, by which our commander had distinguished the several parts of the country seen by him, were memorials of distress. But the anxiety and danger, which he and his people had now experienced, induced him to call a point in sight, which lay to the northward, Cape Tribulation.

The next object, after this event, was to look out for a harbour, where the defects of the ship might be repaired, and the vessel put into proper order for future navigation. On the 14th, a small harbour was happily discovered, which was excellently adapted to the purpose. It was, indeed, remarkable, that, during the whole course of the voyage, our people had seen no place which, in their present circumstances, could have afforded them the same relief. They could not, however, immediately get into it ; and in the midst of all their joy for their unexpected deliverance, they had not forgotten that there was nothing but a lock of wool between them and destruction.

At this time the scurvy, with many formidable symptoms, began to make its appearance among our navigators. Tupia, in particular, was so grievously affected with the disease, that all the remedies prescribed by the surgeon could not retard its progress. Mr. Green, the astronomer, was also upon the decline. These and other circumstances embittered the delay which prevented our commander and his companions from getting on shore. In the morning of the 17th, though the wind was still fresh, the lieutenant ventured to weigh, and to put in for the harbour, the entrance into which was by a very narrow channel. In making the attempt, the ship was twice run aground. At the first time, she went off without any trouble, but the second time she stuck fast. Nevertheless, by proper exertions, in conjunction with the rising of the tide, she floated about one o'clock in the afternoon, and was soon warped into the harbour. The succeeding day was employed in erecting two tents, in landing the provisions and stores, and in making every preparation for repairing the damages which the Endeavour had sustained. In the meanwhile Mr. **Cook,** who had ascended one of the highest hills that overlooked **the harbour,** was by no means entertained with a comfortable prospect ; the low land near the river, being wholly overrun with mangroves, among which the salt water flows at every tide, and the high land appearing to be altogether stony and barren. Mr. Banks also took a walk up the country, and met with the frames of several old Indian houses, and places where the natives, though not recently, had dressed shell fish. The boat, which had this day been dispatched to haul the seine, with a view of procuring some fish for the refreshment of the sick, returned without success. Tupia was more fortunate. Having employed himself in angling, and lived entirely upon what he caught, he recovered in a surprising degree. Mr. Green, to the regret of his friends, exhibited no symptoms of returning health.

On the 19th Mr. Banks crossed the river, to take a farther view of the country, which he found to consist principally of sand hills. Some Indian houses were seen by him, that appeared to have been very lately inhabited, and in his walk he met with large flocks of pigeons and crows. The pigeons were exceedingly beautiful. Of these he shot several; but the crows, which were exactly like those in England, were so shy that they never came within the reach of his gun.

It was not till the 22d, that the tide so far left the Endeavour as to give our people an opportunity of examining her leak. In the place where it was found, the rocks had made their way through four planks, and even into the timbers. Three more planks were greatly damaged, and there was something very extraordinary in the appearance of the breaches. Not a splinter was to be seen, but all was as smooth as if the whole had been cut away by an instrument. It was a peculiarly happy circumstance, that the timbers were here very close, since otherwise the ship could not possibly have been saved. Now also it was that the fragment of the rock was discovered, which, by sticking in the leak of the vessel, had been such a providential instrument of her preservation.

On the same day, some of the people who had been sent to shoot pigeons for the sick, and who had discovered many Indian houses, and a fine stream of fresh water, reported, at their return, that they had seen an animal as large as a greyhound, of a slender make, of a mouse colour, and extremely swift. As the lieutenant was walking, on the morning of the 24th, at a little distance from the ship, he had an opportunity of seeing an animal of the same kind. From the description he gave of it, and from an imperfect view which occurred to Mr. Banks, the latter gentleman was of opinion that its species was hitherto unknown.

The position of the vessel, while she was refitting for sea, was very near depriving the world of that botanical knowledge which Mr. Banks had procured at the expense of so much labour and such various perils. For the greater security of the curious collection of plants which he had made during the whole voyage, he had removed them into the bread room. The room is in the after part of the ship, the head of which, for the purpose of repairing her, was laid much higher than the stern. No one having thought of the danger to which this circumstance might expose the plants, they were found to be under water. However, by the exercise of unremitting care and attention, the larger part of them were restored to a state of preservation.

On the 29th of June, at two o'clock in the morning, Mr. Cook, in conjunction with Mr. Green, observed an emersion of Jupiter's first satellite. The time here was 2h 18' 53", which gave the longitude of the place at 214° 42' 30" west; its latitude is 15° 26' south. The next morning the lieutenant sent some of the young gentlemen to take a plan of the harbour, whilst he himself ascended a hill, that he might gain a full prospect of the sea; and it was a prospect which presented him with a lively view of the difficulties of his situation. To his great concern he saw innumerable sandbanks and shoals, lying in every direction of the coast. Some of them extended as far as he could discern with his glass, and many of them did but just rise above water. To the northward there was an appearance of a passage, and this was the only direction in which our commander could hope to get clear, in the prosecution of his voyage; for as the wind blew constantly from the southeast, to return by the southward would have been extremely difficult, if not absolutely impossible. On this and the preceding day, our people had been very successful in hauling the seine. The supply of fish was so great, that the lieutenant was now able to distribute two pounds and a half to each man. A quantity of greens having likewise been gathered, he ordered them to be boiled with the peas. Hence an excellent mess was produced, which in conjunction with the fish, afforded an unspeakable refreshment to the whole of the ship's company.

Early on the morning of the 2d of July, Lieutenant Cook sent the master out of the harbour, in the pinnace, to sound about the shoals, and to search for a channel to the northward. A second attempt, which was made this day, to heave off the ship, was as unsuccessful as a former one had been. The next day the master returned, and reported, that he had found a passage out to sea between two shoals. On one of these shoals, which consisted of coral rocks, many of which were dry at low water, he had landed, and found there cockles of so enormous a size that a single cockle was more than two men could eat. At the same place he met with a great variety of other shell fish, and brought back with him a plentiful supply for the use of his fellow voyagers. At high water, this day, another effort was made to float the ship, which happily succeeded; but it being found that she had sprung a plank between decks, it became necessary to lay her ashore a second time. The lieutenant, being anxious to attain a perfect knowledge of the state of the vessel, got one of the carpenter's crew, a man in whom he could confide, to dive on the 5th to her bottom, that he might examine the place where the sheathing had been rubbed off. His report, which was that three streaks of the sheathing, about eight feet long, were wanting, and that the main plank had been a little rubbed, was perfectly agreeable to the account that had been given before by the master and others, who had made the same examination; and our commander had the consolation of finding, that in the opinion of the carpenter, this matter would be of little consequence. The other damage therefore being repaired, the ship was again floated at high water, and all hands were employed in taking the stores on board, and in putting her into a condition for proceeding on her voyage. To the harbour in which she refitted for sea, Mr. Cook gave the name of the Endeavour River.

On the morning of the 6th, Mr. Banks, accompanied by Lieutenant Gore, and three men, set out in a small boat up the river, with a view of spending a few days in examining the country. In this expedition nothing escaped his notice which related either to the natural history or the inhabitants of the places he visited. Though he met with undoubted proofs that several of the natives were at no great distance, none of them came within sight. Having found, upon the whole, that the country did not promise much advantage from a farther search, he and his party reëmbarked in their boat, and returned on the 8th to the ship. During their excursion, they had slept upon the ground in perfect security, and without once reflecting upon the danger they would have incurred, if, in that situation, they had been discovered by the Indians.

Lieutenant Cook had not been satisfied with the account which the master had given of his having traced a passage between the shoals into the sea. He sent him out, therefore, a second time, upon the same business; and, on his return, he made a different report. Having been seven leagues out at sea, the master was now of opinion that there was no such passage as he had before imagined. His expedition, however, though in this respect unsuccessful, was not wholly without its advantage. On the very rock where he had seen the large cockles, he met with a great number of turtle; and, though he had no better instrument than a boat-hook, three of them were caught, which together weighed seven hundred and ninety-one pounds. An attempt which, by the order of the lieutenant was made the next morning, to obtain some more turtle, failed, through the misconduct of the same officer who had been so fortunate on the preceding day.

Hitherto the natives of this part of the country had eagerly avoided holding any intercourse with our people: but at length their minds, through the good management of Mr. Cook, became more favourably disposed. Four of them having appeared, on the 10th, in a small canoe, and seeming to be busily employed in striking fish, some of the ship's company were for going over to them in a boat. This, however, the lieutenant would not permit, repeated experience having convinced him that it was more likely to prevent than to procure an interview. He determined to pursue a contrary method, and to try what could be done by letting them alone, and not appearing to make them, in the least degree, the objects of his notice. So successful was this plan, that after some preparatory intercourse, they came alongside the ship, without expressing any fear or distrust. The conference was carried on, by signs, with the utmost cordiality till dinner time, when, being invited by our people to go with them and partake of their provision, they declined it, and went away in their canoe. One of these Indians was somewhat above the middle age; the three others were young. Their stature was of the common size, but their limbs were remarkably small. The colour of their skin was of a dark chocolate. Their hair was black, but not woolly; and their features were far from being disagreeable. They had lively eyes, and their teeth were even and white. The tones of their voices were soft and musical, and there was a flexibility in their organs of speech, which enabled them to repeat, with great facility, many of the words pronounced by the English.

On the next morning our voyagers had another visit from four of the natives. Three of them were the same who had appeared the day before, but the fourth was a stranger, to whom his companions gave the name of Yaparco. He was distinguished by a very peculiar ornament. This was the bone of a bird, nearly as thick as a man's finger, and five or six inches long, which he had thrust into a hole, made in the gristle that divides the nostrils. An instance of the like kind, and only one, had been seen in New Zealand. It was found, however, that among all these people the same part of the nose was perforated; that they had holes in their ears; and that they had bracelets, made of plaited hair, upon the upper part of their arms. Thus the love of ornament takes place among them, though they are absolutely destitute of apparel.

Three Indians, on the 12th, ventured down to Tupia's tent, and were so well pleased with their reception, that one of them went with his canoe to fetch two others, who had never been seen by the English. On his return, he introduced the strangers by name, a ceremony which was never omitted upon such occasions. From a farther acquaintance with the natives, it was found, that the colour of their skins was not so dark as had at first been apprehended, and that all of them were remarkably clean limbed, and extremely active and nimble. Their language appeared to be more harsh than that of the islanders in the South Sea.

On the 14th, Mr. Gore had the good fortune to kill one of the animals before mentioned, and which had been the subject of much speculation. It is called by the natives Kangaroo; and when dressed proved most excellent meat. Indeed, our navigators might now be said to fare sumptuously every day; for they had turtle in great plenty, and it was agreed that these were far superior to any which our people had ever tasted in England. This the gentlemen justly imputed to their being eaten fresh from the sea, before their natural fat had been wasted, or their juices changed, by the situation and diet they are exposed to when kept in tubs. Most of the turtle here caught were of the kind called green turtle, and their weight was from two to three hundred pounds.

In the morning of the 16th, while the men were engaged in their usual employment of getting the ship ready for the sea, our commander climbed one of the heights on the north side of the river, and obtained from it an extensive view of the inland country, which he found agreeably diversified by hills, valleys, and large plains, that in many places were richly covered with wood. This evening, the lieutenant and Mr. Green observed an emersion of the first satellite of Jupiter, which gave 214° 53′ 45″ of longitude. The observation taken on the 29th of June had given 214° 48′ 30″ and the mean was 214° 48′ 7½″, being the longitude of the place west of Greenwich.

On the 17th, Mr. Cook sent the master and one of the mates in the pinnace, to search for a channel northward; after which, accompanied by Mr. Banks and Dr. Solander, he went into the woods on the other side of the water. In this excursion, the gentlemen had a farther opportunity of improving their acquaintance with the Indians, who by degrees became so familiar, that several of them the next day ventured on board the ship. There the lieutenant left them, apparently much entertained, that he might go with Mr. Banks to take a farther survey of the country, and especially to indulge an anxious curiosity they had, of looking round about them upon the sea; of which they earnestly wished, but scarcely dared to hope, that they might obtain a favourable and encouraging prospect. When, after having walked along the shore seven or eight miles to the northward, they ascended a very high hill, the view which presented itself to them inspired nothing but melancholy apprehensions. In every direction they saw rocks and shoals without number, and there appeared to be no passage out to sea, but through the winding channels between them, the navigation of which could not be accomplished without the utmost degree of difficulty and danger. The spirits of the two gentlemen were not raised by this excursion.

On the 19th, our voyagers were visited by ten of the natives, and six or seven more were seen at a distance, chiefly women, who were as naked as the male inhabitants of the country. There being at that time a number of turtles on the deck of the ship, the Indians who came on board were determined to get one of them, and expressed great disappointment and anger when our people refused to comply with their wishes. Several attempts were made by them to secure what they wanted by force; but all their efforts proving unsuccessful, they suddenly leaped into their canoe in a transport of rage, and paddled towards the shore. The lieutenant, with Mr. Banks, and five or six of the ship's crew, immediately went into the boat, and got ashore, where many of the English were engaged in various employments. As soon as the natives reached the land, they seized their arms, which had been laid up in a tree, and having snatched a brand from under a pitch kettle that was boiling, made a circuit to the windward of the few things our people had on shore, and with surprising quickness and dexterity set fire to the grass in their way. The grass, which was as dry as stubble, and five or six feet high, burnt with surprising fury; and a tent of Mr. Banks's would have been destroyed, if that gentleman had not immediately got some of the men to save it, by hauling it down upon the beach. Every part of the smith's forge that would burn was consumed. This transaction was followed by another of the same nature. In spite of threats and entreaties, the Indians went to a different place, where several of the Endeavour's crew were washing, and where the seine, the other nets, and a large quantity of linen, were laid out to dry, and again set fire to the grass. The audacity of this fresh attack rendered it necessary that a musket, loaded with small shot, should be discharged at one of them, who being wounded at the distance of about forty yards, they all betook themselves to flight. In the last instance the fire was extinguished before it had made any considerable progress; but where it had first began, it spread far into the woods. The natives being still in sight, Mr. Cook, to convince them that they had not yet gotten out of his reach, fired a musket, charged with ball, abreast of them among the mangroves, upon which they quickened their pace, and were soon out of view. It was now expected that they would have given our navigators no farther trouble; but in a little time their voices were heard in the woods, and it was perceived that they came nearer and nearer. The lieutenant, therefore, together with Mr. Banks, and three or four more persons, set out to meet them; and the result of the interview, in consequence of the prudent and lenient conduct of our commander and his friends, was a complete reconciliation. Soon after the Indians went away, the woods were seen to be on fire at the distance of about two miles. This accident, if it had happened a little sooner, might have produced dreadful effects; for the powder had been but a few days on board, and it was not many hours since the store tent, with all the valuable things contained in it, had been removed. From the fury with which the grass would burn in this hot climate, and the difficulty of extinguishing the fire, our voyagers determined never to expose themselves to the like danger, but to clear the ground around them, if ever again they should be under the necessity of pitching their tents in such a situation.

In the evening of this day, when everything was gotten on board the ship, and she was nearly ready for sailing, the master returned with the disagreeable account that there was no passage for her to the northward. The next morning, the lieutenant himself sounded and buoyed the bar. At this time, all the hills for many miles round were on fire, and the appearance they assumed at night was eminently striking and splendid.

In an excursion which was made by Mr. Banks, on the 23d, to gather plants, he found the greatest part of the cloth that had been given to the Indians lying in a heap together. This, as well as the trinkets which had been bestowed upon them, they probably regarded as useless lumber. Indeed they seemed to set little value on any thing possessed by our people, excepting their turtle; and that was a commodity which could not be spared.

As Lieutenant Cook was prevented by blowing weather from attempting to get out to sea, Mr. Banks and Dr. Solander seized another opportunity, on the 24th, of pursuing their botanical researches. Having traversed the woods the greater part of the day, without success, as they were returning through a deep valley, they discovered lying upon the ground several marking nuts, the anacardium orientale. Animated with the hope of meeting with the tree that bore them, a tree which perhaps no European botanist had ever seen, they sought for it with great diligence and labor, but to no purpose. While Mr. Banks was again gleaning the country, on the 26th, to enlarge his treasure of natural history, he had the good fortune to take an animal of the opossum tribe, together with two young ones. It was a female, and, though not exactly of the same species, much resembled the remarkable animal which Mon. De Buffon hath described by the name of phalanger.

On the morning of the 29th, the weather becoming calm, and a light breeze having sprung up by land, Lieutenant Cook sent a boat to see what water was upon the bar, and all things were made ready for putting to sea. But, on the return of the boat, the officer reported, that there were only thirteen feet of water on the bar. As the ship drew thirteen feet six inches, and the sea breeze set in again in the evening, all hope of sailing on that day was given up. The weather being more moderate on the 31st, the lieutenant had thoughts of trying to warp the vessel out of the harbour; but upon going out himself in the boat, he found that the wind still blew so fresh that it would not be proper to make the attempt. A disagreeable piece of intelligence occurred on the succeeding day. The carpenter, who had examined the pumps, reported that they were all of them in a state of decay. One of them was so rotten, that, when hoisted up, it dropped to pieces, and the rest were not in a much better condition. The chief confidence, therefore, of our navigators, was now in the soundness of the ship; and it was a happy circumstance, that she did not admit more than one inch of water in an hour.

Early on the 3d of August, another unsuccessful attempt was made to warp the vessel out of the harbour; but in the morning of the next day the efforts of our voyagers were more prosperous, and the Endeavour got once more under sail with a light air from the land, which soon died away, and was followed by sea breezes from the southeast by south. With these breezes the ship stood off to sea, east by north, having the pinnace ahead, which was ordered to keep sounding without intermission. A little before noon the lieutenant anchored in fifteen fathom water, with a sandy bottom; the reason of which was, that he did not think it safe to run in among the shoals, till, by taking a view of them from the mast-head at low water, he might be able to form some judgment which way it would be proper for him to steer. This was a matter of nice and arduous determination. As yet Mr. Cook was in doubt, whether he should beat back to the southward, round all the shoals, or seek a passage to the eastward or the northward: nor was it possible to say, whether each of these courses might not be attended with equal difficulty and danger.

The impartiality and humanity of Lieutenant Cook's conduct in the distribution of provisions ought not to pass unnoticed. Whatever turtle or other fish were caught, they were always equally divided among the whole ship's crew, the meanest person on board having the same share with the lieutenant himself. He hath justly observed, that this is a rule which every commander will find it his interest to follow, in any voyage of a similar nature.

Great difficulties occurred in the navigation from the Endeavour river. On the 5th of August the lieutenant had not kept his course long, before shoals were discovered in every quarter, which obliged him, as night approached, to come to an anchor. In the morning of the sixth, there was so strong a gale, that our voyagers were prevented from weighing. When it was low water, Mr. Cook, with several of his officers, kept a lookout at the mast-head, to see if any passage could be discovered between the shoals. Nothing, however, was in view, excepting breakers, which extended from the south round by the east as far as to the northwest, and reached out to sea, beyond the sight of any of the gentlemen. It did not appear that these breakers were caused by one continued shoal, but by several, which lay detached from each other. On that which was farthest to the eastward, the sea broke very high, so that the lieutenant was induced to think that it was the outermost shoal. He was now convinced, that there was no passage to sea, but through the labyrinth formed by these shoals; and, at the same time he was wholly at a loss what course to steer, when the weather should permit the vessel to sail. The master's opinion was, that our navigators should beat back the way they came; but as the wind blew strongly, and almost without intermission, from that quarter, this would have been an endless labour; and yet, if a passage could not be found to the northward, there was no other alternative. Amidst these anxious deliberations, the gale increased, and continued with little remission till the morning of the 10th, when the weather becoming more moderate, our commander weighed, and stood in for the land. He had now come to a final determination of seeking a passage along the shore to the northward.

In pursuance of this resolution, the Endeavour proceeded in her course, and at noon came between the farthermost headland that lay in sight, and three islands which were four or five leagues to the north of it, out at sea. Here our navigators thought they saw a clear opening before them, and began to hope that they were once more out of danger. Of this hope, however, they were soon deprived, on which account the lieutenant gave to the headland the name of Cape Flattery. After he had steered some time along the shore, for what was believed to be the open channel, the petty officer at the mast-head cried aloud, that he saw land ahead, which extended quite round to the three islands, and that between the ship and them there was a large reef. Mr. Cook, upon this, ran up to the mast-head himself, and plainly discerned the reef, which was so far to the windward that it could not be weathered. As to the land which the petty officer had supposed to be the main, our commander was of opinion that it was only a cluster of small islands. The master, and some others who went up to the mast-head after the lieutenant, were entirely of a different opinion. All of them were positive that the land in sight did not consist of islands, but that it was a part of the main; and they rendered their report still more alarming, by adding, that they saw breakers round them on every side. In a situation so critical and doubtful, Mr. Cook thought proper to come to an anchor, under a high point, which he immediately ascended, that he might have a farther view of the sea and the country. The prospect he had from this place, which he called Point Lookout, clearly confirmed him in his former opinion; the justness of which displayed one of the numerous instances, wherein it was manifest, how much he exceeded the people about him in the sagacity of his judgment concerning matters of navigation.

The lieutenant, being anxious to discover more distinctly the situation of the shoals, and the channel between them, determined to visit the northernmost and largest of the three islands before mentioned; which, from its height, and its lying five leagues out to sea, was peculiarly adapted to his purpose. Accordingly, in company with Mr. Banks, whose fortitude and curiosity stimulated him to take a share in every undertaking, he set out in the pinnace, on the morning of the eleventh, upon this expedition. He sent, at the same time, the master in the yawl, to sound between the low islands and the main land. About one o'clock, the gentlemen reached the place of their destination, and immediately, with a mixture of hope and fear, proportioned to the importance of the business, and the uncertainty of the event, ascended the highest hill they could find. When the lieutenant took a survey of the prospect around him, he discovered, on the outside of the islands, and at the distance of two or three leagues from them, a reef of rocks, upon which the sea broke in a dreadful surf, and which extended farther than his sight could reach. Hence, however, he collected, that there were no shoals beyond them; and as he perceived several breaks or openings in the reef, and deep water between that and the islands, he entertained hopes of getting without the rocks. But though he saw reason to indulge, in some degree, this expectation, the haziness of the weather prevented him from obtaining that satisfactory intelligence which he ardently desired. He determined, therefore, by staying all night upon the island, to try whether the next day would not afford him a more distinct and comprehensive prospect. Accordingly, the gentlemen took up their lodgings under the shelter of a bush, which grew upon the beach. Not many hours were devoted by them to sleep; for, at three in the morning, Mr. Cook mounted the hill a second time, but had the mortification of finding the weather much more hazy than it had been on the preceding day. He had early sent the pinnace, with one of the mates, to sound between the island and the reefs, and to examine what appeared to be a channel through them. The mate, in consequence of its blowing hard, did not dare to venture into the channel, which he reported to be very narrow. Nevertheless, our commander, who judged, from the description of the place, that it had been seen to disadvantage, was not discouraged by this account.

While the lieutenant was engaged in his survey, Mr. Banks, always attentive to the great object of natural history, collected some plants which he had never met with before. No animals were perceived upon the place, excepting lizards, for which reason the gentlemen gave it the name of Lizard Island. In their return to the ship, they landed on a low, sandy island, that had trees upon it, and which abounded with an incredible number of birds, principally sea-fowl. Here they found the nest of an eagle, and the nest of some other bird, of what species they could not distinguish; but it must certainly be one of the largest kinds that exist. This was apparent from the enormous size of the nest, which was built with sticks upon the ground, and was no less than six and twenty feet in circumference, and two feet eight inches in height. The spot which the gentlemen were now upon they called Eagle Island.

When lieutenant Cook got on board, he entered into a very serious deliberation concerning the course he should pursue. After considering what he had seen himself, and the master's report, he was of opinion, that by keeping in with the main land, he should run the risk of being locked in by the great reef, and of being compelled at last to return back in search of another passage. By the delay that would hence be occasioned, our navigators would almost certainly be prevented from getting in time to the East Indies, which was a matter of the utmost importance, and indeed of absolute necessity; for they had now not much more than three months' provision on board, at short allowance. The judgment the lieutenant had formed, together with the facts and appearances on which it was grounded, he stated to his officers, by whom it was unanimously agreed, that the best thing they could do would be to quit the coast entirely, till they could approach it again with less danger.

In pursuance of this resolution, the Endeavour, early in the morning of the 13th, got under sail, and successfully passed through one of the channels or openings in the outer reef, which Mr. Cook had seen from the island. When the ship had gotten without the breakers, there was no ground within one hundred and fifty fathom, and our people found a large sea rolling in upon them from the southeast. This was a certain sign that neither land nor shoals were near them in that direction.

So happy a change in the situation of our voyagers was sensibly felt in every breast, and was visible in every countenance. They had been little less than three months in a state that perpetually threatened them with destruction. Frequently had they passed their nights at anchor within hearing of the surge that broke over the shoals and rocks; and they knew, that if by any accident the anchors should not hold against an almost continual tempest, they must in a few minutes inevitably perish. They had sailed three hundred and sixty leagues, without once, even for a moment, having a man out of the chains heaving the lead. This was a circumstance which perhaps never had happened to any other vessel. But now our navigators found themselves in an open sea, with deep water; and the joy they experienced was proportioned to their late danger, and their present security. Nevertheless, the very waves, which proved by their swell that our people had no rocks or shoals to fear, convinced them, at the same time, that they could not put a confidence in the ship equal to what they had done before she struck. So far were her leaks widened by the blows she received from the waves, that she admitted no less than nine inches of water in an hour. If the company had not been lately in so much more imminent danger, this fact, considering the state of the pumps, and the navigation which was still in view, would have been a matter of very serious concern.

The passage or channel, through which the Endeavour passed into the open sea beyond the reef, lies in latitude 14° 32′ south. It may always be known by the three high islands within it, to which, on account of the use they may be of guiding the way of future voyagers, our commander gave the appellation of the Islands of Direction.

It was not a long time that our navigators enjoyed the satisfaction of being free from the alarm of danger. As they were pursuing their course in the night of the 15th, they sounded frequently, but had no bottom with one hundred and forty fathom, nor any ground with the same length of line. Nevertheless, at four in the morning of the 16th, they plainly heard the roaring of surf, and at break of day saw it foaming to a vast height, at not more than the distance of a mile. The waves which rolled in upon the reef, carried the vessel towards it with great rapidity and, at the same time, our people could reach no ground with an anchor, and had not a breath of wind for the sail. In a situation so dreadful, there was no resource but in the boats; and, most unhappily, the pinnace was under repair. By the help, however, of the long-boat and the yawl, which were sent ahead to tow, the ship's head was got round to the northward, a circumstance which might delay, if it could not prevent destruction. This was not effected till six o'clock, and our voyagers were not then a hundred yards from the rock, upon which the same billow that washed the side of the vessel broke to a tremendous height, the very next time it rose. There was only, therefore, a dreary valley between the English and destruction; a valley no wider than the base of one wave, while the sea under them was unfathomable. The carpenter, in the meanwhile, having hastily patched up the pinnace, she was hoisted out, and sent ahead to tow in aid of the other boats. But all these efforts would have been ineffectual, if a light air of wind had not sprung up, just at the crisis of our people's fate. It was so light an air, that at any other time it would not have been observed: but it was sufficient to turn the scale in favour of our navigators; and in conjunction with the assistance which was afforded by the boats, it gave the ship a perceptible motion obliquely from the reef. The hopes of the company now revived; but in less than ten minutes a dead calm succeeded, and the vessel was again driven towards the breakers, which were not at the distance of two hundred yards. However, before the ground was lost which had already been gained, the same light breeze returned, and lasted ten minutes more. During this time a small opening, about a quarter of a mile distant, was discovered in the reef; upon which, Mr. Cook immediately sent one of mates to examine it, who reported that its breadth was not more than the length of the ship, but that within it there was smooth water. This discovery presented the prospect of a possibility of escape, by pushing the vessel through the opening. Accordingly, the attempt was made, but it failed of success; for when our people, by the joint assistance of their boats and the breeze, had reached the opening, they found that it had become high water; and to their great surprise, they met the tide of ebb running out like a mill-stream. In direct contrariety to their expectations, some advantage was gained by this event. Though it was impossible to go through the opening, the stream, which prevented the Endeavour from doing it, carried her out about a quarter of a mile; and the boats were so much assisted in towing her, by the tide of ebb, that at noon she had gained the distance of nearly two miles. However, there was yet too much reason to despair of deliverance. For even if the breeze, which had now died away, had revived, our navigators were still embayed in the reef: and the tide of ebb being spent, the tide of flood, notwithstanding their utmost efforts, drove the ship back again into her former perilous situation. Happily, about this time, another opening was perceived, nearly a mile to the westward. Our commander immediately sent Mr. Hicks, the first lieutenant, to examine it; and in the meanwhile the Endeavour struggled hard with the flood, sometimes gaining and sometimes losing ground. During this severe service, every man did his duty with as much calmness and regularity as if no danger had been near. At length, Mr. Hicks returned with the intelligence, that the opening, though narrow and hazardous, was capable of being passed. The bare possibility of passing it was encouragement sufficient to make the attempt; and indeed all danger was less to be dreaded by our people, than that of continuing in their present situation. A light breeze having fortunately sprung up, this, in conjunction with the aid of the boats, and the very tide of flood, that would otherwise have been their destruction, enabled them to enter the opening, through which they were hurried with amazing rapidity. Such was the force of the torrent by which they were carried along, that they were kept from driving against either side of the channel, which in breadth was not more than a quarter of a mile. While they were shooting this gulf, their soundings were remarkably irregular, varying from thirty to seven fathom, and the ground at bottom was foul.

As soon as our navigators had gotten within the reef, they came to an anchor; and their joy was exceedingly great at having regained a situation which, three days before, they had quitted with the utmost pleasure and transport. Rocks and shoals, which are always dangerous to the mariner, even when they are previously known and marked, are peculiarly dangerous in seas which have never been navigated before; and in this part of the globe they are more perilous than in any other. Here they consist of reefs of coral rock, which rise like a wall almost perpendicularly out of the deep, and are always overflowed at high water. Here, too, the enormous waves of the vast southern ocean, meeting with so abrupt a resistance, break, with inconceivable violence, in a surf which cannot be produced by any rocks or storms in the northern hemisphere. A crazy ship, shortness of provision, and a want of every necessary, greatly increased the danger to our present voyagers of navigating in this ocean. Nevertheless, such is the ardour of the human mind, and so flattering is the distinction of a first discoverer, that Lieutenant Cook and his companions cheerfully encountered every peril, and submitted to every inconvenience. They chose rather to incur the charge of imprudence and temerity, than to leave a country unexplored which they had discovered, or to afford the least colour for its being said, that they were deficient in perseverance and fortitude. It scarcely needs to be added, that it was the high and magnanimous spirit of our commander, in particular, which inspired his people with so much resolution and vigour.

The lieutenant, having now gotten within the reef, determined, whatever might be the consequence, to keep the main land on board, in his future route to the northward. His reason for this determination was; that, if he had gone without the reef again, he might have been carried by it so far from the coast, as to prevent his being able to ascertain whether this country did, or did not, join to New Guinea; a question which he had fixed upon resolving, from the first moment that he had come within sight of land. To the opening through which the Endeavour had passed, our commander, with a proper sense of gratitude to the Supreme Being, gave the name of Providential Channel. In the morning of the 17th, the boats had been sent out to see what refreshments could be procured; and returned in the afternoon with two hundred and forty pounds of the meat of shell fish, chiefly of cockles. Some of the cockles were as much as two men could move, and contained twenty pounds of good meat Mr. Banks, who had gone out in his little boat, accompanied by Dr. Solander, brought back a variety of curious shells, and many species of corals.

In the prosecution of the voyage, our people, on the 19th, were encompassed on every side with rocks and shoals; but, as they had lately been exposed to much greater danger, and these objects were now become familiar, they began to regard them comparatively with little concern. On the 21st, there being two points in view, between which our navigators could see no land, they conceived hopes of having at last found a passage into the Indian Sea. Mr. Cook, however, that he might be able to determine the matter with greater certainty, resolved to land upon an island which lies at the southeast point of the passage. Accordingly, he went into the boat, with a party of men, accompanied by Mr. Banks and Dr. Solander. As they were getting to shore, some of the natives seemed inclined to oppose their landing, but soon walked leisurely away. The gentlemen immediately climbed the highest hill, from which no land could be seen between the southwest and west-southwest; so that the lieutenant had not the least doubt of finding a channel, through which he could pass to New Guinea. As he was now about to quit the coast of New Holland, which he had traced from latitude thirty-eight to this place, and which he was certain no

European had ever seen before, he once more hoisted English colours. He had, indeed, already taken possession of several particular parts of the country. But he now took possession of the whole eastern coast, with all the bays, harbours, rivers, and islands situated upon it, from latitude 38° to latitude 10° ½' south, in right of his Majesty King George the Third, and by the name of New South Wales. The party then fired three volleys of small arms, which were answered by the same number from the ship. When the gentlemen had performed this ceremony upon the island, which they called Possession Island, they reëmbarked in their boat, and in consequence of a rapid ebb tide, had a very difficult and tedious return to the vessel.

On the 23d, the wind had come round to the southwest; and though it was but a gentle breeze, yet it was accompanied by a swell from the same quarter, which, in conjunction with other circumstances, confirmed Mr. Cook in his opinion that he had arrived to the northern extremity of New Holland, and that he had now an open sea to the westward. These circumstances afforded him peculiar satisfaction, not only because the dangers and fatigues of the voyage were drawing to a conclusion, but because it could no longer be doubted whether New Holland and New Guinea were two separate islands. The northeast entrance of the strait lies in the latitude of 10° 39' south, and in the longitude of 218° 36' west; and the passage is formed by the main land, and by a congeries of islands, to the northwest, called by the lieutenant the Prince of Wales's Islands, and which may probably extend as far as to New Guinea. Their difference is very great, both in height and circuit, and many seemed to be well covered with herbage and wood; nor was there any doubt of their being inhabited. Our commander was persuaded, that among these islands as good passages might be found, as that through which the vessel came, and the access to which might be less perilous. The determination of this matter he would not have left to future navigators, if he had been less harassed by danger and fatigue, and had possessed a ship in better condition for the purpose. To the channel through which he passed, he gave the name of Endeavour Straits.

New Holland, or, as the eastern part of it was called by Lieutenant Cook, New South Wales, is the largest country in the known world which does not bear the name of a continent. The length of coast along which our people sailed, when reduced to a straight line, was no less than twenty-seven degrees of latitude, amounting nearly to two thousand miles. In fact, the square surface of the island is much more than equal to the whole of Europe. We may observe, with regard to the natives, that their number bears no proportion to the extent of their territory. So many as thirty of them had never been seen together but once, and that was at Botany Bay. Even when they appeared determined to engage the English, they could not muster above fourteen or fifteen fighting men; and it was manifest that their sheds and houses did not lie so close together as to be capable of accommodating a larger party. Indeed our navigators saw only the sea-coast on the eastern side; between which and the western shore there is an immense tract of land that is wholly unexplored. But it is evident, from the totally uncultivated state of the country which was seen by our people, that this immense tract must either be altogether desolate, or at least more thinly inhabited than the parts which were visited. Of traffic, the natives had no idea, nor could any be communicated to them. The things which were given them they received, but did not appear to understand the signs of the English requiring a return. There was no reason to believe that they eat animal food raw. As they have no vessel in which water can be boiled, they either broil their meat upon the coals, or bake it in a hole by the help of hot stones, agreeably to the custom of the inhabitants of the South-Sea islands. Fire is produced by them with great facility, and they spread it in a surprising manner. For producing it, they take two pieces of soft wood, one of which is a stick about eight or nine inches long, while the other piece is flat. The stick they shape into an obtuse point at one end, and pressing it upon the flat wood, turn it nimbly by holding it between both their hands. In doing this, they often shift their hands up, and then move them down, with a view of increasing the pressure as much as possible. By this process they obtain fire in less than two minutes, and from the smallest spark they carry it to any height or extent with great speed and dexterity.

It was not possible, considering the limited intercourse which our navigators had with the natives of New South Wales, that much could be learned with regard to their language. Nevertheless, as this is an object of no small curiosity to the learned, and is indeed of peculiar importance in searching into the origin of the various nations that have been discovered, Mr. Cook and his friends took some pains to collect such a specimen of it as might, in a certain degree, answer the purpose. Our commander did not quit the country without making such observations relative to the currents and tides upon the coast, as, while they increase the general knowledge of navigation, may be of service to future voyagers. The irregularity of the tides is an object worthy of notice.

From the coast of New South Wales the lieutenant steered, on the 23rd of August, for the coast of New Guinea, and on the 25th fell upon a dangerous shoal. The ship was in six fathom, but scarcely two were found upon sounding round her, at the distance of half a cable's length. This shoal was of such an extent, reaching from the east round by the north and west to the southwest, that there was no method for the vessel to get clear of it but by going back the way she came. Here was another hair's breadth escape, for it was nearly high water, and there ran a short cockling sea, which, if the ship had struck, must very soon have bulged her. So dangerous was her situation, that if her direction had been half a cable's length more, either to the right or left, she must have struck before the signal for the shoal could have been made.

It had been lieutenant Cook's intention to steer northwest, until he had made the south coast of New Guinea, and it was his purpose to touch upon it, if that could be found practicable. But in consequence of the shoals he met with, he altered his course, in the hope of finding a clearer channel, and deeper water. His hope was agreeably verified; for by noon on the 26th, the depth of water was gradually increased to seventeen fathom. On the 28th, our voyagers found the sea to be in many places covered with a brown scum, such as the sailors usually call spawn. When the lieutenant first saw it, he was alarmed, fearing that the ship was again among shoals; but the depth of water, upon sounding, was discovered to be equal to what it was in other places. The same appearance had been observed upon the coasts of Brazil and New Holland, in which cases it was at no great distance from the shore. Mr. Banks and Dr. Solander examined the scum, but could not determine what it was, any further than as they saw reason to suppose that it belonged to the vegetable kingdom. The sailors, upon meeting with more of it, gave up the notion of its being spawn, and finding a new name for it, called it sea-sawdust.

At daybreak on the 3d of September, our navigators came in sight of New Guinea, and stood in for it, with a fresh gale till nine o'clock, when they brought to, being in three fathom water and within about three or four miles of land. Upon this the pinnace was hoisted, and the lieutenant set off from the ship with the boat's crew, accompanied by Mr. Banks, Dr. Solander, and Mr. Banks's servants, being in all twelve persons, well armed As soon as they came ashore they discovered the prints of human feet, which could not long have been impressed upon the sand. Concluding, therefore, that the natives were at no great distance, and there being a thick wood which reached to within a hundred yards of the water, the gentlemen thought it necessary to proceed with caution lest their retreat to the boat should be cut off. When they had walked some way along the skirts of the wood, they came to a grove of cocoa-nut trees, at the fruit of which they looked very wishfully; but not thinking it safe to climb, they were obliged to leave it without tasting a single nut. After they had advanced about a quarter of a mile from the boat, three Indians rushed out of the wood, with a hideous shout, and as they ran towards the English, the foremost threw something out of his hand which flew on one side of him and burned exactly like gunpowder, though without making any report. The two other natives having at the same instant discharged their arrows, the lieutenant and his party were under under the necessity of firing, first with small shot and a second time with ball. Upon this, the three Indians ran away with great agility. As Mr. Cook had no disposition forcibly to invade this country, either to gratify the appetites or the curiosity of his people, and was convinced that nothing was to be done upon friendly terms, he and his companions returned with all expedition towards their boat. When they were aboard, they rowed abreast of the natives, who had come down to the shore in aid of their countrymen, and whose number now amounted to between sixty and a hundred. Their appearance was much the same as that of the New Hollanders; they nearly resembled them in stature, and in having their hair short and cropped. Like them, also, they were absolutely naked; but the colour of their skin did not seem quite so dark, which, however, might be owing to their being less dirty. While the English gentlemen were viewing them, they were shouting defiance and letting off their fires by four or five at a time. Our people could not imagine what these fires were, or what purposes they were intended to answer. Those who discharged them had in their hands a short piece of stick, which they swung sideways from them, and immediately there issued fire and smoke, exactly resembling those of a musket, and of as short a duration. The men on board the ship, who observed this surprising phenomenon, were so far deceived by it, as to believe that the Indians had fire-arms. To the persons in the boat, it had the appearance of the firing of volleys without a report.

The place where this transaction happened lies in the latitude of 6° 15' south, and is about sixty-five leagues to the northeast of Port Saint Augustine or Walche Cape, and is near what is called in the charts C. de la Colta de St. Bonaventura. In every part of the coast the land is covered with a vast luxuriance of wood and herbage. The cocoa-nut, the bread-fruit, and the plantain-tree, flourish here in the highest perfection; besides which, the country abounds with most of the trees, shrubs, and plants, that are common to the South Sea islands, New Zealand and New Holland.

Soon after Mr. Cook and his party had returned to the ship, our voyagers made sail to the westward, the lieutenant having resolved to spend no more time upon this coast; a resolution which was greatly to the satisfaction of a very considerable majority of his people. Some of the officers, indeed, were particularly urgent that a number of men might be sent ashore, to cut down cocoa-nut trees for the sake of their fruit. This, however our commander absolutely refused, as equally unjust and cruel. It was morally certain, from the preceding behaviour of the natives, that if their property had been invaded they would have made a vigorous effort to defend it; in which case the lives of many of them must have been sacrificed, and perhaps, too, several of the English would have fallen in the contest. The necessity of a quarrel with the Indians would have been regretted by the lieutenant, even if he had been impelled to it by a want of the necessaries of life; but to engage in it for the transient gratification that would arise from obtaining two or three hundred green cocoa-nuts, appeared in his view highly criminal. The same calamity, at least with regard to the natives, would probably have occurred, if he had sought for any other place on the coast to the northward and westward, where the ship might have lain so near the shore as to cover his people with the guns when they had landed. Besides, there was cause to believe, that before such a place could have been found, our navigators would have been carried so far to the westward, as to be obliged to go to Batavia on the north side of Java. This, in Mr. Cook's opinion, would not have been so safe a passage as that to the south of Java, through the straits of Sunda. Another reason for his making the best of his way to Batavia, was the leakiness of the vessel, which rendered it doubtful whether it would not be necessary to heave her down when she arrived at that port. Our commander's resolution was farther confirmed by the consideration that no discovery could be expected in seas which had already been navigated, and where the coast had been sufficiently described both by Spanish and Dutch geographers, and especially by the latter. The only merit claimed by the lieutenant, in this part of his voyage, was the having established it as a fact beyond all controversy, that New Holland and New Guinea are two distinct countries.

Without staying, therefore, on the coast of New Guinea, the Endeavour, on the same day, directed her course to the westward, in pursuing which, Mr. Cook had an opportunity of rectifying the errors of former navigators. Very early in the morning of the 6th of September our voyagers passed a small island, which lay to the north-northwest, and at day-break they discovered another low island, extending from that quarter to north-north-east. Upon the last island, which appeared to be of considerable extent, the lieutenant would have landed to examine its produce, if the wind had not blown so fresh as to render his design impractiable. Unless these two islands belong to the Arrou islands, they have no place in the charts; and if they do belong to the Arrou islands, they are laid down at too great a distance from New Guinea. Some other land which was seen this day, ought, by its distance from New Guinea, to have been part of the Arrou islands; but if any dependance can be placed on former charts, it lies a degree farther to the south.

On the 7th, when the ship was in latitude 9° 30' south, and longitude 229° 34' west, our people ought to have been in sight of the Weasel Isles, which, in the charts, are laid down at the distance of twenty or twenty-five leagues from the coast of New Holland. But as our commander saw nothing of them, he concluded that they must have been placed erroneously. Nor will this be deemed surprising, when it is considered, that not only these islands, but the coast which bounds this sea, have been explored at different times, and by different persons, who had not all the requisites for keeping accurate journals which are now possessed, and whose various discoveries have been delineated upon charts by others, perhaps at the distance of more than a century after such discoveries had been made.

In pursuing their course, our navigators passed the islands of Timor, Timor-lavet, Rottee, and Seman. While they were near the two latter islands, they observed, about ten o'clock at night on the 16th of the month, a phenomenon in the heavens, which in many particulars resembled the Aurora Borealis, though in others it was very different. It consisted of a dull, reddish light, which reached about twenty degrees above the horizon; and though its extent at times varied much, it never comprehended less than eight or ten points of the compass. Through and out of the general appearance, there passed rays of light of a brighter colour, which vanished and were renewed nearly in the same manner as those of Aurora Borealis, but entirely without the tremulous or vibratory motion which is seen in that phenomenon. The body of this light bore south-southeast from the ship, and continued without any diminution of its brightness, till twelve o'clock, and probably a longer time, as the gentlemen were prevented from observing it farther by their retiring to sleep.

By the 16th, Lieutenant Cook had gotten clear of all the islands which had then been laid down in the maps as situated between Timor and Java, and did not expect to meet with any other in that quarter. But the next morning an island was seen bearing west-southwest, and at first he believed he had made a new discovery. As soon as our voyagers had come close in with the north side of it, they had the pleasing prospect of houses and cocoa-nut trees, and of what still more agreeably surprised them, numerous flocks of sheep. Many of the people on board were at this time in a bad state of health, and no small number of them had been dissatisfied with the lieutenant for not having touched at Timor. He readily embraced, therefore, the opportunity of landing at a place which appeared so well calculated to supply the necessities of the company, and to remove both the sickness and the discontent which had spread among them. This place proved to be the island of Savu, where a settlement had lately been made by the Dutch.

The great design of our commander was to obtain provisions, which after some difficulty and some jealousy on the part of Mr. Lange, the Dutch resident, were procured. These provisions were nine buffaloes, six sheep, three hogs, thirty dozen of fowls, many dozens of eggs, some cocoa-nuts, a few limes, a little garlic, and several hundred gallons of palm syrup. In obtaining these refreshments at a reasonable price, the English were not a little assisted by an old Indian, who appeared to be a person of considerable authority under the king of the country. The lieutenant and his friends were one day very hospitably entertained by the king himself, though the royal etiquette did not permit his majesty to partake of the banquet.

So little, in general, had the island of Savu been known, that Mr. Cook had never seen a map or chart in which it is clearly or accurately laid down. The middle of it lies in about the latitude of 10° 35' south, and longitude 237° 30' west; and from the ship it presented a prospect, than which nothing can be more beautiful. This prospect, from the verdure and culture of the country, from the hills richly clothed, which rise in a gentle and regular ascent, and from the stateliness and beauty of the trees, is delightful to a degree that can scarcely be conceived by the most lively imagination. With regard to the productions and natives of the island, the account which our navigators were enabled to give of them, and which is copious and entertaining, was, in a great measure, derived from the information of Mr. Lange.

An extraordinary relation is given of the morals of the people of this island, and which, if true, must fill every virtuous mind with pleasure. Their characters and conduct are represented as irreproachable, even upon the principles of Christianity. Though no man is permitted to have more than one wife, an illicit commerce between the sexes is scarcely known among them. Instances of theft are very rare, and so far are they from revenging a supposed injury by murder, that when any difference arises between them, they immediately and implicitly refer it to the determination of their king. They will not so much as make it the subject of private debate, lest they should hence be provoked to resentment and ill will. Their delicacy and cleanliness are suited to the purity of their morals. From the specimen which is given of the language of Savu, it appears to have some affinity with that of the South Sea islands. Many of the words are exactly the same, and the terms of numbers are derived from the same origin.

On the 21st of September, our navigators got under sail, and having pursued their voyage till the 1st of October, on that day they came within sight of the island of Java. During their course from Savu, Lieutenant Cook allowed twenty minutes a day for the westerly current, which he concluded must run strong at this time, especially on the coast of Java; and accordingly he found that this allowance was exactly equivalent to the effect of the current upon the ship. Such was the sagacity of our commander's judgment in whatever related to navigation.

On the 2d, two Dutch ships being seen to lie off Anger Point, the lieutenant sent Mr. Hicks on board one of them to inquire news concerning England, from which our people had so long been absent. Mr. Hicks brought back the agreeable intelligence that the Swallow, commanded by Captain Carteret, had been at

Batavia two years before. On the morning of the 5th, a prow came along side the Endeavour, with a Dutch officer, who sent down to Mr. Cook a printed paper in English, duplicates of which he had in other languages. This paper was regularly signed, in the name of the governor and council of the Indies, by their secretary, and contained nine questions, very ill expressed, two of which only the lieutenant thought proper to answer. These were what regarded the nation and name of his vessel, and whither she was bound. On the 9th, our voyagers stood in for Batavia Road, where they found the Harcourt Indiaman from England, two English private traders, and a number of Dutch ships. Immediately a boat came on board the Endeavour, and the officer who commanded having inquired who our people were, and whence they came, instantly returned with such answers as were given him. In the mean time Mr. Cook sent a lieutenant ashore to acquaint the governor of his arrival, and to make an apology for not having saluted; a ceremony he had judged better to omit, as he could only make use of three guns, excepting the swivels, which he was of opinion would not be heard.

It being universally agreed that the ship could not safely proceed to Europe without an examination of her bottom, our commander determined to apply for leave to heave her down at Batavia; and for this purpose he drew up a request in writing, which, after he had waited first upon the governor-general, and then upon the council, was readily complied with, and he was told that he should have everything he wanted.

In the evening of the 10th, there was a dreadful storm of thunder, lightning, and rain, during which the main-mast of one of the Dutch East Indiamen was split and carried away by the deck, and the main-top-mast and top-gallant-mast were shivered to pieces. The stroke was probably directed by an iron spindle, which was at the main-top-gallant-mast-head. As this ship lay very near the Endeavour, she could scarcely have avoided sharing the same fate, had it not been for the conducting chain, which fortunately had been just gotten up, and which conveyed the lightning over the side of the vessel. But though she escaped the lightning, the explosion shook her like an earthquake; and the cabin at the same time appeared like a line of fire. Mr. Cook has embraced this occasion of earnestly recommending similar chains to every ship, and hath expressed his hope that all who read his narrative will be warned against having an iron spindle at the mast-head.

The English gentlemen had taken up their lodging and boarding at a hotel, or kind of inn, kept by the order of government. Here they met with those impositions in point of expense and treatment, which are too common to admit of much surprise. It was not long, however, that they submitted to ill usage. By a farther acquaintance with the manner of dealing with their host, and by spirited remonstrances, they procured a better furnished table. Mr. Banks in a few days hired a small house for himself and his party; and as soon as he was settled in his new habitation, sent for Tupia, who had hitherto continued on board on account of sickness. When he quitted the ship and after he came into the boat, he was exceedingly lifeless and dejected; but no sooner did he enter the town, than he appeared to be inspired with another soul. A scene so entirely new and extraordinary filled him with amazement. The houses, carriages, streets, people, and a multiplicity of other objects, rushing upon him at once, produced an effect similar to what is ascribed to enchantment. His boy, Tayeto, expressed his wonder and delight in a still more rapturous manner. He danced along the streets in a kind of ecstasy, examining every object with a restless and eager curiosity, which was excited and gratified every moment. Tupia's attention was particularly excited by the various dresses of the passing multitude; and when he was informed that at Batavia every one wore the dress of his own country, he expressed his desire of appearing in the garb of Otaheite. Accordingly, South

Sea cloth being sent for from the ship, he equipped himself with great expedition and dexterity.

Lieutenant Cook imagined that at Batavia he should find it easy to take up what money he might want for repairing and refitting the Endeavour; but in this he was mistaken. No private person could be found who had ability and inclination to furnish the sum which was necessary. In this exigency the lieutenant had recourse, by a written request to the governor, from whom he obtained an order for being supplied out of the Dutch company's treasury.

When our voyagers had been only nine days at Batavia, they began to feel the fatal effects of the climate and situation. Tupia, after his first flow of spirits had subsided, grew every day worse and worse, and Tayeto was seized with an inflammation upon his lungs. Mr. Banks and Dr. Solander were attacked by fevers, and in a little time almost every person, both on board and on shore, was sick. The distress of our people was indeed very great, and the prospect before them discouraging in the highest degree. Tupia, being desirous of breathing a freer air than among the numerous houses that obstructed it ashore, had a tent erected for him on Cooper's Island, to which he was accompanied by Mr. Banks, who attended this poor Indian with the greatest humanity, till he was rendered incapable of doing it by the violent increase of his own disorder. On the 5th of November, Mr. Monkhouse, the surgeon of the ship, a sensible, skilful man, whose loss was not a little aggravated by the situation of the English, fell the first sacrifice to this fatal country. Tayeto died on the 9th, and Tupia, who loved him with the tenderness of a parent, sunk at once after the loss of the boy, and survived him only a few days. The disorders of Mr. Banks and Dr. Solander grew to such a height that the physicians declared they had no chance of preserving their lives but by removing into the country. Accordingly, a house was hired for them at the distance of about two miles from the town; where, in consequence of enjoying a purer air, and being better nursed by two Malayan women whom they had brought, they recovered by slow degrees. At length Lieutenant Cook was himself taken ill, and out of the whole ship's company not more than ten were able to do duty.

In the midst of these distresses our commander was diligently and vigourously attentive to the repair of his vessel. When her bottom came to be examined, she was found to be in a worse condition than had been apprehended. Her false keel and main keel were both of them greatly injured ; a large quantity of the sheathing was torn off, and among several planks which were much damaged, two of them and the half of a third were so worn for the length of six feet, that they were not above the eighth part of an inch in thickness ; and here the worms had made way quite into the timbers. In this state the Endeavour had sailed many hundred leagues, in a quarter of the globe where navigation is dangerous in the highest degree. It was happy for our voyagers that they were ignorant of their perilous situation ; for it must have deeply affected them to have known that a considerable part of the bottom of the vessel was thinner than the sole of a shoe, and that all their lives depended upon so slight and fragile a barrier between them and the unfathomable ocean.

The repair of the Endeavour was carried on very much to Mr. Cook's satisfaction. In justice to the Dutch officers and workmen, he hath declared, that in his opinion, there was not a marine yard in the world where a ship can be laid with more convenience, safety, and despatch, or repaired with greater diligence and skill. He was particularly pleased with the manner of heaving down by two masts, and gives it a decided preference to the method which had hitherto been practised by the English. The lieutenant was not one of those on whom the bigotry could be charged of adhering to old customs, in opposition to the dictates of reason and experience.

By the 8th of December the Endeavour was perfectly refitted. From that time to the 24th, our people were employed in completing her stock of water, provisions and stores, in erecting some new pumps, and in various other necessary operations. All this business would have been effected much sooner if it had not been retarded by the general sickness of the men.

In the afternoon of the 24th our commander took leave of the governor of Batavia, and of several other gentlemen belonging to the place, with whom he had formed connections, and to whom he had been greatly obliged for their civilities and assistance. In the mean while an accident intervened which might have been attended with disagreeable effects. A seaman, who had run away from one of the Dutch ships in the road, entered on board the Endeavour. Upon his being reclaimed as a subject of Holland, Mr. Cook, who was on shore, declared that if the man appeared to be a Dutchman, he should certainly be delivered up. When, however, the order was carried to Mr. Hicks, who commanded on board, he refused to surrender the seaman, alleging that he was a subject of Great Britain, born in Ireland. In this conduct Mr. Hicks acted in perfect conformity to the lieutenant's intention and directions. The captain of the Dutch vessel, in the next place, by a message from the governor-general, demanded the man as a subject of Denmark. To this Mr. Cook replied, that there must be some mistake in the general's message, since he would never demand of him a Danish seaman, whose only crime was that of preferring the English to the Dutch service. At the same time the lieutenant added, that to show the sincerity of his desire to avoid disputes, if the man was a Dane he should be delivered up as a courtesy; but that if he appeared to be an English subject, he should be kept at all events. Soon after a letter was brought from Mr. Hicks, containing indubitable proofs that the seaman in question was a subject of his Britannic majesty. This letter Mr. Cook sent to the governor, with an assurance to his excellency that he would not part with the man on any terms. A conduct so firm and decisive produced the desired effect, no more being heard of the affair.

In the evening of the 25th, our commander went on board, together with Mr. Banks and the rest of the gentlemen who had resided constantly on shore. The gentlemen, though considerably better, were far from being perfectly recovered. At this time the sick persons in the ship amounted to forty, and the rest of the company were in a very feeble condition. It was remarkable that every individual had been ill excepting the sail-maker, who was an old man between seventy and eighty years of age, and who was drunk every day during the residence of our people at Batavia. Three seamen and Mr. Green's servant died, besides the surgeon, Tupia and Tayeto. Tupia did not entirely fall a sacrifice to the unwholesome, stagnant, and putrid air of the country. As he had been accustomed from his birth to subsist chiefly upon vegetable food, and particularly on ripe fruit, he soon contracted the disorders which are incident to a sea life, and would probably have sunk under them before the voyage of the English could have been completed, even if they had not been obliged to go to Batavia to refit their vessel.

Our navigators did not stay at this place without gaining an extensive acquaintance with the productions of the country and the manners and customs of the inhabitants. The information which was obtained on these heads will be found to constitute a very valuable addition to what was heretofore known upon the subject.

On Thursday, the 27th of December, the Endeavour stood out to sea; and on the 5th of January, 1771, she came to an anchor under the southeast side of Prince's Island. The design of this was to obtain a recruit of wood and water, and to procure some refreshments for the sick, many of whom had become much worse than they were when they left Batavia. As soon as the vessel was secured, the lieutenant, Mr. Banks, and Dr. Solander, went on shore, and were conducted by some Indians they met with to a person who was represented to be the king of the country. After exchanging a few compliments with his majesty, the gentlemen proceeded to business, but could not immediately come to a settlement with him in respect to the price of turtle. They were more successful in their search of a watering-place, having found water conveniently situated, and which they had reason to believe would prove good. As they were going off some of the natives sold them three turtles, under a promise that the king should not be informed of the transaction.

On the next day a traffic was established with the Indians upon such terms as were offered by the English, so that by night our people had plenty of turtle. The three which had been pur-purchased the evening before, were in the mean time dressed for the ship's company, who, excepting on the preceding day, had not, for nearly the space of four months, been once served with salt provisions. Mr. Banks, in the evening, paid his respects to the king at his palace, which was situated in the middle of a rice field. His majesty was busily employed in dressing his own supper; but this did not prevent him from receiving his visitant in a very gracious manner. During the following days, the commerce with the natives for provisions was continued; in the course of which they brought down to the trading place, not only a quantity of turtle, but fowls, fish, monkeys, small deer, and some vegetables.

On the evening of the 11th, when Mr. Cook went on shore to see how those of his people conducted their business, who were employed in wooding and watering, he was informed that an axe had been stolen. As it was a matter of consequence to prevent others from being encouraged to commit thefts of the like kind, he resolved not to pass over the offence, but to insist upon redress from the king. Accordingly, after some altercation, his majesty promised that the axe should be restored in the morning, and the promise was faithfully performed.

On the 15th, our commander weighed, and stood out for sea.

Prince's Island, where he lay about ten days, was formerly much frequented by the India ships of many nations, and especially those of England, but it had lately been forsaken, on account of the supposed badness of its water. This supposition, however, arose from a want of duly examining the brook by which the water is supplied. It is, indeed, brackish at the lower part of the brook, but higher up it will be found excellent. The lieutenant, therefore, was clearly of opinion that Prince's Island is a more eligible place for ships to touch at, than either North Island or New Bay; from neither of which places any considerable quantity of other refreshments can be procured.

As the Endeavour proceeded on her voyage to the Cape of Good Hope, the seeds of disease, which had been received at Batavia, appeared with the most threatening symptoms, and reduced our navigators to a very melancholy situation. The ship was, in fact, nothing better than an hospital, in which those who could go about were not sufficient for a due attendance upon those who were sick. Lest the water which had been taken in at Prince's Island should have had any share in adding to the disorder of the men, the lieutenant ordered it to be purified with lime; and, as a farther remedy against infection, he directed all the parts of the vessel between the decks to be washed with vinegar. The malady had taken too deep root to be speedily eradicated. Mr. Banks was reduced so low by it, that for some time there was no hope of his life; and so fatal was the disease to many others, that almost every night a dead body was committed to the sea. There were buried, in the course of about six weeks, Mr. Sporing, a gentleman who was one of Mr. Banks's assistants; Mr. Parkinson, his natural history painter: Mr. Green, the astronomer; the boatswain, the carpenter, and his mate; Mr. Monkhouse the midshipman, another midshipman, the old jolly sail-maker and his assistant, the ship's cook, the corporal of the marines, two of the carpenter's crew, and nine seamen. In all, the loss amounted to three and twenty persons, besides the seven who died at Batavia. It is probable that these calamitous events, which could not fail of making a powerful impression on the mind of Lieutenant Cook, might give occasion to his turning his thoughts more zealously to those methods of preserving the health of seamen, which he afterwards pursued with such remarkable success.

On Friday, the 5th of March, the Endeavour arrived off the Cape of Good Hope; and as soon as she was brought to an anchor, our commander waited upon the governor, from whom he received assurances that he should be furnished with every supply which the country could afford. His first care was to provide a proper place for the sick, whose number was not small; and a house was speedily found, where it was agreed that they should be lodged and boarded at the rate of two shillings a day for each person.

The run from Java Head to the Cape of Good Hope did not furnish many subjects of remark, that could be of any great use to future voyagers. Such observations, however, as occurred to him, the lieutenant has been careful to record, not being willing to omit the least circumstance that may contribute to the safety and facility of navigation.

The lieutenant, having lain at the Cape to recover the sick, to procure stores, and to refit his vessel, till the 14th of April, then stood out of the bay and proceeded on his voyage homeward. In the morning of the 29th, he crossed his first meridian, having circumnavigated the globe in the direction from east to west. The consequence of which was, that he lost a day, an allowance for which had been made at Batavia. On the 1st of May he arrived at St. Helena, where he staid till the 4th to refresh; during which time Mr. Banks, employed himself in making the complete circuit of the island, and visiting the places most worthy of observation.

The manner in which slaves are described as being treated in this island, must be mentioned with indignation. According to our commander's representation, while every kind of labour is performed by them, they are not furnished either with horses or with any of the various machines which art has invented to facilitate their tasks. Carts might conveniently be used in some parts, and where the ground is too steep for them, wheel-barrows might be employed to great advantage; and yet there is not a wheel-barrow in the whole island. Though everything conveyed from place to place is done by slaves alone, they have not the simple convenience of a porter's knot, but carry their burden upon their heads. They appeared to be a miserable race, worn out by the united operation of excessive labour and ill usage; and Mr. Cook was sorry to observe, and to say, that instances of wanton cruelty were much more frequent among his countrymen at St. Helena, than among the Dutch, who are generally reproached with want of humanity, both at Batavia and the Cape of Good Hope. It is impossible for a feeling mind to avoid being concerned that such an account should be given of the conduct of any who are entitled to the name of Britons. The lieutenant's reproof, if just, hath, it may be hoped, long before this, reached the place, and produced some good effect.* If slavery must still be continued, everything ought to be done which can tend to soften it.

When our commander departed from St. Helena, on the 4th, it was in company with the Portland man of war, and twelve Indiamen. With this fleet he continued to sail till the 10th, when, perceiving that the Endeavour proceeded much more heavily than any of the other vessels, and that she was not likely to get home so soon as the rest, he made a signal to speak with

---

* Near the conclusion of Captain Cook's second voyage, there is the following short note. "In the account given of St. Helena, in the narrative of my former voyage, I find some mistakes. Its inhabitants are far from exercising a wanton cruelty over their slaves; and they have had wheel carriages and porter's knots for many years." This note I insert with pleasure. Nevertheless, I cannot think that the lieutenant could have given so strong a representation of things, if, at the time in which it was written, it had been wholly without foundation.

the Portland. Upon this, Captain Elliot himself came on board, and Mr. Cook delivered to him the common log-books of his ship, and the journals of some of the officers. The Endeavour, however, kept in company with the fleet till the morning of the 23d, at which time there was not a single vessel in sight. On that day died Mr. Hicks, and in the evening his body was committed to the sea, with the usual ceremonies. Mr. Charles Clerke, a young man extremely well qualified for the station, and whose name will hereafter frequently occur, received an order from Mr. Cook to act as lieutenant in Mr. Hicks's room.

The rigging and sails of the ship were now become so bad, that something was continually giving way. Nevertheless, our commander pursued his course in safety; and, on the 10th of June, land, which proved to be the Lizard, was discovered by Nicholas Young, the boy who had first seen New Zealand. On the 11th, the lieutenant ran up the channel. At six the next morning he passed Beachy Head, and in the afternoon of the same day, he came to an anchor in the Downs, and went on shore at Deal.

Thus ended Mr. Cook's first voyage round the world, in which he had gone through so many dangers, explored so many countries, and exhibited the strongest proofs of his possessing an eminently sagacious and active mind; a mind that was equal to every perilous enterprise, and to the boldest and most successful efforts of navigation and discovery.

CHAPTER III.

ACCOUNT OF CAPTAIN COOK DURING THE PERIOD BETWEEN HIS FIRST AND SECOND VOYAGES.

The manner in which Lieutenant Cook had performed his circumnavigation of the globe, justly entitled him to the protection of government, and the favour of his sovereign. Accordingly, he was promoted to be a commander in his majesty's navy, by commission bearing date on the 29th of August, 1771. Mr. Cook, on this occasion, from a certain consciousness of his own merit, wished to have been appointed a post captain. But the Earl of Sandwich, who was now at the head of the Admiralty board, though he had the greatest regard for our navigator, could not accede to his request, because a compliance with it would have been inconsistent with the order of the naval service. The difference was in point of rank only, and not of advantage. A commander has the same pay as a post captain, and his authority is the same when he is in actual employment. The distinction is a necessary step in the progress to the higher honours of the profession.

It cannot be doubted, but that the president and council of the Royal Society were highly satisfied with the manner in which the transit of Venus had been observed. The papers of Mr. Cook and Mr. Green, relative to this subject, were put into the hands of the astronomer royal, to be by him digested, and that he might deduce from them the important consequences to science which resulted from the observation. This was done by him with an accuracy and ability becoming his high knowledge and character. On the 21st of May, 1772, Captain Cook communicated to the Royal Society, in a letter addressed to Dr. Maskelyne, an "Account of the flowing of the Tides in the South Sea, as observed on board of his Majesty's bark, the Endeavour."

The reputation our navigator had acquired by his late voyage was deservedly great; and the desire of the public to be acquainted with the new scenes and new objects which were now brought to light, was ardently excited. It is not surprising, therefore, that different attempts were made to satisfy the general curiosity. There soon appeared a publication entitled, "A Journal of a Voyage round the World." This was the production of some person who had been upon the expedition; and, though his account was dry and imperfect, it served, in a certain degree, to relieve the eagerness of inquiry. The journal of Sydney Parkinson, draftsman to Sir Joseph Banks, to whom it belonged by ample purchase, was likewise printed, from a copy surreptitiously obtained; but an injunction from the Court of Chancery for some time prevented its appearance. This work, though dishonestly given to the world, was recommended by plates. But it was Dr. Hawkesworth's account of Lieutenant Cook's voyage which completely gratified the public curiosity. This account, which was written by authority, was drawn up from the journal of the lieutenant, and the papers of Sir Joseph Banks; and, besides the merit of the composition, derived an extraordinary advantage from the number and excellence of its charts and engravings, which were furnished at the expense of government. The large price given by the booksellers for this work, and the avidity with which it was read, displayed, in the strongest light, the anxiety of the nation to be fully informed in everything that belonged to the late navigation and discoveries.

Captain Cook, during his voyage, had sailed over the Pacific Ocean in many of those latitudes, in which a southern continent had been expected to lie. He had ascertained, that neither New Zealand nor New Holland were parts of such a continent. But the general question concerning its existence had not been deter-

7*

mined by him, nor did he go out for that purpose, though some of the reasons on which the notion of it had been adopted, were dispelled in the course of his navigation. It is well known how fondly the idea of a *Terra Australis incognita* had for nearly two centuries been entertained. Many plausible philosophical arguments have been urged in its support, and many facts alleged in its favour. The writer of this narrative fully remembers how much his imagination was captivated in the more early part of his life, with the hypothesis of a southern continent. He has often dwelt upon it with rapture, and been highly delighted with the authors who contended for its existence, and displayed the mighty consequences which would result from its being discovered. Though his knowledge was infinitely exceeded by that of some able men who paid a particular attention to the subject, he did not come behind them in the sanguineness of his hopes and expectation. Everything, however, which relates to science, must be separated from fancy, and brought to the test of experiment: and here was an experiment richly deserving to be tried. The object, indeed, was of peculiar magnitude, and worthy to be pursued by a great prince, and a great nation.

Happily, the period was arrived in Britain for the execution of the most important scientific designs. A regard to matters of this kind, though so honourable to crowned heads, had heretofore been too much neglected even by some of the best of our princes. Our present sovereign had already distinguished his reign by his patronage of science and literature; but the beginnings which had hitherto been made were only the pledges of future munificence. With respect to the object now in view, the gracious dispositions of his majesty were ardently seconded by the noble lord who had been placed at the head of the board of admiralty. The Earl of Sandwich was possessed of a mind which was capable of comprehending and encouraging the most enlarged views and schemes with regard to navigation and discovery. Accordingly, it was by his particular recommendation that a resolution was formed for the appointment of an expedition, finally to determine the question concerning the existence of a southern continent. Quiros seems to have been the first person who had any idea that such a continent existed, and he was the first that was sent out for the sole purpose of ascertaining the fact. He did not succeed in the attempt ; and the attempts of various navigators down to the present century, were equally unsuccessful.

When the design of accomplishing this great object was resolved upon, it did not admit of any hesitation by whom it was to be carried into execution. No person was esteemed equally qualified with Captain Cook, for conducting an enterprise, the view of which was to give the utmost possible extent to the geography of the globe, and the knowledge of navigation. For the greater advantage of the undertaking, it was determined that two ships should be employed ; and much attention was paid to the choice of them, and to their equipment for the service. After mature deliberation by the navy board, during which particular regard was had to the captain's wisdom and experience, it was agreed that no vessels were so proper for discoveries in distant unknown parts, as those which were constructed like the Endeavour. This opinion concurring with that of the Earl of Sandwich, the admiralty came to a resolution that two ships should be provided of a similar construction. Accordingly two vessels, both of which had been built at Whitby, by the same person who built the Endeavour, were purchased of Captain William Hammond, of Hull. They were about fourteen or sixteen months old at the time when they were bought, and, in Captain Cook's judgment, were as well adapted to the intended service as if they had been expressly constructed for that purpose. The largest of the two, which consisted of four hundred and sixty-two tons burden, was named the Resolution. To the other, which was three hundred and thirty-six tons burden, was given the name of the Adventure. On the 28th of November

1771, Captain Cook was appointed to the command of the former; and, about the same time, Mr. Tobias Furneaux was promoted to the command of the latter. The complement of the Resolution, including officers and men, was fixed at a hundred and twelve persons; and that of the Adventure, at eighty-one. In the equipment of these ships, every circumstance was attended to that could contribute to the comfort and success of the voyage. They were fitted in the most complete manner, and supplied with every extraordinary article which was suggested to be necessary or useful. Lord Sandwich, whose zeal was indefatigable upon this occasion, visited the vessels, from time to time, to be assured that the whole equipment was agreeable to his wishes, and to the satisfaction of those who were to engage in the expedition. Nor were the navy and victualling boards wanting in procuring for the ships the very best of stores and provisions, with some alterations in the species of them, that were adapted to the nature the enterprise; besides which, there was an ample supply of antiscorbutic articles, such as malt, sour krout, salted cabbage, portable broth, saloup, mustard, marmalade of carrots, and inspissated juice of wort and beer.

No less attention was paid to the cause of science in general. The admiralty engaged Mr. William Hodges, an excellent landscape painter, to embark in the voyage, in order to make drawings and paintings of such objects as could not so well be comprehended from written descriptions. Mr. John Reinhold Forster and his son were fixed upon to explore and collect the natural history of the countries which might be visited, and an ample sum was granted by parliament for the purpose. That nothing might be wanting to accomplish the scientific views of the expedition, the board of longitude agreed with Mr. William Wales and Mr. William Bayley, to make astronomical observations. Mr. Wales was stationed in the Resolution, and Mr. Bayley in the Adventure. By the same board they were furnished with the best of instruments, and particularly with four time-pieces, three constructed by Arnold, and one by Mr. Kendal, on Mr. Harrison's principles.

Though Captain Cook had been appointed to the command of the Resolution on the 28th of November, 1771, such were the preparations necessary for so long and important a voyage, and the impediments which occasionally and unavoidably occurred, that the ship did not sail from Deptford till the 9th of April following, nor did she leave Long Reach till the 10th of May. In plying down the river it was found necessary to put into Sheerness, in order to make some alterations in her upper works. These the officers of the yard were directed immediately to take in hand; and Lord Sandwich and Sir Hugh Palliser came down to see them executed in the most effectual manner. The ship being again completed for sea by the 22d of June, Captain Cook on that day sailed from Sheerness, and, on the 3d of July, joined the Adventure in Plymouth Sound. Lord Sandwich, in his return from a visit to the dockyards, having met the Resolution on the preceding evening, his lordship and Sir Hugh Palliser gave the last mark of their great attention to the object of the voyage, by coming on board, to assure themselves that every thing was done which was agreeable to our commander's wishes, and that his vessel was equipped entirely to his satisfaction.

At Plymouth, Captain Cook received his instructions; with regard to which, without entering into a minute detail of them, it is sufficient to say that he was sent out upon the most enlarged plan of discovery that is known in the history of navigation. He was instructed not only to circumnavigate the whole globe, but to circumnavigate it in high southern latitudes, making such traverses from time to time, into every corner of the Pacific Ocean not before examined, as might finally and effectually resolve the much agitated question about the existence of a southern continent in any part of the southern hemisphere, to which access could be had by the efforts of the boldest and most skilful navigators.

CHAPTER IV.

NARRATIVE OF CAPTAIN COOK'S SECOND VOYAGE AROUND THE WORLD.

On the 13th of July, Captain Cook sailed from Plymouth, and on the 29th of the same month anchored in Funchal Road, in the island of Madeira. Having obtained a supply of water, wine, and other necessaries at that island, he left it on the 1st of August, and sailed to the southward. As he proceeded in his voyage he made three puncheons of beer of the inspissated juice of malt; and the liquor produced was very brisk and drinkable. The heat of the weather and the agitation of the ship, had hitherto withstood all the endeavours of our people to prevent this juice from being in a high state of fermentation. If it could be kept from fermenting, it would be a most valuable article at sea.

The captain having found that his stock of water would not last to the Cape of Good Hope, without putting his men to a scanty allowance, resolved to stop at St. Jago, one of the Cape de Verd Islands, for a supply. At Port Praya, in this island, he anchored on the 10th of August, and by the 14th had completed his water and procured some other refreshments, upon which he set sail and prosecuted his course. He embraced the occasion which his touching at St. Jago afforded him, of giving such a delineation and description of Port Praya and of the supplies there to be obtained, as might be of service to future navigators.

On the 20th of the month, the rain poured down upon our voyagers, not in drops, but in streams, and the wind at the same time being variable and rough, the people were obliged to attend so constantly upon the decks that few of them escaped being completely soaked. This circumstance is mentioned to show the method that was taken by Captain Cook to preserve his men from the evil consequences of the wet to which they had been exposed. He had every thing to fear from the rain, which is a great promoter of sickness in hot climates. But to guard against this effect he pursued some hints that had been suggested to him by Sir Hugh Palliser and Captain Campbell, and took care that the ship should be aired and dried with fires made between the decks, and that the damp places of the vessel should be smoked; beside which, the people were ordered to air their bedding, and to wash and dry their clothes whenever there was an opportunity. The result of these precautions was, that there was not one sick person on board the Resolution.

Captain Cook, on the 8th of September, crossed the line in the longitude of 8° west, and proceeded without meeting anything remarkable till the 11th of October, when at 6h. 24m. 12s. by Mr. Kendal's watch, the moon rose about four digits eclipsed; soon after which the gentlemen prepared to observe the end of the eclipse. The observers were the captain himself, and Mr. Forster, Mr. Wales, Mr. Pickersgill, Mr. Gilbert, and Mr. Harvey.

Our commander had been informed before he left England, that he sailed at an improper season of the year, and that he should meet with much calm weather, near and under the line. But though such weather may happen in some years, it is not always, or even generally, to be expected. So far was it from being the case with Captain Cook, that he had a brisk south-west wind in those very latitudes where the calms had been predicted; nor was he exposed to any of the tornadoes which are so much spoken of by other navigators. On the 29th of the month, between eight and nine o'clock at night, when our voyagers were near the Cape of Good Hope, the whole sea within the compass of their sight became at once, as it were, illuminated. The captain had been formerly convinced, by Mr Banks and Dr. Solander, that such appearances in the ocean were occasioned by insects. Mr. Forster, however, seemed disposed to adopt a different opinion. To determine the question, our commander ordered some buckets of water to be drawn up from alongside the ship, which were found full of an innumerable quantity of small globular insects, about the size of a common pin's head, and quite transparent. Though no life was perceived in them, there could be no doubt of their being living animals, when in their own proper element, and Mr. Forster became now well satisfied that they were the cause of the sea's illumination.

On the 30th, the Resolution and Adventure anchored in Table Bay; soon after which Captain Cook went on shore, and accompanied by Captain Furneaux and the two Mr. Forsters, waited on Baron Plattenberg, the governor of the Cape of Good Hope, who received the gentlemen with great politeness, and promised them every assistance the place could afford. From him our commander learned that two French ships from the Mauritius, about eight months before, had discovered land in the latitude of 48° south, along which they sailed forty miles, till they came to a bay, into which they were upon the point of entering when they were driven off and separated in a hard gale of wind. Previously to this misfortune they had lost some of their boats and people that had been sent to sound the bay. Captain Cook was also informed by Baron Plattenberg that in the month of March two other ships from the island of Mauritius had touched at the Cape in their way to the South Pacific Ocean, where they were going to make discoveries under the command of M. Marion.

From the healthy condition of the crews both of the Resolution and Adventure, it was imagined by the captain that his stay at the Cape would be very short. But the necessity of waiting till the requisite provisions could be prepared and collected, kept him more than three weeks at this place; which time was improved by him in ordering both the ships to be caulked and painted, and in taking care that, in every respect, their condition should be as good as when they left England.

On the 22d of November our commander sailed from the Cape of Good Hope, and proceeded on his voyage in search of a southern continent. Having gotten clear of the land, he directed his course for Cape Circumcision; and judging that cold weather would soon approach, he ordered slops to be served to such of the people as were in want of them, and gave to each man the fearnought jacket and trowsers allowed by the admiralty. On the 29th, the wind, which was west-northwest, increased to a storm, that continued with some few intervals of moderate weather, till the 6th of December. By this gale, which was attended with hail and rain, and which blew at times with such violence that the ships could carry no sails, our voyagers were driven far to the eastward of their intended course, and no hopes were left to the captain of reaching Cape Circumcision. A still greater misfortune was the loss of the principal part of the live stock on board, consisting of sheep, hogs and geese. At the same time the sudden transition from warm, mild weather, to weather which was extremely cold and wet, was so severely felt by our people that it was necessary to make some addition to their allowance of spirits, by giving each of them a dram on particular occasions.

Our navigators on the 10th of December began to meet with islands of ice. One of these islands was so much concealed from them by the haziness of the weather, accompanied with snow and sleet, that they were steering directly towards it, and did not see it till it was at a less distance than that of a mile. Captain Cook judged it to be about fifty feet high, and half a mile in circuit. It was flat at the top and its sides rose in a perpendicular direction, against which the sea broke to a great height The weather continuing to be hazy, the captain, on account of the ice islands, was obliged to proceed with the utmost caution Six of them were passed on the 12th, some of which were nearly two miles in circuit, and sixty feet high; nevertheless, such were the force and height of the waves, that the sea broke quite over them. Hence was exhibited a view that for a few moments was pleasing to the eye, but the pleasure was soon swallowed up in the horror which seized upon the mind from the prospect of danger. For if a ship should be so unfortunate as to get on the weather side of one of these islands, she would be dashed to pieces in a moment.

The vessels, on the 14th, were stopped by an immense field or low ice, to which no end could be seen, either to the east, west, or south. In different parts of this field were islands or hills of ice, like those which our voyagers had found floating in the sea, and twenty of which had presented themselves to view the day before. Some of the people on board imagined that they saw land over the ice, and Captain Cook himself at first entertained the same sentiment. But upon more narrowly examining these ice-hills, and the various appearances they made when seen through the haze, he was induced to change his opinion. On the 18th, though in the morning our navigators had been quite embayed, they were, notwithstanding, at length enabled to get clear of the field of ice. They were, however, at the same time, carried in among the ice islands, which perpetually succeeded one another; which were almost equally dangerous, and the avoiding of which was a matter of the greatest difficulty. But perilous as it is to sail in a thick fog, among these floating rocks, as our commander properly called them, this is preferable to the being entangled with immense fields of ice under the same circumstances. In this latter case the great danger to be apprehended is the getting fast in the ice, a situation which would be alarming in the highest degree.

It had been a generally received opinion, that such ice as hath now been described, is formed in bays and rivers. Agreeably to this supposition, our voyagers were led to believe that land was not far distant, and that it lay to the southward, behind the ice

As, therefore they had sailed above thirty leagues along the edge of the ice, without finding a passage to the south, Captain Cook determined to run thirty or forty leagues to the east, and afterwards to endeavour to get to the southward. If, in this attempt, he met with no land or other impediment, his design was to stretch behind the ice, and thus to bring the matter to a decision. The weather at this time affected the senses with a feeling of cold much greater than that which was pointed out by the thermometer, so that the whole crew complained. In order the better to enable them to sustain the severity of the cold, the captain directed the sleeves of their jackets to be lengthened with baize, and had a cap made for each man of the same stuff, strengthened with canvas. These precautions greatly contributed to their comfort and advantage. It is worthy of observation that although the weather was as sharp on the 25th of December, as might have been expected in the same month of the year in any part of England, this was the middle of summer with our navigators. Some of the people now appearing to have symptoms of the scurvy, fresh wort was given them every day, prepared under the direction of the surgeons from the malt which had been provided for the purpose.

By the 29th, it became sufficiently ascertained from the course our commander had pursued, that the field of ice, along which the ships had sailed, did not join to any land as had been conjectured. At this time Captain Cook came to a resolution, provided he met with no impediment, to run as far west as the meridian of Cape Circumcision. While he was prosecuting this design, a gale arose on the 31st, which brought with it such a sea as rendered it very dangerous for the vessels to remain among the ice; and the danger was increased by discovering an immense field to the north, which extended farther than the eye could reach. As our voyagers were not above two or three miles from this field, and were surrounded by loose ice, there was no time to deliberate. They hauled to the south, and though they happily got clear, it was not till the ships had received several hard knocks from the loose pieces which were of the largest kind. On Friday, the 1st of January, 1773, the gale abated, and on the next day in the afternoon, our people had the felicity of enjoying the sight of the moon, the face of which had not been seen by them but once since they had departed from the Cape of Good Hope. Hence a judgment may be formed of the sort of weather they had been exposed to from the time of their leaving that place. The present opportunity was eagerly seized for making several observations of the sun and moon.

Captain Cook was now nearly in the same longitude which is assigned to Cape Circumcision, and about ninety-five leagues to the south of the latitude in which it is said to lie. At the same time the weather was so clear, that land might have been seen at the distance of fourteen or fifteen leagues. He concluded it, therefore, to be very probable, that what Bouvet took for land was nothing but mountains of ice, surrounded by loose or field ice. Our present navigators had naturally been led into a similar mistake. The conjecture, that such ice as had lately been seen was joined to land, was a very plausible one, though not founded on fact. Upon the whole, there was good reason to believe that no land was to be met with under this meridian, between the latitude of fifty-five and fifty-nine, where some had been supposed to exist.

Amidst the obstructions Captain Cook was exposed to, from the ice islands, which perpetually succeeded each other, he derived one advantage, and that was, a supply of fresh water. Though the melting and stowing away of the ice takes up some time, and is indeed, rather tedious, this method of watering is otherwise the most expeditious our commander had ever known. The water produced was perfectly sweet and well tasted. Upon the ice islands, penguins, albatrosses, and other birds were frequently seen. It had hitherto been the received opinion, that such birds never go far from land, and that the sight of them is a sure indication of its vicinity. That this opinion is not well founded, at least where ice islands exist, was now evinced by multiplied experience.

By Sunday, the 17th of January, Captain Cook reached the latitude of 67° 15' south, when he could advance no farther. At this time the ice was entirely closed to the south, in the whole extent from east to west-southwest, without the least appearance of any opening. The captain, therefore, thought it no longer prudent to persevere in sailing southward, especially as the summer was already half spent, and there was little reason to hope that it would be found practicable to get round the ice. Having taken this resolution, he determined to proceed directly in search of the land which had lately been discovered by the French, and as, in pursuing his purpose, the weather was clear at intervals, he spread the ships abreast four miles from each other, in order the better to investigate anything that might lie in their way. On the 1st of February our voyagers were in the latitude of 48° 30' south, and in longitude 58° 7' east, nearly in the meridian of the island of St. Mauritius. This was the situation in which the land, said to have been discovered by the French, was to be expected; but as no signs of it had appeared, our commander bore away to the east. Captain Furneaux, on the same day, informed Cook that he had just seen a large float of sea or rock weed, and about it several of the birds called divers. These were certain signs of the vicinity of land, though whether it lay to the east or west could not possibly be known. Our commander, therefore, formed the design of proceeding in his present latitude four or five degrees of longitude to the west of the meridian he was now in, and then to pursue his researches eastward. The west and northwest winds, which had continued for some days, prevented him from carrying this purpose into execution. However, he was convinced from the perpetual high sea he had lately met with, that there could be no great extent of land to the west.

While Captain Cook, on the next day, was steering eastward, Captain Furneaux told him that he thought the land was to the northwest of them ; as he had at one time observed the sea to be smooth, when the wind blew in that direction. This observation was by no means conformable to the remarks which had been made by our commander himself. Nevertheless, such was his readiness to attend to every suggestion, that he resolved to clear up the point, if the wind would admit of his getting to the west in any reasonable time. The wind, by veering to the north, did admit of his pursuing the search, and the result of it was, his conviction that if any land was near, it could only be an island of no considerable extent.

Captain Cook and his philosophical friends, while they were traversing this part of the Southern ocean, paid particular attention to the variation of the compass, which they found to be from 27° 50′ to 30° 26′ west. Probably the mean of the two extremes, viz. 29° 4′ was the nearest the truth, as it coincided with the variation observed on board the Adventure. One unaccountable circumstance is worthy of notice, though it did not now occur for the first time. It is that when the sun was on the starboard of the ship the variation was the least, and when the larboard side, the greatest.

On the 8th, our commander, in consequence of no signals having been answered by the Adventure, had reason to apprehend that a separation had taken place. After waiting two days, during which guns were kept discharging and false fires were burned in the night, the fact was confirmed, so that the Resolution was obliged to proceed alone in her voyage. As she pursued her course, penguins and other birds from time to time appeared in great numbers ; the meeting with which gave our navigators some hopes of finding land, and occasioned various speculations with regard to its situation. Experience, however, convinced them that no stress was to be laid on such hopes. They were so often deceived that they could no longer look upon any of the oceanic birds, which frequent high latitudes, as sure signs of the vecinity of land.

In the morning of the 17th, between midnight and three o'clock, lights were seen in the heavens similar to those which are known in the northern hemisphere by the name of the Aurora Borealis. Captain Cook had never heard that an Aurora Australis had been seen before. The officer of the watch observed, that it sometimes broke out in spiral rays and in a circular form, at which time its light was very strong, and its appearance beautiful. It was not perceived to have any particular direction; on the contrary, at various times it was conspicuous in different parts of the heavens, and diffused its light throughout the whole atmosphere.

On the 20th, our navigators imagined that they saw land to the southwest. Their conviction of its real existence was so strong, that they had no doubt of the matter, and accordingly they endeavoured to work up to it, in doing which, the weather was favourable to their purpose. However, what had been taken for land proved only to be clouds, that in the evening entirely disappeared and left a clear horizon, in which nothing could be discerned but ice islands. At night the Aurora Australis was again seen, and the appearance it assumed was very brilliant and luminous. It first discovered itself in the east, and in a short time spread over the whole heavens.

In the night of the 23d, when the ship was in latitude 61° 52' south, and longitude 95° 2' east, the weather being exceedingly stormy, thick, and hazy, with sleet and snow, our voyagers were on every side surrounded with danger. In such a situation it was natural for them to wish for day-light; but day-light, when it came, served only to increase their apprehensions, by exhibiting those huge mountains of ice to their view, which the darkness had prevented them from seeing. These unfavourable circumstances, at so advanced a season of the year, discouraged Captain Cook from putting into execution a resolution he had formed of once more crossing the antarctic circle. Accordingly, early in the morning of the 24th, he stood to the north with a very hard gale and a very high sea, which made great destruction among the ice islands. But so far was this incident from being of any advantage to our navigators, that it greatly increased the number of pieces they had to avoid. The large pieces which broke from the ice islands, were found to be much more dangerous than the islands themselves. While the latter rose so high out of the water that they could generally be seen, unless the weather was very thick and hazy, before our people nearly approached them, the others could not be discerned in the night, till they were under the ship's bows. These dangers, however, were now become so familiar to the captain and his company, that the apprehensions they caused were never of long duration; and a compensation was, in some degree, made for them, by the seasonable supplies of fresh water, which the ice islands afforded, and by their very romantic appearance. The foaming and dashing of the waves into the curious holes and caverns which were formed in many of them, greatly heightened the scene; and the whole exhibited a view that at once filled the mind with admiration and horror, and could only be described by the hand of an able painter.

In sailing from the 25th to the 28th, the wind was accompanied with a large hollow sea, which rendered Captain Cook certain that no land of any considerable extent could lie within a hundred or a hundred and fifty leagues from east to southwest. Though this was still the summer season in that part of the world, and the weather was become somewhat warmer than it had been before, yet such were the effects of the cold, that a sow having farrowed nine pigs in the morning, all of them, notwithstanding the utmost care to prevent it, were killed before four o'clock in the afternoon. From this same cause, the captain himself and several of his people had their fingers and toes chilblained. For some days afterward the cold considerably abated, but still it could not be said that there was summer weather, according to our commander's ideas of the summer in the northern hemisphere, as far as sixty degrees of latitude, which was nearly as far as he had then been.

As he proceeded on his voyage, from the 28th of February to the 11th of March, he had ample reason to conclude, from the swell of the sea and other circumstances, that there could be no land to the south but what must lie at a great distance.

The weather having been clear on the 13th and 14th, Mr. Wales had an opportunity of getting some observations of the sun and moon; the results of which, reduced to noon, when the latitude was 58° 22' south, gave 136° 22' east longitude. Mr. Kendal's and Mr. Arnold's watches gave each of them 134° 42', and this was the first and only time in which they pointed out the same longitude since the ship had departed from England. The greatest difference, however, between them, since our voyagers had left the Cape, had not much exceeded two degrees.

From the moderate and what might almost be called pleasant weather, which had occurred for two or three days, Captain Cook began to wish that he had been a few degrees of latitude farther south, and he was even tempted to incline his course that way. But he soon met with weather which convinced him that he had proceeded full far enough, and that the time was approaching when these seas could not be navigated without enduring intense cold. As he advanced in his course he became perfectly assured, from repeated proofs, that he had left no land behind him in the direction of west-southwest, and that no land lay to the south on this side sixty degrees of latitude. He came, therefore, to a resolution on the 17th, to quit the high southern latitudes and to proceed to New Zealand, with a view of looking for the Adventure and of refreshing his people. He had also some thoughts and even a desire of visiting the east coast of Van Diemen's Land, in order to satisfy himself whether it joined the coast of New South Wales. The wind, however, not permitting him to execute this part of his design, he shaped his course for New Zealand, in sight of which he arrived on the 25th, and where he came to anchor on the day following, in Dusky Bay. He had now been a hundred and seventeen days at sea, during which time he had sailed three thousand six hundred and sixty leagues without having once come within sight of land.

After so long a voyage, in a high southern latitude, it might reasonably have been expected that many of Captain Cook's people would be ill of the scurvy. This, however, was not the case. So salutary were the effects of the sweet wort and several articles of provision, and especially of the frequent airing and sweetening of the ship, that there was only one man on board who could be said to be much afflicted with the disease, and even in that man it was chiefly occasioned by a bad habit of body and a complication of other disorders.

As our commander did not like the place in which he had anchored, he sent Lieutenant Pickersgill over to the southeast side of the bay in search of a better, and the lieutenant succeeded in finding a harbour that was in every respect desirable. In the meanwhile, the fishing-boat was very successful, returning with fish sufficient for the whole crew's supper; and in the morning of the next day as many were caught as served for dinner. Hence were derived certain hopes of being plentifully supplied with this article. Nor did the shores and woods appear more destitute of wild-fowl, so that our people had the prospect of enjoying with ease, what, in their situation, might be called the luxuries of life. These agreeable circumstances determined Captain Cook to stay some time in the bay, in order to examine it thoroughly, as no one had ever landed before on any of the southern parts of New Zealand.

On the 27th, the ship entered Pickersgill Harbour, for so it was called from the name of the gentleman by whom it had first been discovered. Here wood for fuel and other purposes, was immediately at hand, and a fine stream of fresh water was not above a hundred yards from the stern of the vessel. Our voyagers being thus advantageously situated, began vigorously to prepare for their necessary occupations, by clearing places in the woods, in order to set up the astronomer's observatory, and the forge for the iron work, and to erect tents for the sail makers and coopers. They applied themselves, also, to the brewing of beer from the branches or leaves of a tree which greatly resembled the American black spruce. Captain Cook was persuaded, from the knowledge which he had of this tree, and from the similarity it bore to the spruce, that, with the addition of inspissated juce of wort and molasses, it would make a very wholesome liquor and supply the want of vegetables, of which the country was destitute. It appeared, by the event, that he was not mistaken in his judgment.

Several of the natives were seen on the 28th, who took little notice of the English, and were very shy of access; and the captain did not choose to force an intercourse with them, as he had been instructed by former experience that the best method of obtaining it was to leave the time and place to themselves. While our commander continued in his present situation he took every opportunity of examining the bay. As he was prosecuting his survey of it, on the 6th of April, his attention was directed to the north side, where he discovered a fine capacious cove, in the bottom of which is a fresh water river. On the west side are several beautiful cascades, and the shores are so steep that the water might directly be conveyed from them into the ship. Fourteen ducks, besides other birds, having been shot in this place, he gave it the name of Duck Cove. When he was returning in the evening he met with three of the natives, one man and two women, whose fears he soon dissipated, and whom he engaged in a conversation that was little understood on either side. The youngest of the women had a volubility of tongue that could not be exceeded, and she entertained Captain Cook and the gentlemen who accompanied him with a dance.

By degrees our commander obtained the good will and confidence of the Indians. His presents, however, were at first received with much indifference, hatchets and spike-nails excepted. At a visit on the 12th, from a family of the natives, the captain, perceiving they approached the ship with great caution, met them in a boat which he quitted when he came near them and went into their canoe. After all, he could not prevail on them to go on board the Resolution, but at length they put on shore in a little creek, and seating themselves abreast of the English vessel, entered into familiar conversation with several of the officers and seamen, in which they paid a much greater regard to some, whom they probably mistook for females, than to others. So well were they reconciled to our voyagers, that they took up their quarters nearly within the distance of a hundred yards from the ship's watering-place. Captain Cook, in his interview with them, had caused the bagpipes and fife to play, and the drum to beat. The two former they heard with apparent insensibility, but the latter excited in them a certain degree of attention.

On the 18th, a chief, with whom some connexions had already been formed, was induced, together with his daughter, to come on board the Resolution. Previously to his doing it, he presented the captain with a piece of cloth and a green talk hatchet. He gave also a piece of cloth to Mr. Forster, and the girl gave another to Mr. Hodges. Though this custom of making presents before any are received, is common with the natives of the South Sea isles, our commander had never till now seen it practised in New Zealand. Another thing performed by the chief, before he went on board, was the taking of a small green branch in his hand, with which he struck the ship's side several times, repeating a speech or prayer. This manner, as it were, of making peace is likewise prevalent among all the nations of the South Seas. When the chief was carried into the cabin, he viewed every part of it with some degree of surprise, but it was not possible to fix his attention to any one object for a single moment. The works of art appeared to him in the same light as those of nature, and were equally distant from his powers of comprehension. He and his daughter seemed to be the most struck with the number of the decks and other parts of the ship.

As Captain Cook proceeded in examining Dusky Bay, he occasionally met with some few more of the natives, with regard to whom he used every mode of conciliation. On the 20th, the chief and his family, who had been more intimate with our navigators than any of the rest of the Indians, went away and never returned again. This was the more extraordinary, as in all his visits he had been gratified with presents. From different persons he had gotten nine or ten hatchets, and three or four times that number of large spike-nails, besides a variety of other articles, so far as these things may be deemed riches in New Zealand, he was undoubtedly become by far the most wealthy man in the whole country.

One employment of our voyagers while in Dusky Bay, consisted in seal-hunting, an animal which was found serviceable for three purposes. The skins were made use of for rigging, the fat afforded oil for the lamps, and the flesh was eaten. On the 24th, the captain having five geese remaining of those he had brought with him from the Cape of Good Hope, went and left them at a place to which he gave the name of Goose Cove. This place he fixed upon for two reasons; first, because there were no inhabitants to disturb them, and secondly, because here was the greatest supply of proper food, so that he had no doubt of their breeding, and hoped that in time they might spread over the whole country, to its eminent advantage. Some days afterward, when everything belonging to the ship had been removed from the shore, he set fire to the topwood in order to dry a piece of ground, which he dug up and sowed with several sorts of garden seeds. The soil indeed, was not such as to promise much success to the planter, but it was the best that could be discovered.

The 25th of April was the eighth fair day our people had successively enjoyed, and there was reason to believe that such a circumstance was very uncommon in the place where they now lay, and at that season of the year. This favourable weather afforded them the opportunity of more speedily completing their wood and water, and of putting the ship into a condition for sea. On the evening of the 25th it began to rain, and the weather was afterward extremely variable, being at times in a high degree wet, cold, and stormy. Nothing, however, prevented Captain Cook from prosecuting, with his usual sagacity and diligence, his search into every part of Dusky Bay; and as there are few places in New Zealand where necessary refreshments may be so plentifully obtained as in this bay, he hath taken care to give such a description of it and of the adjacent country as may be of service to succeeding navigators. Although this country lies far remote from what is now the trading part of the world, yet, as he justly observes, we can by no means tell what use future ages may derive from the discoveries made in the present.

The various anchoring places are delineated on our commander's chart, and the most convenient of them he has particularly described. Not only about Dusky Bay, but through all the southern part of the western coast of Tovy-Poenammo, the country is exceedingly mountainous. A prospect more rude and craggy is rarely to be met with; far inland, there are only to be seen the summits of mountains of a tremendous height, and consisting of rocks that are totally barren and naked excepting where they are covered with snow. But the land which borders on the sea-coast is thickly clothed with wood almost down to the water's edge, and this is the case with regard to all the adjoining islands. The trees are of various kinds, and are fit for almost every possible use. Excepting in the river Thames, Captain Cook had not found finer timber in all New Zealand;

the most considerable species of which is the spruce-tree, for that name he had given it from the similarity of its foliage to the American spruce, though the wood is more ponderous, and bears a greater resemblance to the pitch pine. Many of these trees are so large that they would be able to furnish main-masts for fifty gun ships. Amidst the variety of aromatic trees and shrubs which this part of New Zealand produced, there was none which bore fruit fit to be eaten. The country was not found so destitute of quadrupeds as was formerly imagined.

As Dusky Bay presented many advantages to our navigators, so it was attended with some disagreeable circumstances. There were great numbers of small, black sand flies, which were troublesome to a degree that our commander had never experienced before. Another evil arose from the continual quantity of rain that occurred in the bay. This might, indeed, in part proceed from the season of the year: but it is probable that the country must at all times be subject to much wet weather, in consequence of the vast height and vicinity of the mountains. It was remarkable that the rain, though our people were perpetually exposed to it, was not productive of any evil consequences. On the contrary, such of the men as were sick and complaining when they entered the bay, recovered daily, and the whole crew soon became strong and vigorous. So happy a circumstance could only be attributed to the healthiness of the place and the fresh provisions it afforded, among which the beer was a very material article.

The inhabitants of Dusky Bay are of the same race with the other natives of New Zealand, speak the same language, and adhere nearly to the same customs. Their mode of life appears to be a wandering one, and though they are few in number, no traces were remarked of their families being connected together in any close bonds of union or friendship.

While the Resolution lay in the bay, Mr. Wales made a variety of scientific observations relative to latitude and longtitude, the variation of the compass, and the diversity of the tides.

When Captain Cook left Dusky Bay, he directed his course for Queen Charlotte's Sound, where he expected to find the Adventure. This was on the 11th of May, and nothing remarkable occurred till the 17th, when the wind at once flattened to a calm, the sky became suddenly obscured by dark dense clouds, and there was every prognostication of a tempest. Soon after, six water-spouts were seen, four of which rose and spent themselves between the ship and the land; the fifth was at a considerable distance on the other side of the vessel, and the sixth, the progressive motion of which was not in a straight, but in a crooked line, passed within fifty yards of the stern of the Resolution, without producing any evil effect. As the captain had been informed that the firing of a gun would dissipate water-spouts, he was sorry that he had not tried the experiment. But though he was near enough, and had a gun ready for the purpose, his mind was so deeply engaged in viewing these extraordinary meteors, that he forgot to give the necessary directions.

On the next day the Resolution came within sight of Queen Charlotte's Sound, where Captain Cook had the satisfaction of discovering the Adventure, and both ships felt uncommon joy at thus meeting again after an absence of fourteen weeks. As the events which happened to Captain Furneaux during the separation of the two vessels, do not fall within the immediate design of the present narrative, it may be sufficient to observe, that he had an opportunity of examining, with somewhat more accuracy than had hitherto been done, Van Diemen's Land; and his opinion was, that there are no straits between this land and New Holland, but a very deep bay. He met, likewise, with farther proofs that the natives of New Zealand are eaters of human flesh.

The morning after Captain Cook's arrival in Queen Charlotte's Sound, he went himself at day-break, to look for scurvy-grass, celery, and other vegetables, and he had the good fortune to return with a boat-load in a very short space of time. Having found that a sufficient quantity of these articles might be obtained for the crews of both the ships, he gave orders that they should be boiled with wheat and portable broth every day for breakfast, and with pease and broth for dinner. Experience had taught him that the vegetables now mentioned, when thus dressed, are extremely beneficial to seamen in removing the various scorbutic complaints to which they are subject.

Our commander had entertained a desire of visiting Van Diemen's Land, in order to inform himself whether it made a part of New Holland. But as this point had been, in a great measure, cleared up by Captain Furneaux, he came to a resolution to continue his researches to the east, between the latitudes of 41° and 46°, and he directed accordingly, that the ships should be gotten ready for putting to sea as soon as possible. On the 20th he sent on shore the only ewe and ram that remained of those which, with the intention of leaving them in this country, he had brought from the Cape of Good Hope. Soon after, he visited several gardens, that by order of Captain Furneaux had been made and planted with various articles, all of which were in such a flourishing state, that if duly attended to, they promised to be of great utility to the natives. The next day Captain Cook himself set some men to work to form a garden on Long Island, which he stocked with different seeds, and particularly with the roots of turnips, carrots, parsnips, and potatoes. These were the vegetables that would be of the most real use to the Indians, and of these it was easy to give them an idea, by comparing them with such roots as they themselves knew. On the 22d Captain Cook received the unpleasant intelligence, that the ewe and ram, which with so much care and trouble he had brought to this place, were both of them found dead. It was supposed that they had eaten some poisonous plant, and by this

8*

accident all the captain's hopes of stocking New Zealand with a breed of sheep were instantly blasted.

The intercourse which our great navigator had with the inhabitants of the country during this his second visit to Queen Charlotte's Sound, was of a friendly nature. Two or three families took up their abode near the ships, and employed themselves **daily in** fishing, and in supplying the English with the fruits of their labour. No small advantage hence accrued to our people, who were by no means such expert fishers as the natives, nor were any of our methods of fishing equal to theirs. Thus, in almost every state of society, particular arts of life are carried to perfection, and there is something which the most polished nations may learn from the most barbarous.

On the 2d of June, when the Resolution and Adventure were almost ready to put to sea, Captain Cook sent on shore on the east side of the sound, two goats, a male and female; and Captain Furneaux left, near Cannibal Cove, a boar and two breeding sows. The gentlemen had little doubt but that the country would in time be stocked with these animals, provided they were not destroyed by the Indians before they became wild. Afterwards there would be no danger, and as the natives knew nothing of their being left behind, it was hoped that it might be some time before they would be discovered.

It is remarkable, that during Captain Cook's second visit to Charlotte's Sound, he was not able to recollect the face of any one person whom he had seen there three years before. Nor did it once appear that even a single Indian had the least knowledge of our commander, or any of our people who had been with him in his last voyage. Hence he thought it highly probable, that the greatest part of the natives who inhabited this sound in the beginning of the year 1770, had either since been driven out of it, or had removed of their own accord to some other situation. Not one-third of the inhabitants were there now that had been seen at that time. Their strong hold on the point of Motuara was deserted, and in every part of the sound many forsaken habitations were discovered. In the captain's opinion, there was not any reason to believe that the place had ever been very populous. From comparing the two voyages together, it may be collected that the Indians of Eaheinomauwe are in somewhat of a more improved state of society than those of Tovy-Poenammo.

Part of the 4th of June was employed by Captain Cook in visiting a chief and a whole tribe of the natives, consisting of between ninety and a hundred persons, including men, women, and children. After the captain had distributed some presents among these people, and shown to the chief the gardens which were made, he returned on board and spent the remainder of the day in the celebration of his royal master's nativity. Captain Furneaux and all his officers were invited upon the occasion, and the seamen were enabled, by a double allowance, to partake of the general joy.

As some might think it an extraordinary step in our commander to proceed in discoveries so far south as forty-six degrees of latitude, in the very depth of winter, he has recorded his motives for this part of his conduct. Winter, he acknowledges, is by no means favourable for discoveries. Nevertheless, it appeared to him to be necessary that something should be done in that season in order to lessen the work in which he was engaged, and lest he should not be able to finish the discovery of the southern part of the South Pacific Ocean in the ensuing summer. Besides, if he should discover any land in his route to the east, he would be ready to begin to explore it as soon as ever the season should be favourable. Independently of all these considerations he had little to fear; having two good ships well provided, and both the crews being healthy. Where then could he better employ his time? If he did nothing more, he was at least in hopes of being enabled to point out to posterity, that these seas may be navigated, and that it is practicable to pursue discoveries ever in the depth of winter. Such was the ardour of our navigator for prosecuting the ends of his voyage, in circumstances which would have induced most men to act a more cautious part.

During Captain Cook's stay in the sound, he had observed, that the second visit to this country had not mended the morals of the natives of either sex. He had always looked upon the **females of** New Zealand as more chaste than the generality of Indian women. Whatever favours a few of them might have granted to the people of the Endeavour, such intercourse usually took place in a private manner, and did not appear to be encouraged by the men. But now the captain was told, that the male Indians were the chief promoters of this shameful traffic, and that, for a spike-nail, or any other thing they valued, they would oblige the women to prostitute themselves, whether it were agreeable or contrary to their inclinations. At the same time no regard was paid to the privacy which decency required. The account of this fact must be read with concern by every well-wisher to the good order and happiness of society, even without adverting to considerations of a higher nature.

On the 7th of June, Captain Cook put to sea from Queen Charlotte's Sound, with the Adventure in company. I shall **omit** the nautical part of the route from New Zealand to Otaheite, which continued till the 15th of August, and shall only select such circumstances as are more immediately suitable to the design of the present narrative. It was found, on the 29th of July, that the crew of the Adventure were in a sickly state. Her cook was dead, and about twenty of her best men were rendered incapable of duty by the scurvy and flux. At this time no more than three men were on the sick list on board the Resolution; and only one of these was attacked with the scurvy. Some others, however, began to discover the symptoms of it; and, accordingly, recourse was had to wort, marmalade of carrots, and the rob of lemons and oranges, with the usual success.

Captain Cook could not account for the prevalence of the scurvy being so much greater in the Adventure than in the Resolution, unless it was owing to the crew of the former being more scorbutic when they arrived in New Zealand than the crew of latter, and to their eating few or no vegetables while they lay in Queen Charlotte's Sound. This arose partly from their want of knowing the right sorts, and partly from the dislike which seamen have to the introduction of a new diet. Their aversion to any unusual change of food is so great, that it can only be overcome by the steady and persevering example and authority of a commander. Many of Captain Cook's people, officers as well as common sailors, disliked the boiling of celery, scurvy-grass, and other greens, with pease and wheat; and by some the provision, thus prepared, was refused to be eaten. But, as this had no effect on the captain's conduct, their prejudice gradually subsided: they began to like their diet as much as the rest of their companions; and at length, there was hardly a man in the ship who did not attribute the freedom of the crew from the scurvy, to the beer and vegetables which had been made use of at New Zealand. Henceforward, whenever the seamen come to a place where vegetables could be obtained, our commander seldom found it necessary to order them to be gathered; and, if they were scarce, happy was the person who could lay hold on them first.

On the first of August, when the ships were in the latitude of 25° 1' and the longitude of 134° 6' west, they were nearly in the same situation with that which is assigned by Captain Carteret for Pitcairn's Island, discovered by him in 1767. For this island, therefore, our voyagers diligently looked; but saw nothing. According to the longitude in which he had placed it, Captain Cook must have passed it fifteen leagues to the west. But as this was uncertain, he did not think it prudent to lose any time in searching for it, as the sickly state of the Adventure's people required as speedy an arrival as possible at a place of refreshment. A sight of it, however, would have been **of use in verify** ing or correcting, not only the longitude of Pitcairn's Island, but of the others discovered by Captain Carteret in that neighbourhood. It is a diminution of the value of that gentleman's voyage, that his longitude was not confirmed by astronomical observation, and that hence it was liable to errors, the correction of which was out of his power.

As Captain Cook had now **gotten** to the northward of Captain Carteret's track, he no longer entertained any hopes of discovering a continent. Islands were all that he could expect to find, until he returned again to the south. In this and his former voyage, he had crossed the ocean in the latitude of 40° and upwards, without meeting anything which could in the least, induce him to believe that he should attain the great object of his pursuit. Every circumstance concurred to convince him, that, between the meridian of America and New Zealand, there is no southern continent; and that there is no continent farther to the south, unless in a very high latitude. This, however, was a point too important to be left to opinions and conjectures. It was to be determined by facts; and the ascertainment of it was appointed, by our commander, for the employment of the ensuing summer.

It was the 6th of August before the ships had the advantage of the trade wind. This they got at southeast, being at that time in the latitude of 19° 36' south and the longitude of 131° 32' west. As Captain Cook had obtained the southeast trade wind, he directed his course to the west-northwest; not only with a view of keeping in with the strength of the wind, but also to get to the north of the islands discovered in his former voyage, that he might have a chance of meeting with any other islands which might lie in the way. It was in the track which had been pursued by M. de Bougainville that our commander now proceeded. He was sorry that he could not spare time to sail to the north of this track; but at present, on account of the sickly state of the Adventure's crew, the ariving at a place where refreshments could be procured, was an object superior to that of discovery. To four of the islands which were passed by Captain Cook, he gave the names of Resolution Island, Doubtful Island, Furneaux Island, and Adventure Island. They are supposed to be the same that were seen by M. de Bougainville; and these with several others, which constitute a cluster of low and half-drowned isles, that gentlemen distinguished by the appellation of the Dangerous Archipelago. The smoothness of the sea sufficiently convinced our navigators that they were surrounded by them, and that it was highly necessary to proceed with the utmost caution, especially in the night.

Early in the morning, on the 15th of August, the ships came within sight of Osnaburg Island, or Maitea, which had been discovered by Captain Wallis. Soon after Captain Cook acquainted Captain Furneaux that it was his intention to put into Oaiti-piha Bay, near the southeast end of Otaheite, for the purpose of procuring what refreshments he could from that part of the island, before he went down to Matavia. At six in the evening the island was seen bearing west, and our people continued to advance towards it till midnight, when they brought to till four o'clock in the morning; after which they sailed in for the land, with a fine breeze at east. At daybreak they found themselves within the distance of half a league from the reef; and, at the same time, the breeze began to fail them, and was at last succeeded by a calm. It now became necessary for the boats to be hoisted out, in order to tow off the ships; but all the efforts of our voyagers to keep them from being carried near the reef were insufficient for the purpose. As the calm continued, the situation of the vessels became still more dangerous. Captain Cook, however, entertained hopes of getting round the western point of the reef, and into the bay. But, about two o'clock in the afternoon, when he came before an opening or break in the reef, through which he had flattered himself that he might get with the ships, he found, on sending to examine it, that there was not a sufficient depth of water. Nevertheless this opening caused such an indraught of the tide of flood through it, as was very near proving fatal to the Resolution ; for, as soon as the vessels got into the stream, they were carried towards the reef with great impetuosity. The moment the captain perceived this, he ordered one of the warping machines, which was held in readiness, to be carried out with about four hundred fathoms of rope; but it did not produce the least effect ; and our navigators had now in prospect the horrors of shipwreck. They were not more than two cables' length from the breakers ; and, though it was the only probable method which was left of saving the ships, they could find no bottom to anchor. An anchor, however, they did drop, but before it took hold and brought them up, the Resolution was in less than three fathom water, and struck at every fall of the sea, which broke close under her stern in a dreadful surf, and threatened her crew every moment with destruction. Happliy the Adventure brought up without striking. Presently the Resolution's people carried out **two** kedge-anchors, with hawsers to each ; and these found ground **a** little without the bower. By heaving upon them, and cutting away the bower anchor, the ship was gotten afloat where Captain Cook and his men lay for some time in the greatest anxiety, expecting every minute that either the kedges would come home, or the hawsers be cut in two by the rocks. At length, the tide ceased to act in the same direction : upon which the captain ordered all the boats to try to tow off the vessel. Having found this to be practicable, the two kedges were hove up, and at that moment a light air came off from the land, by which the boats were so much assisted, that the Resolution soon got clear of all danger. Our commander then ordered all the boats **to** assist the Adventure ; but before they reached her, she was under sail with the land breeze, and in a little time joined her companion, leaving behind her three anchors, her coasting cable, and two hawsers, which were never recovered. Thus were our voyagers once more safe at sea, after narrowly escaping being wrecked on the very island, at which, but a few days before, they had most ardently wished to arrive. It was a peculiarly happy circumstance, that the calm continued, after bringing the ships into so dangerous a state. For if the sea breeze, as is usually the case, had set in, the Resolution must inevitably have been lost, and probably the Adventure likewise.

During the time in which the English were in this critical situation, a number of the natives were either on board or near the vessels in their canoes. Nevertheless, they seemed to be insensible of our people's danger, showing not the least surprise, joy, or fear, when the ships were striking; and they went away a little before sunset, quite unconcerned. Though most of them knew Captain Cook again, and many inquired for Mr. Banks and others who had been with the captain before, it was remarkable that not one of them asked for Tupia.

On the 17th, the Resolution and Adventure anchored in Oaitipiha Bay, immediately upon which they were crowded with the inhabitants of the country, who brought with them cocoa-nuts, plantains, bananas, apples, yams, and other roots, which were exchanged for nails and beads. To some, who called themselves chiefs, our commander made presents of shirts, axes, and several articles beside, in return for which they promised to bring him hogs and fowls: a promise which they did not perform, and which, as might be judged from their conduct, they had never had the least intention of performing. In the afternoon of the same day, Captain Cook landed in company with Captain Furneaux, for the purpose of viewing the watering-place, and of sounding the disposition of the natives. The article of water, which was now much wanted on board, he found might conveniently be obtained, and the inhabitants behaved with great civility. Notwithstanding this civility, nothing was brought to market the next day, but fruit and roots, though it was said that many hogs were seen about the houses in the neighbourhood

The cry was, that they belonged to Waheatoua, the earee de hi, or king; who had not yet appeared, nor, indeed, any other chief of note. Among the Indians that came on board the Resolution, and no small number of whom did not scruple to call themselves earees, there was one of this sort who had been entertained in the cabin most of the day, and to all of whose friends Captain Cook had made presents, as well as liberally to himself. At length, however, he was caught taking things which did not belong to him, and handing them out of the quarter galley. Various complaints of the like nature being at the same time made against the natives who were on deck, our commander turned them all out of the ship. His cabin guest was very rapid in his retreat; and the captain was so exasperated at his behaviour, that after the earee had gotten to some distance from the Resolution, he fired two muskets over his head, by which he was so terrified, that he quitted his canoe and took to the water. Captain Cook then sent a boat to take the canoe; but when the boat approached the shore, the people on land began to pelt her with stones. The captain, therefore, being in some pain for her safety, as she was unarmed, went himself in another boat to protect her, and ordered a great gun, loaded with ball, to be fired along the coast, which made all the Indians retire from the shore, and he was suffered to bring away two canoes without the least show of opposition. In a few hours peace was restored, and the canoes were returned to the first person who came for them.

It was not till the evening of this day, that any one inquired after Tupia, and then the inquiry was made by only two or three of the natives. When they learned the cause of his death they were perfectly satisfied, nor did it appear to our commander that they would have felt a moment's uneasiness, if Tupia's decease had proceeded from any other cause than sickness. They were as little concerned about Aotourou, the man who had gone away with M. de Bougainville. But they were continually asking for

Mr. Banks, and for several others who had accompanied Captain Cook in his former voyage.

Since that voyage, very considerabe changes had happened in the country. Toutaha, the regent of the greater peninsula of Otaheite, had been killed in a battle which was fought between the two kingdoms about five months before the Resolution's arrival; and Otoo was now the reigning prince. Tubourai Tomaide, and several more of the principal friends to the English, had fallen in this battle, together with a large number of the common people. A peace subsisted, at present, between the two grand divisions of the island.

On the 20th, one of the natives carried off a musket belonging to the guard on shore. Captain Cook, who was himself a witness to the transaction, sent out some of his people after him; but this **would** have been to very little purpose, if the thief had not been intercepted by several of his own countrymen, who pursued him voluntarily, knocked him down, and returned the musket to the English. This act of justice prevented our commander **from** being placed in a disagreeable situation. If the natives had **not** given their immediate assistance, it would scarcely have been in his power to have recovered the musket by any gentle means whatever; and if he had been obliged to have recourse to other methods, he was sure of losing more than ten times its value.

The fraud of one, who appeared as a chief, is perhaps, not unworthy of notice. This man, in a visit to Captain Cook, presented him with a quantity of fruit; among which was a number of cocoa-nuts, that had already been exhausted of their liquor by our people, and afterwards thrown overboard. These the chief had picked up, and tied so artfully in bundles, that at first the deception was not perceived. When he was informed of it, without betraying the least emotion, and affecting a total ignorance of the matter, he opened two or three of the nuts himself, signified that he was satisfied of the fact, and then went on shore and sent off a quantity of plantains and bananas. The ingenuity and the impudence of fraud are not solely the production of polished society.

Captain Cook, on the 23d, had an interview with Waheatoua, the result of which was that our navigators obtained this day as much pork as furnished a meal to the crews of both vessels. In the captain's **last voyage,** Waheatoua, who was then little more than a boy, was called Tearee; but having succeeded to his father's authority, he had assumed his father's name.

The fruits which **were procured at** Oaiti-piha Bay contributed greatly to the recovery of the sick people belonging **to the** Adventure. Many of them, who had been so ill as to be incapable of moving without assistance, were, in the compass of a few days, so far recovered that they were able to walk about of themselves. When the Resolution entered the **bay,** she had but one scorbutic man on boar. A marine who had long been sick, and who died the second day after her arrival, of a complication of disorders, had not the least mixture of the scurvy.

On the 24th, the ships put to sea, and arrived the next evening in Matavia Bay. Before they could come to an anchor, the decks were crowded with the natives, many of whom Captain Cook knew, and by most of whom he was well remembered. Among a large multitude of people, who were collected together upon the shore, was Otoo, the king of the island. Our commander **paid** him a visit on the following day, **at** Oparree, the place of his residence; and found him to be a fine, personable, well-made man, six feet high, and about thirty years of age. The qualities of his mind were not correspondent to his external appearance; for when Captain Cook endeavoured **to** obtain from him a promise of a visit on board, he acknowledged that he was afraid of the guns, and, indeed, manifested in all his actions that **he** was a prince of a timorous disposition.

Upon the captain's return from Oparree, he found the tents, and the astronomers' observatories, set up on the same spot from which the transit of Venus had been observed in 1769. The sick,

Otaheite Chief, with his Wife, etc., presenting one of his Sisters to CAPT. COOK, on board the Sloop "RESOLUTION." Page 189.

being twenty in number, from the Adventure, and one from the Resolution, all of whom were ill of the scurvy, he ordered to be landed; and he appointed a guard of marines on shore, under the command of Lieutenant Edgcumbe.

On the 27th, Otoo was prevailed upon, with some degree of reluctance, to pay our commander a visit. He came attended with a numerous train, and brought with him fruits, a hog, two large fish, and a quantity of cloth; for which he and all his retinue were gratified with suitable presents. When Captain Cook conveyed his guests to land, he was met by a venerable lady, the mother of the late Toutaha, who seized him by both hands, and burst into a flood of tears, saying, *Toutaha tiyo no tutee matty Toutaha;* that is, "Tutaha, your friend, or the friend of Cook, is dead." He was so much affected with her behaviour, that it would have been impossible for him to have refrained from mingling his tears with hers, had not Otoo, who was displeased with the interview, taken him from her. It was with difficulty that the captain could obtain permission to see her again, when he gave her an axe and some other articles. Captain Furneaux, at this time, presented the king with two fine goats, which, if no accident befel them, might be expected to multiply.

Several days had passed in a friendly intercourse with the natives, and in the procuring of provisions, when, in the evening of the 30th, the gentlemen on board the Resolution were alarmed with the cry of murder, and with a great noise on shore, near the bottom of the bay, and at a distance from the English encampment. Upon this, Captain Cook, who suspected that some of his own men were concerned in the affair, immediately dispatched an armed boat, to know the cause of the disturbance, and to bring off such of his people as should be found in the place. He sent, also, to the Adventure, and to the post on shore, to learn who were missing; for none but those who were upon duty were absent from the Resolution. The boats speedily returned with three marines and a seaman. Some others likewise were taken, belonging to the Adventure ; and all of them being put under confinement, our commander, the next morning, ordered them to be punished according to their deserts. He did not find that any mischief had been done, and the men would confess nothing. Some liberties which had been taken with the women had probably given occasion to disturbance. To whatever cause it was owing, the natives were so much alarmed, that they fled from their habitations in the dead of the night, and the alarm was spread many miles along the **coast.** In the morning when Captain Cook went to visit Otoo, by appointment, he found that he had removed, or rather fled, to a great distance from the usual place of his abode. After arriving where he was, it was some hours before the captain could be admitted to the sight of him ; and then he complained of the riot of the preceding evening.

The sick being nearly recovered, the water completed, and the necessary repairs of the ship finished, Captain Cook determined to put to sea without delay. Accordingly, on the 1st of September, he ordered everything to be removed from the shore, and the vessels to be unmoored, in which employment his people were engaged the greater part of the day. In the afternoon of the same day, Lieutenant Pickersgill returned from Attahourou, to which place he had been sent by the captain, for the purpose of procuring some hogs that had been promised. In this expedition the lieutenant had seen the celebrated Oberea, who has been so much the object of poetical fancy. Her situation was very humble compared with what it had formerly been. She was not only altered much for the worse in her person, but appeared to be poor, and of little or no consequence or authority in the island. In the evening a favourable wind having sprung up, our commander put to **sea** ; on which occasion he was obliged to dismiss his Otaheite friends sooner than they wished to depart ; but well satisfied with his kind and liberal treatment.

From Matavia Bay, Captain Cook directed his course for the

island of Huaheine, where he intended to touch. This island he reached the next day, and, early in the morning of the 3d of September, made sail for the harbour of Owharre, in which he soon came to an anchor. The Adventure, not happening to turn into the harbour with equal facility, got ashore on the north side of the channel; but, by the timely assistance which Captain Cook had previously provided, in case such an accident should occur, she was gotten off again, without receiving any damage. As soon as both the ships were in safety, our commander, together with Captain Furneaux, landed upon the island, and was received by the natives with the utmost cordiality. A trade immediately commenced; so that our navigators had a fair prospect of being plentifully supplied with fresh pork and fowls, which, to people in their situation, was a very desirable circumstance. On the 4th, Lieutenant Pickersgill sailed with the cutter on a trading party, toward the south end of the isle. Another trading party was also sent on shore near the ships, which party Captain Cook attended himself, to see that the business was properly conducted at the first setting out, this being a point of no small importance. Everything being settled in his mind, he went, accompanied by Captain Furneaux and Mr. Foster, to pay a visit to his old friend Oree, the chief of the island. This visit was preceded by many preparatory ceremonies. Among other things the chief sent to our commander the inscription engraved on a small piece of pewter, which he had left with him in July, 1769. It was in the bag that Captain Cook had made for it, together with a piece of counterfeit English coin, and a few beads which had been put in at the same time; whence it was evident what particular care had been taken of the whole. After the previous ceremonies had been discharged, the captain wanted to go to the king, but he was informed that the king would come to him. Accordingly, Oree went up to our commander, and fell on his neck, and embraced him, nor was it a ceremonious embrace, for the tears which trickled down the venerable old man's cheeks sufficiently bespoke the language of his heart. The presents which Captain Cook made to the chief on this occasion, consisted of the most valuable articles he had; for he regarded him as a father. Oree, in return, gave the captain a hog and a quantity of cloth, promising that all the wants of the English should be supplied. And it was a promise to which he faithfully adhered. Indeed, he carried his kindness to Captain Cook so far, as not to fail sending him every day, for his table, a plentiful supply of the very best of ready-dressed fruit and roots.

Hitherto all things had gone on in the most agreeable manner; but on Monday, the 6th, several circumstances occurred, which rendered it an unpleasant and troublesome day. When our commander went to the trading-place, he was informed that one of the inhabitants had behaved with remarkable insolence. The man was completely equipped in a war habit, had a club in each hand, and seemed bent upon mischief. Captain Cook, took, therefore, the clubs from him, broke them before his eyes, and, with some difficulty, compelled him to retire. About the same time, Mr. Sparrman, who had imprudently gone out alone to botanize, was assaulted by two men, who stripped him of everything which he had about him, excepting his trowsers, and struck him again and again with his own hanger, though happily without doing him any harm. When they had accomplished their purpose, they made off; after which, another of the natives brought a piece of cloth to cover him, and conducted him to the trading-place, where the inhabitants, in a large number, were assembled. The instant that Mr. Sparrman appeared in the condition now described, they all fled with the utmost precipitation. Captain Cook having recalled a few of the Indians, and convinced them that he should take no step to injure those who were innocent, went to Oree to complain of the outrage. When the chief had heard the whole affair related, he wept aloud, and many other of the inhabitants did the same. After the first transports of his grief had subsided, he began to expostulate with his people, telling them (for so his language was understood by the English) how well Captain Cook had treated them both in this and his former voyage, and how base it was in them to commit such actions. He then took a minute account of the things of which Mr. Sparrman had been robbed, and, after having promised to use his utmost endeavours for the recovery of them, desired to go into the captain's boat. At this, the natives, apprehensive doubtless for the safety of their prince, expressed the utmost alarm, and used every argument to dissuade him from so rash a measure. All their remonstrances, however, were in vain. He hastened into the boat; and as soon as they saw that their beloved chief was wholly in our commander's power, they set up a great outcry. Indeed, their grief was inexpressible; they prayed, entreated, nay, attempted to pull him out of the boat; and every face was bedewed with tears. Even Captain Cook himself was so moved by their distress, that he united his entreaties with theirs, but all to no purpose. Oree insisted upon the captain's coming into the boat, which was no sooner done, than he ordered it to be put off. His sister was the only person among the Indians who behaved with a becoming magnanimity on this occasion; for, with a spirit equal to that of her royal brother, she alone did not oppose his going. It was his design, in coming into the boat of the English, to proceed with them in search of the robbers. Accordingly, he went with Captain Cook, as far as it was convenient, by water, when they landed, entered the country, and travelled some miles inland; in doing which the chief led the way, and inquired after the criminals of every person whom he saw. In this search he would have gone to the very extremity of the island, if our commander, who did not think the object worthy of so laborious a pursuit, had not refused to proceed any farther. Besides, as he intended to sail the next morning, and all manner of trade was stopped in consequence of the alarm of the natives, it became the more necessary for him to return, that he might restore things to their former state. It was with great reluctance that Oree was prevailed upon to discontinue the search, and to content himself with sending, at Captain Cook's request, some of his people for the things which had been carried off. When he and the captain had gotten back to the boat, they found there the chief's sister and several other persons, who had travelled by land to the place. The English gentlemen immediately stepped into their boat, in order to return on board, without so much as asking Oree to accompany them; notwithstanding which, he insisted upon doing it; nor could the opposition and entreaties of those who were about him induce him to desist from his purpose. His sister followed his example, uninfluenced on this occasion, by the supplications and tears of her daughter. Captain Cook amply rewarded the chief and his sister for the confidence they had placed in him; and, after dinner, conveyed them both on shore, where some hundreds of people waited to receive them, many of whom embraced Oree with tears of joy. All was now peace and gladness; the inhabitants crowded in from every part with such a plentiful supply of hogs, fowls, and vegetable productions, that the English presently filled two boats; and the chief himself presented the captain with a large hog, and a quantity of fruit. Mr. Sparrman's hanger, the only thing of value which he had lost, was brought back, together with part of his coat; and our navigators were told that the remaining articles should be restored the next day. Some things which had been stolen from a party of officers, who had gone out a shooting, were returned in like manner.

The transactions of this day have been the more particularly related, as they show the high opinion which the chief had formed of our commander, and the unreserved confidence that he placed in his integrity and honour. Oree had entered into a solemn friendship with Captain Cook, according to all the forms which were customary in the country; and he seemed to think that this friendship could not be broken by the act of any other persons. It is justly observed by the captain, that another chief may never be found, who, under similar circumstances, will act in the same manner. Oree, indeed, had nothing to fear; for it was not our commander's intention to hurt a hair of his head, or to detain him a moment longer than was agreeable to his own desire. But of this how could he and his people be assured? They were not ignorant that when he was once in Captain Cook's power, the whole force of the island would not be sufficient to recover him, and that they must have complied with any demands, however great, for his ransom. The apprehensions, therefore, of the inhabitants, for their chief's and their own safety, had a reasonable foundation.

Early on the 7th, while the ships were unmooring, the captain went to pay his farewell visit to Oree, and took with him such presents as had not only a fancied value, but a real utility. He left, also, with the chief, the inscription plate that had before been in his possession, and another small copperplate, on which were engraved these words: "Anchored here, his Britannic Majesty's ships Resolution and Adventure, September, 1773." These plates, together with some medals, were put up in a bag, of which Oree promised to take care, and to produce them to the first ship or ships that should arrive at the island. Having, in return, given a hog to Captain Cook, and loaded his boat with fruit, they took leave of each other, when the good old chief embraced our commander with tears in his eyes. Nothing was mentioned, at this interview, concerning the remainder of Mr. Sparrman's property. As it was early in the morning, the captain judged that it had not been brought in, and he was not willing to speak of it to Oree, lest he should give him pain about things which there had not been time to recover. The robbers having soon afterwards been taken, Oree came on board again, to request that our commander would go on shore, either to punish them, or to be present at their punishment; but this not being convenient to him, he left them to the punishment of their own chief. It was from the island of Huaheine that Captain Furneaux received into his ship a young man named Omai, a native of Ulietea, of whom so much hath since been known and written. This choice Captain Cook at first disapproved, as thinking that the youth was not a proper sample of the inhabitants of the Society Islands; being inferior to many of them in birth and acquired rank, and not having any peculiar advantage in point of shape, figure, and complexion. The captain afterwards found reason to be better satisfied with Omai's having accompanied our navigators to England.

During the short stay of the vessels at Huaheine, our people were very successful in obtaining supplies of provisions. No less than three hundred hogs, besides fowls and fruit, were procured, and had the ship continued longer at the place, the quantity might have been greatly increased. Such was the fertility of this small island that none of these articles of refreshment were seemingly diminished, but appeared to be as plentiful as ever.

From Huaheine our navigators sailed for Ulietea, where trade was carried on in the usual manner, and a most friendly intercourse renewed between Captain Cook and Oreo, the chief of the island. Here Tupia was inquired after with particular eagerness, and the inquirers were perfectly satisfied with the account which was given of the occasion of that Indian's decease.

On the morning of the 15th, the English were surprised at finding that none of the inhabitants of Ulietea came off to the ships, as had hitherto been customary. As two men belonging to the Adventure had stayed on shore all night, contrary to orders, Captain Cook's first conjectures were that the natives had stripped them, and were afraid of the revenge that would be taken of the insult. This however was not the case. The men had been treated with great civility, and could assign no cause for the precipitate flight of the Indians. All that the captain could learn was, that several were killed, and others wounded, by the guns of the English. This information alarmed him for the safety of some of our people, who had been sent out in two boats to the island of Otaha. He determined, therefore, if possible, to see the chief himself. When he came up to him, Oreo threw his arms around our commander's neck, and burst into tears, in which he was accompanied by all the women, and some of the men; so that the lamentation became general. Astonishment alone kept Captain Cook from joining in their grief. At last the whole which he could collect from his inquiries was, that the natives had been alarmed on account of the absence of the English boats, and imagined the captain, upon the supposition of the desertion of his men, would use violent means for the recovery of his loss. When the matter was explained, it was acknowledged that not a single inhabitant, or a single Englishman, had been hurt. This groundless consternation displayed in a strong light the timorous disposition of the people of the Society Islands.

Our navigators were as successful in procuring provisions at Ulietea as they had been at Huaheine. Captain Cook judged that the number of hogs obtained amounted to four hundred or upwards; many of them indeed were only roasters, while others exceeded a hundred pounds in weight; but the general run was from forty to sixty. A larger quantity was offered than the ships could contain, so that our countrymen were enabled to proceed on their voyage with no small degree of comfort and advantage.

Our commander, by his second visit to the Society Islands, gained a farther knowledge of their general state, and of the customs of the inhabitants. It appeared that a Spanish ship had been lately at Otaheite, and the natives complained that a disease had been communicated to them by the people of this vessel, which, according to their account, affected the head, the throat, and the stomach, and at length ended in death. With regard to a certain disorder, the effects of which have so fatally been felt in the latter ages of the world, Captain Cook's inquiries could not absolutely determine whether it was known to the islanders before they were visited by the Europeans. If it was of recent origin, the introduction of it was, without a dissentient voice, ascribed to the voyage of M. de Bougainville.

One thing which our commander was solicitous to ascertain, was, whether human sacrifices constituted a part of the religious customs of these people. The man of whom he made his inquiries, and several other natives, took some pains to explain the matter; but, but from our people's ignorance of the language of the country, their explication could not be understood. Captain Cook afterwards learned from Omai that the inhabitants of the Society Islands offer human sacrifices to the Supreme Being. What relates to funeral ceremonies excepted, all the knowledge he could obtain concerning their religion was very imperfect and defective.

The captain had an opportunity, in this voyage, of rectifying the great injustice which had been done to the women of Otaheite and the neighbouring isles. They had been represented as ready, without exception, to grant the last favour to any man who would come up to their price; but our commander found that this was by no means the case. The favours both of the married women, and of the unmarried, of the better sort, were as difficult to be obtained in the Society Islands as in any other country whatever. Even with respect to the unmarried females of the lower class, the charge was not indiscriminately true. There were many of these who would not admit of indecent familiarities. The setting this subject in a proper light must be considered as one of the agreeable effects of Captain Cook's second voyage. Every enlightened mind will rejoice at what conduces to the honour of human nature in general, and of the female sex in particular. Chastity is so eminently the glory of that sex, and, indeed, is so essentially connected with the good order of society, that it must be a satisfaction to reflect that there is no country, however ignorant or barbarous, in which this virtue is not regarded as an object of moral obligation.

This voyage enabled our commander to gain some further knowledge concerning the geography of the Society Isles, and he found it highly probable that Otaheite is of greater extent than he had computed it in his former estimation. The astronomers did not neglect to set up their observatories, and to make observations suited to their purpose.

On the 17th of September Captain Cook sailed from Ulietea, directing his course to the west, with an inclination to the south. Land was discovered on the 23d of the month, to which he gave the name of Harvey's Island. On the 1st of October he reached the island of Middleburg. While he was looking about for a landing-place, two canoes, each of them conducted by two or three men, came boldly alongside the ship, and some of the people entered it without hesitation. This mark of confidence inspired our commander with so good an opinion of the inhabitants, that he determined if possible to pay them a visit, which he did the next day. Scarcely had the vessels gotten to an anchor, before they were surrounded by a great number of canoes, full of the natives, who brought with them cloth and various curiosities, which they exchanged for nails and such other articles as were adapted to their fancy. Among those who came on board was a chief named Tioony, whose friendship Captain Cook immediately gained by proper presents, consisting principally of a hatchet and some spike-nails. A party of our navigators, with the captain at the head of them, having embarked in two boats proceeded to shore, where they found an immense crowd of people, who welcomed them to the island with loud acclamations. There was not so much as a stick, or any other weapon in the hands of a single native, so pacific were their dispositions and intentions. They seemed to be more desirous of giving than receiving, and many of them who could not approach near to the boats, threw into them, over the heads of others, whole bales of cloth, and then retired, without either asking or waiting for any thing in return. The whole day was spent by our navigators in the most agreeable manner. When they returned on board in the evening, every one expressed how much he was delighted with the country and the very obliging behaviour of the inhabitants, who seemed to vie with each other in their endeavours to give pleasure to our people. All this conduct appeared to be the result of the most pure good nature, perhaps without being accompanied with much sentiment or feeling; for when Captain Cook signified to the chief his intention of quitting the island, he did not seem to be in the least moved. Among other articles presented by the captain to Tioony, he left him an assortment of garden-seeds, which, if properly used, might be of great future benefit to the country.

From Middleburg the ships sailed down to Amsterdam, the natives of which island were equally ready with those of the former place to maintain a friendly intercourse with the English. Like the people of Middleburg, they brought nothing with them but cloth, matting, and such other articles as could be of little service, and for these our seamen were so simple as to barter away their clothes. To put a stop, therefore, to so injurious a traffic, and to obtain the necessary refreshments, the captain gave orders that no sort of curiosities should be purchased by any person whatever. This injunction produced the desired effect. When the inhabitants saw that the English would deal with them for nothing but eatables, they brought off bananas and cocoa-nuts in abundance, together with some fowls and pigs; all of which they exchanged for small nails and pieces of cloth. Even a few old rags were sufficient for the purchase of a pig or a fowl.

The method of carrying on trade being settled, and proper officers having been appointed to prevent disputes, our commander's next object was to obtain as complete a knowledge as possible of the island of Amsterdam. In this he was much facilitated by a friendship which he had formed with Attago, one of the chiefs of the country. Captain Cook was struck with admiration when he surveyed the beauty and cultivation of the island. He thought himself transported into the most fertile plains of Europe. There was not an inch of waste ground. The roads occupied no larger a space than was absolutely necessary, and the fences did not take up above four inches each. Even such a small portion of ground was not wholly lost, for many of the fences themselves contained useful trees or plants. The scene was everywhere the same, and nature, assisted by a little art, nowhere assumes a more splendid appearance than in this island.

Friendly as were the natives of Amsterdam, they were not entirely free from the thievish disposition which hath so often been remarked in the islanders of the Southern Ocean. The instances, however, of this kind which occurred, were not of such a nature as to produce any extraordinary degree of trouble, or to involve our people in a quarrel with the inhabitants.

Captain Cook's introduction to the king of the island afforded a scene somewhat remarkable. His majesty was seated with so much sullen and stupid gravity, that the captain took him for an idiot, whom the Indians, from some superstitious reasons, were ready to worship. When our commander saluted and spoke to him, he neither answered nor took the least notice of him, nor did he alter a single feature of his countenance. Even the presents which were made to him could not induce him to resign a bit of his gravity, or to speak one word, or to turn his head either to the right hand or to the left. As he was in the prime of life, it was possible that a false sense of dignity might engage him to assume so solemn a stupidity of appearance. In the history of mankind instances might probably be found which would confirm this supposition.

It is observable that the two islands of Middleburg and Am-

9*

sterdam are guarded from the sea by a reef of coral rocks, which extend out from the shore about one hundred fathoms. On this reef the force of the sea is spent before it reaches the land. The same, indeed, is in a great measure the situation of all the tropical isles which our commander had seen in that part of the globe; and hence arises an evidence of the wisdom and goodness of Providence, as by such a provision nature has effectually secured them from the encroachments of the sea, though many of them are mere points, when compared with the vast ocean by which they are surrounded.

In Amsterdam Mr. Forster not only found the same wants that are at Otaheite and the neighbouring islands, but several others, which are not to be met with in those places. Captain Cook took care, by a proper assortment of garden seeds and pulse, to increase the vegetable stock of the inhabitants.

Hogs and fowls were the only domestic animals that were seen in these islands. The former are of the same sort with those which had been met with in other parts of the Southern Ocean, but the latter are far superior, being as large as any in Europe, and equal, if not preferable, with respect to the goodness of their flesh.

Both men and women are of a common size with Europeans. Their colour is that of a lightish copper, and with a greater uniformity than occurs among the natives of Otaheite and the Society Isles. Some of the English gentlemen were of opinion that the inhabitants of Middleburg and Amsterdam were a much handsomer race, while others, with whom Captain Cook concurred, maintained a contrary sentiment. However this may be, their shape is good, their features regular, and they are active, brisk, and lively. The women, in particular, are the merriest creatures our commander had ever met with; and provided any person seemed pleased with them, they would keep chattering by his side without the least invitation, or considering whether they were understood. They appeared in general to be modest, though there were several amongst them of a different character. As there were yet on board some complaints of a certain disorder, the captain took all possible care to prevent its communication. Our navigators were frequently entertained by the women with songs, and this in a manner which was by no means disagreeable. They had a method of keeping time by snapping their fingers. Their music was harmonious as well as their voices, and there was a considerable degree of compass in their notes.

A singular custom was found to prevail in these islands. The greater part of the people were observed to have lost one or both of their little fingers, and this was not peculiar to rank, age, or sex; nor was the amputation restricted to any specific period of life. Our navigators endeavoured in vain to discover the reason of so extraordinary a practice.

A very extensive knowledge of the language of Middleburg and Amsterdam could not be obtained during the short stay which was made there by the English. However, the more they inquired into it, the more they found that it was, in general, the same with that which is spoken at Otaheite and the Society Isles. The difference is not greater than what frequently occurs betwixt the most northern and western parts of England.

On the 7th of October, Captain Cook proceeded on his voyage. His intention was to sail directly to Queen Charlotte's Sound, in New Zealand, for the purpose of taking in wood and water, after which he was to pursue his discoveries to the south and the east. The day after he quitted Amsterdam he passed the island of Pilstart, an island which had been discovered by Tasman.

On the 21st, he made the land of New Zealand, at the distance of eight or ten leagues from Table Cape. As our commander was very desirous of leaving in the country such an assortment of animals and vegetables as might greatly contribute to the future benefit of the inhabitants, one of the first things which he did was to give to a chief, who had come off in a canoe, two boars, two sows, four hens, and two cocks, together with a quantity of seeds. The seeds were of the most useful kind, such as wheat, French and kidney beans, pease, cabbage, turnips, onions, carrots, parsnips, and yams. The man to whom these several articles were presented, though he was much more enraptured with a spike-nail half the length of his arm, promised, however, to take care of them, and in particular, not to kill any of the animals. If he adhered to his promise, they would be sufficient, in a due course of time, to stock the whole island.

It was the 3d of November before Captain Cook brought the Resolution into Ship Cove, in Queen Charlotte's Sound. He had been beating about the island from the 21st of October, during which time his vessel was exposed to a variety of tempestuous weather. In one instance he had been driven off the land by a furious storm, which lasted two days, and which would have been dangerous in the highest degree, had it not fortunately happened that it was fair overhead, and that there was no reason to be apprehensive of a lee-shore. In the course of the bad weather which succeeded this storm, the Adventure was separated from the Resolution, and was never seen nor heard of through the whole remainder of the voyage.

The first object of our commander's attention after his arrival in Queen Charlotte's Sound, was to provide for the repair of his ship, which had suffered in various respects, and especially in her sails and rigging. Another matter which called for his notice was the state of the bread belonging to the vessel, and he had the mortification of finding that a large quantity of it was damaged. To repair this loss in the best manner he was able, he ordered all the casks to be opened, the bread to be picked, and such parcels of it to be baked in the copper oven, as could by that means be recovered. Notwithstanding this care, four thousand two hundred and ninety-two pounds were found totally unfit for use, and about three thousand pounds more could only be eaten by people in the situation of our navigators.

Captain Cook was early in his inquiries concerning the animals which had been left at New Zealand in the former part of his voyage. He saw the youngest of the two sows that Captain Furneaux had put on shore in Cannibal Cove. She was in good condition, and very tame. The boar and other sow, if our commander was rightly informed, were taken away and separated, but not killed. He was told that the two goats, which he had landed up the sound, had been destroyed by a rascally native of the name of Goubiah, so that the captain had the grief of discovering that all his benevolent endeavours to stock the country with useful animals were likely to be frustrated by the very people whom he was anxious to serve. The gardens had met with a better fate. Everything in them, excepting potatoes, the inhabitants had left entirely to nature, who had so well performed her part, that most of the articles were in flourishing condition.

Notwithstanding the inattention and folly of the New Zealanders, Captain Cook still continued his zeal for their benefit. To the inhabitants who resided at the cove, he gave a boar, a young sow, two cocks, and two hens, which had been brought from the Society Islands. At the bottom of the West Bay he ordered to be landed without the knowledge of the Indians, four hogs, being three sows and one boar, together with two cocks and two hens. They were carried a little way into the woods, and as much food was left them as would serve them for ten or twelve days, which was done to prevent their coming down to the shore in search of sustenance, and by that means being discovered by the natives. The captain was desirous of replacing the two goats which Goubiah was understood to have killed, by leaving behind him the only two that yet remained in his possession. But he had the misfortune, soon after his arrival at Queen Charlotte's Sound, to lose the ram, and this in a manner for which it was not easy to assign the cause. Whether it was owing to anything he had eaten, or to his being stung with nettles, which were very plentiful in the place, he was seized with fits that bordered upon madness. In one of these fits, he was supposed to have run into the sea, and to have been drowned; and thus every method which our commander had taken to stock the country with sheep and goats, proved ineffectual. He hoped to be more successful with respect respect to the boars and sows, and the cocks and hens, which he left on the island.

While the boatswain, one day, and a party of men, were employed in cutting broom, some of them stole several things from a private hut of the natives, in which was deposited most of the treasures they had received from the English, as well as property of their own. Complaint being made by the Indians to Captain Cook, and a particular man of the boatswain's party having been pointed out to the captain as the person who had committed the theft, he ordered him to be punished in their presence. With this they went away seemingly satisfied, although they did not recover any of the articles which they had lost. It was always a maxim with our commander, to punish the least crimes which any of his people were guilty of with regard to uncivilized nations. Their robbing us with impunity he by no means considered as reason for our treating them in the same manner. Addicted as the New Zealanders were, in a certain degree, to stealing, a disposition which must have been very much increased by the novelty and allurement of the objects presented to their view, they had, nevertheless, when injured themselves, such a sense of justice as to apply to Captain Cook for redress. The best method, in his opinion, of preserving a good understanding with the inhabitants of countries in this state of society, is, first to convince them of the superiority we have over them in consequence of our fire-arms, and then to be always upon our guard. Such a conduct, united with strict honesty and gentle treatment, will convince them that it is their interest not do disturb us, and prevent them from forming any general plan of attack.

In this second visit of our navigators to New Zealand, they met with indubitable evidence that the natives were eaters of human flesh. The proofs of this fact had a most powerful influence on the mind of Oedidee, a youth of Bolabola, whom Captain Cook had brought in the Resolution from Ulietea. He was so affected, that he became perfectly motionless, and exhibited such a picture of horror that it would have been impossible for art to describe that passion, with half the force with which it appeared in his conntenance. When he was roused from this state by some of the English, he burst into tears, continued to weep and scold by turns, told the New Zealanders that they were vile men, and assured them that he would not be any longer their friend. He would not so much as permit them to come near him; and he refused to accept, or even to touch, the knife with which some human flesh had been cut off. Such was Oedidee's indignation against the abominable custom; and our commander has justly remarked, that it was an indignation worthy to be imitated by every rational being. The conduct of this young man, upon the present occasion, strongly points out the difference which had taken place, in the progress of civilization, between the inhabitants of the Society Islands and those of New Zealand. It was our commander's firm opinion, that the only human flesh which was eaten by these people was that of their enemies, who had been slain in battle.

During the stay of our voyagers in Queen Charlotte's Sound, they were plentifully supplied with fish, procured from the natives at a very easy rate; and, besides the vegetables afforded by their own gardens, they everywhere found plenty of scurvy-grass and celery. These the captain ordered to be dressed every day for all his hands. By the attention which he paid to his men in the article of provisions, they had for three months lived principally on a fresh diet, and, at this time there was not a sick or scorbutic person on board.

The morning before the captain sailed, he wrote a memorandum, containing such information as he thought necessary for Captain Furneaux, in case he should put into the sound. This memorandum was buried in a bottle under the root of a tree in the garden; and in such a manner, that it could not avoid being discovered, if either Captain Furneaux, or any other European, should chance to arrive at the cove.

Our commander did not leave New Zealand without making such remarks on the coast between Cape Teerawhitte and Cape Palliser as may be of service to future navigators. It being now the unanimous opinion that the Adventure was nowhere upon the island, Captain Cook gave up all expectation of seeing her any more during the voyage. This circumstance, however, did not discourage him from fully exploring the southern parts of the Pacific Ocean, in the doing of which he intended to employ the whole of the ensuing season. When he quitted the coast, he had the satisfaction to find that not a man of the crew was dejected, or thought that the dangers they had yet to go through were in the least augmented by their being alone. Such was the confidence they placed in their commander, that they were as ready to proceed cheerfully to the south, or wherever he might lead them, as if the Adventure, or even a larger number of ships, had been in company.

On the 26th of November, Captain Cook sailed from New Zealand in search of a continent, and steered to the south, inclining to the east. Some days after this, our navigators reckoned themselves to be antipodes to their friends in London, and consequently were at as great a distance from them as possible. The first ice island was seen on the 12th of December, farther south than the first ice which had been met with after leaving the Cape of Good Hope, in the preceding year. In the progress of the voyage, ice islands continually occurred, and the navigation became more and more difficult and dangerous. When our people were in the latitude of 67° 5' south, they all at once got within such a cluster of these islands, together with a large quantity of loose pieces, that to keep clear of them was a matter of the utmost difficulty. On the 22d of the month, the Resolution was in the highest latitude she had yet reached; and circumstances now became so unfavourable, that our commander thought of returning more to the north. Here there was no probability of finding any land, or a possibility of getting farther south. To have proceeded, therefore, to the east in this latitude, must have been improper, not only on account of the ice, but because a vast space of sea to the north must have been left unexplored, in which there might lie a large tract of country. It was only by visiting those parts, that it could be determined whether such a supposition was well founded. As our navigators advanced to the northeast on the 24th, the ice islands increased so fast upon them, that, at noon, they could see nearly a hundred around them, besides an immense number of small pieces. In this situation they spent Christmas-day, much in the same manner as they had done in the former year. Happily our people had continual day-light, and clear weather; for had it been as foggy as it was on some preceding days, nothing less than a miracle could have saved them from being dashed to pieces.

While the Resolution was in the high latitudes, many of her company were attacked with a slight fever, occasioned by colds The disorder, however, yielded to the simplest remedies, and was generally removed in a few days. On the 5th of January, 1774, the ship not being then in much more than fifty degrees of latitude, there were only one or two persons on the sick list.

After Captain Cook, agreeably to his late resolution, had traversed a large extent of ocean, without discovering land, he again directed his course to the southward. By the 30th of the month, through obstructions and difficulties which, from their similar nature to those already mentioned, it would be tedious to repeat, he reached to the seventy-first degree of latitude. Thus far had he gone; but to have proceeded farther would have been the height of folly and madness. It would have been exposing himself, his men, and his ship, to the utmost danger, and perhaps to destruction, without the least prospect of advantage. The captain was of opinion, as indeed were most of the gentlemen on board, that the ice now in sight extended quite to the pole, or might join to some land, to which it might be fixed from the earliest time. If, however, there be such land, it can afford no better retreat for birds, or any other animals, than the ice itself, with which it must be wholly covered. Though our commander had not only the ambition of going farther than any one had done before, but of proceeding as far as it was possible for man to go, he was the less satisfied with the interruption he now met with, as it shortened the dangers and hardships inseparable from the navigation of the southern polar regions. In fact he was impelled by inevitable necessity to tack and stand back to the north.

The determination which Captain Cook now formed was to spend the ensuing winter within the tropic, if he met with no employment before he came there. He was well satisfied that no continent was to be found in this ocean, but what must lie so far to the south as to be wholly unaccessible on account of ice. If there existed a continent in the South Atlantic Ocean, he was sensible that he could not explore it without having the whole summer before him. Upon a supposition, on the other hand, that there is no land there, he might undoubtedly have reached the Cape of Good Hope by April. In that case he would have put an end to the finding of a continent; which was indeed the first object of the voyage. But this could not satisfy the extensive and magnanimous mind of our commander. He had a good ship, expressly sent out on discoveries, a healthy crew, and was not in want either of stores or provisions. In such circumstances to have quitted this Southern Pacific Ocean, would, he thought, have been betraying not only a want of perseverance, but of judgment, in supposing it to have been so well explored that nothing farther could be done. Although he had proved that there was no continent but what must lie far to the south, there remained, nevertheless, room for very large islands in places wholly unexamined. Many, likewise, of those which had formerly been discovered had been but imperfectly explored, and their situations were as imperfectly known. He was also persuaded that his continuing some time longer in this sea would be productive of improvements in navigation and geography, as well as in other sciences.

In consequence of these views, it was Captain Cook's intention first to go in search of the land said to have been discovered by Juan Fernandez in the last century. If he should fail in finding this land, he proposed to direct his course in quest of Easter Island, or Davis's Land, the situation of which was known with so little certainty, that none of the attempts lately made for its discovery had been successful. He next intended to get within the tropic, and then to proceed to the west, touching at, and settling the situations of such islands as he might meet with till he arrived at Otaheite, where it was necessary for him to stop, to look for the Adventure. It was also in his contemplation to run as far west as the Tierra Austral del Espiritu Santo, which was discovered by Quiros, and to which M. de Bougainville has given the name of the Great Cyclades. From this land it was the captain's plan to steer to the south, and so back to the east, between the latitudes of fifty and sixty. In the execution of this plan, it was his purpose, if possible, to attain the length of Cape Horn in the ensuing November, when he should have the best part of the summer before him to explore the southern part of the Atlantic Ocean. Great as was this design, our commander thought it capable of being carried into execution; and when he communicated it to his officers, he had the satisfaction of finding that it received their zealous and cheerful concurrence. They displayed the utmost readiness in executing, in the most effectual manner, every measure he thought proper to adopt. With such good examples to direct them, the seamen were always obedient and alert; and on the present occasion, so far were they from wishing the voyage to be concluded, that they rejoiced at the prospect of its being prolonged another year, and of soon enjoying the benefits of a milder climate.

In pursuing his course to the north, Captain Cook became well assured that the discovery of Juan Fernandez, if any such was ever made, could be nothing more than a small island. At this time the captain was attacked by a bilious colic, the violence of which confined him to his bed. The management of the ship, upon this occasion, was left to Mr. Cooper, the first officer, who conducted her entirely to his commander's satisfaction. It was several days before the most dangerous symptoms of Captain Cook's disorder were removed, during which time Mr. Patten, the surgeon, in attending upon him, manifested not only the skilfulness of a physician, but the tenderness of a nurse. When the captain began to recover, a favourite dog, belonging to Mr. Forster, fell a sacrifice to his tender stomach. There was no other fresh meat whatever on board, and he could eat not only of the broth which was made of it, but of the flesh itself, when there was nothing else that he was capable of tasting. Thus did he derive nourishment and strength from food, which, to most people in Europe, would have been in the highest degree disgusting, and productive of sickness. The necessity of the case overcame every feeling of dislike.

On the 11th of March our navigators came within sight of Easter Island, or Davis's Land, their transactions at which place were of too little moment to deserve a particular recital. The inhabitants are, in general, a slender race. In colour, features, and language, they bear such an affinity to the people of the more western isles, that there can be no doubt of their having been descended from one common original. It is indeed extraordinary that the same nation should have spread themselves to so wide an extent, as to take in almost a fourth part of the circumference of the globe. With regard to the disposition of the natives of Easter Island, it is friendly and hospitable; but they are as much addicted to stealing as any of their neighbours. The island itself hath so little to recommend it, that no nation need to contend for the honour of its discovery. So sparing has nature been of her favours to this spot, that there is in it no safe anchorage, no wood for fuel, no fresh water worth taking on board. The most remarkable objects in the country are some surprising gigantic statues, which were first seen by Roggewein.

It was with pleasure that our commander quitted a place which could afford such slender accommodations to voyagers, and directed his course for the Marquesas Islands. He had not been long at sea before he was again attacked by his bilious disorder. The attack, however, was not so violent as the former one had been. He had reason to believe that the return of his disease was owing to his having exposed and fatigued himself too much at Easter Island.

On the 6th and 7th of April, our navigators came within sight of four islands, which they knew to be the Marquesas. To one of them, which was a new discovery, Captain Cook gave the name of Hood's Island, after that of the young gentleman by whom it was first seen. As soon as the ship was brought to an anchor in Madre de Dios, or Resolution Bay, in the Island of St. Christina, a traffic commenced, in the course of which the natives would frequently keep our goods, without making any return. At last the captain was obliged to fire a musket ball over one man who had several times treated the English in this manner. This produced only a temporary effect. Too many of the Indians having come on board, our commander, who was going in a boat to find a convenient place for mooring the ship, said to the officers, " You must look well after these people, or they will certainly carry off something or other." Scarcely had he gotten into the boat, when he was informed that they had stolen an iron stanchion from the opposite gangway, and were carrying it off. Upon this he ordered his men to fire over the canoe, till he could get around in the boat, but not to kill any one. Such, however, was the noise made by the natives, that the order was not heard, and the unhappy thief was killed at the first shot. All the Indians having retired with precipitation, in consequence of this unfortunate accident, Captain Cook followed them into the bay, prevailed upon some of them to come alongside his boat, and, by suitable presents, so far conciliated their minds that their fears seemed to be in a great measure allayed. The death of their countryman did not cure them of their thievish disposition; but at length it was somewhat restrained by their conviction that no distance secured them from the reach of our muskets. Several smaller instances of their talent at stealing the captain thought proper to overlook.

The provisions obtained at St. Christina were yams, plantains, bread-fruit, a few cocoa-nuts, fowls and small pigs. For a time the trade was carried on upon reasonable terms, but the market was at last ruined by the indiscretion of some young gentlemen, who gave away in exchange various articles which the inhabitants had not seen before, and which captivated their fancy above nails, or more useful iron tools. One of the gentlemen had given for a pig a very large quantity of red feathers, which he had gotten at Amsterdam. The effect of this was particularly fatal. It was not possible to support the trade in the manner in which it was now begun, even for a single day. When, therefore, our commander found that he was not likely to be supplied on any conditions, with sufficient refreshments, and that the island was neither very convenient for taking in wood and water, nor for affording the necessary repairs of the ship, he determined to proceed immediately to some other place where the wants of his people could be effectually relieved. After having been nineteen weeks at sea, and having lived all that time upon salt diet, a change in their food could not avoid being peculiarly desirable ; and yet on their arrival at St. Christina, it could scarcely be asserted that a single man was sick, and there were but a few who had the least complaint of any kind. " This," says Captain Cook, " was undoubtedly owing to the many antiscorbutic articles we had on board, and to the great attention of the surgeon, who was remarkably careful to apply them in time." It may justly be added, that this was likewise owing to the singular care of the captain himself, and to the exertion of his authority in enforcing the excellent regulations which his wisdom and humanity had adopted.

The chief reason for our commander's touching at the Marquesas Islands was to fix their situation, that being the only circumstance in which the nautical account of them, given in Mr. Dalrymple's collection, is deficient. It was farther desirable to settle this point, as it would lead to a more accurate knowledge of Mendana's other discoveries. Accordingly Captain Cook has marked the situation of the Marquesas with his usual correctness. He has also taken care to describe the particular cove in Resolution Bay, in the Island of St. Christina, which is most convenient for obtaining wood and water.

It is remarkable with respect to the inhabitants of the Marquesas Islands, that collectively taken, they are, without exception, the finest race of people in this sea. Perhaps they surpass all other nations in symmetry of form and regularity of features. It is plain, however, from the affinity of their language to that of Otaheite and the Society Isles, that they are of the same origin Of this affinity the English were fully sensible, though they could not converse with them; but Oedidee was capable of doing it tolerably well.

From the Marquesas Captain Cook steered for Otaheite, with a view of falling in with some of the islands discovered by former navigators, and especially by the Dutch, the situation of which had not been accurately determined. In the course of the voyage, he passed a number of low islets, connected together by reefs of coral rocks. One of the islands, on which Lieutenant Cooper went ashore with two boats, well armed, was called by the natives Tiookea. It had been discovered and visited by Captain Byron. The inhabitants of Tiookea are of a much darker colour than those of the higher islands, and appeared to be more fierce in their dispositions. This may be owing to their manner of gaining their subsistence, which is chiefly from the sea, and to their being much exposed to the sun and the weather. Our voyagers observed that they were stout, well-made men, and that they had marked on their bodies the figure of a fish, which was a good emblem of their profession.

Besides passing by St. George's Islands, which had been so named by Captain Byron, our commander made the discovery of four others. These he called Palliser's Isles, in honour of his particular friend, Sir Hugh Palliser. The inhabitants seemed to be the same sort of people as those of Tiookea, and like them, were armed with long pikes. Captain Cook could not determine, with any degree of certainty, whether the group of isles he had lately seen were, or were not, any of those that had been discovered by the Dutch navigators. This was owing to the neglect of recording, with sufficient accuracy, the situation of their discoveries. Our commander hath, in general, observed, with regard to this part of the ocean, that, from the latitude of twenty down to fourteen or twelve, and from the meridian of a hundred and thirty-eight to a hundred and forty-eight or a hundred and fifty west, it is so strewed with low isles, that a navigator cannot proceed with too much caution.

On the 22d of April, Captain Cook reached the Island of Otaheite, and anchored in Matavia Bay. As his chief reason for putting in at this place was to give Mr. Wales an opportunity of ascertaining the error of the watch by the known longitude, and to determine anew her rate of going, the first object was to land the instruments, and to erect tents for the reception of a guard, and such other people as it was necessary to have on shore. Sick there were none; for the refreshments which had been obtained at the Marquesas had removed every complaint of that kind.

From the quantity of provisions which, contrary to expectation, our commander now found at Otaheite, he determined to make a longer stay in the island than he had at first intended. Accordingly, he took measures for the repairs of the ship, which the high southern latitudes had rendered indispensably necessary.

During Captain Cook's stay at Otaheite, he maintained a most friendly connexion with the inhabitants, and a continual interchange of visits was preserved between him and Otoo, Towha, and other chiefs of the country. His traffic with them was greatly facilitated by his having fortunately brought with him some red parrot feathers from the Island of Amsterdam. These were jewels of high value in the eyes of the Otaheitans. The captain's stock in trade was by this time greatly exhausted; so that if it had not been for the feathers, he would have found it difficult to have supplied the ship with the necessary refreshments.

Among other entertainments which our commander and the rest of the English gentlemen met with at Otaheite was a grand naval review. The vessels of war consisted of a hundred and sixty large double canoes, well equipped, manned and armed. They were decorated with flags and streamers, and the chiefs, together with all those who were on the fighting stages, were dressed in their war habits. The whole fleet made a noble appearance, and such as our voyagers had never seen before in this sea, or could ever have expected. Besides the vessels of war, there were a hundred and seventy sail of smaller double canoes, which seemed to be designed for transports and victuallers. Upon each of them was a little house, and they were rigged with mast and sail, which was not the case with the war canoes. Captain Cook guessed that there were no less than seven thousand seven hundred and sixty men in the whole fleet. He was not able to obtain full information concerning the design of this armament.

Notwithstanding the agreeable intercourse that was in general maintained between our commander and the people of Otaheite, circumstances occasionally happened which called for peculiar exertions of his prudence and resolution. One of the natives, who had attempted to steal a water-cask from the watering place, was caught in the act, sent on board and put in irons. In this situation he was seen by King Otoo and other chiefs. Captain Cook having made known to them the crime of their countryman, Otoo entreated that he might be set at liberty. This the captain however refused, alleging that since he punished his own people when they committed the least offence against Otoo's, it was but just that this man should also be punished. As Captain Cook knew that Otoo would not punish him, he resolved to do it himself. Accordingly, he directed the criminal to be carried on shore to the tents, and having himself followed, with the chiefs and other Otaheitans, he ordered the guard out, under arms, and commanded the man to be tied up to a post. Otoo again solicited the culprit's release, and in this he was seconded by his sister, but in vain. The captain expostulated with him on the conduct of the man, and of the Indians in general, telling him, that neither he, nor any of the ship's company, took the smallest matter of property from them without first paying for it; enumerating the articles which the English had given in exchange for such and such things, and urging that it was wrong in them to steal from those who were their friends. He added, that the punishing of the guilty person would be the means of saving the lives of several of Otoo's people by deterring them from committing crimes of the like nature, and thus preventing them from the danger of being shot to death, which would certainly happen, at one time or other, if they persisted in their robberies. With these arguments the king appeared to be satisfied, and only desired that the man might not be killed. Captain Cook then directed that the crowd, which was very great, should be kept at a proper distance, and in the presence of them all, ordered the fellow two dozen of lashes with a cat-o'-nine tails. This punishment the man sustained with great firmness, after which he was set at liberty. When the natives were going away, Towha called them back, and with much gracefulness of action, addressed them in a speech of nearly half an hour in length, the design of which was to condemn their present conduct, and to recommend a different one for the future. To make a farther impression upon the minds of the inhabitants, our commander ordered his marines to go through their exercises, and to load and fire in volleys with balls. As they were very quick in their manœuvres, it is more easy to conceive than to describe the amazement which possessed the Indians during the whole time, and especially those of them who had not seen anything of the kind before.

The judicious will discern, with regard to this narrative, that it throws peculiar light upon Captain Cook's character. Nor is it an uncurious circumstance in the history of human society, that a stranger should thus exercise jurisdiction over the natives of a country, in the presence of the prince of that country, without his authority and even contrary to his solicitations.

Another disagreeable altercation with the inhabitants of Otaheite, arose from the negligence of one of the English sentinels on shore. Having either slept, or quitted his post, an Indian seized the opportunity of carrying off his musket. When any extraordinary theft was committed, it immediately excited such an alarm among the natives in general, from their fear of Captain Cook's resentment, they fled from their habitations, and a stop was put to the traffic for provisions. On the present occasion, the captain had no small degree of trouble; but by his prudent conduct the musket was recovered, peace restored, and commerce again opened. In the differences which happened with the several people he met with in his voyages, it was a rule with him never to touch the least article of their property, any farther than to detain their canoes for a while when it became absolutely necessary. He always chose the most mild and equitable methods of bringing them to reason; and in this he not only succeeded, but frequently put things upon a better footing than if no contention had taken place.

During this visit to Otaheite, fruit and other refreshments were obtained in great plenty. The relief arising from them was the more agreeable and salutary, as the bread of the ship was in a bad condition. Though the biscuit had been aired and picked at New Zealand, it was now in such a state of decay, that it was necessary for it to undergo another airing and cleaning, in which much of it was found wholly rotten, and unfit to be eaten. This decay was judged to be owing to the ice our navigators had frequently taken in when to the southward, which made the hold of the vessel cold and damp, and to the great heat that succeeded when they came to the north. Whatever was the cause, the loss was so considerable, that the men were put to a scanty allowance in this article, with the additional mortification of the bread being bad that could be used.

Two goats that had been given by Captain Furneaux to Otoo, in **the** former part of the voyage, seemed to promise fair for answering the purposes for which they were left upon the island. The ewes, soon after, had two female kids, which were now so far grown as to be almost ready to propagate. At the same time **the old** ewe was again with kid. The people were very fond of them, and they were **in excellent** condition. From these circumstances Captain Cook entertained a hope, that in the course of years, they **would** multiply so much as to be extended over all the isles of the Southern Ocean. The like success did not attend the sheep which had been left in the country. These speedily died, one excepted, which was said to be yet alive. Our navigators also furnished the natives with cats, having given away no less than twenty at Otaheite, besides some which had been made presents of at Ulietea and Huaheine.

With regard to the number of the inhabitants of Otaheite, our commander collected, from comparing several facts together, that, including women and children, there could not be less, in the whole island, than two hundred and four thousand. This number, at first sight, exceeded his belief. But when he came to reflect on the vast swarms of people that appeared wherever he went, he was convinced that the estimate was agreeable to truth.

Such was the friendly treatment which our voyagers met with at Otaheite, that one of the gunner's mates was induced to form a plan for remaining in the country. As he knew that he could not execute his scheme with success while the Resolution continued in Matavia Bay, he took the opportunity, when she was ready to quit it, and the sails were set for that purpose, to slip overboard. Being a good swimmer, he had no doubt of getting safe to a canoe, which was at some distance ready to receive him, for his design was concerted with the natives, and had even been encouraged by Otoo. However, he was discovered before he had gotten clear of the ship, and a boat being presently hoisted out, he was taken up and brought back to the vessel. When our commander reflected on the man's situation, he did not think him very culpable, or his desire of staying in the island so extraordinary, as might at first view be imagined. He was a native of Ireland, and had sailed in the Dutch service. Captain Cook, on his return from his former voyage, had picked him up at Batavia, and had kept him in his employment ever since. It did not appear that he had either friends or connections which could bind him to any particular part of the world. All nations being alike to him, where could he be more happy than at Otaheite? Here, in one of the finest climates of the globe, he could enjoy not only the necessaries, but the luxuries of life, in ease and plenty. The captain seems to think, that if the man had applied to him in time he might have given his consent to his remaining in the country.

On the 15th of May Captain Cook anchored in O'Wharre Harbour, in the Island of Huaheine. He was immediately visited by his friend Oree, and the same agreeable intercourse subsisted between the captain and this good old chief, which had formerly taken place. Red feathers were not here in such estimation as they had been at Otaheite; the natives of Huaheine having the good sense to give a preference to the more useful articles of nails and axes. During the stay of our voyagers in the island, some alarms were occasioned by the thievish disposition of several of the inhabitants, but matters subsided without any material consequences. A solemn march, which our commander made through part of the country, at the head of forty-eight men, tended to impress the Indians with a sense of his power and authority. In fact, their attempts at stealing had been too much invited by the indiscretion of some of the English, who unguardedly separated themselves in the woods, for the purpose of killing birds, and who managed their muskets so unskillfully as to render them less formidable in the eyes of the natives.

I cannot persuade myself to omit a dramatic entertainment, at which several of the gentlemen belonging to the Resolution attended one evening. The piece represented a girl as running away with our navigators from Otaheite, and the story was partly founded in truth; for a young woman had taken a passage in the ship, down to Ulietea. She happened to be present at the representation of her own adventures, which had such an effect upon her, that it was with great difficulty that she could be prevailed upon by the English gentlemen to see the play out, or to refrain from tears while it was acting. The piece concluded with the reception she was supposed to meet with from her friends at her return, and it was a reception that was by no means favourable. As these people, when they see occasion, can add little extempore pieces to their entertainments, it is reasonable to imagine that the representation now described was intended as a satire against the girl, and to discourage others from following her steps. Such is the sense which they entertain of the propriety of female decorum.

During Captain Cook's stay at Huaheine, bread-fruit, cocoa-nuts, and other vegetable productions, were procured in abundance, but not a sufficiency of hogs to supply the daily expense of the ship. This was partly owing to a want of proper articles for traffic. The captain was obliged, therefore, to set the smiths at work, to make different sorts of nails, iron tools, and instruments, in order to enable him to obtain refreshments at the islands he was yet to visit, and to support his credit and influence among the natives.

When our commander was ready to sail from Huaheine, Oree was the last man that went out of the vessel. At parting, Captain Cook told him that they should meet each other no more, at which he wept, and said, "Let your sons come, we will treat them well."

At Ulietea, to which the captain next directed his course, the events that occurred were nearly similar to those which had already been related. He had always been received by the people of this island in the most hospitable manner, and they were justly entitled to everything which it was in his power to grant. They expressed the deepest concern at his departure, and were continually importuning him to return. Oreo, the chief, and his wife and daughter, but especially the two latter, scarcely ever ceased weeping. Their grief was so excessive, that it might perhaps be doubted whether it was entirely sincere and unaffected ; but our commander was of opinion that it was real. At length, when he was ready to sail, they took a most affectionate leave. Oreo's last request to Captain Cook was, that he would return ; and when he could not obtain a promise to that effect, he asked the name of his burying place. To this strange question the captain answered, without hesitation, that it was Stepney, that being the parish in which he lived when in London. Mr. Forster, to whom the same question was proposed, replied, with greater wisdom and recollection, that no man, who used the sea, could say where he should be buried.

As our commander could not promise, or even then suppose, that more English ships would be sent to the southern isles, Oedidee, who for so many months had been the faithful companion of our navigators, chose to remain in his native country. But he left them with a regret fully demonstrative of his esteem and affection, nor could anything have torn him from them, but the fear of never returning. When Oreo pressed so ardently Captain Cook's return, he sometimes gave such answers as left room for hope. At these answers Oedidee would eagerly catch, take him on one side, and ask him over again. The captain declares that he had not words to describe the anguish which appeared in this young man's breast when he went away. He looked up at the ship, burst into tears, and then sunk down into the canoe. Oedidee was a youth of good parts, and of a docile, gentle, and humane disposition; but as he was almost wholly ignorant of the religion, government, manners, customs, and traditions of his countrymen, and neighbouring islands, no material knowledge could have been collected from him, had our commander brought him away. He would, however, in every respect, have been a better specimen of the nation than Omai.

When Captain Cook first came to these islands, he had some thoughts of visiting Tupia's famous Bolabola. But having obtained a plentiful supply of refreshments, and the route he had in view allowing him no time to spare, he laid this design aside, and directed his course to the west. Thus did he take his leave, as he then thought, forever, of these happy isles, on which benevolent nature has spread her luxuriant sweets with a lavish hand, and in which the natives, copying the bounty of Providence, are equally liberal, being ready to contribute plentifully and cheerfully to the wants of navigators.*

On the 6th of June, the day after our voyagers left Ulietea, they saw land, which they found to be a low reef island, about four leagues in compass, and of a circular form. This was Howe Island, which had been discovered by Captain Wallis. Nothing remarkable occurred from this day to the 16th, when land was again seen. It was another reef island; and being a new discovery, Captain Cook gave it the name of Palmerston Island, in honour of Lord Palmerston. On the 20th, fresh land appeared, which was perceived to be inhabited. This induced our commander to go on shore with a party of gentlemen; but the natives were found to be fierce and untractable. All endeavours to bring them to a parley were to no purpose; for they came on with the ferocity of wild boars, and instantly threw their darts. Two or three muskets discharged in the air did not prevent one of them from advancing still further, and throwing another dart, or rather a spear, which passed close over Captain Cook's shoulder. The courage of this man had nearly cost him his life. When he threw his spear, he was not five paces from the captain, who had resolved to shoot him for his own preservation. It happened, however, that his musket missed fire: a circumstance on which he afterward reflected with pleasure. When he joined his party, and tried his musket in the air, it went off perfectly well. This island, from the disposition and behaviour of the natives, with whom no intercourse could be established, and from whom no benefit could be received, was called by our commander Savage Island. It is about eleven leagues in circuit; is of a round form and good height; and has deep waters close to its shores. Among its other disadvantages, it is not furnished with a harbour.

---

* From Mr. Wales's observations it appeared that, during five months, in which their watch had passed through the extremes of heat and cold, it went better in the cold than in the hot climates.

In pursuing his course to the west-southwest, Captain Cook passed by a number of small islands, and, on the 26th, anchored on the north side of Anamocka, or Rotterdam. A traffic immediately commenced with the natives, who brought what provisions they had, being chiefly yams and shaddocks, which they exchanged for nails, beads, and other small articles. Here, as in many former cases, the captain was put to some trouble, on account of the thievish disposition of the inhabitants. As they had gotten possession of an adze and two muskets, he found it necessary to exert himself with peculiar vigour, in order to oblige them to make restitution. For this purpose, he commanded all the marines to be armed, and sent on shore; and the result of this measure was, that the things which had been stolen were restored. In the contest, Captain Cook was under the necessity of firing some small shot at a native, who had distinguished himself by his resistance. His countrymen afterwards reported that he was dead; but he was only wounded, and that not in a dangerous manner. Though his sufferings were the effects of his own misbehaviour, the captain endeavoured to soften them, by making him a present, and directing his wounds to be dressed by the surgeon of the ship.

The first time that our commander landed at Anamocka, an old lady presented him with a girl, and gave him to understand, that she was at his service. Miss, who had previously been instructed, wanted a spike-nail, or a shirt, neither of which he had to give her: and he flattered himself, that, by making the two women sensible of his poverty, he should easily get clear of their importunities. In this, however, he was mistaken. The favours of the young lady were offered upon credit; and on his declining the proposal, the old woman began to argue with him and then to abuse him. As far as he could collect from her countenance and her actions, the design of her speech was both to ridicule and reproach him, for refusing to entertain so fine a young woman. Indeed, the girl was by no means destitute of beauty; but Captain Cook found it more easy to withstand her allurements than the abuse of the ancient matron, and therefore hastened into his boat.

While the captain was on shore at Anamocka, he got the names of twenty islands, which lie between the northwest and northeast. Some of them were in sight; and two of them, which are most to the west, are remarkable on account of their great height. These are Amattafoa and Oghao. From a continual column of smoke which was seen daily ascending from the middle of Amattafoa, it was judged that there was a volcano in that island.

Anamocka was first discovered by Tasman, and by him was named Rotterdam. It is of a triangular form, and each side extends about three and a half or four miles. From the northwest to the south of the island, round by the east and north, it is encompassed by a number of small isles, sand-banks, and breakers. An end could not be seen to their extent to the north, and they may possibly reach as far to the south as Amsterdam, or Tongataboo. Together with Middleburg, or Eaoowe, and Pilsart, these form a group, containing about three degrees of latitude, and two of longitude. To this group Captain Cook had given the name of the Friendly Isles, or Archipelago, from the firm alliance and friendship which seemed to subsist among their inhabitants, and from their courteous behaviour to strangers. The same group may perhaps be extended much farther, even down to Boscawen and Keppel's Isles, which were discovered by Captain Wallis, and lie nearly in the same meridian.

Whilst our commander was at Anamocka, he was particularly assiduous to prevent the introduction of a certain disorder. As some of his people brought with them the remains of this disease from the Society Isles, he prohibited them from having any female intercourse; and he had reason to believe that his endeavours were successful.

The productions of Rotterdam, and the persons, manners, and

customs of its inhabitants, are similar to those of Amsterdam. It is not, however, equally plentiful in its fruits, nor is every part of it in so high a state of cultivation. Neither hath it risen to the same degree of wealth, with regard to cloth, matting, ornaments, and other articles, which constitute the chief riches of the islanders of the Southern Ocean.

Pursuing their course to the west, our navigators discovered land on the 1st of July; and, upon a nearer approach, found it to be a small island, to which, on account of the number of turtle that were seen upon the coast, Captain Cook gave the name of Turtle Isle. On the 16th, high land was seen bearing south-west, which no one doubted to be the Australis del Espiritu Santo of Quiros, and which is called by M. de Bougainville the Great Cyclades. After exploring the coast for some days, the captain came to anchor, in a harbour near the island of Mallicollo. One of his first objects was to commence a friendly intercourse with the natives; but, while he was thus employed, an accident occurred, which threw all into confusion, though in the end it was rather advantageous than hurtful to the English. A fellow in a canoe having been refused admittance into one of our boats, bent his bow to shoot a poisoned arrow at the boat-keeper. Some of his countrymen having prevented his doing it at that instant, time was given to acquaint our commander with the transaction, who immediately ran upon deck. At this minute the Indian had directed his arrow at the boat-keeper; but being called to by Captain Cook, he pointed it at him. Happily the captain had a musket in his hand loaded with small shot, and gave him the contents. By this, however, he was only staggered for a moment; for he still held his bow in the attitude of shooting. A second discharge of the same nature made him drop it, and obliged him, together with the other natives who were in the canoe, to paddle off with all possible celerity. At this time, some of the inhabitants began to shoot arrows from another quarter. A musket discharged in the air had no effect upon them; but no sooner was a four-pound ball shot over their heads than they fled in the utmost confusion.

A few hours after these transactions, the English put off in two boats, and landed in the face of four or five hundred people, who were assembled on the shore; and who, though they were all armed with bows and arrows, clubs and spears, made not the least opposition. On the contrary, when they saw Captain Cook advance with nothing but a green branch in his hand, one of them, who appeared to be a chief, giving his bows and arrows to another, met the captain in the water, bearing also a green branch. These being mutually exchanged in token of friendship, the chief led our commander to the crowd, to whom he immediately distributed presents. The marines, in the meantime, were drawn up on the beach. Captain Cook then acquainted the Indians, by signs, that he wanted wood; and in the same manner permission was granted him to cut down the trees.

Much traffic could not be carried on with these people, because they set no value on nails, or iron tools, or, indeed, on any articles which our navigators could furnish. In such exchanges as they did make, and which were principally of arrows for pieces of cloth, they distinguished themselves by their honesty. When the ship had begun to sail from the island, and they might easily, in consequence of their canoes dropping astern, have avoided delivering the things they had been paid for, they used their utmost efforts to get up with her, that they might discharge their obligations. One man, in particular, followed the Resolution a considerable time, and did not reach her till the object which brought him was forgotten. As soon as he came alongside the vessel, he held up the thing which had been purchased; and, though several of the crew offered to buy it, he insisted upon delivering to the person to whom it had been sold. That person, not knowing him again, would have given something in return: but this he refused, and showed him what he had before received. There was only a single instance in which the natives took, or even attempted to take, anything from our voyagers, by any means whatever; and in that case restitution was immediately made, without trouble and without altercation.

The inhabitants of Mallicollo, in general, are the most ugly and ill-proportioned people that Captain Cook had ever seen, and are in every respect different from all the nations that had been met with in the Southern Ocean. They are a very dark-coloured, and rather a diminutive race, with long heads, flat faces, and countenances which have some resemblance to that of the monkey. Their hair, which is mostly black or brown, is short and curly; but not altogether so soft and woolly as that of a negro. The difference of this people from any whom our commander had yet visited, appeared not only in their persons but their language. Of about eighty words, which were collected by Mr. Forster, scarcely one was found to bear any affinity to the language spoken in any country or island hitherto described. It was observed by Captain Cook, that the natives could pronounce most of the English words with great ease. They had not so much as a name for a dog, and knew nothing of that animal; for which reason the captain left them a dog and bitch; and as they were very fond of them, it was highly probable that the breed would be fostered and increased.

To the harbour, in which our commander anchored, while he lay at Mallicollo, he gave the name of Fort Sandwich. It has many advantages, with regard to depth of water, shelter from winds, and lying so near the shore as to be a cover to those of the ship's company who may be carrying on any necessary operations on land.

Soon after our navigators had gotten to sea, which was on the 23d of July, they discovered three or four small islands, that before had appeared to be connected. At this time the Resolution was not far from the Isle of Ambrym, the Isle of Paoom, and the Isle of Apee. On the next morning, several more islands were discovered, lying off the southeast point of Apee, and constituting a group, which Captain Cook called Shepherd's Isles, in honour of his learned and valuable friend, Dr. Shepherd, Plumian professor of Astronomy at Cambridge. The ship was this day in some danger. It suddenly fell calm, and our voyagers were left to the mercy of the current, close by the isles, where no sounding could be found with a line of a hundred and eighty fathoms. The lands or islands, which lay around the vessel in every direction, were so numerous, that they could not be counted. At this crisis a breeze sprung up, which happily relieved the captain and his company from the anxiety the calm had occasioned.

Amidst the number of islands, that were continually seen by our navigators, there was only one on which no inhabitants were discerned. This consisted chiefly of a remarkable peaked rock, which was only accessible to birds, and which obtained the name of the Monument.

In the farther course of the ship to the southward, our navigators drew near to certain lands, which they found to consist of one large island, the southern and western extremities of which extended beyond their sight. Three or four smaller ones lay off its north side. To the two principal of these Captain Cook gave the name of Montagu and Hinchinbrook; and the large island he named Sandwich, in honour of his noble patron the Earl of Sandwich. This island, which was spotted with woods and lawns, agreeably diversified over the whole surface, and which had a gentle slope from the hills down to the sea-coast, exhibited a most beautiful and delightful prospect. The examination of it was not, however, so much an object with our commander, as to proceed to the south, in order to find the southern extremity of the Archipelago.

Pursuing his discoveries, Captain Cook came in sight of an island, which was afterwards known to be called by the natives Erromango. After coasting it for three days, he brought his vessel to anchor in a bay there, on the 3d of August. The nex day, he went with two boats to examine the coast, and to look for a proper landing-place, that he might obtain a supply of wood and water. At this time, the inhabitants began to assemble on the shore, and by signs to invite our people to land. Their behaviour was apparently so friendly, that the captain was charmed with it; and the only thing which could give him the least suspicion was, that most of them were armed with clubs, spears, darts, and bows and arrows. He did not, therefore, remit his vigilance; but kept his eye continually upon the chief, watching his looks, as well as his actions. It soon was evident, that the intentions of the Indians were totally hostile. They made a violent attempt to seize upon one of the boats; and though, on our commander's pointing a musket at them, they in some measure desisted, yet they returned in an instant, seemingly determined to carry their design into execution. At the head of the party was the chief: while others, who could not come at the boat, stood behind with darts, stones, and bows and arrows in hand, ready to support their countrymen. As signs and threats had no effect, the safety of Captain Cook and his people became the only object of consideration, and yet he was unwilling to fire on the multitude. He resolved, therefore, to make the chief alone the victim of his own treachery, and accordingly aimed his musket at him; but at this critical moment it missed fire. This circumstance encouraged the natives to despise our weapons, and to show the superiority of their own, by throwing stones and darts, and by shooting arrows. Hence it became absolutely necessary for the captain to give orders to his men to fire upon the assailants. The first discharge threw them into confusion; but a second was scarcely sufficient to drive them off the beach. In consequence of this skirmish, four of the Indians lay, to all appearance, dead on the shore. However, two of them were afterwards perceived to crawl into the bushes; and it was happy for these people, that not half of the muskets of the English would go off, since otherwise many more must have fallen. The inhabitants were, at length, so terrified, as to make no farther appearance; and two oars which had been lost in the conflict, were left standing up against the bushes.

It was observed of these islanders, that they seemed of a different race from those of Mallicollo, and that they spoke a different language. They are of a middle size, with a good shape and tolerable features. Their colour is very dark; and their aspect is not mended by a custom they have of painting their faces, some with a black, and others with a red pigment. As to their hair, it is curly and crisp, and somewhat woolly. The few women who were seen, and who appeared to be ugly, wore a kind of petticoat, made either of palm leaves, or of a plant similar in its nature; but the men, like those of Mallicollo, were almost entirely naked. On account of the treacherous behaviour of the inhabitants of Erromango, Captain Cook called a promontory, or peninsula, near which the skirmish happened, *Traitor's Head*.

From this place the captain sailed for an island which had been discovered before, at a distance, and at which, on account of his wanting a large quantity of wood and water, he was resolved to make some stay. At first the natives were disposed to be very hostile; but our commander, with equal wisdom and humanity, contrived to terrify them, without danger to their lives. This was principally effected by firing a few great guns, at which they were so much alarmed, as afterwards to be brought to tolerable order. Among these islanders, many were inclined to be on friendly terms with our navigators, and especially the old people; whilst most of the younger were daring and insolent, and obliged the English to keep to their arms. It was natural enough that age should be prudent and cautious, and youth bold and impetuous; and yet this distinction, with regard to the behaviour of the various nations which had been visited by Captain Cook, had not occurred before.

The island, where the captain now stayed, was found, upon inquiry, to be called, by the inhabitants, Tanna; and three others in its neighbourhood, and which could be seen from it, were distinguished by the names of Immer, Erronan or Footoona, and Annatom.

From such information of the natives, as our commander could see no reason to doubt, it appeared that circumcision was practised among them, and that they were eaters of human flesh. Concerning the latter subject, he should never have thought of asking them a single question, if they had not introduced it themselves, by inquiring whether the English had the same custom. It hath been argued, that necessity alone could be the origin of this horrid practice. But as the people of Tanna are possessed of fine pork and fowls, together with an abundance of roots and fruits, the plea of necessity cannot be urged in their behalf. In fact, no instance was seen of their eating human flesh; and, therefore, there might, perhaps, be some reason to hesitate in pronouncing them to be cannibals.

By degrees the inhabitants grew so courteous and civil, as to permit the English gentlemen to ramble about the skirts of the woods, and to shoot in them, without offering them the least molestation or showing any dislike. One day, some boys of the island having gotten behind thickets, and thrown two or three stones at our people, who were cutting wood, they were fired at by the petty officers on duty. Captain Cook, who was then on shore, was alarmed at the report of the muskets; and, when he was informed of the cause, was much displeased, that so wanton a use should be made of our fire-arms. Proper measures were taken by him to prevent such conduct for the future.

In the island of Tanna was a volcano, which sometimes made a dreadful noise, and, at each explosion, which happened every three or four minutes, threw up fire and smoke in prodigious columns. At one time, great stones were seen high in the air At the foot of the hill were several hot springs; and on the side of it Mr. Forster found some places whence smoke of a sulphurous smell issued, through cracks or fissures of the earth. A thermometer, that was placed in a little hole made in one of them, and which in the open air stood only at eighty, rose to a hundred and seventy. In another instance, the mercury rose to a hundred and ninety-one. Our commander, being desirous of getting a near and good view of the volcano, set out with a party for that purpose. But the gentlemen met with so many obstructions from the inhabitants, who were jealous of their penetrating far into the country, that they thought proper to return.

It is observable, with respect to the volcano of Tanna, that it is not on the ridge of the hill to which it belongs, but on its side. Nor is that hill the highest in the country, for there are others near it of more than double its height. It was in moist and wet weather that the volcano was most violent.

When our commander was ready to sail from Tanna, an event happened, which gave him much concern. Just as our people were getting some logs into the boat, four or five of the natives stepped forward to see what they were doing. In consequence of the Indians not being allowed to come within certain limits, the sentinel ordered them back, upon which they readily complied. At this time, Captain Cook, who had his eyes fixed upon them, observed the sentry present his piece to the men. The captain was going to reprove him for this action, when to his inexpressible astonishment, the sentry fired. An attack so causeless and extraordinary, naturally threw the natives into great confusion. Most of them fled, and it was with difficulty that our commander could prevail upon a few of them to remain. As they ran off, he perceived one of them to fall who was immediately lifted up by two others, who took him into the water, washed his wound, and then led him off. The wounded person not being carried far, Captain Cook then sent for the surgeon of the ship and accompanied him to the man, whom they found expiring. The rascal that had fired pretended, that an Indian had laid an arrow across his bow, and was going to shoot at him; so that he apprehended himself to be in danger. This however, was no more than what the islanders had always done, to show that they were armed as well as our voyagers. What rendered the present incident the more unfortunate was, that it was not the man who bent the bow, but one who stood near him, that was shot by the sentry.

The harbour where the captain anchored, during his stay at Tanna, was called by him Port Resolution, after the name of the ship, she being the first vessel by which it was ever entered. It was no more than a little creek, three quarters of a mile in length and about half that space in breadth. No place can exceed it in its convenience for taking in wood and water, which are both close to the shore. The inhabitant of the island, with whom our commander had the most frequent and friendly connexions, was named Paowang.

Very little trade could be carried on with the people of Tanna. They had not the least knowledge of iron; and consequently, nails, tools, and other articles made of that metal, and which are so greedily sought for in the more eastern isles, were here of no consideration. Cloth could be made of no service to persons who go naked.

Among the productions of the island, there is reason to believe that the nutmeg-tree might be mentioned. This is collected from the circumstance of Mr. Forster's having shot a pigeon in the craw of which a wild nutmeg was discovered. However, though he took some pains to find the tree, his endeavours were not attended with success.

It was at first thought by our navigators, that the inhabitants of Tanna were a race between the natives of the Friendly Islands and those of Mallicollo; but by a short acquaintance with them they were convinced that they had but little or no affinity to either, excepting in the hair. Some few women and children were seen, whose hair resembled that of the English. With regard, however, to these persons, it was obvious that they were of another nation; and it was understood that they came from Erronan. Two languages were found to be spoken in Tanna. One of them, which appeared to have been introduced from Erronan, is nearly, if not exactly, the same with that of the Friendly Islands. The other, which is the proper language of the country, and which is judged to be peculiar to Tanna, Erromango, and Anaton, is different from any other that had hitherto been met with by our voyagers.

The people of Tanna, are of the middle size, and for the most part slender. There are few tall or stout men amongst them. In general, they have good features and agreeable countenances. Like all the tropical race, they are active and nimble; and seem to excel in the use of arms, but not to be fond of labour. With respect to the management of their weapons, Mr. Wales hath made an observation so honourable to Homer, that were I to omit it I should not be forgiven by my classical readers. "I must confess," says Mr. Wales, "I have often been led to think the feats which Homer represents his heroes as performing with their spears, a little too much of the marvellous to be admitted into an heroic poem; I mean when confined within the strait stays of Aristotle. Nay, even so great an advocate for him as Mr. Pope, acknowledges them to be surprising. But since I have seen what these people can do with their wooden spears, and them badly pointed, and not of a hard nature, I have not the least exception to any one passage in that great poet on this account. But if I see fewer exceptions, I can find infinitely more beauties in him; as he has, I think, scarcely an action, circumstance or description of any kind whatever, relating to a spear, which I have not seen and recognized among these people; as, their whirling motion, and whistling noise, as they fly; their quivering motion, as they stick in the ground when they fall; their meditating their aim, when they are going to throw; and their shaking them in their hand, as they go along."

On the 20th of August, Captain Cook sailed from Tanna, and employed all the remainder of the month in a further examination of the islands around him. He had now finished his survey of the whole Archipelago, and had gained a knowledge of it, infinitely superior to what had ever been attained before. The northern islands of this Archipelago were first discovered in 1606, by that eminent navigator Quiros, who considered them as part of the southern continent, which at that time, and till very lately, was supposed to exist. M. de Bougainville was the next person by whom they were visited, in 1768. This gentleman, however, besides landing on the Isle of Lepers, only made the discovery, that the country was not connected, but composed of islands which he called the Great Cyclades. Captain Cook, besides ascertaining the situation and extent of these islands, added to them several new ones which had hitherto been unknown, and explored the whole. He thought, therefore, that he had obtained a right to name them; and accordingly he bestowed upon them the appellation of the *New Hebrides*. His title to this honour will not be disputed in any part of Europe, and certainly not by so enlightened and liberal a people as the French nation.

The season of the year now rendered it necessary for our commander to return to the south, while he had yet some time to explore any land he might meet with between the New Hebrides and New Zealand; at which last place he intended to touch, that he might refresh his people, and renew his stock of wood and water for another southern course. With this view, he sailed on the first of September, and on the 4th land was discovered; in a harbour belonging to which the Resolution came to an anchor the next day. The design of Captain Cook was not only to visit the country, but to have an opportunity of observing an eclipse of the sun, which was soon to happen. An intercourse immediately commenced with the inhabitants, who, during the whole of the captain's stay, behaved in a very civil and friendly manner. In return, he was solicitous to render them every service in his power. To Teabooma, the chief, he sent, among other articles, a dog and a bitch, both young, but nearly full grown. It was some time before Teabooma could believe that the two animals were intended for him; but when he was convinced of it, he was lost in an excess of joy. Another and still more valuable present, was that of a young boar and sow; which, on account of the absence of the chief when they were brought to land, were received with great hesitation and ceremony.

The last time that our commander went on shore at this place, he ordered an inscription to be cut out on a large tree, setting forth the name of the ship, the date of the year, and other circumstances, which testified that the English were the first discoverers of the country. This he had before done, wherever such a ceremony seemed necessary. How the island was called by the natives, our voyagers could never learn; and, therefore Captain Cook gave it the name of New Caledonia. The inhabitants are strong, robust, active, and well made. With regard to the origin of the nation, the captain judged them to be a race between the people of Tanna and the Friendly Isles; or between those of Tanna and the New Zealanders; or all three. Their language is in some respects a mixture of them all. In their disposition they are courteous and obliging; and they are not in the least addicted to pilfering, which is more than can be asserted concerning any other nation in this sea.

The women of New Caledonia, and those likewise of Tanna, were found to be much chaster than the females of the more eastern islands. Our commander never heard that the least favor was obtained from them by any one of his company. Sometimes, indeed, the women would exercise a little coquetry, but they went no farther.

The botanists of the ship did not here complain for want of employment. They were diligent in their researches, and their labours were amply rewarded. Every day brought some new accession to botanical knowledge, or that of other branches of natural history.

Everything being ready to put to sea, Captain Cook weighed anchor on the 13th of September, with the purpose of examining the coast of New Caledonia. In pursuing this object, by which he was enabled to add greatly to nautical and geographical knowledge, the Resolution was more than once in danger of being lost; and particularly, in the night of the 28th of the month, she had a narrow escape. Our navigators, on this occasion, were much alarmed, and day-light showed that their fears had not been ill founded. Indeed, breakers had been continually under their lee, and at a small distance from them; so that they were in the most imminent danger. "We owed our safety," says the captain, "to the interposition of Providence, a good look-out, and the very brisk manner in which the ship was managed."

Our commander now began to be tired of a coast which he could no longer explore but at the risk of losing the vessel, and ruining the whole voyage. He determined, however, not to leave it, till he knew of what kind some groves of trees were, which, by their uncommon appearance, had occasioned much speculation, and had been mistaken by several of the gentlemen, for bisaltes. Captain Cook was the more solicitous to ascertain the point, as these trees appeared to be of a sort which might be useful to shipping, and had not been seen any where but in the southern parts of New Caledonia. They proved to be a species of spruce pine, very proper for spars, which were then wanted. The discovery was valuable, as excepting New Zealand, there was not an island known, in the South Pacific Ocean, where the ship could supply herself with a mast or yard, to whatever distress she might be reduced. It was the opinion of the carpenter of the Resolution, who was a mast-maker as well as a shipwright, that very good masts might be made from the trees in question. The wood of them, which is white, close-grained, tough, and light, is well adapted to that purpose. One of the small islands where the trees were found, was called by the captain the Isle of Pines. To another, on account of its affording sufficient employment to the botanists, during the little time they staid upon it, he gave the name of Botany Isle.

Captain Cook now took into serious consideration what was further to be done. He had pretty well determined the extent of the southwest coast of New Caledonia, and would gladly have proceeded to a more accurate survey of the whole, had he not been deterred not only by the dangers he must encounter, but by the time required for the undertaking, and which he could not possibly spare. Indeed, when he considered the vast ocean he had to explore to the south; the state and condition of the ship; the near approach of summer; and that any material accident might detain him in the sea even for another year, he did not think it advisable to make New Caledonia any longer the object of his attention. But though he was thus obliged by necessity for the first time to leave a coast which he had discovered, before it was fully surveyed, he did not quit it till he had ascertained the extent of the country, and proved, that excepting New Zealand, it was perhaps the largest island in the South Pacific Ocean.

As the Resolution pursued her course from New Caledonia, land was discovered, which, on a nearer approach, was found to be an island of good height, and five leagues in circuit. Captain Cook named it Norfolk Isle, in honour to the noble family of Howard. It was uninhabited; and the first persons that ever set foot on it were unquestionably our English navigators. Various trees and plants were observed that are common at New Zealand; and, in particular, the flax plant, which is rather more luxuriant here than in any part of that country. The chief produce of the island is a kind of spruce pine, exceeding straight and tall, which grows in great abundance. Such is the size of many of the trees, that, breast high, they are thick as two men can encircled. Among the vegetables of the place, the palm-cabbage afforded both a wholesome and palatable refreshment; and, indeed, proved the most agreeable repast that our people had for a considerable time enjoyed. In addition to this gratification they had the pleasure of procuring some excellent fish.

From Norfolk Isle our commander steered for New Zealand, it being his intention to touch at Queen Charlotte's Sound, that he might refresh his crew, and put the ship in a condition to encounter the southern latitudes. On the 18th of October, he anchored before Ship Cove in that sound; and the first thing he did, after landing, was to look for the bottle he had left on the shore, in which was a memorandum. It was taken away; and, it soon appeared, from indubitable circumstances, that the Adventure had been in the cove after it was quitted by the Resolution.

Upon visiting the gardens which had been formed at Motuara, they were found almost in a state of nature, having been wholly neglected by the inhabitants. Many, however, of the articles were in a flourishing condition, and showed how well they liked the soil in which they were planted. It was several days before any of the natives made their appearance, but when they did so, and recognized Captain Cook and his friends, joy succeeded to fear. They hurried in numbers out of the woods, and embracing the English over and over again, leaping and skipping about like madmen. Amidst all this extravagance of joy, they were careful to preserve the honour of their females; for they would not permit some women, who were seen at a distance, to come near our people. The captain's whole intercourse with the New Zealanders, during this his third visit to Queen Charlotte's Sound, was peaceable and friendly, and one of them, a man apparently of consequence, whose name was Pedro, presented him with a staff of honour, such as the chiefs generally carry. In return, our commander dressed Pedro, who had a fine person, and a good presence, in a suit of old clothes, of which he was not a little proud.

Captain Cook still continued his solicitude to stock the island with useful animals; and accordingly, in addition to what he had formerly done, he ordered two pigs, a boar and sow, to be put on shore. There was reason to believe, that some of the cocks and hens which had formerly been left here still existed. None of them, indeed were seen; but a hen's egg was found, which had not long been laid.

Mr. Wales had now an opportunity of completing his observations with regard to Queen Charlotte's Sound, so as to ascertain its latitude and longitude with the utmost accuracy. In the captain's former voyage there had been an error in this respect. Such were Mr. Wales's abilities and assiduity, that the same correctness was maintained by him, in determining the situations of all the other places which were visited by our navigators.

On the 10th of November, Captain Cook took his departure from New Zealand, in farther pursuit of his great object, the determination of the question concerning the existence of a southern continent. Having sailed, the 27th, in different degrees of latitude, extending from 43° to 55° 48′ south, he gave up all hopes of finding any more land in this ocean. He came, therefore, to the resolution of steering directly for the west entrance of the Straits of Magalhaens, with a view of coasting the south side of Terra del Fuego, round Cape Horn, to the Strait Le Maire. As the world had hitherto obtained but a very imperfect knowedge of this shore, the captain thought that the full survey of it would be more advantageous, both to navigation and geography, than anything he could expect to find in a higher latitude.

In the prosecution of this voyage, our commander, on the 17th of December, reached the west coast of Terra del Fuego; and having continued to range it till the 20th, he came to an anchor in a place to which he afterwards gave the name of Christmas Sound. . Through the whole course of his various navigations, he had never seen so desolate a coast. It seems to be entirely composed of rocky mountains, without the least appearance of vegetation. These mountains terminate in horrible precipices, the craggy summits of which spire up to a vast height; so that scarcely anything in nature can appear with a more barren and savage aspect, than the whole of the country.

The run which Captain Cook had made directly across the ocean in a high southern latitude, was believed by him to be the first of the kind that had ever been carried into execution. He was, therefore, somewhat particular in remarking every circumstance, which seemed to be in the least material. However, he could not but observe, that he had never made a passage any where of such length, or even of a much shorter extent, in which so few things occurred, that were of an interesting nature. Excepting the variation of the compass, he knew of nothing else that was worthy of notice. The captain had now done with the Southern Pacific Ocean; and he had explored it in such a manner, that it would be impossible for any one to think that more could be performed in a single voyage, towards obtaining that end, than had actually been accomplished.

Barren and dreary as the land is about Christmas Sound, it was not wholly destitute of some accommodations, which could not fail of being agreeable to our navigators. Near every harbour they found fresh water and wood for fuel. The country abounds likewise with wild fowl, and particularly with geese; which afforded a refreshment to the whole crew, that was the more acceptable **on** account of the approaching festival. Had not Providence thus happly provided **for** them, their Christmas cheer must have been salt beef and pork. Some Madeira wine, the only article of provision that was mended by keeping, was still left. This in conjunction with the geese, which were cooked in every variety of method, enabled our people to celebrate Christmas as cheerfully as, perhaps, was done by their friends in England.

The inhabitants of Terra del Fuego, Captain Cook found to be the same nation that he had formerly seen in Success Bay; and the same whom M. de Bougainville has distinguished by the name of Pecharas. They are a little, ugly, half starved, beardless race, and go almost naked. It is their own fault that they are not better clothed, nature having furnished them with ample materials for that purpose. By lining their seal-skin cloaks with the skins and feathers of aquatic birds; by making the cloaks themselves larger; and by applying the same materials to different parts of clothing, they might render their dress much more warm and comfortable. But while they are doomed to exist in one of the most inhospitable climates in the globe, they have not sagacity enough to avail themselves of those means of adding to the conveniences of life, which Providence has put into their power. In short, the captain, after having been a witness to so many varieties of the human race, hath pronounced, that of all the nations he had seen, the Pecharas are the most wretched.

Notwithstanding the barrenness of the country it abounds with a variety of unknown plants, and gave sufficient employment to the botanists of the Resolution. "Almost every plant," says Mr. Forster, "which we gathered" on the rocks "was new to us, and some species were remarkable for the beauty of their flowers, or their smell."

On the 28th of December, our commander sailed from Christmas Sound, and proceeded on his voyage, round Cape Horn, through Strait le Maire, to Staten Land. This famous Cape, was passed by him on the next day, when he entered the southern Atlantic Ocean. In some charts, Cape Horn is laid down as belonging to a small island; but this was neither confirmed, nor could it be contradicted by our navigators; for several breakers appeared on the coast, both to the east and west of it, and the hazy weather rendered every object very indistinct. Though the summits of some of the hills were rocky, the sides and valleys seemed covered with a green turf, and wooded in tufts.

In ranging Staten Island, a good port was found, situated three leagues to the westward of St. John, and in a northern direction. Upon account of the day on which the discovery of this port was made (being the first of January), Captain Cook gave it the name of New Year's Harbour. The knowledge of it may be of service to future navigators. Indeed, it would be more convenient for ships bound to the west, or round Cape Horn if its situation would permit them to put to sea, with an easterly and northerly wind. But this inconvenience is not of great consequence, since these winds are seldom known to be of long duration. The captain, however, has declared, that if he were on a voyage round Cape Horn to the west, and not in want of wood or water, or any other thing which might make it necessary to put into port, he would not approach the land at all. By keeping out at sea the currents would be avoided, which, he was satisfied, would lose their force at ten or twelve leagues from land, and be totally without influence at a greater distance.

The extent of Terra del Fuego, and consequently that of the Straits of Magalhaens, our commander ascertained to be less than has been laid down by the generality of navigators. Nor was the coast upon the whole, found to be so dangerous as has often been represented. The weather, at the same time, was remarkably temperate.

In one of the little isles near Staten Land, and which had been called, by Captain Cook, New Year's Isle, there was observed a harmony between the different animals of the place, which is too curious to be omitted. It seemed as if they had entered into a league not to disturb each other's tranquillity. The greater part of the sea-coast is occupied by sea-lions; the sea-bears take up their abode in the isle; the shags are posted in the highest cliffs; the penguins fix their quarters where there is the most easy communication to and from the sea; and the rest of the birds choose more retired places. All these animals were occasionally seen to mix together, like domestic cattle and poultry in a farm-yard, without one attempting to molest the other. Nay, the captain had often observed the eagles and vultures sitting on the hills among the shags, while none of the latter, whether old or young, appeared to be the least disturbed at their presence. It may be asked, then, how do these birds of prey live? This question our commander hath answered, by supposing that they feed on the carcases of seals and birds which die by various causes. It is probable, from the immense quantity of animals with which this island abounds, that such carcases exist in great numbers.

From Staten Island, Captain Cook sailed, on the 4th of January with a view in the first place, of discovering that extensive coast, laid down by Mr. Dalrymple in his chart, in which is the gulf of St. Sebastian. In order to have all other parts before him, the captain designed to make the western point of that gulf. As he had some doubt of the existence of such a coast, this appeared to him the best route for determining the matter, and for exploring the southern part of this ocean. When he came to the situations assigned to the different points of the gulf of St. Sebastian, neither land nor any unequivocal signs of land were discovered. On the contrary, it was evident, that there could not be any extensive tract of country in the direction which had been supposed.

Proceeding in his voyage, land was seen on the 14th, which was at first mistaken for an island of ice. It was in a manner wholly covered with snow. From the person by whom it was first discovered, it obtained the name of Wallis's Island. It is a high rock, of no great extent, near to which are some rocky islets. Another island of a larger compass, on account of the vast number of birds which were upon it, was called Bird Isle. A more extensive range of country had been seen for some time, which Captain Cook reached on the 17th, and where he landed, on the same day, in three different places. The head of the bay, in which he came to shore, was terminated by particular ice-cliffs, of considerable height. Pieces were continually breaking off, and floating out to sea; and while our navigators were in the bay, a great fall happened, which made a noise like a cannon. No less savage and horrible were the inner parts of the country. The wild rocks raised their summits till they were lost in the clouds, and the valleys lay covered with everlasting snow. There was not a tree to be seen, or a shrub found, that was even big enough to make a tooth-pick. The only vegetation, that was met with, was a coarse strong-bladed grass, growing in tufts, wild burnet, and a plant like moss, which sprang from the rocks.

When our commander landed in the bay, he displayed the English colours; and, under a discharge of small arms, took possession of the country in his majesty's name. It was not, however, a discovery which was ever likely to be productive of any considerable benefit. In his return to the ship, Captain Cook brought with him a quantity of seals and penguins, which were an acceptable present to the crew; not from the want of provisions, which were plentiful in every kind, but from a change of diet. Any sort of fresh meat was preferred by most on board to salt. The captain himself was now, for the first time, tired of the salted meats of the ship; and though the flesh of the penguins could scarcely vie with bullock's liver, its freshness was sufficient to render it comparatively agreeable to the palate. To the bay in which he had been, he gave the name of Possession Bay.

The land in which this bay lies, was at first judged by our

navigators to be part of a great continent. But upon coasting round the whole country, it was proved to a demonstration that it was only an island of seventy leagues in circuit. In honour to his majesty, Captain Cook called it the Isle of Georgia. It could scarcely have been thought, that an island of no greater extent than this, situated between latitude of fifty-four and fifty-five, should, in a manner, be wholly covered, many fathoms deep, with frozen snow, in the height of summer. The sides and summits of the lofty mountains were cased with snow and ice ; and an incredible quantity lay in the valleys. So immense was the quantity, that our commander did not think that it could be the produce of the island. Some land, therefore, which he had seen at a distance, induced him to believe, that it might belong to an extensive tract ; and gave him hopes of discovering a continent. In this respect, however, he was disappointed ; but the disappointment did not sit heavily upon him ; since, to judge of the bulk by the apprehended sample, it would not have been worth the discovery. It was remarkable, that our voyagers did not see a river, or a stream of fresh water, on the whole coast of the Isle of Georgia. Captain Cook judged it to be highly probable, that there are no perennial springs in the country ; and that the interior parts, in consequence of their being much elevated, never enjoy heat enough to melt the snow in sufficient quantities to produce a river or stream of water. In sailing round the island, our navigators were almost continually involved in a thick mist ; so that, for anything they knew to the contrary, they might be surrounded with dangerous rocks.

The captain, on the 25th of the month, steered from the Isle of Georgia, and, on the 27th, computed that he was in latitude sixty, south. Farther than this he did not intend to go, unless some certain signs of soon meeting with land should be discovered. There was now a long hollow swell from the west, which was a strong indication that no land was to be met with in that direction ; and hence arose an additional proof of what has already been remarked, that the extensive coast laid down in Mr. Dalrymple's chart of the ocean between Africa and America and the Gulf of St. Sebastian, doth not exist. Not to mention the various islands which were seen in the prosecution of the voyage, and the names that were given to them, I shall only advert to a few of the more material circumstances. On an elevated coast, which appeared in sight on the 31st, our commander bestowed the appellation of Southern Thule. The reason of his giving it this name was, that it is the most southern land that had ever been yet discovered. It is everywhere covered with snow, and displays a surface of vast height. On this day, our voyagers were in no small danger from a great westerly swell, which set right upon the shore, and threatened to carry them on the most horrible coast in the world. Happily, the discovery of a point to the north, beyond which no land could be seen, relieved them from their apprehensions. To the more distinguished tracts of country, which were discovered from the 31st of January to the 6th of February, Captain Cook gave the names of Cape Bristol, Cape Montagu, Saunder's Isle, Candlemas Isles, and Sandwich's Land. The last is either a group of islands, or else a point of the continent. For that there is a tract of land near the pole, which is the source of most of the ice that is spread over this vast Southern Ocean, was the captain's firm opinion. He also thought it probable, that this land must extend farthest to the north, where it is opposite to the Southern **Atlantic and** Indian Oceans. Ice had always been found by him farther to the north in these oceans, than anywhere else, and this he judged could not be the case, if there were not land of considerable extent to the south. However, the greatest part of this southern continent, if it actually exists, must lie within the polar circle, where the sea is so encumbered with ice, that the land is rendered inaccessible. So great is the risk which is run, in examining a coast in these unknown and icy seas, that our commander, with a modest and well-grounded boldness, could assert, that no man would ever venture farther than he had done ; and that the lands which may lie to the south will never be explored. Thick fogs, snow storms, intense cold, and every thing beside, that can render navigation dangerous, must be encountered ; all which difficulties are greatly heightened by the inexpressibly horrid aspect of the country. It is a country doomed by nature never once to feel the warmth of the sun's rays, but to lie buried in everlasting snow and ice. Whatever ports there may be on the coast, they are almost entirely covered with frozen snow of a vast thickness. If, however, any one of them should be so far open as to invite a ship into it, she would run the risk of being fixed there for ever, or of coming out in an ice island. To this it may be added that the islands and floats on the coast, the great falls from the ice cliffs in the port, or a heavy snow storm, attended with a sharp frost, might be equally fatal.

Nothing could exceed the inclination of Captain Cook, if it had been practicable, to penetrate farther to the south ; but difficulties like these were not to be surmounted. If he had risked all that had been done during the voyage, for the sake of discovering and exploring a coast which, when discovered and explored, would have answered no end whatever, or have been of the least use either to navigation or geography, or indeed to any other science, he would justly have been charged with inexcusable temerity. He determined, therefore, to alter his course to the east, and to sail in quest of Bouvet's Land, the existence of which was yet to be settled. Accordingly, this was the principal object of his pursuit, from the 6th to the 22d of the month. By that day he had run down thirteen degrees of longitude, in the very latitude assigned for Bouvet's Land. No such land, however, was discovered ; nor did any proofs occur of the existence of Cape Circumcision. Our commander was at this time no more than two degrees of longitude from the route he had taken to the south, when he left the Cape of Good Hope. It would, therefore, have been to no purpose to proceed any farther to the east in this parallel. But being desirous of determining the question concerning some land that was supposed to have been seen more to the south, he directed his course for the situation in which the discovery of it might be expected. Two days were spent by him in this pursuit, to no effectual purpose. After having run over the place where the land was imagined to lie, without meeting with the least signs of any, it became certain that the ice islands had deceived our navigators, as well as Mr. Bouvet.

Captain Cook had now made the circuit of the southern ocean in a high latitude, and traversed it in such a manner as to leave not the least room for the possibility of there being a continent, unless near the pole, and out of the reach of navigation. By twice visiting the tropical sea, he had not only settled the situation of some old discoveries, but made many new ones; and, indeed, even in that part had left little more to be accomplished. The intention of the voyage had, in every respect, been fully answered, and the southern hemisphere sufficiently explored. A final end was hereby put to the searching after a southern continent, which for nearly two centuries past, had occasionally engrossed the attention of some of the maritime powers, and had been urged with great ardour by philosophers and geographers in different ages.

The great purpose of his navigation round the globe being thus completed, the captain began to direct his views towards England. He had, indeed, some thoughts of protracting his course a little longer, for the sake of revisiting the place where the French discovery is said to be situated. But, upon mature deliberation, he determined to lay aside his intention. He considered that if the discovery had really been made, the end would be as fully answered, as if it had been done by himself. It could only be an island; and, if a judgment might be formed from the degree of cold which our voyagers had experienced in that latitude, it could not be a fertile one. Besides, our commander would hereby have been kept two months longer at sea, and that in a tempestuous latitude, with which the ship was not in a condition to struggle. Her sails and rigging were so much worn that something was giving way every hour; and there was nothing left, either to repair or to replace them. The provisions of the vessel were in such a state of decay, that they afforded very little nourishment, and the company had been long without refreshments. Indeed the crew were yet healthy, and would cheerfully have gone wherever the captain judged it proper to lead them; but he was fearful lest the scurvy should lay hold of them, at a time when none of the remedies were left by which it could be removed. He thought, likewise, that it would have been cruel in him to have continued the fatigues and hardships they were perpetually exposed to, longer than was absolutely necessary. Throughout the whole voyage, they had merited by their behaviour every indulgence which it was in his power to bestow. Animated by the conduct of the officers, they had shown that no difficulties or dangers which came in their way were incapable of being surmounted; nor had their activity, courage, and cheerfulness been in the least abated by the separation from them of their consort the Adventure.

From all these considerations, which were evidently the dictates of wisdom and humanity, Captain Cook was induced to spend no longer time in searching for the French discoveries, but to steer for the Cape of Good Hope. He determined, however, to direct his course in such a manner, as to look for the Isles of Denia and Marseveen, which are laid down in Dr. Halley's variation chart. After sailing in the proper latitudes from the 25th of February to the 13th of March, no such islands were discovered. Nothing, indeed, had been seen that could encourage our voyagers to persevere in a search after them; and much time could not now be spared, either for the purpose of finding them or of proving their non-existence. Every one on board was for good reasons impatient to get into port. The captain, therefore, could no longer avoid yielding to the general wishes, and resolved to proceed to the Cape, without further delay.

Soon after our commander had come to this determination, he demanded of the officers and petty officers, in pursuance of his instructions, the log-books and journals they had kept; which were delivered to him accordingly, and sealed up for the inspection of the admiralty. He enjoined them also, and the whole crew, not to divulge where they had been, till they were permitted by their lordships; an injunction, a compliance with which might probably be rendered somewhat difficult, from the natural tendency there is in men, to relate the extraordinary enterprises and adventures wherein they have been concerned.

As the Resolution approached towards the Cape of Good Hope, she fell in first with a Dutch East Indiaman from Bengal, commanded by Captain Bosch; and next with an English Indiaman being the True Briton, from China, of which Captain Broadly was the commander. Mr. Bosch very obligingly offered to our navigators sugar, arrack, and whatever he had to spare; and Captain Broadly, with the most ready generosity, sent them fresh provisions, tea, and various articles which could not fail of being peculiarly acceptable to people in their situation. Even a parcel of old newspapers furnished no slight gratification to persons, who had so long been deprived of obtaining any intelgence concerning their country and the state of Europe. From these vessels Captain Cook received some information with regard to what had happened the Adventure after her separation from the Resolution.

On Wednesday, the 22d of March,* he anchored in Table Bay; where he found several Dutch ships, some French, and the Ceres, an English East Indiaman, bound directly for England, under the command of Captain Newte. By this gentleman he sent a copy of the preceding part of the journal, some charts, and other drawings to the admiralty.

During the circumnavigation of the globe, from the period of our commander's leaving the Cape of Good Hope to his return to it again, he had sailed no less than twenty thousand leagues. This was an extent of voyage nearly equal to three times the equatorial circumference of the earth, and which had never been accomplished before, by any ship, in the same compass of duration. In such a case, it could not be a matter of surprise that the rigging and sails of the Resolution should be essentially damaged, and even worn out: and yet, in all this great run, which had been made in every latitude between nine and seventy-one, she did not spring either low mast, top-mast, lower or top-sail yard; nor did she so much as break a lower or top-mast shroud. These happy circumstances were owing to the good properties of the vessel, and the singular care and abilities of her officers.

On the remainder of the voyage it is not necessary to enlarge. Though it was conducted with the same attention to navigation and geography, and with the same sagacity in making whatever was worthy of observation, nevertheless, as it was not employed in traversing unknown seas, or in discovering countries that had not been heard of before, it may be sufficient briefly to mention the places at which Captain Cook touched, before his arrival in England. The repairs of the ship having been completed, and the necessary stores gotten on board, together with a fresh supply of provisions and water, he left the Cape of Good Hope on the 27th of April, and reached the island of St. Helena on the

---

* With our navigators, who had sailed round the world, it was Wednesday, the 22d of March; but at the Cape of Good Hope it was Tuesday the 21st.

15th of May. Here he staid till the 21st, when he sailed for the island of Ascension, where he anchored on the 28th. From this place he directed his course, on the 31st, for the island of Fernando de Noronha, at which he arrived on the 9th of June.

In the progress of the voyage, our commander made an experiment upon the still for procuring fresh water; and the result of the trial was, that the invention is useful upon the whole, but that to trust entirely to it would by no means be advisable. Indeed, provided there is not a scarcity of fuel, and the coppers are good, as much water may be obtained as will support life; but no efforts will be able to procure a quantity sufficient for the preservation of health, especially in hot climates. Captain Cook was convinced, by experience, that nothing contributes more to the health of seamen, than having plenty of water.

On the 14th of July, the captain came to an anchor in the Bay of Fayal, one of the Azores islands. His sole design of stopping here was to give Mr. Wales an opportunity of finding the rate of the watch, that hereby he might be enabled to fix the longitude of these islands with the greater degree of certainty. No sooner, therefore, had our commander anchored, than he sent an officer to wait on the English consul, and to acquaint the governor with the arrival of our navigators, requesting his permission for Mr. Wales to make observations on shore, for the purpose now mentioned. Mr. Dent, who then acted as consul, not only obtained this permission, but accommodated Mr. Wales with a convenient place in his garden, to set up his intruments.

This object being accomplished, Captain Cook proceeded, on the 19th, with all expedition for England. On the 30th of the same month, he anchored at Spithead, and landed at Portsmouth; having been absent from Great Britain three years and eighteen days, in which time, and under all changes of climate, **he had** lost but **four** men, and only one of them by sickness.

CHAPTER V.

ACCOUNT OF CAPTAIN COOK DURING THE PERIOD BETWEEN HIS SECOND VOYAGE AND HIS VOYAGE TO THE PACIFIC OCEAN.

The able manner in which Captain Cook had conducted the preceding voyage, the discoveries he had made, and his complete determination of the grand point he had been sent to ascertain, justly and powerfully recommended him to the protection and encouragement of all those who had patronized the undertaking.

No alteration had occurred, during his absence, in the presidency of the admiralty department. The noble lord, whose extensive views had taken such a lead in the plans of navigation and discovery, still continued at the head of that board ; and it could not be otherwise than a high satisfaction to him, that so extraordinary a degree of success had attended his designs for the enlargement of science. His lordship lost no time in representing Captain Cook's merits to the king ; nor did his majesty stand in need of solicitations to show favour to a man, who had so eminently fulfilled his royal and munificent intentions. Accordingly our navigator, on the 9th of August, was raised to the rank of post captain. Three days afterwards, he received a more distinguished and substantial mark of the approbation of government ; for he was then appointed a captain in Greenwich Hospital—a situation which was intended to afford him a pleasing and honourable reward for his illustrious labours and services.

It will easily be supposed, that the lovers of science would, in general, be peculiarly attentive to the effects resulting from Captain Cook's discoveries. The additions he had made to knowledge of geography, navigation and astronomy, and the new views he had opened of the diversified state of human life and manners, could not avoid commanding their esteem, and exciting their admiration. With many persons of philosophic literature he was in the habits of intimacy and friendship; and he was particularly accquainted with Sir John Pringle, at that time president of the Royal Society. It was natural, therefore, that his scientific friends should wish him to become a member of this learned body; the consequence of which was, that, in the latter end of the year 1775, he was proposed as a candidate for election. On the 29th of February, 1776, he was unanimously chosen: and he was admitted on the 7th of March. The same evening, a paper was read, which he had addressed to Sir John Pringle, containing an account of the method he had taken to preserve the health of the crew of his majesty's ship the Resolution, during her voyage round the world. Another paper, at the request of the president, was communicated by him, on the 18th of April, relative to the tides in the South Seas. The tides particularly considered were those in the Endeavour River, on the east coast of New Holland.

A still greater honour was in reserve for Captain Cook, than the election of him to be a common member of the Royal Society. It was resolved by Sir John Pringle and the council of the society, to bestow upon him the estimable prize of the gold medal, for the best experimental paper of the year; and no determination could be founded in greater wisdom and justice. If Captain Cook had made no important discoveries, if he had not determined the question concerning a southern continent, his name would have been entitled to immortality on account of his humane attention to, and his unparalleled success in preserving the lives and health of his seamen.

He had good reason, upon this head, to assume the pleasureable, but modest language, with which he has concluded his narrative of his second navigation round the globe : " Whatever," says he, " may be the public judgment about other matters, it is with real satisfaction, and without claiming any merit, but that of attention to my duty, that I can conclude this account with an observation, which facts enable me to make, that our having discovered the possibility of preserving health among a numerous ship's company, for such a length of time, in such varieties of climate, and amidst such continued hardships and fatigues, will make this voyage remarkable, in the opinion of every benevolent person, when the disputes about the southern continent shall have ceased to engage the attention, and to divide the judgment of philosophers."

It was the custom of Sir John Pringle, at the delivery of Sir Godfrey Copley's annual medal, to give an elaborate discourse, containing the history of that part of science for the improvement of which the medal was conferred. Upon the present occasion, the president had a subject to enlarge upon, which was perfectly congenial to his disposition and studies. His own life had been much employed in pointing the means which tended not only to cure, but to prevent the diseases of mankind ; and, therefore, it was with peculiar pleasure and affection, that he celebrated the conduct of his friend, who, by precautions equally wise and simple, had rendered the circumnavigation of the globe, so far as health is concerned, quite a harmless undertaking. Towards the beginning of his discourse, Sir John justly asks, " What inquiry can be so useful as that which hath for its object the saving the lives of men ? and when shall **we** find one more successful than that before us ? Here," adds the president, " **are** no vain boastings of the empiric, nor ingenious and delusive theories of the dogmatist : but a concise and artless, and an incontested relation of the means, by which, under divine favour, Captain Cook, with a company of a hundred and eighteen men, performed a voyage of three years and eighteen days, throughout all the climates, from fifty-two degrees north to twenty-one degrees south, with the loss of only one man by sickness.—I would inquire," proceeds Sir John Pringle, "of the most conversant in the study of bills of mortality, whether, in the most healthful climate, and in the best condition of life, they have ever found so small a number of deaths, within that space of time? How great and agreeable then must our surprise be, after perusing the histories of long navigations in former days, when so many perished by marine diseases, to find the air of the sea acquitted of all malignity; and, in fine, that a voyage round the world may be undertaken with less danger, perhaps, to health, than a common tour in Europe!"

In the progress of his discourse, the president recounted the dreadful calamities and destruction the scurvy had heretofore brought upon mariners in voyages of great length; after which he pointed out at large, and illustrated with his own observations, the methods pursued by Captain Cook for preserving the health of his men. In conclusion, Sir John remarked, that the Royal Society never more cordially or more meritoriously bestowed the gold medal, that faithful symbol of their esteem and affection. "For if," says he, "Rome decreed the *civic crown* to him who saved the life a single citizen, what wreaths are due to that man, who, having himself saved many, perpetuates in your transactions the means by which Britain may now, on the most distant voyages, preserve numbers of her intrepid sons, her *mariners*, who, braving every danger, have so liberally contributed to the fame, to the opulence, and to the maritime empire of their country." *

---

* "It cannot but be acceptable to insert here, Captain Cook's enumeration of the several causes, to which, under the care of Providence, the uncommon good state of health, experienced by his people was owing. I shall not trespass upon the reader's time in mentioning them all, but confine myself to such as were found the most useful.

"We were furnished with a quantity of malt, of which was made *sweet wort*. To such of the men as showed the least symptoms of the scurvy; and also to such as were thought to be threatened with that disorder, this was given, from one to two or three pints a day, each man; or in such proportion as the surgeon found necessary, which sometimes

One circumstance alone was wanting to complete the pleasure and celebrity arising from the assignment of Sir Godfrey Copley's

amounted to three quarts. This is, without doubt, one of the best anti-scorbutic sea medicines yet discovered; and if used in time, will, with proper attention to other things, I am persuaded, prevent the scurvy from making any great progress for a considerable while. But I am not altogether of opinion that it will cure at sea.

"*Sour krout*, of which we had a large quantity, is not only a wholesome vegetable food, but, in my judgment, highly anti-scorbutic; and it spoils not by keeping. A pound of this was served to each man, when at sea, twice a week, or oftener, as was thought necessary.

"*Portable broth* was another great article of which we had a large supply. An ounce of this to each man, or such other proportion as circumstances pointed out, was boiled in their peas, three days in the week; and when we were in places where vegetables were to be got, it was boiled with them, and wheat or oatmeal, every morning for breakfast, and also with peas and vegetables for dinner. It enabled us to make several nourishing and wholesome messes, and was the means of making the people eat a greater quantity of vegetables, than they would otherwise have done.

"*Rob of Lemon and Orange* is an anti-scorbutic we were not without. The surgeon made use of it in many cases, with great success.

"Among the articles of victualling, we were supplied with *sugar* in the room of *oil*, and with *wheat* for a part of our *oatmeal*; and were certainly gainers by the exchange. Sugar, I apprehend, is a very good anti-scorbutic; whereas oil (such as the navy is usually supplied with), I am of opinion, has the contrary effect.

"But the introduction of the most salutary articles, either as provisions or medicines, will generally prove unsuccessful, unless supported by certain regulations. On this principle, many years' experience, together with some hints I had from Sir Hugh Palliser, Captains Campbell, Wallis, and other intelligent officers, enabled me to lay a plan whereby all was to be governed.

"The crew were at three watches, except upon some extraordinary occasions. By this means they were not so much exposed to the weather, as if they had been at watch and watch; and had generally dry clothes to shift themselves, when they happened to get wet. Care was also taken to expose them as little to wet weather as possible.

"Proper methods were used to keep their persons, hammocks, bedding, clothes, etc., constantly clean and dry. Equal care was taken to keep the ship clean and dry betwixt decks. Once or twice a week she was aired with fires; and when this could not be done, she was smoked with gunpowder, mixed with vinegar or water. I had also, frequently, a fire made in an iron pot at the bottom of the well, which was of great use in purifying the air in the lower parts of the ship. To this, and to cleanliness, as well in the ship as among the people, too great attention cannot be paid; the least neglect occasions a putrid and disagreeable smell below, which nothing but fires will remove.

"Proper attention was paid to the ship's coppers, so that they were kept constantly clean.

"The fat which boiled out of the salt beef and pork, I never suffered to be given to the people; being of opinion that it promotes the scurvy.

"I was careful to take in water wherever it was to be got, even though we did not want medal. Captain Cook was not himself present, to hear the discourse of the president, and to receive the honour conferred upon him. Some months before the anniversary of St. Andrew's day, he had sailed on his last expedition. The medal, therefore, was delivered into the hands of Mrs. Cook, whose satisfaction at being intrusted with so valuable a pledge of her husband's reputation, cannot be questioned. Neither can it be doubted, but that the captain, before his departure from England, was fully apprised of the mark of distinction which was intended for him by the Royal Society.

Captain Cook, after the conclusion of his second voyage, was called upon to appear in the world in the character of an author. In the account that was published, by authority, of his former circumnavigation of the globe, as well as of those which had been performed by the Captains Byron, Carteret, and Wallis, it

---

it Because I look upon fresh water from the shore to be more wholesome, than that which has been kept some time on board a ship. Of this essential article we were never at an allowance, but had always plenty for every necessary purpose. Navigators in general cannot, indeed, expect, nor would they wish to meet with such advantages, in this respect, as fell to my lot. The nature of our voyage carried us into very high latitudes. But the hardships and dangers inseparable from that situation, were in some degree compensated by the singular felicity we enjoyed, of extracting inexhaustible supplies of fresh water from an ocean strewed with ice.

" We came to few places, where either the art of man, or the bounty of nature, had not provided some sort of refreshment or other, either in the animal or vegetable way. It was my first care to procure whatever of any kind could be met with, by every means in my power; and to oblige our people to make use thereof, both by my example and authority; but the benefits arising from refreshments of any kind soon became so obvious, that I had little occasion to recommend the one, or to exert the other "

In a letter which Captain Cook wrote to Sir John Pringle, just before he embarked on his last voyage, dated Plymouth Sound, July 7, 1776, he expressed himself as follows: " I entirely agree with you, that the dearness of the rob of lemons and of oranges will hinder them from being furnished in large quantities But I do not think this so necessary; for, though they may assist other things, I have no great opinion of them alone. Nor have I a higher opinion of vinegar. My people had it very sparingly during the late voyage, and, towards the latter part, none at all; and yet we experienced no ill effect from the want of it. The custom of washing the inside of the ship with vinegar, I seldom observed; thinking that fire and smoke answered the purpose much better."—*Sir John Pringle's Six Discourses.*

was thought requisite to procure the assistance of a professed literary man, whose business it should be to draw up a narrative from the several journals of these commanders. Accordingly Dr. Hawkesworth, as is universally known, was employed for the purpose. In the present case, it was not esteemed necessary to have recourse to such an expedient. Captain Cook was justly regarded as sufficiently qualified to relate his own story. His journal only required to be divided into chapters, and perhaps be amended by a few verbal corrections. It is not speaking extravagantly to say, that, in point of composition, his history of his voyage reflects upon him no small degree of credit. His style is natural, clear, and manly; being well adapted to the subject and to his own character; and it is possible, that a pen of more studied elegance would not have given any additional advantage to the narration. It was not till some time after Captain Cook's leaving England that the work was published; but, in the meanwhile, the superintendence of it was undertaken by his learned and valuable friend, Dr. Douglas, whose late promotion to the mitre hath afforded pleasure to every literary man, of every denomination. When the Voyage appeared, it came recommended by the accuracy and excellence of its charts, and by a great variety of engravings, from the curious and beautiful drawings of Mr. Hodges. This work was followed by the publication of the original astronomical observations, which had been made by Mr. Wales in the Resolution, and by Mr. Bayley in the Adventure. It was at the expense of the commissioners of longitude that these observations were made, and it was by their order that they were printed. The book of Mr. Wales and Mr. Bayley displays, in the strongest light, the scientific use and value of Captain Cook's voyage.

Some of the circumstances which have now been mentioned have designedly been brought forward more early in point of time than should otherwise have been done, in order to prevent any interruption in the course of the subsequent narrative.

Though Captain Cook was expected to sit down in repose, after his toils and labours, the design of farther discoveries was not laid aside. The illusion, indeed, of a *Terra Australis incognita*, to any purpose of commerce, colonization, and utility had been dispelled : but there was another grand question which remained to be determined ; and that was the practicability of a northern passage to the Pacific Ocean.

It had long been a favourite object with navigators, and particularly with the English, to discover a shorter, a more commodious, and a more profitable course of sailing to Japan and China, and, indeed, to the East Indies in general, than by making the tedious circuit of the Cape of Good Hope. To find a western passage round North America, had been attempted by several bold adventurers, from Frobisher's first voyage, in 1576, to those of James and of Fox, in 1631. By these expeditions a large addition was made to the knowledge of the northern extent of America, and Hudson's and Baffin's Bays were discovered. But the wished-for-passage, on that side, into the Pacific Ocean, was still unattained. Nor were the various attempts of our countrymen and of the Dutch, to find such a passage, by sailing round the north of Asia, in an eastern direction, attended with better success. Wood's failure, in 1676, appears to have concluded the long list of unfortunate expeditions in that country. The discovery, if not absolutely despaired of, had been unsuccessful in such a number of instances, that it ceased, for many years, to be an object of pursuit.

The question was again revived in the present century. Mr. Dobbs, a warm advocate for the probability of a northwest passage through Hudson's Bay, once more recalled the attention of this country to that undertaking. In consequence of the spirit by him excited, Captain Middleton was sent out by government in 1741, and Captains Smith and More, in 1746. But, though an act of parliament had been passed, which secured a reward of twenty thousand pounds to the discovery of a passage, the accomplishment of this favourite object continued at as great a distance as ever.

To ascertain a matter of such importance and magnitude in navigation, was reserved to be another glory of his present majesty's reign. The idea was peculiarly suited to the enlightened mind of the noble lord at the head of the admiralty, and he adopted it with ardour. Preparatory to the execution of the design, Lord Mulgrave sailed with two ships to determine how far navigation was practicable towards the north pole. In this expedition, his lordship met with the same insuperable difficulties which had been experienced by former voyagers. Nevertheless, the expectation of opening a communication between the Pacific and Atlantic Oceans, by a northerly course, was not abandoned; and it was resolved that a voyage should be undertaken for that purpose.

For the conduct of an enterprise, the operations of which were intended to be so new, so extensive, and so various, it was evident that great ability, skill, and experience were indispensably necessary. That Captain Cook was of all men the best qualified for carrying it into execution, was a matter that could not be called in question. But however ardently it might be wished that he would take upon him the command of the service, no one (not even his friend and patron, Lord Sandwich himself) presumed to solicit him upon the subject. The benefits he had already conferred on science and navigation, and the labours and dangers he had gone through, were so many and great, that it was not deemed reasonable to ask him to engage in fresh perils. At the same time, nothing could be more natural, than to consult him upon everything relative to the business; and his advice was particularly requested with regard to the properest person for conducting the voyage. To determine this point, the captain, Sir Hugh Palliser, and Mr. Stephens were invited to Lord

Sandwich's to dinner. Here, besides taking into consideration what officer should be recommended to his majesty for accomplishing the purposes in view, many things were said concerning the nature of the design. Its grandeur and dignity, the consequences of it to navigation and science, and the completion it **would** give to the whole system of discoveries, were enlarged upon in a course of the conversation. Captain Cook was so fired with the contemplation and representations of the object, that he started up, and declared that he himself would undertake the direction of the enterprise. It is easy to suppose, with what pleasure the noble lord and the other gentlemen received a proposal, which was so agreeable to their secret wishes, and which they thought of the highest importance towards attaining the ends of the voyage. No time was lost by the Earl of Sandwich, in laying the matter before the king; and Captain Cook was appointed to the command of the expedition on the 10th of February, 1776. At the same time it was agreed, that on his return to England, he should be restored to his situation at Greenwich; and, if no vacancy occurred during the interval, the officer who succeeded him was to resign in his favour.

The command and the direction of the enterprise being thus happily settled, it became an object of great importance to determine what might be the best course that could be given to the voyage. All former navigators round the globe had returned to Europe by the Cape of Good Hope. But to Captain Cook the arduous task was now assigned, of attempting it by reaching the high northern latitudes between Asia and America; and the adoption of this resolution was, I believe, the result of his own reflections upon the subject. The usual plan, therefore, of discovery was reversed; so that, instead of a passage from the Atlantic to the Pacific, one from the latter to the former was to be tried. Whatever openings or inlets there might be on the east side of America, that lie in a direction which could afford any hopes of passage, it was wisely foreseen, that the ultimate success of the expedition would depend upon there being an open sea between the west side of that continent and the extremities of Asia. Accordingly, Captain Cook was ordered to proceed into the Pacific Ocean, through the chain of the new islands which had been visited by him in the southern tropic. After having crossed the equator into the northern parts of that ocean, he was then to hold such a course as might probably fix many interesting points in geography, and produce intermediate discoveries, in his progress northward to the principal scene of his operations. With regard to his grand object, it was determined, for the wisest reasons, and after the most mature deliberation and inquiry, that upon his arrival on the coast of New Albion, he should proceed northward as far as the latitude of 65°, and not lose any time in exploring rivers or inlets, or upon any other account, until he had gotten into that latitude.

To give every possible encouragement to the prosecution of the great design in view, the motives of interest were added to the obligations of duty. In the act of parliament which passed in 1745, the reward of twenty thousand pounds had only been held out to the ships *belonging to any of his majesty's subjects*, while his majesty's own ships were excluded. Another, and more capital defect of the act was, that it confined the reward to such ships alone as should discover a passage through Hudson's Bay. By a new law, which passed in 1776, both these deficiencies were effectually remedied. It was now enacted, "That if any ship belonging to any of his majesty's subjects, or *to his majesty*, shall find out, and sail through any passage by sea, between the Atlantic and Pacific Oceans, in *any direction*, or parallel of the northern hemisphere, to the northward of the 52° of northern latitude, the owners of such ships, if belonging to any of his majesty's subjects, or *the commander, officers, and seamen, of such ship belonging to his majesty*, shall receive, as a reward for such discovery, the sum of twenty thousand pounds."

That everything might be done which could facilitate the success of the grand expedition, Lieutenant Pickersgill was sent out in 1776, with directions to explore the coast of Baffin's Bay; and in the next year, Lieutenant Young was commissioned not **only to** examine the western parts of that bay, but to endea**vour** to find a passage on that side, from the Atlantic to the Pacific Ocean. Nothing was performed by either of these gentlemen that promoted the purposes of Captain Cook's voyage.

Two vessels were fixed upon by government for the intended service; the Resolution and the Discovery. The command of the former was given to Captain Cook, and of the other to Captain Clerke. To the Resolution was assigned the same complement of officers and men which she had during her preceding voyage; **and the** only difference in the establishment of the Discovery from that of the Adventure, was in the single instance of her having no marine officer on board.

From the time of the two ships being put into commission, the greatest degree of attention and zeal was exerted by the Earl of Sandwich, and the rest of the board of admiralty, to have them equipped in the most complete manner. Both the vessels were supplied with as much of every necessary article as could conveniently be stowed, and with the best of each kind that could be procured. Whatever, likewise, the experience of the former voyages had shown to be of any utility in preserving the health of the seamen, was provided in a large abundance. That some permanent benefit might be conveyed to the inhabitants of Otaheite, and of the other islands of the Pacific Ocean, whom our navigators might happen to visit, it was graciously commanded by his majesty, that an assortment of useful animals should be carried out to those countries. Accordingly, a bull, two cows with their calves, and several sheep, with hay and corn for their subsistence, were taken on board; and it was in tended to add other serviceable animals to these when Captain Cook should arrive at the Cape of Good Hope. With the same benevolent purposes, the captain was furnished with a sufficient quantity of such of our European garden seeds, as could not fail of being a valuable present to the newly discovered islands, by adding fresh supplies of food to their own vegetable productions. By order of the board of admiralty, many articles besides were delivered to our commander, which were calculated, in various ways, to improve the condition of the natives of the other hemisphere. Still farther to promote a friendly intercourse with them, and to carry on a traffic that might be profitable on both sides, an ample assortment was provided of iron tools and trinkets. An attention no less humane was extended to the wants of our own people. Some additional clothing, adapted to cold climates, was ordered for the crews of the two ships, and nothing was denied to our navigators, that could be supposed to be in the least conducive to their health, or even to their convenience.

It was not to these things only, that the extraordinary care of Lord Sandwich and of the other gentlemen at the head of the naval department, was confined. They were equally solicitous to afford every assistance that was calculated to render the expedition of public utility. Several astronomical and nautical instruments were intrusted, by the board of longitude, to Captain Cook, and Mr. King his second lieutenant; who had undertaken to make the necessary observations, during the voyage, for the improvement of astronomy and navigation. It was originally intended that a professed observator should be sent out in the Resolution; but the scientific abilities of the captain and his lieutenant rendered the appointment of such a person absolutely unnecessary. The case was somewhat different with regard to the Discovery. Mr. William Bayley, who had already given satisfactory proofs of his skill and diligence as an observator, while he was employed in Captain Furneaux's ship, during the late voyage, was engaged a second time, in that capacity, and appointed to sail on board Captain Clerke's vessel. The department of natural history was assigned to Mr. Anderson, the surgeon of the Resolution, who was as willing, as he was well qualified, to describe everything in that branch of science which should occur worthy of notice. From the remarks of this gentleman, Captain Cook had derived considerable assistance in his last navigation; especially with regard to the very copious vocabulary of the language of Otaheite, and the comparative specimen of the languages of the other islands which had then been visited. There were several young men among our commander's sea officers, who, under his direction, could be usefully employed in constructing charts, in taking views of the coasts and headlands near which our voyagers might pass, and in drawing plans of the bays and harbours in which they should anchor. Without a constant attention to this object, the captain was sensible, that his discoveries could not be rendered profitable to future navigators. That he might go out with every help, which could serve to make the result of the voyage entertaining to the generality of readers, as well as instructive to the sailor and the scholar, Mr. Webber was fixed upon, and engaged to embark in the Resolution, for the express purpose of supplying the unavoidable imperfections of written accounts, by enabling our people to preserve and to bring home such drawings of the most memorable scenes of their transactions, as could only be executed by a professed and skilful artist.

As the last mark of the extraordinary attention which the Earl of Sandwich, Sir Hugh Palliser, and others of the board of admiralty had uniformly shown to the preparations for the expedition, they went down to Long Reach, and paid a visit to the ships, on the 8th of June to examine whether every ing was completed conformably to their intentions and orders and to the satisfaction of all who were to embark in the voyage. His lordship and the rest of the admiralty board, together with several noblemen and gentlemen of their acquaintance, honoured Captain Cook on that day with their company at dinner. Both upon their coming on board, and their going ashore, they were **saluted with** seventeen guns, and with three cheers.

As the ships were to touch at Otaheite and the Society Islands, it had been determined not to omit the only opportunity which might ever offer of carrying Omai back to his native country. Accordingly, he left London, on the 24th of June, in company with Captain Cook ; and it was with a mixture of regret and satisfaction that he took his departure. When England, and those who, during his stay had honoured him with their protection or friendship were spoken of, his spirits were sensibly affected, and it was with difficulty that he could refrain from tears. But his eyes began to sparkle with joy, as soon as ever the conversation was turned to his own islands. The good treatment he received in England had made a deep impression upon his mind ; and he entertained the highest ideas of the country and of the people. Nevertheless, the pleasing prospect he now had before him of returning home, loaded with what, he well knew, would there be esteemed invaluable treasures, and the flattering hope, which the possession of these afforded him, of attaining to a distinguished superiority among his countrymen, were considerations which operated, by degrees, to suppress every uneasy sensation. By the time he had gotten on board the ship, he appeared to be quite happy.

His majesty had furnished Omai with an ample provision of every article which our English navigators, during their former intercourse with Otaheite and the Society Islands, had observed to be in any estimation there, either as useful or ornamental. Many presents, likewise, of the same nature, had been made him by Lord Sandwich, Sir Joseph Banks and several other gentlemen and ladies of his acquaintance. In short, both during his residence in England, and at his departure from it, no method had been neglected, which could be calculated to render him the instrument of conveying to the inhabitants of the islands of the Pacific Ocean, the most exalted ideas of the greatness and generosity of the British nation.

CHAPTER VI.

NARRATIVE OF CAPTAIN COOK'S VOYAGE TO THE PACIFIC OCEAN, TO THE PERIOD OF HIS DEATH.

EVERY preparation for the voyage being completed, Captain Cook received an order to proceed to Plymouth, and to take the Discovery under his command. Having, accordingly, given the proper directions to Captain Clerke, he sailed from the Nore to the Downs, on the 25th of June. On the 30th of the same month, he anchored in Plymouth Sound, where the Discovery was already arrived. It was the 8th day of July before our commander received his instructions for the voyage; and, at the same time, he was ordered to proceed with the Resolution to the Cape of Good Hope. Captain Clerke, who was detained in London, by some unavoidable circumstances, was to follow as soon as he should join his ship.

In the evening of the 12th, Captain Cook stood out of Plymouth Sound, and pursued his course down the channel. It was very early that he began his judicious operations for preserving the health of his crew; for on 17th, the ship was smoked between decks with gunpowder, and the spare sails were well aired. On the 30th, the moon being totally eclipsed, the captain observed it with a night telescope. He had not, on this occasion, an opportunity of making many observations. The reason was, that the moon was hidden behind the clouds the greater part of the time; and this was particularly the case, when the beginning and the end of total darkness, and the end of the eclipse, **happened.**

It being found, that there were not hay and corn sufficient for the subsistence of the stock of animals on board, till the arrival of our people at the Cape of Good Hope, Captain Cook determined to touch at Teneriffe. This island he thought better adapted to the purposes of procuring these articles, and other refreshments, than Madeira. On the 1st of August, he anchored in the road of Santa Cruz, and immediately dispatched an officer to the governor, who, with the utmost politeness, granted everything which our commander requested.

Were a judgment to be formed from the appearance of the country in the neighbourhood of Santa Cruz, it might be concluded that Teneriffe is so barren a spot as to be insufficient for the maintenance even of its own inhabitants. It was proved, however, by the ample supplies which our navigators received, that the islanders had enough to spare for visitors. The necessary articles of refreshment were procured at such moderate prices, as to confirm Captain Cook in his opinion that Teneriffe is a more eligible place than Madeira for ships to touch at which are bound on long voyages. Indeed, the wine of the latter island is far superior to that of the former; but then it can only be purchased by **a sum of money** proportionably larger.

During the short stay which the captain made at Teneriffe, he continued with great assiduity his astronomical observations; and Mr. Anderson has not a little contributed to our farther knowledge of the country, by his remarks on the general state, its natural appearances, its productions, and its inhabitants. He learned, from a sensible and well-informed gentleman, who resided in the island, that a shrub is common there which agrees exactly with the description given by Tournefort and Linnæus of the *tea shrub*, as growing in China and Japan. It is reckoned a weed, and every year is rooted out in large quantities from the vineyards. The Spaniards, however, sometimes use it as tea, and ascribe to it all the qualities of that which is imported from China. They give it also the name of tea, and say that it was found in the country when the islands were first discovered. Another botanical curiosity is called the *impregnated lemon;* which is a perfect and distinct lemon enclosed within another, and differing from the outer one only in being a little more globular.

The air and climate of Teneriffe, are, in general, remarkably healthful, and particularly adapted to give relief in pulmonary complaints. This the gentleman before mentioned endeavoured to account for, from its being always in a person's power to procure a different temperature of the air, by residing at different heights in the island. He expressed, therefore, his surprise that the physicians of England should never have thought of sending their consumptive patients to Teneriffe, instead of Nice or Lisbon.

Although it is not understood that there is any great similarity between the manners of the English and those of the Spaniards, it was observable, that the difference between them was very little perceived by Omai. He only said, that the Spaniards did not appear to be so friendly as the English; and that, in their persons, they approached to some resemblance of his own countrymen.

On the 4th, Captain Cook sailed from Teneriffe, and proceeded on his voyage. Such was his attention, both to the discipline and the health of his company, that twice in the space of five days, he exercised them at great guns and small arms, and cleared and smoked the ship below decks. On the evening of the 10th, when the Resolution was at a small distance from the island of Bonavista, she ran so close upon a number of sunken rocks, that she did but just weather the breakers. The situation of our voyagers, for a few minutes, was very alarming. In this situation the captain, with the intrepid coolness which distinguished his character, did not choose to sound, as that, without any possibility of lessening, might have heightened the danger.

While our commander was near the Cape de Verde Islands, he had an opportunity of correcting an assertion of Mr. Nichelson with regard to the manner of sailing by those islands, which, if implicitly trusted to, might prove of dangerous consequence. On the 13th, our navigators arrived before Port Praya, in the Island of St. Jago: but as the Discovery was not there, and little water had been expended in the passage from Teneriffe, Captain Cook did not think proper to go in, but stood to the southward.

In the course of the voyage, between the latitudes of 12° and 7° north, the weather was generally dark and gloomy. The rains were frequent, and accompanied with that close and sultry weather which too often brings on sickness in this passage. At such a time the worst consequences are to be apprehended; and commanders of ships cannot be too much on their guard. It is necessary for them to purify the air between decks with fires and smoke, and to oblige their people to dry their clothes at every opportunity. The constant observance of these precautions on board the Resolution was attended with such success, that the captain had now fewer sick men than on either of his former voyages. This was the more remarkable, as, in consequence of the seams of the vessel having opened so wide as to admit the rain when it fell, there was scarcely a man who could lie dry in his bed; and the officers in the gun-room were all driven out of their cabins by the water that came through the sides. When settled weather returned, the caulkers were employed in repairing these defects, by caulking the decks and the inside weather-works of the ship; for the humanity of our commander would not trust the workmen over the sides, while the Resolution was at sea.

On the 1st of September, our navigators crossed the equator. While, on the 8th, Captain Cook was near the eastern coast of Brazil, he was at considerable pains to settle its longitude, which, till some better astronomical observations are made on shore in that country, he concluded to be thirty-five degrees and a half, or thirty-six degrees west, at most.

As our people proceeded on their voyage, they frequently saw, in the night, those luminous marine animals, which have formerly been mentioned and described. Some of them appeared to be considerably larger than any which the captain had met with before; and sometimes they were so numerous, that hundreds of them were visible at the same moment.

On the 18th of October, the Resolution came to an anchor in Table Bay, at the Cape of Good Hope: and the usual compliments having been paid to Baron Plettenberg, the governor, Captain Cook immediately applied himself to his customary operations. Nothing remarkable occurred till the evening of the 31st, when a tempest arose from the southeast, which lasted three days, and which was so violent that the Resolution was the only ship in the bay that rode out the gale without dragging her anchors. The effects of the storm were sensibly felt by our people on shore; for their tents and observatory were torn to pieces, and their astronomical quadrant narrowly escaped irreparable damage. On the 3d of November, the tempest ceased, and the next day the English were enabled to resume their different employments.

It was not till the 10th of the month, that Captain Cook had the satisfaction of seeing the Discovery arrive in the bay and effect her junction with the Resolution. She had sailed from England on the 1st of August, and would have reached the Cape of Good Hope a week sooner, if she had not been driven from the coast by the late storm. Every assistance was immediately given to put her into a proper condition for proceeding on the voyage.

While the necessary preparations for the future navigation were completing, a disaster happened with regard to the cattle which had been carried out in the Resolution. They had been conveyed on shore for the purpose of grazing. The bull, and two cows, with their calves, had been sent to graze along with some other cattle; but Captain Cook was advised to keep the sheep, which were sixteen in number, close to the tents, where they were penned up every evening. During the night preceding the 14th, some dogs having gotten in among them, forced them out of the pen, killed four, and dispersed the rest. Six of them were recovered the next day; but the two rams, and two of the finest ewes in the whole flock, were amongst those which were missing. Baron Plettenberg being at this time in the country, our commander applied to Mr. Hemmey, the lieutenant-governor, and to the fiscal, for redress; and both these gentlemen promised to use their endeavours for the recovery of the lost sheep. It is the boast of the Dutch, that the police at the Cape is so carefully executed, that it is scarcely possible for a slave, with all his cunning and knowledge of the country, to effectuate his escape. Nevertheless, Captain Cook's sheep evaded all the vigilance of the fiscal's officers and people. At length after much trouble and expense, by employing some of the meanest and lowest scoundrels in the place, he recovered all but the two ewes, of which he never could hear the least tidings. The character given of the fellows to whom the captain was obliged to have recourse, by the person who recommended their being applied to, was, that for a ducaton they would cut their master's throat, burn the house over his head, and bury him and the whole family in the ashes.

During the stay of our voyagers at the Cape, some of the officers, accompanied by Mr. Anderson, made a short excursion into the neighbouring country. This gentlemen, as usual, was very diligent in recording everything which appeared to him worthy of observation. His remarks, however, in the present case, will be deemed of little consequence, compared with the full, accurate, and curious account of the Cape of Good Hope, with which Dr. Sparrman hath lately favoured the literary world.

With respect to Captain Cook, besides the unavoidable care which lay upon him, in providing his ships with whatever was requisite for the commodious and successful prosecution of the voyage, his attention was eminently directed to scientific objects. He was anxious to ascertain the currents, the variations of the compass, and the latitude and longitude of the places to which he came. The observations which he collected, and recorded in his journal, while he was at the Cape of Good Hope, will be esteemed of the greatest importance by judicious navigators.

After the disaster which had happened to the sheep, it may well be supposed that our commander did not long trust on shore those which remained. Accordingly, he gave orders to have them, and the other cattle, conveyed on board as fast as possible. He made an addition, also, to the original stock, by the purchase of two young bulls, two heifers, two young stallions, two mares, two rams, several ewes and goats, and some rabbits and poultry. All these animals were intended for New Zealand, Otaheite, and the neighbouring islands; and indeed, for any other places, in the course of the voyage, where the leaving of any of them might be of service to posterity.

In the supplies which were provided at the Cape, Captain Cook paid a particular regard to the nature and extent of his undertaking. As it was impossible to tell when or where he might meet with a place which could so amply contribute to his necessities, he thought proper to lay in such a store of provisions for both ships, as would be sufficient to last them for two years and upwards.

Our commander, having given a copy of his instructions to Captain Clerke, and an order directing him how to proceed in case of a separation, weighed from Table Bay on the 30th of November, though it was not till the third of December that he got clear of the land. On the sixth the ships passed through several spots of water, nearly of a red colour. When some of this was taken up, it was found to contain a large quantity of small animals of a reddish hue, and which the microscope discovered to resemble a crag-fish. As our navigators pursued their course to the southeast, a very strong gale, which they had from the westward, was followed by a mountainous sea, in consequence of which, the Resolution rolled and tumbled so much that the cattle on board were preserved with the utmost difficulty. Soon after, several of the goats, especially the males, together with some sheep, died, notwithstanding all the care to prevent it, that was exercised by our people. This misfortune was chiefly owing to the coldness of the weather, which now began to be felt in the most sensible manner.

On the 12th land was seen, which, upon a nearer approach, was found to consist of two islands. That which lies most to the south, and is the largest, was judged by Captain Cook to be about fifteen leagues in circuit. The northerly one is about nine leagues in circuit: and the two islands are at the distance of five leagues from each other. As the ships passed through the channel between them, our voyagers could not discover, with the assistance of their best glasses, either tree or shrub on either of them. They seemed to have a rocky and bold shore, and their surface is for the most part composed of barren mountains, the summits and sides of which were covered with snow. These two islands, together with four others which lie from nine to twelve degrees of longitude more to the east and nearly in the same latitude, had been discovered by Captains Marion du Fresne and Crozet, French navigators, in January, 1772, on their passage, in two ships from the Cape of Good Hope to the Philippine Islands. As no names had been assigned to them in a chart of the Southern Ocean, which Captain Crozet communicated to **Captain** Cook in 1775, our commander distinguished the two larger ones by calling them Prince Edward's Islands, after his majesty's fourth son. To the other four, with a view of commemorating the discoverers, he gave the name of Marion's and Crozet's Islands.

Though it was now the middle of summer in this hemisphere, the weather was not less severe than what is generally met with in England in the very depth of winter. Instead, however, of being discouraged by this circumstance, the captain shaped his course in such a manner as to pass to the southward of Marion's and Crozet's Islands, that he might get into the latitude of land which had been discovered by M. de Kerguelen, another French navigator. It was part of our commander's instructions to examine whether a good harbour might not here be found.

As our voyagers, on the 24th, were steering to the eastward, a fog clearing up a little, which had involved them for some time, and which had rendered their navigation both tedious and dangerous, land was seen, bearing south-southeast. Upon a nearer approach, it was found to be an island of considerable height, and about three leagues in circuit. Another island, of the same magnitude, was soon after discovered, and in a short space a third, besides some smaller ones. At times, as the fog broke away, there was the appearance of land over the small islands, and Captain Cook entertained thoughts of steering for it, by running in between them. But, on drawing nearer, he found that, so long as the weather contined foggy, this would be a perilous attempt. For if there should be no passage, or if our people should meet with any sudden danger, there was such a prodigious sea, breaking on all the shores in a frightful surf, that it would have been impossible for the vessels to be gotten off. At the same time, the captain saw another island ; and as he did not know how many more might succeed, he judged it prudent in order to avoid getting entangled among unknown lands in a thick fog, to wait for clearer weather.

The island last mentioned is a high round rock, which was named Blighe's Cap. Our commander had received some very slight information concerning it at Teneriffe, and his sagacity for tracing it was such, as immediately to determine, that it was the same that M. de Kerguelen had called the Isle of Rendezvous. His reason for giving it that name is not very apparent: for nothing can rendezvous upon it but the fowls of the air, it being certainly inaccessible to every other animal. The weather beginning to clear up, Captain Cook steered in for the land, of which a faint view had been obtained in the morning. This was Kerguelen's Land. No sooner had our navigators gotten off Cape Francois than they observed the coast, to the southward, to be much indented by projecting points and bays ; from which circumstance they were sure of finding a good harbour. Accordingly, such a harbour was speedily discovered, in which the ships came to anchor on the 25th, being Christmas day. Upon landing, our commander found the shore almost covered with penguins and other birds, and with seals. The latter, which were not numerous, having been unaccustomed to visitors, were so insensible of fear, that as many as were wanted, for the purpose of making use of their fat or blubber, were killed without difficulty. Fresh water was so plentiful, that every gully afforded a large stream ; but not a single tree or shrub, or the least sign of it, could be met with, and but very little herbage of any sort. Before Captain Cook returned to his ship, he ascended the first ridge of rocks, that rise in a kind of amphitheatre, above one another, in hopes of obtaining a view of the country ; in which, however, he was disappointed: for, previously to his reaching the top, there came on so thick a fog, that he could scarcely find his way down again. In the evening, the seine was hauled at the head of the harbour, but only half a dozen small fish were caught. As no better success attended a trial which was made the next day with hook and line, the only resource for fresh provisions was in birds, the store of which was inexhaustible.

The people having wrought hard for two days, and nearly completed their water, the captain allowed them the 27th as a day of rest, to celebrate Christmas. Many of them, in consequence of this indulgence, went on shore, and made excursions in different directions, into the country, which they found barren and desolate in the highest degree. One of them, in his ramble, discovered, and brought to our commander, in the evening, a quart bottle, fastened with some wire to a projecting rock, on the north side of the harbour. This bottle contained a piece of parchment, on which was written the following inscription:

> LUDOVICO XV. GALLIARUM
> REGE ET D. DE BOYNES
> REGI A SECRETIS AD RES
> MARITIMAS ANNIS 1772 ET
> 1773.

It was clear from this inscription, that our English navigators were not the first who had been in the place. As a memorial of our people's having touched at the same harbour, Captain Cook wrote as follows, on the other side of the parchment:

> NAVES RESOLUTION
> ET DISCOVERY
> DE REGE MAGNÆ BRITANNÆ,
> DECEMBRIS, 1776.

He then put it again into a bottle, together with a silver two-penny piece of 1772. Having covered the mouth of the bottle with a leaden cap, he placed it the next morning in a pile of stones erected for the purpose, upon a little eminence on the north shore of the harbour, and near to the place where it was first found. In this position, it cannot escape the notice of any European, whom accident or design may bring into the port. Here the captain displayed the British flag, and named the place Christmas Harbour, from our voyagers having arrived in it on that festival.

After our commander had finished the business of the inscription, he went in his boat round the harbour, to examine what the shore afforded. His more particular object was to look for drift-wood; but he did not find a single piece throughout the whole extent of the place. On the same day, accompanied by Mr. King, his second-lieutenant, he went upon Cape Francois, with the hope, that from this elevation, he might obtain a view of the sea-coast, and of the adjoining islands. But, when he had gotten up, he found that every distant object below him was obscured in a thick fog. The land on the same plain, or of a greater height, was sufficiently visible, and appeared naked and desolate in the highest degree, some hills to the southward excepted, which were covered with snow.

On the 29th Captain Cook departed from Christmas Harbour, and proceeded to range along the coast, with a view of discovering its position and extent. In pursuing his course, he met with several promontories and bays, together with a peninsula, all of which he has described and named, chiefly in honour of his various friends. Such was the danger of the navigation, that the ships had more than once a very narrow escape. On the same day, another harbour was discovered, in which the vessels came to an anchor for one night. Here the captain, Mr. Gore, and Mr. Bayley went on shore to examine the country, which they found, if possible, more barren and desolate than the land that lies about Christmas Harbour; and yet, if the least fertility were anywhere to be expected, it ought to have existed in this place, which is completely sheltered from the bleak and predominating southerly and westerly winds. Our commander observed, with regret, that there was neither food nor covering for cattle of any sort; and that, if he left any, they must inevitably perish. Finding no encouragment to continue his researches, he weighed anchor and put to sea on the 30th, having given to the harbour the name of Port Palliser. On the same day, he came to a point, which proved to be the very eastern extremity of Kerguelen's Land. In a large bay, near this point, there was a prodigious quantity of sea-weed, some of which is of a most extraordinary length. It seemed to be the same kind of vegetable production that Sir Joseph Banks had formerly distinguished by the appellation of *fucas giganteus*. Although the stem is not much thicker than a man's hand, Captain Cook thought himself well warranted to say, that a part of it grows to the length of sixty fathoms and upward.

The result of the examination of Kerguelen's Land was, that the quantity of latitude which it occupies doth not much exceed one degree and a quarter. Its extent from east to west, still remains undecided. At its first discovery it was probably supposed to belong to a southern continent; but, in fact, it is an island, and that of no great extent. If our commander had not been unwilling to deprive M. Kerguelen of the honour of its bearing his name, he would have been disposed, from its sterility, to call it the land of Desolation.

It should here be mentioned, that M. de Kerguelen, made two visits to the coast of this country; one in 1772, and another in 1773. With the first of these voyages, Captain Cook had only a very slight acquaintance, and to the second he was totally a stranger; so that he scarcely had any opportunity of comparing his own discoveries with those of the French navigator. M. de

Kerguelen was peculiarly unfortunate, in having done but little to complete what he had begun; for though he discovered a new land, he could not, in two expeditions to it, once bring his ships to an anchor upon any part of its coasts. Captain Cook had either had fewer difficulties to struggle with, or was more successful in surmounting them.

During the short time in which our voyagers lay in Christmas Harbour, Mr. Anderson lost no opportunity of searching the country in every direction. Perhaps no place, hitherto discovered, under the same parallel of latitude, affords so scanty a field for a natural historian. All that could be known in the space of time allotted him, and probably all that will ever be worthy to be known, was collected by this gentleman. A verdure, which had been seen at a little distance from the shore, gave our people the flattering expectation of meeting with a variety of herbage; but in this they were greatly deceived. On landing, it was perceived that the lively colour which had imposed upon them, was occasioned only by one small plant, not unlike some sort of *saxifrage*. It grows in large spreading tufts, a considerable way up the hills. The whole catalogue of plants does not exceed sixteen or eighteen, including several kinds of moss, and a beautiful species of lichen, which rises higher up from the rocks than the rest of the vegetable productions. There is not the appearance of a shrub in the whole country. Nature has been somewhat more bountiful in furnishing it with animals; though, strictly speaking, they are not inhabitants of the place, being all of the marine kind. In general, the land is only used by them for breeding, and as a resting-place. Of these animals the most considerable are seals; being of that sort which is called the ursine seal. The birds, which have already been mentioned as very numerous, chiefly consist of penguins, ducks, petrels, albatrosses, shags, gulls, and sea-swallows. Penguins, which are far superior in number to the rest, are of three kinds, one of which had never been seen by any of our voyagers before. The rocks, or foundations of the hills, are principally composed of that dark blue and very hard stone, which seems to be one of the most universal productions of nature. Nothing was discovered that had the least appearance of ore or metal.

From this desolate coast Captain Cook took his departure on the 31st, intending, agreeably to his instructions, to touch next at New Zealand; that he might obtain a recruit of water, take in wood, and make hay for the cattle. Their number was now considerably diminished; for two young bulls, one of the heifers, two rams, and several of the goats had died while our navigators were employed in exploring Kerguelen's Land. For some time they had fresh gales, and tolerably clear weather. But on the 3d of January, 1777, the wind veered to the north, where it continued eight days, and was attended with so thick a fog, that the ships ran above three hundred leagues in the dark. Occasionally the weather would clear up, and give our people a sight of the sun; but this happened very seldom, and was always of short continuance. However, amidst all the darkness produced by the fog, the vessels, though they seldom saw each other were so fortunate, in consequence of frequently firing guns as signals, that they did not lose company. On the 12th, the northerly winds ended in a calm. This was succeeded, in a little time, by a wind from the southward, which brought on a rain, that continued for twenty-four hours. At the end of the rain, the wind freshened, and veering to the west and northwest, was followed by rain and clear weather.

Nothing very remarkable occurred to our voyagers till the 24th, when they discovered the coast of Van Dieman's Land; and, on the 26th, the ships came to an anchor in Adventure Bay. Captain Cook, as soon as he had anchored, ordered the boats to be hoisted out; in one of which he went himself, to look for the most commodious place for obtaining the necessary supplies

Wood and water were found in abundance, and in places sufficiently convenient; but grass, which was most wanted, was scarce, and, at the same time very coarse. Necessity, however, obliged our people to take up with such as could be procured.

On the 28th, the English, who were employed in cutting wood, were agreeably surprised with a visit from some of the natives. They consisted of eight men and a boy, who approached our voyagers not only without fear, but with the most perfect confidence and freedom. There was only a single person among them who had anything which bore the least appearance of a weapon, and that was no more than a stick about two feet long, and pointed at one end. These people were quite naked, and wore no kind of ornaments; unless some large punctures, or ridges, raised in different parts of their bodies, either in straight or curved lines, may be considered in that light. Most of them had their hair and beards smeared with a red ointment; and the faces of some of them were painted with the same composition. Every present which Captain Cook made them they received without the least appearance of satisfaction. Of bread and elephant fish, which were offered them, they refused to taste, but showed that they were fond of birds, as an article of food. Two pigs, which the captain had brought on shore, having come within their reach, they seized them by the ears, as a dog would have done, and would have carried them off immediately, apparently with no other intention than to kill them. Our commander being desirous of knowing the use of the stick which one of the Indians had in his hands, he signified by signs, his wishes to that purpose. His intimations so far succeeded, that one of them set up a piece of wood as a mark, and threw it at the distance of about twenty yards. There was but little reason to commend his dexterity; for, after repeated trials, he was still very wide from his object. Omai, to convince the natives how much our weapons were superior to theirs, then fired his musket at the mark, by which they were so greatly terrified, that, notwithstanding all the endeavours of the English to quiet their minds, they ran instantly into the woods.

After the retreat of the Indians, Captain Cook, judging that their fears would prevent their remaining near enough to observe what passed, ordered the two pigs, being a boar and a sow, to be carried about a mile within the head of the bay, and saw them left there, by the side of a fresh-water brook. It was, at first, his benevolent intention to make an additional present to Van Dieman's Land, of a young bull and a cow, together with some sheep and goats. But, upon reflection, he laid aside his design; being persuaded that the natives would destroy them, from their incapacity of entering into his views with regard to the improvement of their country. As pigs are animals which soon become wild, and are fond of the thickest cover of the woods, there was the greater probability of their being preserved. For the accommodation of the other cattle, an open place must have been chosen; in which situation they could not possibly have been concealed many days.

On the 29th, about twenty of the inhabitants, men and boys, joined Captain Cook and such of his people as had landed with him, without manifesting the least sign of fear or distrust. It was remarkable, that one of the Indians was conspicuously deformed; nor was he more distinguished by the hump upon his back, than by the drollery of his gestures, and the humour of his speeches; which had the appearance of being intended for the entertainment of our voyagers. Unfortunately, the language in which he spoke to them was wholy unintelligible. To each of the present group the captain gave a string of beads and a medal, which they seemed to receive with some satisfaction. On iron, and iron tools, they appeared to set no value. There was reason to believe, that they were even ignorant of fish-hooks; and yet it is difficult to suppose, that a people who inhabit a sea-coast, and who were not observed to derive any of their sustenance from the production of the ground, should be unacquainted with some mode of catching fish. However, they were never seen to be thus employed; nor was any canoe or vessel discovered by which they could go upon the water. Though they had rejected the kind of fish which had been offered them, it was evident that shell fish made a part of their food.

After Captain Cook had left the shore, several women and children made their appearance, and were introduced to Lieutenant King by some of the men that attended them. These females (a kangaroo skin excepted, which was tied over their shoulders, and seemed to be intended to support their infants) were as naked and as black as the men, and had their bodies marked with scars in the same manner. Many of the children had fine features, and were thought to be pretty; but a less favourable report was made of the women, and especially of those who were advanced in years. Some of the gentlemen, however, belonging to the Discovery, as our commander was informed, paid their addresses and made liberal offers of presents, which were rejected with great disdain. It is certain that this gallantry was not very agreeable to the men: for an elderly man, as soon as he observed it, ordered the women to retire. The order was obeyed; but, on the part of some of the females, with the appearance of a little reluctance.

On the present occasion, Captain Cook made some proper and pertinent reflections, which I shall deliver in his own words: "This conduct," says he, "of Europeans among savages, to their women, is highly blameable; as it creates a jealousy in their men, that may be attended with consequences fatal to the success of the common enterprise, and to the whole body of adventurers, without advancing the private purpose of the individual, or enabling him to gain the object of his wishes. I believe it has generally been found, amongst uncivilized people, that where the women are easy of access, the men are the first to offer them to strangers ; and that, where this it not the case, neither the allurement of presents, nor the opportunity of privacy, will be likely to have the desired effect. This observation, I am sure, will hold good throughout all the parts of the South Sea where I have been. Why then should men act so absurd a part, as to risk their own safety and that of all their companions, in pursuit of a gratification which they have no probability of obtaining ?"

While our navigators were at Van Dieman's Land, they were successful in obtaining a plentiful crop of grass for their cattle, and such as was far more excellent than what they had met with at their first going on shore. The quantity collected was judged by the captain to be sufficient to last till his arrival in New Zealand.

Van Dieman's Land had been visited twice before. That name had been given it by Tasman, who discovered it in 1642 ; from which time it had escaped all notice of European navigators, till Captain Furneaux touched at it, in 1773. It is well known that it is the southern part of New Holland, which is by far the largest island in the world ; indeed, so large an island, almost as to deserve the appellation of a continent.

While Captain Cook was at this country, he neglected nothing which could promote the knowledge of science and navigation. **Here,** as everywhere else, he settled the latitude and longitude of places ; marked the variations of the compass, and recorded the nature of the tides. He corrected, likewise, an error of Captain Furneaux, with respect to the situation of Maria's Island ; on which subject he hath candidly remarked, that his own idea is not the result of a more faithful, but merely of a second examination.

Mr. Anderson, during the few days in which the ship remained in the Adventure Bay, exerted his usual diligence in collecting as full an account as could be obtained in so short a period of time.

of the natural productions and the inhabitants of the country. Little can be said concerning either the personal activity or genius of the natives. The first they do not seem to possess in any remarkable degree ; and, to all appearance, they have less of the last, than even the half-animated inhabitants of Terra del Fuego. Their not expressing that surprise which might have been expected from their seeing men so much unlike themselves and things to which they had hitherto been utter strangers ; their indifference for the presents of our people, and their general inattention, were sufficient testimonies that they are not endowed with any acuteness of understanding. What the ancient poets tell us of Fauns and Satyrs living in hollow trees, is realized at Van Dieman's Land. Some wretched constructions of sticks, covered with bark, and which did not deserve the name of huts, were indeed found near the shore : but these seemed only to have been erected for temporary purposes. The most comfortable habitations of the natives were afforded by the largest trees. These had their trunks hollowed out by fire, to the height of six or seven feet ; and there was room enough in them for three or four persons to sit round a hearth, made of clay. At the same time, these places of shelter are durable ; for the people take care to leave one side of the tree sound, which is sufficient to keep it in luxuriant growth. The inhabitants of Van Dieman's Land are undoubtedly from the same stock with those of the northern parts of New Holland. Their language, indeed, appeared to be different ; but how far the difference extended, our voyagers could not have an opportunity of determining. With regard to the New Hollanders in general, there is reason to suppose that they originally came from the same **place** with all the Indians of **the South Sea.**

On the 30th of January, 1777, Captain Cook sailed from Adventure Bay, and on the 12th of February came to anchor at his old station of Queen Charlotte's Sound, in New Zealand. Being unwilling to lose any time, he commenced his operations that very afternoon. By his order, several of the empty water casks were landed, and a place was begun to be cleared for setting up the two observatories, and the erection of tents, to accommodate a guard, and the rest of the company, whose business might require them to remain on shore. Our navigators had not long been at anchor, before a number of canoes, filled with natives, came alongside of the ships. However, very few of them would venture on board; which appeared the more extraordinary, as the captain was well known to them all, and they could not be insensible how liberally he had behaved to them on former occasions. There was one man in particular, whom he had treated with remarkable kindness, during the whole of his last stay in this place, and yet, neither professions of friendship, nor presents, could prevail upon him to enter the Resolution.

There was a real cause for this shyness on the part of the New Zealanders. A dreadful event had happened to some of Captain Furneaux's crew, while he lay in Queen Charlotte's Sound, after he had finally separated from Captain Cook, in the former voyage. Ten men, who had been sent out in the large cutter to gather wild greens, for the ship's company, were killed in a skirmish with the natives. What was the cause of the quarrel could not be ascertained, as not one of the company survived to relate the story. Lieutenant Burney, who was ordered to go in search of them, found only some fragments of their bodies; from which it appeared, that they had been converted into the food of the inhabitants. It was the remembrance of this event, and the fear of its being revenged, which now rendered the New Zealanders so fearful of entering the English vessels. From the conversation of Omai, who was on board the Adventure when the melancholy affair happened, they knew that it could not be unknown to Captain Cook. The captain, therefore, judged it necessary to use every endeavour to assure them of the continuance of his friendship, and that he should not disturb them on account of the catastrophe. It was most probably in consequence of this assurance, that they soon laid aside all manner of restraint and distrust.

In the meanwhile, the operations for refitting the ships, and for obtaining provisions, were carried on with great vigour. For the protection of the party on shore, our commander appointed a guard of ten marines, and ordered arms for all the workmen, with whom Mr. King, and two or three petty officers, constantly remained. A boat was never sent to a considerable distance without being armed, or without being under the direction of such officers as might be depended upon, and who were well acquainted with the natives. In Captain Cook's former visits to this country, he had never made use of such precautions; nor was he now convinced of their absolute necessity. But after the tragical fate of the crew of the Adventure's boat in this sound, and of Captain Marion du Fresne, and some of his people in **the** Bay of Islands (in 1772), it was impossible to free our navigators from all apprehensions of experiencing a similar calamity.

Whatever suspicions the inhabitants might at first entertain, that their acts of barbarity would be revenged, they very speedily became so perfectly easy upon the subject, as to take up their residence close to our voyagers: and the advantage of their coming to live with the English was not inconsiderable. Every day, when the weather would permit, some of them went out to catch fish, and our people generally obtained, by exchanges, a good share of the produce of their labours, in addition to **the** supply which was afforded by our own nets and lines. **Nor was** there a deficiency of vegetable refreshments; to which was **united** spruce-beer for drink; so that if the seeds of the scurvy had been contracted by any of the crew, they would speedily have been removed by such a regimen. The fact, however, was, that there were only two invalids upon the sick lists in both ships.

Curiosities, fish, and women, were the articles of commerce supplied by the New Zealanders. The two first always came to a good market; but the latter did not happen, at this time, to be an acceptable commodity. Our seamen had conceived a dislike to these people, and were either unwilling or afraid to associate with them; the good effect of which was, that our commander knew no instance of a man's quitting his station, to go to the habitations of the Indians. A connexion with women it was out of Captain Cook's power to prevent; but he never encouraged it, and always was fearful of its consequences. Many, indeed, are of opinion, that such an intercourse is a great security among savages. But if this should ever be the case with those who remain and settle among them, it is generally otherwise with respect to travellers and transient visitors. In such a situation as was that of our navigators, a connexion with the women of the natives, betrays more men than it saves. "What else," says the captain, "can reasonably be expected, since all their views are selfish, without the least mixture of regard or attachment? My own experience, at least, which hath been pretty extensive, hath not pointed out to me one instance to the contrary."

Amongst the persons who occasionally visited the English, was a chief of the name of Kahoora, who, as the captain was informed, had headed the party that cut off Captain Furneaux's people, and had himself killed Mr. Rowe, the officer who commanded. This man our commander was strongly solicited to put to death, even by some of the natives; and Omai was perfectly eager and violent upon the subject. To these solicitations the captain paid not the least degree of attention. He even admired Kahoora's courage, and was not a little pleased with the confidence with which he had put himself into his power. Kahoora had placed his whole safety in the declarations that Captain Cook had uniformly made to the New Zealanders; which were, that he had always been a friend to them all, and would continue to be so, unless they gave him cause to act otherwise; that as to their inhuman treatment of our people, he should think no more of it, the transaction having happened long ago, and when he was not **present**; but that, if ever they made a second attempt of the same kind, they might rest assured of feeling the weight of his resentment.

While our commander, on the 16th, was making an excursion for the purpose of collecting food for his cattle, he embraced the opportunity to inquire, as accurately as possible, into the circumstances which had attended the melancholy fate of our countrymen. Omai was his interpreter on this occasion. The result of the inquiry was, that the quarrel first took its rise from some thefts, in the commission of which the natives were detected; that there was no premeditated plan of bloodshed; and that if these thefts had not, unfortunately, been too hastily resented, no mischief would have happened. Kahoora's greatest enemies, and even the very men that had most earnestly solicited his destruction, confessed, at the same time, that he had no intention of quarrelling with Captain Furneaux's people, and much less of killing any of them, till the fray had actually commenced

Captain Cook continued, in this his last visit to New Zealand, the solicitude he had formerly shown to be of some essential future service to the country. To one chief he gave two goats, a male and a female, with a kid; and to another two pigs, a boar and a sow. Although he obtained a promise from both these chiefs, that they would not kill the animals which had been presented to them, he **could** not venture to place any great reliance upon their assurances. It was his **full** intention, on his present arrival in Queen Charlotte's Sound, to have left not only goats and hogs, but sheep, together with a young bull and two heifers. The accomplishment, however, of this resolution depended either upon his finding a chief, who was powerful enough to protect and keep the cattle, or upon his meeting with a place where there might be a probability of their being concealed from those who would ignorantly attempt to destroy them. Neither of these circumstances happened to be conformable to his wishes. At different times he had left in New Zealand ten or a dozen hogs, besides those which had been put on shore by Captain Furneaux. It will, therefore, be a little extraordinary, if this race of animals should not increase and be preserved, either in a wild or domestic state, or in both. Our commander was informed that Tiratou, a popular chief among the natives, had a number of cocks and hens, and one sow, in his separate possession. With regard to the gardens which had formerly been planted, though they had almost entirely been neglected, and some of them destroyed, they were not wholly unproductive. They were found to contain cabbages, onions, leeks, purslain, radishes, mustard, and a few potatoes. The potatoes, which had first been brought from the Cape of Good Hope, were greatly meliorated by change of soil; and, with proper cultivation, would be superior to those produced in most other countries.

A great addition of knowledge was obtained, during this voyage, with respect to the productions of New Zealand, and the manners and customs of its inhabitants. The zeal of Captain Cook upon the subject was admirably seconded by the sedulous diligence of Mr. Anderson, who omitted no opportunity of collecting every kind and degree of information. I shall only so far trespass on the patience of my readers, as to mention a few circumstances tending to delineate the character of the natives. They seemed to be a people perfectly satisfied with the little they already possess; **nor** are they remarkably curious either in their observations **or their** inquiries. New objects are so far from striking them with such **a** degree of surprise as might naturally be expected, that **they** scarcely fix their attention even for a moment. In the **arts** with which they are acquainted, they show as much ingenuity, both in invention and execution, as any uncivilized nations under similar circumstances. Without the least use of those tools which are formed of metal, they make everything that is necessary to procure their subsistence, clothing, and military weapons; and all this is done by them with a neatness, a strength, and a convenience, that are well adapted to the accomplishment of the several purposes they have in view. No people can have a quicker sense of an injury done to them than the New Zealanders, or be more ready to resent it; and yet they want one characteristic of true bravery; for they will take an opportunity of being insolent, when they think there is no danger of their being punished. From the number of their weapons, and their dexterity in using them, it appears, that war is their principal profession. Indeed, their public contentions are so frequent, or rather so perpetual, that they must live under continual apprehensions of being destroyed by each other. From their horrid custom of eating the flesh of their enemies, **not only** without reluctance but with peculiar satisfaction, it would be natural to suppose that they must be destitute of every human feeling, even with regard to their own party. This, however, is not the case; for they lament the loss of their friends with a violence of expression which argues the most tender remembrance of them. At a very early age the children are initiated into all the practices, whether good or bad, of their fathers; so that a boy or girl, when only nine or ten years old, can perform the motions, and imitate the frightful gestures, by which the more aged are accustomed to inspire their enemies with terror. They can keep likewise the strictest time in their song; and it is with some degree of melody that they sing the traditions of their forefathers, their actions in war, and other subjects. The military achievements of their ancestors, the New Zealanders celebrate with the highest pleasure, and spend much of their time in diversions of this sort, and in playing upon a musical instrument.

which partakes of the nature of a flute. With respect to their language, it is far from being harsh or disagreeable, though the pronunciation of it is frequently guttural; nor, if we may judge from the melody of some kinds of their songs, is it destitute of those qualities, which fit it to be associated with music. Of its identity with the languages of the other islands, throughout the South Sea, fresh proofs were exhibited during the present voyage.

At the request of Omai, Captain Cook consented to take with him two youths from New Zealand. That they might not quit their native country under any deluding ideas of visiting it again, the captain took care to inform their parents, in the strongest terms, that they would never return. This declaration seemed, however, to make no kind of impression. The father of the youngest lad resigned him with an indifference, which he would scarcely have shown at parting with his dog, and even stripped the boy of the little clothing he possessed, delivering him quite naked into the hands of our voyagers. This was not the case with the mother of the other youth. She took her leave of him with all the marks of tender affection, that might be expected between a parent and a child on such an occasion; but she soon resumed her cheerfulness, and went away wholly unconcerned.

On the 25th of the month, Captain Cook stood out of Queen Charlotte's Sound, and by the 27th got clear of New Zealand. No sooner had the ships lost sight of the land, than the two young adventurers from that country, one of whom was nearly eighteen years of age, and the other about ten, began deeply to repent of the step they had taken. It was the experience of the sea-sickness which gave this turn to their reflections; and all the soothing encouragement the English could think of, was but of little avail. They wept, both in public and in private, and made their lamentation in a kind of song, that seemed to be expressive of the praises of their country and people, from which they were to be separated forever. In this disposition they continued for many days; but as their sea-sickness wore off, and the tumult of their minds subsided, the fits of the lamentation became less and less frequent, and at length entirely ceased. By degrees, their native country and their friends were forgotten, and they appeared to be as firmly attached to our navigators, as if they had been born in England.

In the prosecution of the voyage, Captain Cook met with unfavourable winds; and it was not till the 29th of March that land was discovered. It was found to be an inhabited island, the name of which, as was learned from two of the natives, who came off in a canoe, is Mangeea. Our commander examined the coast with his boats, and had a short intercourse with some of the inhabitants. Not being able to find a proper harbour for bringing the ships to an anchorage, he was obliged to leave the country unvisited, though it seemed capable of supplying all the wants of our voyagers. The island of Mangeea is full five leagues in circuit, and of a moderate and pretty equal height. It has upon the whole, a pleasing aspect, and might be made a beautiful spot by cultivation. The inhabitants, who appeared to be both numerous and well fed, seemed to resemble those of Otaheite and the Marquesas in the beauty of their persons; and the resemblance, as far as could be judged in so short a compass of time, takes place with respect to their general disposition and character.

From the coast of Mangeea our commander sailed in the afternoon of the 30th, and on the next day land was again seen, within four leagues of which the ships arrived on the 1st of April. Our people could then pronounce it to be an island, nearly of the same appearance and extent with that which had so lately been left. Some of the natives speedily put off in their canoes, and three of them were persuaded to come on board the Resolution; on which occasion, their whole behaviour marked that they were quite at their ease, and felt no kind of apprehension that they should be detained, or ill used. In a visit from several others of the inhabitants, they manifested a dread of approaching near the cows and horses; nor could they form the least conception of their nature. But the sheep and goats did not, in their opinion, surpass the limits of their ideas; for they gave our navigators to understand that they knew them to be birds. As there is not the most distant resemblance between a sheep or a goat, and any winged animal, this may be thought to be almost an incredible example of human ignorance. But it should be remembered, that, excepting hogs, dogs, and birds, these people were strangers to the existence of any other land animal.

In a farther intercourse with the natives, who had brought a hog, together with some plantains and cocoa-nuts, they demanded a dog from our voyagers, and refused everything besides which was offered in exchange. One of the gentlemen on board happened to have a dog and a bitch which were great nuisances in the ship; and these he might now have disposed of in a manner that would have been of real future utility to the island. But he had no such views in making them the companions of his voyage. Omai, however, with a good nature that reflects honour upon him, parted with a favourite dog which he had brought from England; and with this acquisition the people departed highly satisfied.

On the 3d of April, Captain Cook despatched Mr. Gore, with three boats, to endeavour to get upon the island. Mr. Gore himself, Omai, Mr. Anderson, and Mr. Burney, were the only persons that landed. The transactions of the day, of which Mr. Anderson drew up an ingenious and entertaining account, added to the stock of knowledge gained by our navigators, but did not accomplish Captain Cook's principal object. Nothing was procured by the gentlemen, from the island, that supplied the wants of the ships. In this expedition, Omai displayed that turn for exaggeration, with which travellers have so frequently been charged. Being asked by the natives concerning the English, their ships, their country, and the arms they made use of, his answers were not a little marvellous. He told these people, that our country had ships as large as their island; on board which were instruments of war (describing our guns) of such dimensions, that several persons might sit within them. At the same time, he assured the inhabitants, that one of these guns was sufficient to crush their whole island at a single shot. Though he was obliged to acknowledge that the guns on board the vessels upon their coast were but small, he contrived by an explosion of gunpowder, to inspire them with a formidable idea of their nature and effect. It is probable, that this representation of things contributed to the preservation of the gentlemen, in their enterprise on shore; for a strong disposition to retain them had been shown by the natives.

It seemed destined that this day should give Omai more occasions than one of bearing a principal part in its transactions. The island, though never visited by Europeans before, happened to have other strangers residing in it; and it was entirely owing to Omai's having attended on the expedition, that a circumstance so curious came to the knowledge of the English. Scarcely had he been landed upon the beach, when he found, among the crowd which had assembled there, three of his own countrymen, natives of the Society Islands. That, at the distance of about two hundred leagues from those islands, an immense unknown ocean intervening, with the wretched boats their inhabitants are known to make use of, and fit only for a passage where sight of land is hardly ever lost, such a meeting, at such a place, so accidentally visited, should occur, may be well regarded as one of those unexpected situations with which the writers of feigned adventures love to surprise their readers. When events of this kind really happen in common life, they deserve to be recorded for their singularity. It may easily be supposed with what mutual surprise and satisfaction this interview of Omai with his countrymen was attended. Twelve years before, about twenty persons in number, of both sexes, had embarked on board a canoe at Otaheite, to cross over to the neighbouring island of Ulieta. A violent storm having arisen, which drove them out of their course, and their provisions being very scanty, they suffered incredible hardships, and the greatest part of them perished by famine and fatigue. Four men only survived when the boat overset, and then the destruction of this small remnant appeared to be inevitable. However, they kept hanging by the side of the vessel, which they continued to do for some days, when they were providentially brought within sight of the people of this island, who immediately sent out canoes, and brought them on shore. The three men, who now survived, expressed a strong sense of the kind treatment they had received; and so well satisfied were they with their present situation, that they refused an offer which was made them of being conveyed to their native country. A very important instruction may be derived from the preceding narrative. It will serve to explain, better, than a thousand conjectures of speculative reasoners, how the detached parts of the earth, and in particular, how the islands of the South Sea, though lying remote from any inhabited continent, or from each other, may have originally been peopled. Similar adventures have occurred in the history of navigation and shipwrecks.

The island on which Mr. Gore, Mr. Anderson, Mr. Burney, and Omai, had landed, is called Wateeoo by the natives, and is a beautiful spot, having a surface composed of hills and plains which are covered with a verdure rendered extremely pleasant by the diversity of its hues. Its inhabitants are very numerous; and many of the young men were perfect models in shape, besides which, they had complexions as delicate as those of the women, and appeared to be equally amiable in their dispositions. In their manners, their general habits of life, and their religious ceremonies and opinions, these islanders have a near resemblance to the people of Otaheite, and its neighbouring isles; and their language was well understood, both by Omai and the two New Zealanders.

The next place visited by Captain Cook was a small island, called Wennooaette, or Otakootaia, to which Mr. Gore was sent, at the head of a party who procured about a hundred cocoa-nuts for each ship, and some grass, together with a quantity of the leaves and branches of young trees, for the cattle. Though at this time, no inhabitants were found in Wennooaette, yet, as there remained indubitable marks of its being, at least, occasionally frequented, Mr. Gore left a hatchet, and several nails, to the full value of what had been taken away.

On the 5th, our commander directed his course for Harvey's Island, which was only at the distance of fifteen leagues, and where he hoped to procure some refreshments. This island had been discovered by him, in 1773, during his last voyage, when no traces were discerned of its having any inhabitants. It was now experienced to be well peopled, and by a race of men who appeared to differ much, both in person and disposition, from the natives of Wateeoo. Their behaviour was disorderly and clamorous: their colour was of a deeper cast; and several of them had a fierce and rugged aspect. It was remarkable, that not one of them had adopted the practice, so generally prevalent among the people of the Southern Ocean, of puncturing or *tatooing* their bodies. But, notwithstanding this singularity, the most unequivocal proofs were exhibited of their having the same common origin; and their language, in particular, approached still nearer to the dialect of Otaheite, than that of Wateeoo, or Maugeea. No anchorage for the ships being found in Harvey's Island, Captain Cook quitted it without delay.

The captain being thus disappointed at all the islands he had met with, since his leaving New Zealand, and his progress having unavoidably been retarded by unfavourable winds, and other unforeseen circumstances, it became impossible to think of doing anything this year in the high latitudes of the northern hemisphere, from which he was still at so great a distance, though the season for his operations there was already begun. In this situation, it was absolutely necessary, in the first place, to pursue such measures as were most likely to preserve the cattle that were on board. A still more capital object was to save the stores and provisions of the ships, that he might the better be enabled to prosecute his discoveries to the north, which could not now be commenced till a year later than was originally intended. If he had been so fortunate as to have procured a supply of water, and of grass, at any of the islands he had lately visited, it was his purpose to have stood back to the south, till he had met with a westerly wind. But the certain consequence of doing this, without such a supply, would have been the loss of all the cattle; while, at the same time, not a single advantage would have been gained, with regard to the grand ends of the voyage. He determined, therefore, to bear away for the Friendly Islands, where he was sure of being abundantly provided.

In pursuing his course, agreeably to this resolution, our commander, on the 14th, reached Palmerston Island, where, and at a neighbouring islet, both of which were uninhabited, some little relief was obtained. The boats soon procured a load of scurvy-grass and young cocoa-nut trees, which was a feast for the cattle; and the same feast with the addition of palm cabbage, and the tender branches of the *wharra* tree, was continued for several days. On the 16th, Omai, being on shore with the captain, caught, with a scoop-net, in a very short time, as much fish as served the whole party for dinner, besides sending a quantity to both the ships. Birds, too, and particularly men-of-war and tropic birds, were plentifully obtained; so that our navigators had sumptuous entertainment. Omai acted as cook upon the occasion. The fish and the birds he dressed with heated stones, after the manner of his country; and performed the operation with a dexterity and good humour which were greatly to his credit. From the islet before mentioned, twelve hundred cocoanuts were procured, which being equally divided among the crew, were of great use to them, both on account of the juice and the kernel. There is no water in the islets which are comprehended under the name of Palmerston's Island. If that article could be obtained, and good anchorage could be accomplished within the reef, Captain Cook would prefer this island to any of the uninhabited ones, for the mere purpose of refreshment. The quantity of fish that might be caught would be sufficient; and a ship's company could roam about unmolested by the petulance of the inhabitants.

Different opinions have been entertained concerning the formation of the low islands in the great ocean. From the observations which our commander now made, he was convinced, that such islands are formed from shoals, or coral banks, and, consequently, that they are always increasing.

After leaving Palmerston's Island, Captain Cook steered to the west, with a view of making the best of his way to Annamooka. During his course, the showers were so copious, that our navigators saved a considerable quantity of water. Finding that a greater supply could be obtained by the rain in one hour, than could be gotten by distillation in a month, the captain laid aside the still as a thing which was attended with more trouble than profit. At this time, the united heat and moisture of the weather, in addition to the impossibility of keeping the ships dry, threatened to be noxious to the health of our people. It was, however, remarkable, that neither the constant use of salt food, nor the vicissitudes of climate, were productive of any evil effects. Though the only material refreshment our voyagers had received, since their leaving the Cape of Good Hope, was that which they had procured at New Zealand, there was not, as yet, a single sick person on board. This happy situation of things was undoubtedly owing to the unremitting attention of our commander, in seeing that no circumstance was neglected, which could contribute to the preservation of the health of his company.

On the 28th of April, Captain Cook touched at the Island of Komango; and, on the 1st of May, he arrived at Annamooka. The station he took was the very same which he had occupied when he visited the country three years before; and it was probably almost in the same place where Tasman, the first discoverer of this and some of the neighbouring islands, anchored in 1643. A friendly intercourse was immediately opened with the natives, and everything was settled to the captain's satisfaction. He received the greatest civilities from Toobou, the chief of Annamooka; and Taipa, a chief from the island of Komango, attached himself to the English in so extraordinary a manner, that, in order to be near them in the night, as well as in the day, he had a house brought on men's shoulders, a full quarter of a mile, and placed close to the shed, which was occupied by our party on shore. On the 6th, our commander was visited by a great chief from Tongataboo, whose name was Feenou, and who was falsely represented, by Taipa, to be the king of all the Friendly Isles. The only interruption to the harmony which subsisted between our people and the natives of Annamooka arose from the thievish disposition of many of the inhabitants. They afforded frequent opportunities of remarking how expert they were in the business of stealing. Even some of the chiefs did not think the profession unbecoming their dignity. One of them was detected in carrying a bolt out of the ship, concealed under his clothes; for which Captain Cook sentenced him to receive a dozen lashes, and kept him confined till he had paid a hog for his liberty. After this act of justice, our navigators were no longer troubled with thieves of rank: but their servants, or slaves, were still employed in the dirty work; and upon them a flogging seemed to make no greater impression, than it would have done upon the mainmast. When any of them happened to be caught in the act, so far were their masters from interceding in their favour, that they often advised our gentlemen to kill them. This, however, being a punishment too severe to be inflicted, they generally escaped without being punished at all; for of the shame, as well as of the pain of corporal chastisement, they appeared to be equally insensible. At length, Captain Clerke invented a mode of treatment, which was thought to be productive of some good effect. He put the thieves into the hands of the barber, and completely shaved their heads. In consequence of this operation, they became objects of ridicule to their own countrymen; and our people, by keeping them at a distance, were enabled to deprive them of future opportunities for a repetition of their rogueries.

The island of Annamooka being exhausted of its articles of food, Captain Cook proposed, on the 11th, to proceed directly for Tongataboo. From this resolution, however, he was diverted at the instance of Feenou, who warmly recommended, in preference to it, an island, or rather group of islands, called Hapaee, lying on the northeast. There, he assured our voyagers, they could be plentifully supplied with every refreshment, in the easiest manner; and he enforced his advice by engaging to attend them thither in person. Accordingly, Hapaee was made choice of for the next station; and the examination of it became an object with the captain, as it had never been visited by any European ships.

On the 17th, our commander arrived at Hapaee, where he met with a most friendly reception from the inhabitants, and from

Earoupa, the chief of the island. During the whole stay of our navigators, the time was spent in a reciprocation of presents, civilities, and solemnities. On the part of the natives were displayed single combats with clubs, wrestling and boxing-matches, female combatants, dances performed by men, and night entertainments of singing and dancing. The English, on the other hand, gave pleasure to the Indians by exercising the mariners, and, excited their astonishment by the exhibition of fire-works. After curiosity had, on both sides, been sufficiently gratified, Captain Cook applied himself to the examination of Hapaee, Leefooga, and other neighbouring islands. As the ships were returning, on the 31st, from these islands to Annamooka, the Resolution was very near running full upon a low sandy isle, called Pootoo Pootooa, surrounded with breakers. It fortunately happened, that the men had just been ordered upon deck to put the vessels about, and were most of them at **their** stations ; so that the necessary movements were executed not only with judgment but also with alertness. This alone saved the ship and her company from destruction. "Such hazardous situations," says the captain, " are the unavoidable companions of the man who goes upon a voyage of discovery."

During our commander's expedition to Hapaee, he was introduced to Poulaho, the real king of the Friendly Isles ; in whose presence it instantly appeared how groundless had been Feenou's pretensions to that character. Feenou, however, was a chief of great note and influence. By Poulaho Captain Cook was invited to pass over to Tongataboo, which request he complied with after he had touched two or three days at Annamooka. In the passage the Resolution was insensibly drawn upon a large flat, on which lay innumerable coral rocks of different depths below the surface of the water. Notwithstanding all the care and attention of our people to keep her clear of them, they could not prevent her from striking on one of these rocks. The same event happened to the Discovery; but fortunately neither of the ships stuck fast, or received any damage.

On the 10th of June, Captain Cook arrived at Tongataboo, where the king was waiting for him upon the beach, and immediately conducted him to a small but neat house, which he was told, was at his service, during his stay upon the island. The house was situated a little within the skirts of the woods, and had a fine large area before it; so that a more agreeable spot could not have been provided. Our commander's arrival at Tongataboo was followed by a succession of entertainments, similar to those which had occurred at Hapaee, though somewhat diversified in circumstances, and exhibited with additional splendour. The pleasure, however, of the visit was occasionally interrupted by the thieveries of many of the inhabitants. Nothing could prevent their plundering our voyagers, in every quarter; and they did it in the most daring and insolent manner. There was scarcely anything which they did not attempt to steal; and yet, as the crowd was always great, the captain would not permit the sentinels to fire, lest the innocent should suffer with the guilty.

Captain Cook, on the 19th, made a distribution of the animals which he had selected as presents for the principal men of the island. To Poulaho, the king, he gave a young English bull and cow, together with three goats; to Marewagee, a chief of consequence, a Cape ram and two ewes; and to Feenou, a horse and a mare. He likewise left in the island a young boar and three young sows, of the English breed; and two rabbits, a buck and a doe. Omai, at the same time was instructed to represent the importance of these animals, and to explain as far as he was capable of doing it, the manner in which they should be preserved and treated. Even the generosity of the captain was not without its inconveniences. It soon appeared that some were dissatisfied with the allotment of the animals; for next morning, two kids and two turkey-cocks were missing. As our commander could not supppose that this was an accidental loss, he determined to have them again. The first step he took was to seize on three canoes that happened to be alongside the ships; after which, he went on shore, and having found the king, his brother Feenou, and some other chiefs, he immediately put a guard over them, and gave them to understand, that they must remain under restraint, till not only the kid and the turkeys, but the rest of the things which at different times had been stolen from our voyagers, should be restored. This bold step of Captain Cook was attended with a very good effect. Some of the articles which had been lost were instantly brought back, and such good assurances were given with regard to the remainder, that, in the afternoon, the chiefs were released. It was a happy circumstance, with respect to the transaction, that it did not abate the future confidence of Poulaho and his friends in the captain's kind and generous treatment.

On the 5th of July was an eclipse of the sun, which, however, in consequence of unfavourable weather, was very imperfectly observed. Happily, the disappointment was of little consequence, as the longitude was more than sufficiently determined by lunar observations.

Captain Cook sailed from Tongataboo on the 10th, and, two days after, came to anchor at the island of Middleburgh, or Eooa, as it is called by the inhabitants. Here he was immediately visited by Taoofa, the chief with whom he had formerly been acquainted. The intercourse now renewed was friendly in the highest degree, both with Taoofa and the rest of the natives; and our commander endeavoured to meliorate their condition by planting a pine-apple and sowing the seeds of melons, and other vegetables, in the chief's plantation. To this he was encouraged by a proof that his last endeavours had not been wholly unsuccessful. He had, one day, served up to him at his dinner, a dish of turnips, being the produce of the seeds which he had left at Eooa in his last voyage.

The stay which Captain Cook made at the Friendly Islands was between two and three months; during which time, some accidental difference excepted, there subsisted the utmost cordiality between the English and the natives. These differences were never attended with any fatal consequences; which happy circumstance was principally owing to the unremitting attention of the captain, who directed all his measures with a view to the prevention of such quarrels as would be injurious either to the inhabitants or to his own people. So long as our navigators staid at the islands, they expended very little of their sea provisions, subsisting, in general, upon the produce of the country, and carrying away with them a quantity of refreshments, sufficient to last till their arrival at another station, where they could depend upon a fresh supply. It was a singular pleasure to our commander, that he possessed an opportunity of adding to the happiness of these good Indians, by the useful animals which he left among them. Upon the whole, the advantages of having touched at the Friendly Islands were very great; and Captain Cook reflected upon it with peculiar satisfaction, that these advantages were obtained without retarding, for a single moment, the prosecution of the great object of his voyage; the season for proceeding to the north having been previously lost.

Besides the immediate benefits which both the natives and the English derived from their mutual intercourse on the present occasion, such a large addition was now made to the geographical knowledge of this part of the Pacific Ocean, as may render no small service to future navigators. Under the denomination of the Friendly Islands, must be included not only the group at Hapaee, but all those islands that have been discovered nearly under the same meridian, to the north, as well as some others, which though they have never hitherto been seen by any European voyagers, are under the dominion of Tongataboo. From the information which our commander received, it appears, that this Archipelago is very extensive. Above one hundred and fifty islands were reckoned by the natives, who made use of bits of leaves to ascertain their number; and Mr. Anderson, with his usual diligence procured all their names. Fifteen of them are said to be high or hilly, and thirty-five of them large. Concerning the size of the thirty-two which were unexplored, it can only be mentioned, that they must be larger than Annamooka, which was ranked among the smaller isles. Several, indeed, of those which belong to this latter denomination, are mere spots, without inhabitants. Captain Cook had not the least doubt but that Prince William's Island, discovered and so named by Tasman, was comprehended in the list furnished by the natives. He had also good authority for believing that Keppel's and Boscawen's Islands, two of Captain Wallis's discoveries in 1765, were included in the same list; and that they were under the sovereignty of Tangataboo, which is the grand seat of government. It must be left to future navigators to extend the geography of this part of the South Pacific Ocean, by ascertaining the extent situation and size of nearly a hundred islands in the neighbourhood, which our commander had no opportunity of exploring.

During the present visit to the Friendly Islands, large additions were made to the knowledge which was obtained in the last voyage, of the natural history and productions of the country, and the manners and customs of its inhabitants. Though it does not fall within the plan of this narrative to enter into a detail of the particulars recorded, I cannot help taking notice of the explanation which Captain Cook has given of the thievish disposition of the natives. It is an explanation which reflects honour upon his sagacity, humanity, and candour; and therefore I shall relate it in his own words: "The only defect," says he, "sullying their character, that we know of, is a propensity to thieving;

to which we found those of all ages, and both sexes, addicted, to an uncommon degree. It should, however, be considered, that this exceptionable part of their conduct seems to exist merely with respect to us; for, in their general intercourse with one another, I had reason to be of opinion, that thefts do not happen more frequently (perhaps less so) than in other countries, the dishonest practices of whose worthless individuals are not supposed to authorise any indiscriminate censure on the whole body of the people. Great allowances should be made for the foibles of these poor natives of the Pacific Ocean, whose minds we overpowered with the glare of objects, equally new to them as they were captivating. Stealing, among civilized nations of the world, may well be considered as denoting a character deeply stained with moral turpitude; with avarice, unrestrained by the known rules of right; and with profligacy, producing extreme indigence, and neglecting the means of relieving it. But at the Friendly and other islands which we visited, the thefts so frequently committed by the natives, of what we had brought along with us, may be fairly traced to less culpable motives. They seemed to arise solely from an intense curiosity or desire to possess something which they had not been accustomed to before, and belonging to a sort of people so different from themselves. And perhaps, if it were possible, that a set of beings, seemingly as superior in our judgment as we are in theirs, should appear among us, it might be doubted, whether our natural regard to justice would be able to restrain many from falling into the same error. That I have assigned the true motive for their propensity to this practice, appears from their stealing everything indiscriminately at first sight, before they could have the least conception of converting their prize to any one useful purpose. But I believe, with us, no person would forfeit his reputation, or expose himself to punishment, without knowing, beforehand, how to employ the stolen goods. Upon the whole, the pilfering disposition of these islanders, though certainly disagreeable and troublesome to strangers, was the means of affording us some information as to the quickness of their intellects.

With respect to the religion of these Indians, Mr. Anderson maintains, that they have very proper sentiments concerning the immateriality and immortality of the soul; and thinks himself sufficiently authorised to assert, that they do not worship anything which is the work of their own hands, or any visible part of the creation. The language of the Friendly Islands has the greatest imaginable conformity with that of New Zealand, of Wateeoo, and Mangeea. Several hundred of the words of it were collected by Mr. Anderson; and amongst these are terms that express numbers reaching to a hundred thousand. Beyond this limit they never went, and probably were not able to go farther; for it was observed, that when they had gotten thus far, they commonly used a word which expresses an indefinite number.

On the 17th of July, our commander took his final leave of the Friendly Islands, and resumed his voyage. An eclipse was observed in the night between the 20th and 21st; and on the 8th of August land was discovered. Some of the inhabitants who came off in canoes seemed earnestly to invite our people to go on shore; but Captain Cook did not think proper to run the risk of losing the advantage of a fair wind, for the sake of examining an island, which appeared to be of little consequence. Its name, as was learned from the natives, who spoke the Otaheite language, is Toobouai.

Pursuing his course, the captain reached Otaheite on the 12th, and steered for Oheitepha Bay, with an intention to anchor there, in order to draw what refreshments he could from the southeast part of the island, before he went down to Matavia. Omai's first reception among his countrymen was not entirely of a flattering nature. Though several persons came on board who knew him, and one of them was his brother-in-law, there was nothing remarkably tender or striking in their meeting. An interview which Omai had, on the 13th, with his sister, was agreeable to the feelings of nature; for their meeting was marked with expressions of tender affection, more easy to be conceived than described. In a visit, likewise, which he received from an aunt, the old lady threw herself at his feet, and plentifully bedewed them with tears of joy.

Captain Cook was informed by the natives, that, since he was last at the island, in 1774, two ships had been twice in the Oheitepha Bay, and had left animals in the country. These, on further inquiry, were found to be hogs, dogs, goats, one bull, and a ram. That the vessels which had visited Otaheite were Spanish, was plain from an inscription that was cut upon a wooden cross, standing at some distance from the front of a house which had been occupied by the strangers. On the transverse part of the cross was inscribed,

CHRISTUS VINCIT.

And on the perpendicular part,

CAROLUS III. IMPERAT. 1774.

Our commander took this occasion to preserve the memory of the prior visits of the English, by inscribing, on the other side of the post,

GEORGIUS TERTIUS, REX,
ANNIS 1767,
1769, 1773, 1774, & 1777.

Whatever might be the intentions of the Spaniards in their visit to the island, it ought to be remembered to their honour, that they behaved so well to the inhabitants, as always to be spoken of in the strongest expressions, of esteem and veneration.

Captain Cook had at this time an important affair to settle. As he knew that he could now be furnished with a plentiful supply of cocoa-nuts, the liquor of which is an excellent and wholesome beverage, he was desirous of prevailing upon his people to consent to their being abridged, during their stay at Otaheite and the neighbouring islands, of their stated allowance of spirits to mix with water. But as this stoppage of a favourite article, without assigning some reason for it, might occasion a general murmur, he thought it most prudent to assemble the ship's company, and to make known to them the design of the voyage, and the extent of future operations. To animate them in undertaking with cheerfulness and perseverance what lay before them, he took notice of the rewards offered by parliament, to such of his majesty's subjects as should first discover a communication between the Atlantic and Pacific Oceans, in any direction whatever, in the northern hemisphere; and also such as should first penetrate beyond the eighty-ninth degree of northern latitude. The captain made no doubt, he told them, that he should find them willing to coöperate with him in attempting, as far as might be possible, to become entitled to one or both of these rewards; but that, to give the best chance of success, it would be necessary to observe the utmost economy in the expenditure of the stores and provisions, particularly the latter, as there was no probability of getting a supply anywhere, after leaving these islands. He strengthened his argument, by reminding them, that, in consequence of the opportunity's having been lost of getting to the north this summer, the voyage must last at least a year longer than had originally been supposed. He entreated them to consider the various obstructions and difficulties they might still meet with, and the aggravated hardships they would endure, if it should be found necessary to put them to short allowance, of any species of provisions, in a cold climate. For these very substantial reasons, he submitted to them, whether it would not be better to be prudent in time, and, rather than to incur the hazard of having no spirits left, when such a cordial would most be wanted, to consent to give up their grog now, when so excellent a liquor as that of cocoa-nuts, could be substituted in its place. In conclusion, our commander left the determination of the matter entirely to their own choice.

This speech, which certainly partook much of the nature of true eloquence, if a discourse admirably calculated for persuasion be entitled to that character, produced its full effect on the generous minds of English seamen. Captain Cook had the satisfaction of finding that his proposal did not remain a single moment under consideration; being unanimously and immediately approved of, without the least objection. By our commander's order, Captain Clerke made the same proposal to his people, to which they likewise agreed. Accordingly, grog was no longer served, excepting on Saturday nights; when the companies of both ships had a full allowance of it, that they might drink the health of their friends in England.

On the 24th Captain Cook quitted the southeast part of Otaheite, and resumed his old station in Matavia Bay. Immediately upon his arrival, he was visited by Otoo, the king of the whole island, and their former friendship was renewed; a friendship which was continued without interruption, and cemented by a perpetual succession of civilities, good offices, and entertainments. One of our commander's first objects was to dispose of all the European animals which were in the ships. Accordingly, he conveyed to Oparee, Otoo's place of residence, a peacock and hen: a turkey cock and hen, one gander and three geese, a drake and four ducks. The geese and ducks began to breed before our navigators left their present station. There were already at Otoo's, several goats, and the Spanish bull; which was one of the finest animals of the kind that was ever seen. To the bull Captain Cook sent the three cows he had on board, together with a bull of his own; to all which were added the horse and mare, and the sheep that had still remained in the vessels.

The captain found himself lightened of a very heavy burthen, in having disposed of these passengers. It is not easy to conceive the trouble and vexation, which had attended the conveyance of this living cargo, through such various hazards, and to so immense a distance. But the satisfaction which our commander felt, in having been so fortunate as to fulfil his majesty's humane designs, in sending such valuable animals, to supply the wants of two worthy nations, afforded him an ample recompense for the many anxious hours he had passed, before this subordinate object of his voyage could be carried into execution.

At this time, a war was on the point of breaking out between the inhabitants of Eimeo and those of Otaheite; and by the latter Captain Cook was requested to take a part in their favour. With this request, however, though enforced by frequent and urgent solicitations, the captain, according to his usual wisdom, refused to comply. He alleged, that as he was not thoroughly acquainted with the dispute, and the people of Eimeo had never offended him, he could not think himself at liberty to engage in hostilities against them. With these reasons Otoo and most of the chiefs appeared to be satisfied; but one of them, Towha, was so highly displeased, that our commander never afterwards recovered his friendship.

Upon the present occasion, Captain Cook had full and undeniable proof, that the offering of human sacrifices forms a part of the religious institutions of Otaheite. Indeed, he was a witness to a solemnity of this kind; the process of which he had particularly described, and has related it with the just sentiments of indignation and abhorrence. The unhappy victim, who was now offered to the object of worship, seemed to be a middle-aged man, and was said to be one of the lowest class of people. But the captain could not learn, after all his inquiries, whether the wretch had been fixed upon on account of his having committed any crime, which was supposed to be deserving of death. It is certain, that a choice is generally made, either of such guilty persons for the sacrifices, or of common low fellows, who stroll about from place to place, without any visible methods of obtaining an honest subsistence. Those who are devoted to suffer, are never apprised of their fate, till the blow is given, that puts an end to their being. Whenever upon any particular emergency, one of the great chiefs considers a human sacrifice to be necessary, he pitches upon the victim, and then orders him to be suddenly fallen upon and killed, either with clubs or stones. Although it should be supposed, that no more than one person is ever devoted to destruction on any single occasion, at Otaheite, it will still be found that these occurrences are so frequent, as to cause a shocking waste of the human race; for our commander counted no less than forty-nine skulls of former victims, lying before the Morai, where he had seen another added to the number. It was apparent, from the freshness of these skulls, that no great length of time had elapsed, since the wretches to whom they belonged had been offered upon the altar of blood.

There is reason to fear that this custom is as extensive as it is horrid. It is highly probable, that it prevails throughout the widely-diffused islands of the Pacific Ocean; and Captain Cook had particular evidence of its subsisting at the Friendly Islands. To what an extent the practice of human sacrifices was carried in the ancient world, is not unknown to the learned. Scarcely any nation was free from it in a certain state of society; and, as religious reformation is one of the last efforts of the human mind, the practice may be continued, even when the manners are otherwise far removed from savage life. It may have been a long time before civilization has made such a progress as to deprive superstition of its cruelty, and to divert it from barbarous rites to ceremonies, which, though foolish enough, are comparatively mild, gentle, and innocent.

On the 5th of September, an accident happened which, though slight in itself, was of some consequence from the situation of things. A young ram of the Cape breed, which had been lambed and brought up with great care on board the ship, was killed by a dog. Desirous as Captain Cook was of propagating so useful a race, among the Society Islands, the loss of a ram was a serious misfortune. It was the only one he had of that breed; and of the English breed a single ram was all that remained.

Captain Cook and Captain Clerke, on the 14th, mounted on horseback, and took a ride round the plain of Matavia to the great surprise of a large number of the natives, who attended upon the occasion, and gazed upon the gentlemen with as much astonishment as if they had been Centaurs. What the two captains had begun was afterwards repeated every day, by one and another of our people; notwithstanding which, the curiosity of the Otaheitans still continued unabated. They were exceedingly delighted with these animals, after they had seen the use which was made of them. Not all the novelties put together, which European visitors had carried amongst the inhabitants, inspired them with so high an idea of the greatness of distant nations.

Though Captain Cook would not take a part in the quarrels between the islands, he was ready to protect his particular friends, when in danger of being injured. Towha, who commanded the expedition against Eimeo, had been obliged to submit to a disgraceful accommodation. Being full of resentment, on account of his not having been properly supported, he was said to have threatened, that as soon as the captain should leave the island, he would join his forces to those of Tiaraboo, and attack Otoo, at Matavia or Oparre. This induced our commander to declare, in the most public manner, that he was determined to espouse the interest of his friend, against any such combination ; and that, whoever presumed to assault him, should feel the weight of his heavy displeasure, when he returned again to Otaheite. Captain Cook's declaration had probably the desired effect ; for, if Towha had formed hostile intentions, no more was heard of the matter.

The manner in which our commander was freed from a rheumatic complaint, that consisted of a pain extending from the hip to the foot, deserves to be recorded. Otoo's mother, his three sisters, and eight other women went on board, for the express purpose of undertaking the cure of his disorder. He accepted of their friendly offer, had a bed spread for them on the cabin-floor, and submitted himself to their directions. Being desired to lay himself down amongst them, then, as many of them as could get round him began to squeeze him with both hands, from head to foot, but more particularly in the part where the pain was lodged, till they made his bones crack, and his flesh become a perfect mummy. After undergoing this discipline about a quarter of an hour, he was glad to be released from the women. The operation, however, gave him immediate relief ; so that he was encouraged to submit to another rubbing down before he went to bed ; the consequence of which was, that he was tolerably easy all the succeeding night. His female physicians repeated their prescription the next morning, and again in the evening ; after which his pains were entirely removed, and the cure was perfected. This operation, which is called *romee*, is universally practised among these islanders ; being sometimes performed by the men, but more generally by the women.

Captain Cook, who now had come to the resolution of departing soon from Otaheite, accompanied, on the 27th, Otoo to Oparre, and examined the cattle and poultry, which he had consigned to his friend's care at that place. Everything was in a promising way, and properly attended. The captain procured from Otoo four goats; two of which he designed to leave at Ulietea, where none had as yet been introduced; and the other two he proposed to reserve for the use of any islands he might chance to meet with in his passage to the north. On the next day, Otoo came on board, and informed our commander that he had gotten a canoe, which he desired him to carry home, as a present to the Earree rahie no Pretane. This, he said, was the only thing he could send which was worthy of his majesty's acceptance. Captain Cook was not a little pleased with Otoo, for this mark of his gratitude; and the more, as the thought was entirely his own. Not one of our people had given him the least hint concerning it; and it showed, that he was fully sensible to whom he stood indebted for the most valuable presents that he had received. As the canoe was too large to be taken on board, the captain could only thank him for his good intentions; but it would have given him a much greater satisfaction, if his present could have been accepted.

During this visit of our voyagers to Otaheite, such a cordial friendship and confidence subsisted between them and the natives, as never once to be interrupted by any untoward accident. Our commander had made the chiefs fully sensible, that it was their interest to treat with him on fair and equitable terms, and to keep their people from plundering or stealing. So great was Otoo's attachment to the English, that he seemed pleased with the idea of their having a permanent settlement at Matavia; not considering, that from that time he would be deprived of his kingdom, and the inhabitants of their liberties. Captain Cook had too much gratitude and regard for these islanders, to wish that such an event should ever take place. Though our occasional visits may, in some respects, have been of advantage to the natives, he was afraid that a durable establishment among them, conducted as most European establishments amongst Indian nations have unfortunately been, would give them just cause to lament that they had been discovered by our navigators. It is not, indeed, likely, that a measure of this kind should at any time seriously be adopted, because it cannot serve either the purposes of public ambition, or private avarice; and, without such inducements, the captain has ventured to pronounce that it will never be undertaken.

From Otaheite our voyagers sailed, on the 30th, to Eimeo, where they came to an anchor on the same day. At this island, the transactions which happened were, for the most part, very unpleasant. A goat, which was stolen, was recovered without any extraordinary difficulty, and one of the thieves was, at the same time, surrendered; being the first instance of the kind that our commander had met with in his connexions with the Society Islands. The stealing of another goat was attended with an uncommon degree of perplexity and trouble. As the recovery of it was a matter of no small importance, Captain Cook was determined to effect this at any rate; and accordingly he made an expedition across the island, in the course of which he set fire to six or eight houses, and burned a number of war canoes. At last, in consequence of a peremptory message to Maheine, the chief of Eimeo, that not a single canoe should be left in the country, or an end be put to the contest, unless the animal in his possession should be restored, the goat was brought back. This quarrel was as much regretted on the part of the captain, as it could be on that of the natives. It grieved him to reflect, that, after refusing the pressing solicitations of his friends at Otaheite to favour their invasion of this island, he should find himself so speedily reduced to the necessity of engaging in hostilities against its inhabitants; and in such hostilities as, perhaps, had been more injurious to them than Towha's expedition.

On the 11th of October, the ships departed from Eimeo, and

the next day arrived at Owharre Harbour, on the west side of Huaheine. The grand business of our commander at this island was the settlement of Omai. In order to obtain the consent of the chiefs of the island, the affair was conducted with great solemnity. Omai dressed himself very properly on the occasion ; brought with him a suitable assortment of presents ; went through a variety of religious ceremonies ; and made a speech, the topics of which had been dictated to him by our commander. The result of the negotiation was, that a spot of ground was assigned him, the extent of which, along the shore of the harbour, was about two hundred yards ; and its depth to the foot of the hill somewhat more. A proportionable part of the hill was included in the grant. This business having been adjusted in a satisfactory manner, the carpenters of both ships were employed in building a small house for Omai, in which he might secure his European commodities. At the same time, some of the English made a garden for his use, in which they planted shaddocks, vines, pine-apples, melons and the seeds of several other vegetable articles. All of these Captain Cook had the satisfaction of seeing in a flourishing state before he left the island.

At Huaheine, Omai found a brother, a sister, and a brother-in-law, by whom he was received with great regard and tenderness. But though these people were faithful and affectionate in their attachment to him, the captain discovered, with concern, that they were of too little consequence in the island to be capable of rendering him any positive service. They had not either authority or influence to protect his person or property ; and in such a situation, there was reason to apprehend that he might be in danger of being stripped of all his possessions as soon as he should cease to be supported by the power of the English. To prevent this evil, if possible, our commander advised him to conciliate the favour and engage the patronage and protection of two or three of the principal chiefs, by a proper distribution of some of his moveables; with which advice he prudently complied. Captain Cook, however did not entirely trust to the operations of gratitude, but had recourse to the more forcible motive of intimidation. With this view, he took every opportunity of signifying to the inhabitants that it was his intention to return to the island again, after being absent the usual time; and that if he did not find Omai in the same state of security in which he left him, all those whom he should then discover to have been his enemies, should feel the weight of his resentment. As the natives had now formed an opinion that their country would be visited by the ships of England at stated periods, there was ground to hope, that this threatening declaration would produce no inconsiderable effect.

When Omai's house was near finished, and many of his moveables were carried ashore, a box of toys excited the admiration of the multitude in a much higher degree than articles of a more useful nature. With regard to his pots, kettles, dishes, plates, drinking-mugs, glasses, and the whole train of domestic accommodation, which in our estimation are so necessary and important, scarcely any one of his countrymen would condescend to look upon them. Omai himself, being sensible that these pieces of English furniture would be of no great consequence in his present situation, wisely sold a number of them, among the people of the ships, for hatchets, and other iron tools which had a more intrinsic value in this part of the world, and would give him a more distinguished superiority over those with whom he was to pass the remainder of his days.

Omai's family, when he settled at Huaheine, consisted of eight or ten persons, if that can be called a family to which a single female did not as yet belong, nor was likely to belong, unless its masters should become less volatile. There was nothing in his present temper which seemed likely to dispose him to look out for a wife; and perhaps it is to be apprehended, that his residence in

England had not contributed to improve his taste for the sober felicity of a domestic union with some woman of his country.

The European weapons of Omai consisted of a musket, bayonet and cartouch-box ; a fowling-piece, two pair of pistols, and two or three swords or cutlasses. With the possession of these warlike implements, he was highly delighted ; and it was only to gratify his eager desire for them that Captain Cook was induced to make him such presents. The captain would otherwise have thought it happier for him to be without fire-arms, or any European weapons, lest an imprudent use of them (and prudence was not his most distinguishing talent) should rather increase his dangers than establish his superiority. Though it was no small satisfaction to our commander to reflect, that he had brought Omai safe back to the very spot from which he had been taken, this satisfaction was, nevertheless, somewhat diminished by the consideration, that his situation might now be less desirable than it was before his connexion with the English. It was to be feared, that the advantages which he had derived from his visit to England would place him in a more hazardous state, with respect to his personal safety.

Whatever faults belonged to Omai's character, they were overbalanced by his good-nature and his gratitude. He had a tolerable share of understanding, but it was not accompanied with application and perseverance ; so that his knowledge of things was very general, and in most instances imperfect : nor was he a man of much observation. He would not, therefore, be able to introduce many of the arts and customs of England among his countrymen, or greatly to improve those to which they have long been habituated. Captain Cook, however, was confident, that he would endeavour to bring to perfection the fruits and vegetables which had been planted in his garden. This of itself would be no small acquisition to the natives. But the greatest benefit which these islands are likely to receive from Omai's travels, will be in the animals that are left upon them; and which, had it not been for his coming to England, they might probably never have obtained. When these multiply, of which Captain Cook thought there was little reason to doubt, Otaheite and the Society Islands will equal, if not exceed, any country in the known world, for plenty of provisions.

Before our commander sailed from Huaheine he had the following inscription cut on the outside of Omai's house:

Georgius Tertius Rex, 2 Novembris, 1777.

Naves { Resolution, Jac. Cook, Pr.
Discovery, Car. Clerke, Pr.

On the same day, Omai took his final leave of our navigators, in doing which, he bade farewell to all the officers in a very affectionate manner. He sustained himself with a manly resolution, till he came to Captain Cook, when his utmost efforts to conceal his tears failed; and he continued to weep all the time that the boat was conveying him to shore. Not again to resume the subject, I shall here mention, that when the captain was at Ulietea a fortnight after this event, Omai sent two men with the satisfactory intelligence, that he remained undisturbed by the people of Huaheine, and that everything succeeded well with him, excepting in the loss of his goat, which had died in kidding. This intelligence was accompanied with a request, that another goat might be given him, together with two axes. Our commander, esteeming himself happy in having an additional opportunity of serving him, despatched the messengers back with the axes and a couple of kids, male and female, which were spared for him out of the Discovery.

The fate of the two youths, who had been brought from New Zealand, must not be forgotten. As they were extremely desirous of continuing with our people, Captain Cook would have carried them to England with him, if there had appeared the most distant probability of their ever being restored to their own country. Tiarooa, the eldest of them, was a very well-disposed young man, with strong natural sense, and a capacity of receiving any instruction. He seemed to be fully convinced of the inferiority of New Zealand to these islands, and resigned himself, though not without some degree of reluctance, to end his days, in ease and plenty, at Huaheine. The other had formed so strong an attachment to our navigators, that it was necessary to take him out of the ship, and carry him ashore by force. This necessity was the more painful, as he was a witty, smart boy; and, on that account, a great favourite on board. Both these youths became a part of Omai's family.

Whilst our voyagers were at Huaheine, the atrocious conduct of one particular thief occasioned so much trouble, that the captain punished him more severely than he had ever done any culprit before. Besides having his head and beard shaved, he ordered both his ears to be cut off, and then dismissed him. It can scarcely be reflected upon without regret, that our commander should have been compelled to such an act of severity.

On the 3rd of November, the ships came to an anchor in the harbour of Ohamaneno, in the island of Ulietea. The observatories being set up on the 6th, and the necessary instruments having been carried on shore, the two following days were employed in making astronomical observations. In the night between the 12th and 13th, John Harrison, a marine, who was sentinel at the observatory, deserted, taking with him his arms and accoutrements. Captain Cook exerted himself on this occasion, with his usual vigour. He went himself in pursuit of the deserter, who, after some evasion on the part of the inhabitants, was surrendered. He was found sitting between two women, with the musket lying before him; and all the defence he was able to make was, that he had been enticed away by the natives. As this account was probably the truth, and as it appeared, besides, that he had remained upon his post till within ten minutes of the time when he was to have been relieved, the punishment which the captain inflicted upon him was not very severe.

Some days after, a still more troublesome affair happened, of the same nature. On the morning of the 24th, the captain was informed that a midshipman and a seaman, both belonging to the Discovery, were missing; and it soon appeared, that they had gone away in a canoe in the preceding evening, and had now reached the other end of the island. As the midshipman was known to have expressed a desire of remaining at these islands, it was evident that he and his companion had gone off with that intention. Though Captain Clerke immediately set out in quest of them with two armed boats and a party of marines, his expedition proved fruitless, the natives having amused him the whole day with false intelligence. The next morning an account was brought that the deserters were at Otaha. As they were not the only persons in the ships who wished to spend their days at these favourite islands, it became necessary, for the purpose of preventing any further desertion, to recover them at all events. Captain Cook, therefore, in order to convince the inhabitants that he was in earnest, resolved to go after the fugitives himself; to which measure he was determined, from having observed, in repeated instances, that the natives had seldom offered to deceive him with false information.

Agreeably to this resolution, the captain set out the next morning, with two armed boats, being accompanied by Oreo, the chief of Ulietea, and proceeded immediately to Otaha. But when he had gotten to the place where the deserters were expected to be found, he was acquainted they were gone over to Bolabola. Thither our commander did not think proper to follow them, having determined to pursue another measure, which he judged would more effectually answer his purpose. This mea sure was to put the chief's son, daughter, and son-in-law, into confinement, and to detain them till the fugitives should be restored. As to Oreo, he was informed, that he was at liberty to leave the ship whenever he pleased, and to take such methods as he esteemed best calculated to get our two men back; that, if he succeeded, his friends should be released; if not, that Captain Cook was resolved to carry them away with him. The captain added, that the chief's own conduct, as well as that of many of his people, in assisting the runaways to escape, and in enticing others to follow them, would justify any step that could be taken to put a stop to such proceedings. In consequence of this explanation of our commander's views and intentions, Oreo zealously exerted himself to recover the deserters; for which purpose he despatched a canoe to Bolabola, with a message to Opoony, the sovereign of that island, acquainting him with what had happened, and requesting him to seize the two fugitives, and send them back. The messenger, who was no less a person than the father of Pootoe, Oreo's son-in-law, came, before he set out, to Captain Cook, to receive his commands, which were, not to return without the runaways, and to inform Opoony, that, if they had left Bolabola, he must despatch canoes in pursuit of them, till they should finally be restored. These vigorous measures were at length successful. On the 28th, the deserters were brought back; and as soon as they were on board, the three prisoners were released. Our commander would not have acted so resolutely on the present occasion, had he not been peculiarly solicitous to save the son of a brother officer from being lost to his country.

While this affair was in suspense, some of the natives, from their anxiety on account of the confinement of the chief's relations, had formed a design of a very serious nature; which was no less than to seize upon the persons of Captain Clerke, and Captain Cook. With regard to Captain Clerke, they made no secret of speaking of their scheme, the day after it was discovered. But their first and grand plan of operations was to lay hold of Captain Cook. It was his custom to bathe every evening in fresh water ; in doing which he frequently went alone, and always without arms. As the inhabitants expected him to go, as usual, on the evening of the 26th, they had determined at that time to make him a prisoner. But he had thought it prudent, after confining Oreo's family, to avoid putting himself in their power ; and had cautioned Captain Clerke and the officers not to venture themselves far from the ships. In the course of the afternoon, the chief asked Captain Cook three several times, if he would not go to the bathing-place ; and when he found at last, that the captain could not be prevailed upon, he went off, with all his people. He was apprehensive, without doubt, that the design was discovered ; though no suspicion of it was then entertained by our commander, who imagined, that the natives were seized with some sudden fright, from which as usual they would quickly recover. On one occasion, Captain Clerke and Mr. Gore were in particular danger. A party of the inhabitants armed with clubs advanced against them ; and their safety was principally owing to Captain Clerke's walking with a pistol in his hand, which he once fired. The discovery of the conspiracy, especially so far as respected Captain Clerke and Mr. Gore, was made by a girl, whom one of the officers had brought from Huaheine. On this account, those who were charged with the execution of the design were so greatly offended with her that they threatened to take away her life, as soon as our navigators should leave the island ; but proper methods were pursued for her security. It was a happy circumstance that the affair was brought to light ; since a scheme could not have been carried into effect without being, in its consequences, productive of much distress and calamity to the natives.

Whilst Captain Cook was at Ulietea, he was visited by his old friend Oree, who, in the former voyages, was chief, or rather regent, of Huaheine. Notwithstanding his now being, in some degree, reduced to the rank of a private person, he still preserved his consequence, never appeared without a numerous body of attendants, and was always provided with such presents as indicated his wealth, and were highly acceptable.

The last of the Society Islands to which our commander sailed was Bolabola, where he arrived on the 8th of December. His chief view in passing over to this island was to procure from its monarch, Opoony, an anchor which Monsieur de Bougainville had lost at Otaheite, and which had been conveyed to Bolabola. It was not from a want of anchors, that Captain Cook was desirous of making the purchase, but to convert the iron of which it consisted into a fresh assortment of trading articles, these being now very much exhausted. The captain succeeded in his negotiation, and amply rewarded Opoony for giving up the anchor.

Whilst our commander was at Bolabola, he received an account of those military expeditions of the people of this country, which he had heard much of in each of his three voyages, and which had ended in the complete conquest of Ulietea and Otaha. The Bolabola men, in consequence of these enterprises, were in the highest reputation for their valour; and, indeed, were deemed so invincible, as to be the objects of terror to all the neighbouring islands. It was an addition to their fame, that their country was of such small extent, being not more than eight leagues in compass, and not half so large as Ulietea.

Captain Cook continued to the last his zeal for furnishing the natives of the South Sea with useful animals. At Bolabola, where there was already a ram, which had originally been left by the Spanish at Otaheite, he carried ashore an ewe, that had been brought from the Cape of Good Hope, and he rejoiced in the prospect of laying a foundation, by this present, for a breed of sheep in the island. He left also at Ulietea, under the care of

Oreo, an English boar and sow, and two goats. It may, therefore, be regarded as certain, that not only Otaheite, but all the neighbouring islands, will, in a few years, have their race of hogs considerably improved; and it is probable that they will be stocked with all the valuable animals, which have been transported thither by their European visitors. When this shall be accomplished, no part of the world will equal these islands, in the variety and abundance of the refreshments which they will be able to afford to navigators; nor did the captain know any place that excelled them, even in their present state.

It is an observation of great importance, that the future felicity of the inhabitants of Otaheite, and the Society Islands, will not a little depend on their continuing to be visited from Europe. Our commander could not avoid expressing it as his real opinion, that it would have been far better for these poor people never to have known our superiority in the accommodations and arts which render life comfortable, than, after once knowing it, to be again left and abandoned to their original incapacity of improvement. If the intercourse between them and us should wholly be discontinued, they cannot be restored to that happy mediocrity, in which they lived before they were first discovered. It seemed to Captain Cook, that it was become, in a manner, incumbent upon the Europeans to visit these islands once in three or four years, in order to supply the natives with those conveniences which we have introduced among them, and for which we have given them a predilection. Perhaps they may heavily feel the want of such occasional supplies, when it may be too late to go back to their old and less perfect contrivances; contrivances which they now despise, and which they have discontinued since the introduction of ours. It is, indeed, to be apprehended, that by the time that the iron tools of which they had become possessed, are worn out, they will have almost lost the knowledge of their own. In this last voyage of our commander, a stone hatchet was as rare a thing among the inhabitants as an iron one was eight years before; and a chisel of bone or stone was not to be seen. Spike-nails had succeeded in their place; and of spike-nails the natives were weak enough to imagine they had gotten an inexhaustible store. Of all our commodities, axes and hatchets remained the most unrivalled; and they must ever be held in the highest estimation through the whole of the islands. Iron tools are so strikingly useful, and are now become so necessary to the comfortable existence of the inhabitants, that should they cease to receive supplies of them, their situation, in consequence of their neither possessing the materials, nor being trained up to the art of fabricating them, would be rendered completely miserable. It is impossible to reflect upon this representation of things without strong feelings of sympathy and concern. Sincerely it is to be wished, that such may be the order of events, and such the intercourse carried on with the southern islanders, that, instead of finally suffering by the acquaintance with us, they may rise to a higher state of civilization, and permanently enjoy blessings far superior to what they had heretofore known.

Amidst the various subordinate employments which engaged the attention of Captain Cook and his associates, the great objects of their duty were never forgotten. No opportunity was lost of making astronomical and nautical observations; the consequence of which was, that the latitude and longitude of the places where the ship anchored, the variations of the compass, the dips of the needle, and the state of the tides, were ascertained with an accuracy that forms a valuable addition to philosophical science, and will be of eminent service to future navigators.

Our commander was now going to take his final departure from Otaheite and the Society Islands. Frequently as they had been visited, it might have been imagined, that their religious, political, and domestic regulations, manners and customs, must, by this time, be thoroughly understood. A great accession of knowledge was undoubtedly gained in the present voyage ; and yet it was confessed, both by Captain Cook and Mr. Anderson, that their accounts of things were still imperfect in various respects ; and that they continued strangers to many of the most important institutions which prevailed among the natives. There was one part of the character of several of these people, on which the well-regulated mind of the captain would not permit him to enlarge. "Too much," says he, "seems to have been already known, and published in our former relations, about some of the modes of life, that made Otaheite so agreeable an abode to many on board our ships ; and if I could now add any finishing strokes to a picture, the outlines of which have been already drawn with sufficient accuracy, I should still have hesitated to make this journal the place for exhibiting a view of licentious manners, which could only serve to disgust those for whose information I write."

From Mr. Anderson's account of the Otaheitans, it appears, that their religious system is extensive, and in various instances singular. They do not seem to pay respect to one God as possessing preëminence, but believe in a plurality of divinities, all of whom are supposed to be very powerful. In different parts of the island, and in the neighbouring islands, the inhabitants choose those deities for the objects of their worship, who, they think, are most likely to protect them, and to supply all their wants. If, however, they are disappointed in their expectations, they deem it no impiety to change their divinity, by having recourse to another, whom they hope to find more propitious and successful. In general, their notions concerning Deity are extravagantly absurd. With regard to the soul, they believe it according to Mr. Anderson, to be both immaterial and immortal ; but he acknowledges, that they are far from entertaining those sublime expectations of future happiness which the Christian revelation affords, and which even reason alone, duly exercised, might teach us to expect.

Although seventeen months had elapsed since Captain Cook's departure from England, during which time he had not, upon the whole, been unprofitably employed, he was sensible that, with respect to the principal object of his instructions, it was now only the commencement of his voyage; and that, therefore, his attention was to be called anew to every circumstance which might contribute towards the safety of his people, and the ultimate success of the expedition. Accordingly, he had examined into the state of the provisions, whilst he was at the Society Islands, and, as soon as he had left them, and had gotten beyond the extent of his former discoveries, he ordered a survey to be taken of all the boatswain's and carpenter's stores which were in the ships, that he might be fully informed of their quantity and condition; and, by that means, know how to use them to the greatest advantage.

It was on the 8th of December, the very day on which he had touched there, that our commander sailed from Bolabola. In the night between the 22d and 23d, he crossed the line, in the longitude of 203° 15' east; and on the 24th, land was discovered, which was found to be one of those low uninhabited islands, that are so frequent in this ocean. Here our voyagers were successful in catching a large quantity of turtle, which supplied them with an agreeable refreshment; and here, on the 28th, an eclipse of the sun was observed by Mr. Bayley, Mr. King, and Captain Cook. On account of the season of the year, the captain called the land where he now was, and which he judged to be about fifteen or twenty leagues in circumference, Christmas Island. By his order, several cocoa-nuts and yams were planted, and some melon-seeds sown in proper places; and a bottle was left, containing this inscription:

GEORGIUS TERTIUS, REX, 31 DECEMBRIS, 1777.

NAVES { RESOLUTION, JAC. COOK, PR.
{ DISCOVERY, CAR. CLERKE, PR.

On the 2d of January, 1778, the ships resumed their course to the northward, and though several evidences occurred of the vicinity of land, none was discovered till the 18th, when an island made its appearance, bearing northeast by east. Soon after, more land was seen, lying towards the north, and entirely detached from the former. The succeeding day was distinguished by the discovery of a third island, in the direction of west-northwest, and as far distant as the eye could reach. In steering towards the second island, our voyagers had some doubt whether the land before them was inhabited; but this matter was speedily cleared up, by the putting off of some canoes from the shore, containing from three to six men each. Upon their approach, the English were agreeably surprised to find that they spoke the language of Otaheite, and of the other countries which had lately been visited. These people were at first fearful of going on board; but when, on the 20th, some of them took courage, and ventured to do it, they expressed an astonishment, on entering the ship, which Captain Cook had never experienced in the natives of any place, during the whole course of his several voyages. Their eyes continually flew from object to object; and, by the wildness of their looks and gestures, they fully manifested their entire ignorance with relation to everything they saw, and strongly marked to our navigators, that, till this time, they had never been visited by Europeans, or been acquainted with any of our commodities, excepting iron. Even with respect to iron, it was evident that they had only heard of it, or at most, had known it in some small quantity, brought to them at a distant period; for all they understood concerning it was, that it was a substance much better adapted to the purposes of cutting, or the boring of holes, than anything their own country produced. The ceremonies on entering the ship, their gestures and motions, and their manner of singing, were similar to those which our voyagers had been accustomed to see in the places lately visited.

There was, likewise, a farther circumstance in which these people perfectly resembled the other islanders; and that was, in their endeavouring to steal whatever came within their reach; or rather to take it openly, as what would either not be resented, or not hindered. The English soon convinced them of their mistake, by keeping such a watchful eye over them, that they afterwards were obliged to be less active in appropriating to themselves every object that struck upon their fancy, and excited the desire of possession.

One order given by Captain Cook at this island was, that none of the boats' crews should be permitted to go on shore; the reason of which was, that he might do everything in his power to prevent the importation of a fatal disease, which unhappily had already been communicated in other places. With the same view, he directed that all female visitors should be excluded from the ships. Another necessary precaution, taken by the captain, was a strict injunction, that no person, known to be capable of propagating disorder, should be sent upon duty out of the vessels. Thus zealous was the humanity of our commander, to prevent an irreparable injury from being done to the natives. There are men who glory in their shame, and who do not care how much evil they communicate. Of this there was an instance at Tongataboo, in the gunner of the Discovery, who had been stationed on shore to manage the trade for that ship; and who, though he was well acquainted with his own situation, continued to have connexions with different women. His companions expostulated with him without effect, till Captain Clerke, hearing of the dangerous irregularity of his conduct, ordered him on board. If I knew the rascal's name, I would hang it up, as far as lies in my power, to everlasting infamy.

Mr. Williamson being sent with the boats to search for water, and attempting to land, the inhabitants came down in such numbers, and were so violent in their endeavours to seize upon the **oars,** muskets, and, in **short** everything they could lay hold of, that he was obliged to fire, by which one man was killed. This unhappy circumstance was not known to Captain Cook till after he had left the island; so that all his measures were directed as if nothing of the kind had happened.

When the ships were brought to an anchor, our commander went on shore; and, at the very instant of his doing it, the collected body of the natives all fell flat upon their faces, and continued in that humble posture, till, by expressive signs, he prevailed upon them to rise. Other ceremonies followed; and the next day a trade was set on foot for hogs and potatoes, which the people of the island gave in exchange for nails and pieces of iron, formed into something like chisels. So far was any obstruction from being met with in watering, that, on the contrary, the inhabitants assisted our men in rolling the casks to and from the pool; and readily performed whatever was required.

Affairs thus going on to the captain's satisfaction, he made an excursion into the country, accompanied by Mr. Anderson and Mr. Webber, the former of whom was as well qualified to describe with the pen, as the latter was to represent with his pencil, whatever might occur worthy of observation. In this excursion, the gentlemen, among other objects that called for their attention, found a *Morai*. On the return of our commander, he had the pleasure of finding that a brisk trade for pigs, fowls and roots was carrying on with the greatest good order, and, without any attempt to cheat or steal, on the part of the natives. The rapacious disposition they at first displayed, was entirely corrected by their conviction that it could not be exercised with impunity. Among the articles which they brought to barter, the most remarkable was a particular sort of cloak and cap, that might be reckoned elegant, even in countries where dress is eminently the object of attention. The cloak was richly adorned with red and yellow feathers, which in themselves were highly beautiful, and the newness and freshness of which added not a little to their beauty.

On the 22d, a circumstance occurred, which gave the English room to suspect that the people of the island are eaters of human flesh Not, however, to rest the belief of the existence of so horrid a practice on the foundation of suspicion only, Captain Cook was anxious to inquire into the truth of the fact, the result of which was its being fully confirmed. An old man, in particular, who was asked upon the subject, answered in the affirmative, and seemed to laugh at the simplicity of such a question. His answer was equally affirmative on a repetition of the inquiry ; and he added, that the flesh of men was excellent food, or, as he expressed it, "savoury eating." It is understood that enemies slain in battle are the sole objects of this abominable custom.

The island at which our voyagers had now touched, was called Atooi by the natives. Near it was another island, named Oneeheow, where our commander came to an anchor on the 29th of the month. The inhabitants were found to resemble those of Atooi in their dispositions, manners, and customs ; and proofs, too convincing, appeared, that the horrid banquet of human flesh is here as much relished, amidst plenty, as it is in New Zealand. From a desire of benefiting these people, by furnishing them with additional articles of food, the captain left them a ram goat and two ewes, a boar and sow pig of the English breed, and the seeds of melons, pumpkins and onions. These benevolent presents would have been made to Atooi, the larger island, had not our navigators been unexpectedly driven from it by stress of weather. Though the soil of Oneeheow seemed in general poor, it was observable, that the ground was covered with shrubs and plants, some of which perfumed the air with a more delicious fragrancy, than what Captain Cook had met with at any other of the countries that had been visited by him in this part of the world.

It is a curious circumstance, with regard to the islands in the

Pacific Ocean which the late European voyages have added to the geography of the globe, that they have generally been found to lie in groups, or clusters. The single intermediate islands, which have as yet been discovered, are few in proportion to the others; though there are probably many more of them that are still unknown, and may serve as steps, by which the several clusters are, in some degree, connected together. Of the Archipelago now first visited, there were five only with which our commander became at this time acquainted. The names of these, as given by the natives, were Woahoo, Atooi, Oneeheow, Oreehoua, and Tahoora. To the whole group Captain Cook gave the appellation of Sandwich Islands, in honour of his great friend and patron, the Earl of Sandwich.

Concerning the island of Atooi, which is the largest of the five, and which was the principal scene of the captain's operations, he collected, in conjunction with Mr. Anderson, a considerable degree of information. The land, as to its general appearance, does not in the least resemble any of the islands that our voyagers had hitherto visited within the tropic, on the south side of the equator; excepting so far as regards its hills near the centre, which slope gentle towards the sea. Hogs, dogs, and fowls, were the only tame domestic animals that were here found; and these were of the same kind with those which exist in the countries of the South Pacific Ocean. Among the inhabitants (who are of a middle stature, and firmly made), there is a more remarkable equality in the size, colour, and figure of both sexes, than our commander had observed in most other places. They appeared to be blessed with a frank and cheerful disposition; and, in Captain Cook's opinion, they are equally free from the fickle levity which distinguishes the natives of Otaheite, and the sedate cast discernible amongst many of those at Tongataboo. It is a very pleasing circumstance in their character, that they pay a particular attention to their women, and readily lend assistance to their wives in the tender offices of maternal duty. On all occasions, they seemed to be deeply impressed with a consciousness of their own inferiority; being alike strangers to the preposterous pride of the more polished Japanese, and of the ruder Greenlander. Contrary to the general practice of the countries that had hitherto been discovered in the Pacific Ocean, the people of the Sandwich Islands have not their ears perforated; nor have they the least idea of wearing ornaments in them, though, in other respects, they are sufficiently fond of adorning their persons. In everything manufactured by them there is an uncommon degree of neatness and ingenuity; and the elegant form and polish of some of their fishing-hooks could not be exceeded by any European artist, even if he should add all his knowledge in design to the number and convenience of his tools. From what was seen of their agriculture, sufficient proofs were afforded, that they are not novices in that art; and that the quantity and goodness of their vegetable productions may as much be attributed to skilful culture, as to natural fertility of soil. Amidst all the resemblances between the natives of Atooi, and those of Otaheite, the coincidence of their languages was the most striking; being almost word for word the same. Had the Sandwich Islands been discovered by the Spainards, at an early period, they would undoubtedly have taken advantage of so excellent a situation, and have made use of them as refreshing places for their ships, which sail annually from Acapula for Manilla. Happy, too, would it have been for Lord Anson, if he had known, that there existed a group of islands, half way between America and Tinian where all his wants could have been effectually supplied, and the different hardships to which he was exposed have been avoided.

On the second of February, our navigators pursued their course to the northward, in doing which the incidents they met with were almost entirely of a nautical kind. The long-looked for coast of New Albion was seen on the 7th of March, the ships being then in the latitude of 44° 33' north, and in the longitude of 235° 20' east. As the vessels ranged along the west side of America, Captain Cook gave names to several capes and headlands which appeared in sight. At length, on the 29th, the captain came to an anchor at an inlet, where the appearance of the country differed much from what had been seen before; being full of mountains, the summits of which were covered with snow; while the valleys between them, and the grounds on the sea-coast, high as well as low, were covered to a considerable breadth, with high, straight trees, which formed a beautiful prospect, as of one vast forest. It was immediately found, that the coast was inhabited; and there soon came off to the Resolution three canoes, containing eighteen of the natives; who could not, however, be prevailed upon to venture themselves on board. Notwithstanding this, they displayed a peaceable disposition; showed great readiness to part with anything they had, in exchange for what was offered them; and expressed a stronger desire for iron, than for any other of our commercial articles, appearing to be perfectly acquainted with the use of that metal. From these favourable circumstances, our voyagers had reason to hope, that they should find this a comfortable station to supply all their wants, and to make them forget the hardships and delays which they had experienced during a constant succession of adverse winds, and boisterous weather, almost ever since their arrival upon the coast of America.

The ships having happily found an excellent inlet, the coasts of which appeared to be inhabited by a race of people who were disposed to maintain a friendly intercourse with strangers, Captain Cook's first object was to search for a commodious harbour; and he had little trouble in discovering what he wanted. A trade having immediately commenced, the articles which the inhabitants offered to sale were the skins of various animals, such as bears, wolves, foxes, deer, raccoons, pole-cats, martins ; and, in particular, of the sea-otters. To these were added, besides the skins in their natural shape, garments made of them ; another sort of clothing, formed from the bark of a tree ; and various different pieces of workmanship. But of all the articles brought to market, the most extraordinary were human skulls, and hands not yet quite stripped of their flesh ; some of which had evident marks of their having been upon the fire. The things which the natives took in exchange for their commodities, were knives, chisels, pieces of iron and tin, nails, looking-glasses, buttons, or any kind of metal. Glass beads did not strike their imaginations ; and cloth of every sort they rejected. Though commerce, in general, was carried on with mutual honesty, there were some among these people who were as much inclined to thievery as the islanders in the Southern Ocean. They were, at the same time, far more dangerous thieves ; for, possessing sharp iron instruments, they could cut a hook from a tackle, or any other piece of iron from a rope, the moment that the backs of the English were turned. The dexterity with which they conducted their operations of this nature, frequently eluded the most cautious viligance. Some slighter instances of deception, in the way of traffic, Captain Cook thought it better to bear with, than to make them the foundation of a quarrel ; and to this he was the rather determined, as the English articles were now reduced to objects of a trifling nature. In the progress of the commerce, the natives would deal for nothing but metal ; and, at length, brass was so eagerly sought for, in preference to iron, that, before our navigators quitted the place, scarcely a bit of it was left in the ships, excepting what belonged to the necessary instruments. Whole suits of clothes were stripped of every button ; bureaus were deprived of their furniture ; copper kettles, tin canisters, candlesticks, and whatever of the like kind could be found, all went to wreck ; so that these Americans became possessors of a greater medley and variety of things from our people, than any other nation that had been visited in the course of the voyage.

Of all the uncivilized tribes which our commander had met with in his several navigations, he never found any who had such strict notions of their having a right to the exclusive property of everything which their country produces, as the inhabitants of the sound where he was now stationed. At first, they wanted to be paid for the wood and water that were carried on board; and had the captain been upon the spot, when these demands were made, he would certainly have complied with them: but the workmen in his absence, maintained a different opinion, and refused to submit to any such claims. When some grass, which appeared to be of no use to the natives, was wanted to be cut, as food for the few goats and sheep which still remained on board, they insisted that it should be purchased, and were very unreasonable in their terms; notwithstanding which Captain Cook consented to gratify them, as far as he was able. It was always a sacred rule with him, never to take any of the property of the people whom he visited, without making them an ample compensation.

The grand operation of our navigators, in their present station, was to put the ships into a complete repair for the prosecution of the expedition. While this business was carrying on, our commander took the opportunity of examining every part of the sound; in the course of which he gained a farther knowledge of the inhabitants, who, in general, received him with great civility. In one instance he met with a surly chief, who could not be softened with presents, though he condescended to accept of them. The females of the place over which he presided showed a more agreeable disposition; for some of the young women expeditiously dressed themselves in their best apparel, and assembling in a body, welcomed the English to their village, by joining in a song, which was far from being harsh or disagreeable. On another occasion, the captain was entertained with singing. Being visited by a number of strangers, on the 22d of April, as they advanced towards the ships, they all stood up in their canoes, and began to sing. Some of their songs, in which the whole body joined, were in a slow, and others in a quicker time ; and their notes were accompanied with the most regular motions of their hands ; or with beating in concert, with their paddles, on the sides of their canoes ; to which were added other very expressive gestures. At the end of each song, they continued silent for a few moments, and then began again, sometimes pronouncing the word *Hooee!* forcibly as a chorus.

Among the natives of the country, there was one chief who attached himself to our commander in a particular manner. Captain Cook having, at parting, bestowed upon him a small present, received, in return, a beaver skin, of much greater value. This called upon the captain to make some addition to his present, with which the chief was so much pleased, that he insisted on our commander's acceptance of the beaver-skin cloak which he then wore ; and of which he was particularly fond. Admiring this instance of generosity, and desirous that he should not suffer by his friendship, the captain gave him a new broad sword, with a brass hilt ; the possession of which rendered him completely happy.

On Captain Cook's first arrival in this inlet, he had honoured it with the name of King George's Sound ; but he afterwards found that it is called Nootka by the natives. During his stay in the place, he displayed his usual sagacity and diligence, in conjunction with Mr. Anderson, in collecting everything that could be learned concerning the neighbouring country and its inhabitants ; and the account is interesting, as it exhibits a picture of productions, people, and manners, very different from what had occurred in the Southern Ocean. I can only, as on former occasions, slightly advert to a few of the more leading circumstances. The climate, so far as our navigators had experience of it, was found to be in an eminent degree milder than that on the east coast of America, in the same parallel of latitude; and it was remarkable, that the thermometer, even in the night, never fell lower than 42°; while in the day it frequently rose to 60°. With regard to trees, those of which the woods are chiefly composed, are the Canadian pine, the white cypress, and the wild pine, with two or three different sorts of pine that are less common. In the other vegetable productions there appeared but little variety; but it is to be considered, that, at so early a season, several might not yet have sprung up; and that many more might be concealed from our voyagers, in consequence of the narrow sphere of their researches. Of the land animals, the most common were bears, deer, foxes, and wolves. The sea animals, which were seen off the coast, were whales, porpoises, and seals. Birds, in general, are not only rare as to the different species, but very scarce as to numbers; and the few which are to be met with are so shy, that, in all probability, they are continually harassed by the natives either to eat them as food, or to get possession of their feathers, which are used as ornaments. Fish are more plentiful in quantity than birds, but were not found in any great variety; and yet, from several circumstances, there was reason to believe, that the variety is considerably increased at certain seasons. The only animals that were observed of the reptile kind were snakes and water-lizards; but the insect tribe seemed to be more numerous.

With respect to the inhabitants of the country, their persons are generally under the common stature; but not slender in proportion, being usually pretty full or plump, though without being muscular. From their bringing for sale human skulls and bones, it may justly be inferred, that they treat their enemies with a degree of brutal cruelty: notwithstanding which, it does not follow, that they are to be reproached with any charge of pecu liar inhumanity; for the circumstance now mentioned only marks a general agreement of character with that of almost every tribe of uncivilized men, in every age, and in every part of the globe. Our navigators had no reason to complain of the disposition of the natives, who appeared to be a docile, courteous, good-natured people; rather phlegmatic in the usual cast of their tempers, but quick in resenting what they apprehend to be an injury, and easily permitting their anger to subside. Their other passions, and especially their curiosity, seemed to lie in some measure dormant: one cause of which may be found in the indolence, that, for the most part, is prevalent amongst them. The chief employments of the men, are those of fishing, and of killing land or sea-animals, for the sustenance of their families; while the women are occupied in manufacturing their flaxen or woollen garments, or in other domestic offices. It must be mentioned to their honour, that they were always properly clothed, and behaved with the utmost decorum; justly deserving all commendation, for a bashfulness and modesty becoming their sex; and this was the more meritorious in them, as the male inhabitants discovered no sense of shame. In their manufactures and mechanic arts, these people have arrived to a greater degree of extent and ingenuity, both with regard to the design and execution, than could have been expected from their natural disposition, and the little progress to which they have arrived in general civilization. Their dexterity, in particular, with respect to works of wood, must principally be ascribed to the assistance they receive from iron tools, which are in universal use amongst them, and in the application of which they are very dexterous. Whence they have derived their knowledge of iron, was a matter of speculation with Captain Cook. The most probable opinion, is, that this and other metals may have been introduced by way of Hudson's Bay and Canada, and thus successively have been conveyed across the continent, from tribe to tribe. Nor is it unreasonable to suppose, that these metals may sometimes be brought, in the same manner, from the northwestern parts of Mexico.* The language of Nootka is by no means harsh or disagreeable; for it abounds, upon the whole, rather with what may be called labial and dental, than with guttural sounds. A large vocabulary of it was collected by Mr. Anderson.

Whilst Captain Cook was at Nootka Sound, great attention was paid by him as usual, to astronomical and nautical subjects. The observations which he had an opportunity of making, were, indeed, so numerous, as to form a very considerable addition to geographical and philosophical science.

On the 26th, the repairs of the ships having been completed, everything was ready for the captain's departure. When, in the afternoon of that day, the vessels were upon the point of sailing, the mercury in the barometer fell unusually low; and there was every other presage of an approaching storm, which might reasonably be expected to come from the southward. This circumstance induced our commander in some degree to hesitate, and especially as night was at hand, whether he should venture to sail or wait till the next morning. But his anxious impatience to proceed upon the voyage and the fear of losing the present opportunity of getting out of the sound, made a greater impression upon his mind, than any apprehension of immediate danger. He determined, therefore, to put to sea at all events; and accordingly carried his design into execution that evening. He was not deceived in his expectations of a storm. Scarcely were the vessels out of the Sound before the wind increased to a strong gale, with squalls and rain, accompanied by so dark a sky, that the length of the ships could not be seen. Happily the wind took a direction that blew our navigators from the

---

* Two silver spoons, of a construction similar to what may sometimes be seen in Flemish pictures of still life, were procured here by Mr. Gore, who bought them from a native, who wore them, tied together with a leathern thong, as an ornament round his neck. Mr. Gore gave the **spoons to Sir Joseph Banks.**

coast; and though, on the 27th, the tempest rose to a perfect hurricane, and the Resolution sprang a leak, no material damage ensued.

In the prosecution of the voyage to the north, and back again to the Sandwich Islands, the facts that occurred were chiefly of a nautical kind. Minutely to record these is not the purpose of the present work, and indeed would extend it to an unreasonable length.

From this long and important navigation, I can only select some few incidents, that may be accommodated to the tastes and expectations of the generality of readers.

One thing it is not improper here to observe; which is that the captain, in his passage along the coast of America, kept at a distance from that coast, whenever the wind blew strongly upon it, and sailed on till he could approach it again with safety. Hence several great gaps were left unexplored, and particularly between the latitudes of 50° and 55°. The exact situation, for instance, of the supposed Straits of Anian was not ascertained. Every one who is acquainted with the character of our commander will be sensible, that if he had lived to return again to the north in 1779, he would have endeavoured to explore the parts which had been left unexamined.

The first place at which Captain Cook landed, after his departure from Nootka Sound, was at an island, of eleven or twelve leagues in length, the southwest point of which lies in the latitude of 59° 49' north, and the longitude of 216° 58' east. Here, on the 11th of May, at the foot of a tree, on a little eminence not far from the shore, he left a bottle, with a paper in it on which were inscribed the names of the ships and the date of the discovery. Together with the bottle he enclosed two silver two-penny pieces of his majesty's coin, which had been struck in 1772. These, with many others, had been given him by the Reverend Dr. Kaye, the present Dean of Lincoln;

and our commander, as a mark of his esteem and regard for that learned and respectable gentleman, named the island, after him, Kaye's Island.

At an inlet where the ships came to an anchor on the 12th, and to which Captain Cook gave the appellation of Prince William's Sound, he had an opportunity not only of stopping the leak which the Resolution had sprung in the late storm, and of prosecuting his nautical and geographical discoveries, but of making considerable additions to his knowledge of the inhabitants of the American coast. From every observation which was made concerning the persons of the natives of this part of the coast, it appeared, that they had a striking resemblance to those of the Esquimaux and Greenlanders. Their canoes, their weapons, and their instruments for fishing and hunting, are likewise exactly the same, in point of materials and construction, that are used in Greenland. The animals in the neighbourhood of Prince William's Sound are, in general, similar to those which are found at Nootka. One of the most beautiful skins here offered for sale, was, however, that of a small animal, which seemed to be peculiar to the place. Mr. Anderson was inclined to think that it is the animal which is described by Mr. Pennant, under the name of the *casan* marmot. Among the birds seen in this country, were the white headed eagle, the shag, and the *alcedo*, or great king-fisher, the colours of which were very fine and bright. The humming-bird, also, came frequently and flew about the ship, while at anchor ; but it can scarcely be supposed, that it can be able to subsist here during the severity of winter. Water-fowl, upon the whole, are in considerable plenty ; and there is a species of diver about the size of a partridge, which seems peculiar to the place. Torsk and halibut were almost the only kinds of fish that were obtained by our voyagers. Vegetables, of any sort, were few in number ; and the trees were chiefly the Canadian and spruce pine, some of which were of a considerable height and thickness. The beads and iron, that were found among the people of the coast, must undoubtedly have been derived from some civilized nation ; and yet there was ample reason to believe, that our English navigators were the first Europeans with whom the natives had ever held a direct communication. From what quarter then had they gotten our manufactures ? Most probably, through the intervention of the more inland tribes, from Hudson's Bay, or the settlements on the Canadian lakes. This, indeed, must certainly have been the case, if iron was known amongst the inhabitants of this part of the American coast prior to the discovery of it by the Russians, and before there was any traffic with them carried on from Kamtschatka. From what was seen of Prince William's Sound, Captain Cook judged that it occupied at least a degree and a half of latitude, and two of longitude, exclusively of the arms or branches, the extent of which is not known.

Some days after leaving this sound our navigators came to an inlet, from which great things were expected. Hopes were strongly entertained, that it would be found to communicate either with the sea to the north or with Baffin's or Hudson's Bay to the east, and accordingly it became the object of very accurate and serious examination. The captain was soon persuaded that the expectations formed from it were groundless ; notwithstanding which, he persisted in the search of a passage, more, indeed, to satisfy other people, than to confirm his own opinion. In consequence of a complete investigation of the inlet, indubitable marks occurred of its being a river. This river, without seeing the least appearance of its source, was traced by our voyagers, as high as the latitude of 61° 34′ and the longitude of 210°, being seventy leagues from its entrance. During the course of the navigation, on the 1st of June, Lieutenant King was ordered on shore to display the royal flag, and to take pos session of the country in his majesty's name. The lieutenant at the same time buried in the ground a bottle containing some pieces of English coin, of the year 1772, and a paper, on which the names of the ship were inscribed, and the date of the present discovery. The great river now discovered, promises to vie with the most considerable ones already known ; and, by itself and its branches, lies open to a very extensive inland communication. If, therefore, the knowledge of it should be of future service, the time which was spent in exploring it ought the less to be regretted. But to Captain Cook, who had a much greater object in view, the delay that was hence occasioned was a real loss, because the season was advancing apace. It was, however, a satisfaction for him to reflect, that if he had not examined this very considerable inlet, it would have been assumed, by speculative fabricators of geography, as a fact, that there was a passage through it to the North Sea, or to Baffin's or Hudson's Bay. Perhaps, too, it would have been marked, on future maps of the world, with greater precision, and more certain signs of reality, than the invisible, because imaginary, Straits of de Fuca and de Fonte. In describing the inlet, our commander had left a blank which was not filled up with any particular name ; and, therefore, the Earl of Sandwich directed, with the greatest propriety, that it should be called Cook's River.

All the natives who were met with, during the examination of this river, appeared, from every mark of resemblance, to be of the same nation with the inhabitants of Prince William's Sound ; but from the people of Nootka, or King George's Sound, they essentially differed, both in their persons and their language. The only things which were seen among them, that were not of their own manufacture, were a few glass beads, the iron points of their spears, and knives of the same metal. Whencesoever, these articles might be derived, it was evident, that they had never had any immediate intercourse with the Russians ; since if that had been the case, our voyagers would scarcely have found them clothed in such valuable skins as those of the sea-otter. A very beneficial fur-trade might undoubtedly be carried on with the inhabitants of this vast coast. But without a practicable northern passage, the situation is too remote to render it probable, that Great Britain should hence ever derive any material advantage; though it is impossible to say, with certainty, how far the spirit of commerce, for which the English nation is so eminently distinguished, may extend. The most valuable, or rather the only valuable skins, which Captain Cook saw on the west side of America, were those of the sea-otter; for as to the skins of all the other animals of the country, and especially of the foxes and martins, they seemed to be of an inferior quality.

It was on the 6th of June that our navigators got clear of Cook's River. Proceeding in the course of their discoveries, when they were sailing, on the 19th, amidst the group of islands, which were called by Beering, Schumagin's Islands, Captain Clerke fired three guns, and brought to, expressing by the proper signals, that he wished to speak with Captain Cook. At this our commander was not a little alarmed, and, as no apparent danger had been remarked in the passage, through the channel where the vessels now were, it was apprehended that some accident, such as springing a leak, must have happened. On Captain Clerke's coming on board the Resolution, he related that several of the natives had followed his ship; that one of them had made many signs, taking of his cap, and bowing after the manner of Europeans; and that, at length, he had fastened to a rope, which was handed down to him, a small thin wooden case or box. Having delivered his parcel safe, and spoken something, accompanied with more signs, the canoes dropped astern, and left the Discovery. On opening the box, a piece of paper was found, folded up carefully, upon which something was written, that was reasonably supposed to be in the Russian language. To the paper was prefixed the date 1778, and in the body of the note there was a reference to the year 1776. Although no person on board was learned enough to decipher the alphabet of the writer, his numerals sufficiently marked, that others had preceded our voyagers in visiting this dreary part of the globe; and the prospect of soon meeting with men, who were united to them in ties somewhat closer than those of our common nature, and who were not strangers to the arts and commerce of civilized life, could not but afford a sensible satisfaction to people who, for such a length of time, had been conversant with the savages of the Pacific Ocean, and of the North American continent. Captain Clerke, was, at first, of opinion that some Russians had been shipwrecked; but no such idea occurred to Captain Cook. He rather thought that the paper contained a note of information left by some Russian traders, to be delivered to the next of their countrymen who should arrive; and that the natives, seeing the English pass, and supposing them to be Russians, had resolved to bring off the note. Accordingly, our commander pursued his voyage, without inquiring farther into the matter.

On the 21st, amongst some hills, on the main land, that towered above the clouds to a most amazing height, one was discovered to have a volcano, which constantly threw up vast columns of black smoke. It doth not stand far from the coast; and it lies in the latitude of 54° 48', and the longitude of 195° 45'. This mountain was rendered remarkable by its figure, which is a complete cone, and the volcano is at the very summit. While, in the afternoon of the same day, during a calm of three hours, the English were fishing with great success for halibuts, a small canoe, conducted by one man, came to them from an island in the neighbourhood. On approaching the ship, he took off his cap and bowed, as the native had done, who had visited the Discovery a day or two before. From the acquired politeness of these people, as well as from the note already mentioned, it was evident that the Russians must have a communication and traffic with them; and of this a fresh proof occurred in the present visitor; for he wore a pair of green cloth breeches, and a jacket of black cloth, or stuff, under the gut-shirt or frock of his own country.

In the prosecution of the voyage, on the 26th, there was so thick a fog, that our navigators could not see a hundred yards before them; notwithstanding which, as the weather was moderate, the captain did not intermit his course. At length, however, being alarmed at the sound of breakers on one side the ship, he immediately brought her to, and came to an anchor; and the Discovery, by his orders, did the same. A few hours after, the fog having in some degree cleared away, it appeared that both the vessels had escaped a very imminent danger. Providence, in the dark, had conducted them between rocks which our commander would not have ventured to pass through in a clear day, and had conveyed them to an anchoring-place, as good as he could possibly have fixed upon, had the choice been entirely at his option.

On the 27th, our voyagers reached an island, that is known by the name, of Oonalashka; the inhabitants of which behaved with a degree of politeness uncommon to savage tribes. A young man, who had overset his canoe, being obliged by this accident to come on board the ship, went down into Captain Cook's cabin upon the first invitation, without expressing the least reluctance or uneasiness. His own clothes being wet, the captain gave him others, in which he dressed himself with as much ease as any Englishman could have done. From the behaviour of this youth, and that of some of the rest of the natives, it was evident that these people were no strangers to Europeans, and to several of their customs. There was something, however, in the English ships, that greatly excited their attention; for such as could not come off in canoes, assembled on the neighbouring hills to look at them. In one instance it was apparent that the inhabitants were so far from having made any progress in politeness, that they were still immersed in the most savage manners. For, as our commander was walking along the shore, on the 29th, he met with a group of them, of both sexes, who were seated on the grass, at a repast, consisting of a raw fish, which they seemed to eat with as much relish, as persons in civilized life would experience from a turbot, served up in the richest sauce. Soon after the vessels had come to an anchor at Oonalashka, a native of the island brought on board such another note as had been given to Captain Clerke. He presented it to Captain Cook; but as it was written in the Russian language, and could be of no use to the English, though it might be of consequence to others, the captain returned it to the bearer, and dismissed him with a few presents; for which he expressed his thanks by making several low bows as he retired.

On the 2d of July, our voyagers put to sea from Oonalashka; and, pursuing their course of navigation and discovery, came, on the 16th, within sight of a promontory, near which our commander ordered Lieutenant Williamson to land, that he might see in what direction the coast took beyond it, and what the country produced. Accordingly, Mr. Williamson went on shore, and reported on his return, that, having landed on the point, and climbed the highest hill, he found that the farthest part of the coast in sight bore nearly north. At the same time, he took possession of the country in his majesty's name, and left a bottle, in which was enclosed a piece of paper, containing an inscription of the names of the ships, together with the date of the discovery. To the promontory he gave the name of Cape Newenham. The land, as far as Mr. Williamson could see, produced neither tree nor shrub; but the lower grounds were not destitute of grass, and of some other plants, very few of which were in flower

When our navigators, on the 3d of August, had advanced to the latitude of 62° 34′, a great loss was sustained by them in the death of Mr. Anderson, the surgeon of the Resolution, who had been lingering under a consumption for more than twelve months. He was a young man of a cultivated understanding and agreeable manners, and was well skilled in his own profession; besides which, he had acquired a considerable degree of knowledge in other branches of science. How useful an assistant he was to Captain Cook, hath often appeared in the present narrative. Had his life been spared, the public would undoubtedly have received from him such communications, on various parts of the natural history of the several places that had been visited, as would justly have entitled him to very high commendation. The proofs of his abilities that now remain, will hand down the name of Anderson, in conjunction with that of Cook, to posterity. Soon after he had breathed his last, land having been seen at a distance, which was supposed to be an island, our commander honored it with the appellation of Anderson's Island. The next day he removed Mr. Law, the surgeon of the Discovery, into the Resolution, and appointed Mr. Samwell, the surgeon's first mate of the Resolution, to be surgeon of the Discovery.

On the 9th, Captain Cook came to an anchor under a point of land, to which he gave the name of Cape Prince of Wales, and which is remarkable by being the most western extremity of America hitherto explored. This extremity is distant from the eastern Cape of Siberia only thirteen leagues: and thus our commander had the glory of ascertaining the vicinity of the two continents, which had only been conjectured from the reports of the neighbouring Asiatic inhabitants, and the imperfect observations of the Russian navigators.

Resuming his course on the 10th, Captain Cook anchored in a bay, the land of which was at first supposed to be part of the island of Alaschka, which is laid down in Mr. Stæhlin's map. But, from the figure of the coast, from the situation of the opposite shore of America, and from the longitude, the captain soon began to think, that it was more probably the country of the Tschutski, on the eastern extremity of Asia, which had been explored by Beering in 1728. In the result it appeared, that this was in fact the case. Our commander became fully satisfied in the farther progress of his voyage, that Mr. Stæhlin's map must be erroneous; and he had the honour of restoring the American continent to that space which the geographer now mentioned had occupied with his imaginary island of Alaschka.

From the Bay of St. Lawrence, belonging to the country of the Tschutski, our navigators steered, on the 11th, to the east, in order to get nearer to the coast of America. After that, proceeding to the north, they reached on the 17th, the latitude of 70° 33'. On this day, a brightness was perceived in the northern horizon, like that which is reflected from ice, and is commonly called the *blink*. This was at first but little noticed, from a supposition that there was no probability of meeting with ice so soon: and yet the sharpness of the air and the gloominess of the weather, had, for two or three days past, seemed to indicate a sudden change. In about an hour's time, the sight of a large field of ice left Captain Cook no longer in doubt with regard to the cause of the brightness of the horizon. The ships, in the same afternoon, being then in the latitude of 70° 41', were close to the edge of the ice, and not able to stand on any farther. On the 18th, when the vessels were in the latitude of 70° 44', the ice on the side of them was as compact as a wall, and was judged to be at least ten or twelve feet in height. Further to the north, it appeared to be much higher Its surface was extremely rugged, and in different places there were seen upon it pools of water. A prodigious number of sea horses lay upon the ice; and some of them, on the nineteenth, were procured for food, there being at this time a want of fresh provisions. When the animals were brought to the vessels, it was no small disappointment to many of the seamen, who had feasted their eyes for several days with the prospect of eating them, to find that they were not sea-cows, as they had supposed, but sea-horses. This disappointment would not have been occasioned, or the difference known, had there not happened to be one or two sailors on board who had been in Greenland, and who declared what these animals were, and that it never was customary to eat of them. Such, however, was the anxiety for a change of diet, as to overcome this prejudice. Our voyagers lived upon the sea-horses as long as they lasted; and there were few who did not prefer them to the salt meat.

Captain Cook continued, to the 29th, to traverse the Icy Sea beyond Beering's Strait, in various directions, and through numberless obstructions and difficulties. Every day the ice increased so as to preclude all hopes of attaining, at least during the present year, the grand object of the voyage. Indeed, the season was now so far advanced, and the time in which the frost was expected to set in was so near at hand, that it would have been totally inconsistent with prudence, to have made any farther attempts, till the next summer, at finding a passage into the Atlantic. The attention, therefore, of our commander was now directed to other important and necessary concerns. It was of great consequence to meet with a place where our navigators might be supplied with wood and water. But the point which principally occupied the captain's thoughts was, how he should spend the winter, so as to make some improvements in geography and navigation, and, at the same time, to be in a condition to return to the north, in farther search of a passage, in the ensuing summer.

Before Captain Cook proceeded far to the south, he employed a considerable time in examining the sea and coasts in the neighbourhood of Beering's Strait, both on the side of Asia and America. In this examination, he ascertained the accuracy of Beering, so far as he went; demonstrated the errors with which Stæhlin's map of the New Northern Archipelago abounds; and made large additions to the geographical knowledge of this part of the world. "It reflects," as Mr. Coxe justly observes, "the highest honour even on the British name, that our navigator extended his discoveries much farther in one expedition, and at so great a distance from the point of his departure, than the Russians accomplished in a long series of years, and in parts belonging or contiguous to their own empire."

On the 2d of October, our voyagers came within sight of the island of Oonalashka, and anchored the next day in Samganoodha harbor. Here the first concern was to put the ships under the necessary repair; and, while the carpenters were employed in this business, one third of the people had permission, by turns, to go and collect the berries with which the island abounds, and which, though now beginning to be in a state of decay, did not a little contribute, in conjunction with spruce-beer, effectually to eradicate every seed of the scurvy, that might exist in either of the vessels. Such a supply of fish was likewise procured, as not only served for present consumption, but afforded a quantity to be carried out to sea; so that hence a considerable saving was made of the provisions of the ships, which was at this time an object of no small importance.

Captain Cook, on the 8th, received by the hands of an Oonalashka man, named Derramoushk, a very singular present, which was that of a rye loaf, or rather a pie in the form of a loaf, for it enclosed some salmon, highly seasoned with pepper. This man had the like present for Captain Clerke, and a note for each of the two captains, written in a character which none on board could understand. It was natural to suppose that the presents came from some Russians in the neighbourhood; and therefore a few bottles of rum, wine, and porter, were sent to these unknown friends in return; it being rightly judged, that such articles would be more acceptable than anything besides, which it was in the power of our navigators to bestow. Corporal Lediard of the marines,* an intelligent man, was, at the same time directed to accompany Derramoushk, for the purpose of gaining farther

---

* This Corporal Lediard is an extraordinary man, something of whose history cannot fail of being entertaining to my readers. In the winter of 1786, he set out on the singular undertaking of walking across the continent of America; for the accomplishment of which purpose, he determined to travel by the way of Siberia, and to procure a passage from that country to the opposite American coast. Being an American by birth, and having no means of raising the money necessary for his expenses, a subscription was raised for him by Sir Joseph Banks, and some other gentlemen, amounting, in the whole, to a little more than fifty pounds. With this sum he proceeded to Hamburgh, from which place he went to Copenhagen, and thence to Petersburgh, where he arrived in the beginning of March, 1787. In his journey from Copenhagen to Petersburgh, finding that the gulf of Bothnia was not frozen over, he was obliged to walk round the whole of it, by Tornæo. At Petersburgh he stayed till the 21st of May, when he obtained leave to accompany a convoy of military stores, which at that time was proceeding to Mr. Billings, who had been his shipmate in Captain Cook's voyage, and who was then employed by the Empress of Russia, for the purpose of making discoveries in Siberia, and on the northwest coast of America. With this convoy Mr. Lediard set out, and in August reached the city of Irkutsk in Siberia. After that, he proceeded to the town of Yakutsk, where he met with Captain Billings. From this place he went back to Irkutsk, to spend a part of the winter; proposing in the spring, to return to Yakutsk, in order to proceed in the summer to Okotsk.

Hitherto, Mr. Lediard had gone on prosperously, and flattered himself with the hopes of succeeding in his undertaking. But, in January last (1788,) in consequence of an express from the empress, he was arrested, and, in half an hour's time, carried away, under the guard of two soldiers and an officer, in a post sledge, for Moscow, without his clothes, money, and papers. From Moscow he was conveyed to the city of Moialoff in White Russia, and thence to the town of Tolochin in Poland. There he was informed, that her majesty's orders were, that he was never to enter her dominions again without her express permission. During all this time, he suffered the greatest hardships, from sickness, fatigue and want of rest; so that he was almost reduced to a skeleton. From Tolochin he made his way to Konigsberg; having had, as he says, a miserable journey in a miserable country, in a miserable season, in miserable health, and a malerable purse; and disappointed of his daring enterprise. Mr. Lediard informs Sir Joseph Banks, to whom he sent from time to time, a full account of his transactions, that, though he had been retarded in his pursuits by malice, he had not travelled totally in vain; his observations in Asia, being, perhaps, as complete as a longer visit would have rendered them. From his last letter it appears, that he proposed to return, as speedily as possible, from Konigsberg to England.

information; and with orders, if he met with any Russians, that he should endeavour to make them understand that our voyagers were Englishmen, and the friends and allies of their nation. On the 10th, the corporal returned with three Russian seamen or furriers, who with several others, resided at Egoochshac, where they had a dwelling-house, some store-houses, and a sloop of about thirty tons burden. One of these men was either master or mate of this vessel; another of them wrote a very good hand, and was acquainted with figures: and all of them were sensible and well-behaved persons, who were ready to give Captain Cook every possible degree of information. The great difficulty, in the reception and communication of intelligence, arose from the want of an interpreter. On the 14th, a Russian landed at Oonalashka, whose name was Erasim Gregorioff Sin Ismyloff, and who was the principal person among his countrymen in this and the neighbouring islands. Besides the intelligence which our commander derived from his conversation with Ismyloff, and which was carried on by signs, assisted by figures and other characters, he obtained from him the sight of two charts, and was permitted to copy them. Both of them were manuscripts, and bore every mark of authencity. The first included the Penshinskian Sea; the coast of Tartary, down to the latitude of 41°; the Curil Islands; and the peninsula of Kamtschatka. But it was the second chart that was the most interesting to Captain Cook; for it comprehended all the discoveries made by the Russians to the eastward of Kamtschatka, towards America; which, however, exclusively of the voyages of Beering and Tscherikoff, amounted to little or nothing. Indeed, all the people with whom the captain conversed at Oonalashka, agreed in assuring him, over and over again, that they knew of no other islands, besides those which were laid down upon this chart: and that no Russian had ever seen any part of the continent of America to the northward, excepting that which lies opposite to the country of Tschutskis.

When, on the 1st, Mr. Ismyloff took his final leave of the English navigators, our commander intrusted to his care a letter to the lords commissioners of the admiralty, in which was enclosed a chart of all the northern coasts the captain had visited. It was expected, that there would be an opportunity of sending this letter, in the ensuing spring, to Kamtschatka or Okotsk, and that it would reach Petersburgh during the following winter. Mr. Ismyloff, who faithfully and successfully discharged the trust our commander had reposed in him, seemed to possess abilities, that might entitle him to a higher station in life than that which he occupied. He had a considerable knowledge of astronomy, and was acquainted with the most useful branches of the mathematics. Captain Cook made him a present of a Hadley's octant; and though it was probably the first he had ever seen, he understood, in a very short time, the various uses to which that instrument can be applied.

While the ships lay at Oonalashka, our voyagers did not neglect to make a diligent inquiry into the productions of the island, and the general manners of the inhabitants. On these, as being in a great measure similar to objects which have already been noticed, it is not necessary to enlarge. There is one circumstance, however, so honourable to the natives, that it must not be omitted. They are, to all appearance, the most peaceable and inoffensive people our commander had ever met with; and, with respect to honesty, they might serve as a pattern to countries that are in the highest state of civilization. A doubt was suggested, whether this disposition may not have been the consequence of their present subjection to the Russians. From the affinity which was found to subsist between the dialects of the Greenlander and Esquimaux, and those of the inhabitants of Norton's Sound and Oonalashka, there is strong reason to believe, that all these nations are of the same extraction; and, if that be the case, the existence of a northern communication of some kind, by sea, between the west side of America and the east side, through Baffin's Bay, can scarcely be doubted; which communication, nevertheless, may effectually be shut up against ships, by ice and other impediments.

While the vessels lay in Samganoodha harbour, Captain Cook exerted his usual diligence in making nautical and astronomical observations. All things, on the 26th, having been gotten ready for his departure, he put to sea on that day, and sailed for the Sandwich Islands, it being his intention to spend a few months there, and then to direct his course to Kamtschatka, so as to endeavour to reach that country by the middle of May, in the ensuing summer.

On the 26th of November, when the ships had proceeded southward till they came to the latitude of 20° 55′ land was discovered, which proved to be an island of the name of Mowee, that had not hitherto been visited. It is one of the group of the Sandwich Islands. As it was of the last importance to procure a supply of provisions at these islands, and experience had taught our commander, that he could have had no chance of succeeding in his object if it were left to every man's discretion to traffic for what he pleased, and in what manner he pleased; the captain published an order, prohibiting all persons from trading, excepting such as should be appointed by himself and Captain Clerke. Even these persons were enjoined to trade only for provisions and refreshments. While our navigators lay off Mowee, which was for some days, a friendly intercourse was maintained with the inhabitants.

Another island was discovered on the 30th, which is called by the natives Owyhee. As it appeared to be of greater extent and importance than any of the islands which had yet been visited in this part of the world, Captain Cook spent nearly seven weeks in sailing round, and examining its coast. Whilst he was thus employed, the inhabitants came off, from time to time, in their canoes, and readily engaged in traffic with our voyagers. In the conduct of this business, the behaviour of the islanders was more entirely free from suspicion and reserve than our commander had ever yet experienced. Not even the people of Otaheite itself, with whom he had been so intimately and repeatedly connected, had displayed such a full confidence in the integrity and good treatment of the English.

Among the articles procured from the natives, was a quantity of sugar-cane. Upon a trial, Captain Cook found that a strong decoction of it produced a very palatable beer; on which account, he ordered some more to be brewed for general use. When, however, the barrel was broached, not one of the crew would taste of the liquor. As the captain had no motive in preparing this beverage, but that of sparing the rum and other spirits for a colder climate, he did not exert either authority or persuasion to prevail upon the men to change their resolution; for he knew, that there was no danger of the scurvy, so long as a plentiful supply could be obtained of different vegetables. Nevertheless, that he might not be disappointed in his views, he gave orders that no grog should be served in the ships; and he himself, together with the officers, continued to make use of the sugar-cane beer, which was much improved by the addition of a few hops, that chanced to be still on board. There could be no reasonable doubt of its being a very wholesome liquor; and yet the inconsiderate crew alleged that it would be injurious to their health. No people are more averse to every kind of innovation than seamen, and their prejudices are extremely difficult to be conquered. It was, however, by acting contrary to these prejudices, and by various deviations from established practice, that Captain Cook had been enabled to preserve his men from that dreadful distemper, the scurvy, which, perhaps, has destroyed more of our sailors, in their peaceful voyages, than have fallen by the enemy in military expeditions.

As the captain was pursuing his examination of the coast of

Owyhee, it having fallen calm at one o'clock in the morning of the 19th of December, the Resolution was left to the mercy of a northeasterly swell, which impelled her fast towards the land; so that long before day-break, lights were seen from the land, which was not more than a league distant. The night, at the same time, was dark, with thunder, lightning, and rain. As soon as it was light, a dreadful surf, within half a league of the vessel, appeared breaking from the shore, and it was evident that our navigators had been in the most perilous situation; nor was the danger yet over, for, in consequence of the veering of the wind, they were but just able to keep their distance from the coast. What rendered their situation more alarming was, that a rope of the main-top sail having given way, this occasioned the sail to be rent in two. In the same manner, the two top-gallant sails gave way, though they were not half worn out. However, a favourable opportunity was seized of getting others to the yards; and the Resolution again proceeded in safety.

On the 16th of January, 1779, canoes arrived in such numbers from all parts, that there were not fewer than a thousand about the two ships, most of them crowded with people, and well laden with hogs and other productions of the island. It was a satisfactory proof of their friendly intentions, that there was not a single person amongst them who had with him a weapon of any kind; trade and curiosity alone appeared to be the motives which actuated their conduct. Among such multitudes, however, as, at times, were on board, it will not be deemed surprising, that some should betray a thievish disposition. One of them took out of the Resolution a boat's rudder, and made off with it so speedily that it could not be recovered. Captain Cook judged this to be a favourable opportunity of showing these people the use of fire-arms; and accordingly he ordered two or three muskets and as many four-pounders, to be fired over the canoe, which carried off the rudder. It not being intended that any of the shot should take effect, the surrounding multitude of the natives seemed to be more surprised than terrified.

Mr. Bligh, having been sent to examine a neighbouring bay, reported, on his return, that it had good anchorage and fresh water, and that it was in an accessible situation. Into this bay, therefore, the captain resolved to carry the ships, in order to refit, and to obtain every refreshment which the place could afford. As night approached, the greater part of the Indians retired on shore; but numbers of them requested permission to sleep on board; in which request, curiosity (at least with regard to several of them) was not their sole motive; for it was found the next morning, that various things were missing; on which account our commander determined not to entertain so many persons another night.

On the 17th, the ships came to an anchor in the bay which had been examined by Mr. Bligh, and which is called Karakakooa by the inhabitants. At this time, the vessels continued to be much crowded with natives, and were surrounded with a multitude of canoes. Captain Cook, in the whole course of his voyages, had never seen so numerous a body of people assembled in one place. For, besides those who had come off to the English in their canoes, all the shore of the bay was covered with spectators, and many hundreds were swimming round the ships like shoals of fish. Our navigators could not avoid being greatly impressed with the singularity of this scene; and perhaps there were few on board that now lamented the want of success which had attended the endeavours of getting homeward, the last summer, by a northern passage. "To this disappointment," says the captain, "we owed our having it in our power to revisit the Sandwich Islands, and to enrich our voyage with a discovery, which, though the last, seemed, in many respects to be the most important that had hitherto been made by Europeans, throughout the extent of the Pacific Ocean."

Such is the sentence that concludes our commander's journal: and the satisfaction with which this sentence appears to have been written, cannot fail of striking the mind of every reader. Little did Captain Cook then imagine, that a discovery which promised to add no small honour to his name, and to be productive of very agreeable consequences, should be so fatal in the result. Little did he think, that the island of Owyhee was destined to be the last scene of his exploits, and the cause of his destruction.

The reception which the captain met with from the natives, on his proceeding to anchor in Karakakooa Bay, was flattering in the highest degree. They came off from the shore in astonishing numbers, and expressed their joy by singing and shouting, and by exhibiting a variety of wild and extravagant gestures. Pareea, a young man of great authority, and Kaneena, another chief, had already attached themselves to our commander, and were very useful in keeping their countrymen from being troublesome.

During the long cruise of our navigators off the island of Owyhee, the inhabitants had almost universally behaved with great fairness and honesty in their dealings, and had not shown the slightest propensity to theft: and this was a fact the more extraordinary, as those with whom our people had hitherto maintained any intercourse, were of the lowest rank, being either servants or fishermen. But, after the arrival of the Resolution and Discovery in Karakakooa Bay, the case was greatly altered. The immense crowd of islanders that blocked up every part of the ships, not only afforded frequent opportunities of pilfering without risk of detection; but held out, even if they should be detected, a prospect of escaping with impunity, from the superiority of their numbers to that of the English. Another circumstance, to which the alteration in the conduct of the natives might be ascribed, arose from the presence and encouragement of their chiefs, into whose possession the booty might be traced, and whom there was reason to suspect of being the instigators of the depredations that were committed.

Soon after the Resolution had gotten into her station, Pareea and Kaneena brought on board a third chief, named Koah, who was represented as being a priest, and as having, in his early youth, been a distinguished warrior. In the evening, Captain Cook, attended by Mr. Bayley and Mr. King, accompanied Koah on shore. Upon this occasion, the captain was received with very peculiar and extraordinary ceremonies; with ceremonies that indicated the highest respect on the part of the natives, and which, indeed, seemed to fall little short of adoration.

One principal object that engaged our commander's attention at Owyhee, was the salting of hogs for seastore; in which his success was far more complete than had been attained in any former attempt of the same kind. It doth not appear, that experiments relative to this subject had been made by the navigators of any nation before Captain Cook. His first trials were in 1774, during his second voyage round the world; when his success, though very imperfect, was nevertheless, sufficient to encourage his farther efforts in a matter of so much importance. As the present voyage was likely to be protracted a year beyond the time for which the ships were victualled, he was under a necessity of providing, by some such method, for the subsistence of the crews, or of relinquishing the prosecution of his discoveries. Accordingly, he lost no opportunity of renewing his attempts; and the event answered his most sanguine expectations. Captain King brought home with him some of the pork, which was pickled at Owyhee in January, 1779; and, upon its being tasted by several persons in England about Christmas, 1780, it was found to be perfectly sound and wholesome. It seemed to be destined, that in every instance Captain Cook should excel all who had gone before him, in promoting the purposes of navigation.

On the 26th, the captain had his first interview with Terreeoboo, the king of the island. The meeting was conducted with a variety of ceremonies, among which, the custom of making an exchange of names, which, amongst all the islanders of the Pacific Ocean is the strongest pledge of friendship, was observed When the formalities of the interview were over, our commander carried Terreeoboo, and as many chiefs as the pinnace could hold, on board the Resolution. They were received, on this occasion, with every mark of respect that could be shown them; and, in return for a beautiful and splendid feathered cloak which the king had bestowed on Captain Cook, the captain put a linen shirt on his majesty, and girt his own hanger round him.

In the progress of the intercourse which was maintained between our voyagers and the natives, the quiet and inoffensive behaviour of the latter took away every apprehension of danger; so that the English trusted themselves among them at all times, and in all situations. The instances of kindness and civility which our people experienced from them were so numerous, that they could not easily be recounted. A society of priests, in particular, displayed a generosity and munificence, of which no equal example had hitherto been given : for they furnished a constant supply of hogs and vegetables to our navigators, without ever demanding a return, or even hinting at it in the most distant manner. All this was said to be done at the expense of a great man among them, who was at the head of their body, whose name was Kaoo, and who on other occasions manifested his attachment to the English. There was not always so much reason to be satisfied with the conduct of the warrior chiefs, or earees, as with that of the priests. Indeed, the satisfaction that was derived from the usual gentleness and hospitality of the inhabitants, was frequently interrupted by the propensity of many of them to stealing ; and this circumstance was the more distressing, as it sometimes obliged our commander and the other officers to have recourse to acts of severity, which they would willingly have avoided, if the necessity of the case had not absolutely called for them.

Though the kind and liberal behaviour of the natives continued without remission, Terreeoboo, and his chiefs, began at length to be very inquisitive about the time in which our voyagers were to take their departure. Nor will this be deemed surprising, when it is considered, that, during sixteen days in which the English had been in the bay of Karakakooa, they had made an enormous consumption of hogs and vegetables. It did not appear, however, that Terreeboo had any other view in his inquiries, than a desire of making sufficient preparation for dismissing our navigators with presents suitable to the respect and kindness towards them which he had always displayed. For, on his being informed, that they were to leave the island in a day or two, it was observed, that a kind of proclamation was immediately made through the villages, requiring the people to bring in their hogs and vegetables, for the king to present to the orono,* on his quitting the country. Accordingly, on the 3d of February, being the day preceding the time which had been fixed for the sailing of the ships, Terreeoboo invited Captain Cook and Mr. King to attend him to the place where Kaoo resided. On their arrival, they found the ground covered with parcels of cloth, at a small distance from which lay an immense quantity of vegetables ; and near them was a large herd of hogs. At the close of the visit, the greater part of the cloth, and the whole of the hogs and vegetables, were given by Terreeoboo to the captain and Mr. King ; who were astonished at the value and magnificence of the present ; for it far exceeded everything of the kind which they had seen, either at the Friendly or Society Islands. Mr. King had in so high a degree conciliated the affections and gained the esteem of the inhabitants of Owyhee,

---

* Orono was a title of high honour, which had been bestowed on Captain Cook.

that, with offers of the most flattering nature, he was strongly solicited to remain in the country. Terreeoboo and Kaoo waited upon Captain Cook, whose son they supposed Mr. King to be, with a formal request that he might be left behind. To avoid giving a postive refusal to an offer which was so kindly intended, the captain told them that he could not part with Mr. King at that time, but that, on his return to the island in the next year, he would endeavour to settle the matter to their satisfaction.

Early on the 4th, the ships sailed out of Karakakooa Bay, being followed by a large number of canoes. It was our commander's design, before he visited the other islands, to finish the survey of Owyhee, in hopes of meeting with a road better sheltered than the bay he had just left. In case of not succeeding in this respect, he purposed to take a view of the southeast part of Mowee, where he was informed that he should find an excellent harbor.

The circumstances which brought Captain Cook back to Karakakooa Bay, and the unhappy consequences that followed, I shall give from Mr. Samwell's narrative of his death. This narrative was, in the most obliging manner, communicated to me in manuscript, by Mr. Samwell, with entire liberty to make such use of it as I should judge proper. Upon a perusal of it, its importance struck me in so strong a light, that I wished to have it separately laid before the world. Accordingly, with Mr. Samwell's concurrence, I procured its publication, that, if any objections should be made to it, I might be able to notice them in my own work. As the narrative had continued for more than two years unimpeached and uncontradicted, I esteem myself fully authorised to insert it in this place, as containing the most complete and authentic account of the melancholy catastrophe, which, at Owyhee, befel our illustrious navigator and commander.

"On the 6th we were overtaken by a gale of wind; and the

next night, the Resolution had the misfortune of springing the head of the foremast, in such a dangerous manner, that Captain Cook was obliged to return to Keragegooah,* in order to have it repaired; for we could find no other convenient harbour on the island. The same gale had occasioned much distress among some canoes, that had paid us a visit from the shore. One of them, with two men and a child on board, was picked up by the Resolution, and rescued from destruction: the men, having toiled hard all night, in attempting to reach the land, were so much exhausted, that they could hardly mount the ship's side. When they got upon the quarter-deck, they burst into tears, and seemed much affected with the dangerous situation from which they had escaped; but the little child appeared lively and cheerful. One of the Resolution's boats was also so fortunate, as to save a man and two women, whose canoe had been upset by the violence of the waves. They were brought on board, and, with the others, partook of the kindness and humanity of Captain Cook.

"On the morning of Wednesday, the 10th, we were within a few miles of the harbour; and were soon joined by several canoes, in which appeared many of our old acquaintance, who seemed to have come to welcome us back. Among them was Coo, aha, a priest; he had brought a small pig, and some cocoa nuts in his hand, which, after having chanted a few sentences, he presented to Captain Clerke. He then left us, and hastened on board the Resolution, to perform the same friendly ceremony before Captain Cook. Having but light winds all that day, we

---

* It is proper to take notice, that Mr. Samwell spells the names of several persons and places differently from what is done in the history of the voyage. For instance,

Karakakooa	he calls	Ke, rag, e, goo, ah,
Terreeoboo,	"	Kariopoo,
Kowrowa,	"	Kavaroah,
Kaneecab areea,	"	Kaneekapo, herei,
Maiha maiha,	"	Ka, mea, mea.

could not gain the harbour. In the afternoon, a chief of the first rank, and nearly related to Kariopoo, paid us a visit on board the Discovery. His name was Ka, mea, mea: he was dressed in a very rich feathered cloak, which he seemed to have brought for sale, but would part with it for nothing except iron daggers. These, the chiefs, some time before our departure, had preferred to every other article; for, having received a plentiful supply of hatchets and other tools, they began to collect a store of warlike instruments. Kameamea procured nine daggers for his cloak; and, being pleased with his reception, he and his attendants slept on board that night.

"In the morning of the 11th of February, the ships anchored again in Keragegooah bay, and preparation was immediately made for landing the Resolution's foremast. We were visited but by few of the Indians, because there were but few in the bay. On our departure, those belonging to other parts had repaired to their several habitations, and were again to collect from various quarters, before we could expect to be surrounded by such multitudes as we had once seen in that harbour. In the afternoon, I walked about a mile into the country, to visit an Indian friend, who had, a few days before, come near twenty miles, in a small canoe, to see me, while the ship lay becalmed. As the canoe had not left us long before a gale of wind came on, I was alarmed for the consequences: however, I had the pleasure to find, that my friend had escaped unhurt, though not without some difficulties. I take notice of this short excursion, merely because it afforded me an opportunity of observing, that there appeared no change in the disposition or behaviour of the inhabitants. I saw nothing that could induce me to think, that they were displeased with our return, or jealous of the intention of our second visit. On the contrary, that abundant good nature, which had always characterised them, seemed still to glow in every bosom, and to animate every countenance.

"The next day, February the 12th, the ships were put under a taboo, by the chiefs: a solemnity, it seems, that was requisite to be observed, before Kariopoo, the king, paid his first visit to Captain Cook, after his return. He waited upon him the same day, on board the Resolution, attended by a large train, some of which bore the presents designed for Captain Cook; who received him in his usually friendly manner, and gave him several articles in return. This amicable ceremony being settled, the taboo was dissolved: matters went on in the usual train; and the next day, February the 13th, we were visited by the natives in great numbers: the Resolution's mast was landed, and the astronomical observatories erected on their former situation. I landed, with another gentleman at the town of Kavoroah, where we found a great number of canoes, just arrived from different parts of the island, and the Indians busy in constructing temporary huts on the beach, for their residence during the stay of the ships. On our return on board the Discovery, we learned, than an Indian had been detected in stealing the armorer's tongs from the forge, for which he received a pretty severe flogging, and was sent out of the ship. Notwithstanding the example made of this man, in the afternoon another had the audacity to snatch the tongs and chisel from the same place, with which he jumped overboard, and swam for the shore. The master and a midshidman were instantly dispatched after him, in the small cutter. The Indian, seing himself pursued, made for a canoe; his countrymen took him on board, and paddled as swift as they could towards the shore; we fired several muskets at them, but to no effect, for they soon got out of reach of our shot. Pareah, one of the chiefs, who was at that time on board the Discovery, understanding what had happened, immediately went ashore, promising to bring back the stolen goods. Our boat was so far distanced, in chasing the canoe which had taken the thief on board, that he had time to make his escape into the country

Captain Cook, who was then ashore, endeavoured to intercept his landing; but, it seems, that he was led out of the way by some of the natives, who had officiously intruded themselves as guides. As the master was approaching near the landing-place he was met by some of the Indians in a canoe: they had brought back the tongs and chisel, together with another article, that we had not missed, which happened to be the lid of the water-cask. Having recovered these things, he was returning on board, when he was met by the Resolution's pinnace, with five men in her, who, without any orders, had come from the observatories to his assistance. Being thus unexpectedly reinforced, he thought himself strong enough to insist upon having the thief, or the canoe which took him in, delivered up as reprisals. With that view he turned back; and having found the canoe on the beach, he was preparing to launch it into the water, when Pareah made his appearance, and insisted upon his not taking it away, as it was his property. The officer not regarding him, the chief seized upon him, pinioned his arms behind, and held him by the hair of his head; on which one of the sailors struck him with an oar: Pareah instantly quitted the officer, snatched the oar out of the man's hand, and snapped it in two across his knee. At length the multitude began to attack our people with stones. They made some resistance, but were soon overpowered, and obliged to swim for safety to the small cutter, which lay farther out than the pinnace. The officers, not being expert swimmers, retreated to a small rock in the water, where they were closely pursued by the Indians. One man darted a broken oar at the master; but his foot slipping at the time, he missed him, which fortunately saved that officer's life. At last, Pareah interfered, and put an end to their violence. The gentlemen, knowing that his presence was their only defence against the fury of the natives, entreated him to stay with them, till they could get off in the boats: but that he refused, and left them. The master went to seek assistance from the party at the observatories; but the midshipman chose to remain in the pinnace. He was very rudely treated by the mob, who plundered the boat of everything that was loose on board, and then began to knock her to pieces, for the sake of the iron-work; but Pareah fortunately returned in time to prevent her destruction. He had met the other gentleman on his way to the observatories, and suspecting his erraud, had forced him to return. He dispersed the crowd again, and desired the gentlemen to return on board; they represented, that all the oars had been taken out of the boat, on which he brought some of them back, and the gentlemen were glad to get off without farther molestation. They had not proceeded far, before they were overtaken by Pareah, in a canoe: he delivered the midshipman's cap, which had been taken from him in the scuffle, joined noses with them, in token of reconciliation, and was anxious to know if Captain Cook would kill him for what had happened. They assured him of the contrary, and made signs of friendship to him in return. He then left them, and paddled over to the town of Kavaroah, and that was the last time we ever saw him. Captain Cook returned on board soon after, much displeased with the whole of this disagreeable business; and the same night sent a lieutenant on board the Discovery to learn the particulars of it, as it had originated in that ship.

It was remarkable, that in the midst of the hurry and confusion attending this affair, Kanynah (a chief who had always been on terms particularly friendly with us) came from the spot where it happened, with a hog to sell on board the Discovery; it was of an extraordinary large size, and he demanded for it a pahowa, or dagger, of an unusual length. He pointed to us, that it must be as long as his arm. Captain Clerke not having one of that length, told him he would get one made for him by the morning; with which being satisfied, he left the hog, and went ashore without making any stay with us. It will not be altogether foreign to the subject, to mention a circumstance that happened to-day on board the Resolution. An Indian chief asked Captain Cook, at his table, if he was a Tata Toa ; which means a fighting man, or a soldier. Being answered in the affirmative, he desired to see his wounds. Captain Cook held out his right hand, which had a scar upon it, dividing the thumb from the finger, the whole length of the metacarpal bones. The Indian, being thus convinced of his being a Toa, put the same question to another gentleman present, but he happened to have none of those distinguishing marks : the chief then said, that he himself was a Toa, and showed the scars of some wounds he had received in battle. Those who were on duty at the observatories, were disturbed, during the night, with shrill and melancholy sounds, issuing from the adjacent villages, which they took to be the lamentations of the women. Perhaps the quarrel between us might have filled their minds with apprehensions for the safety of their husbands ; but be that as it may, their mournful cries struck the sentinels with unusual awe and terror.

" To widen the breach between us, some of the Indians, in the night, took away the Discovery's large cutter, which lay swamped at the buoy of one of her anchors : they had carried her off so quietly that we did not miss her till the morning, Sunday, February the 14th. Captain Clerke lost no time in waiting upon Captain Cook, to acquaint him with the accident ; he returned on board with orders for the launch and small cutter to go, under the command of the second lieutenant, and lie off the east point of the bay, in order to intercept all canoes that might attempt to get out ; and, if he found it necessary, to fire upon them. At the same time, the third lieutenant of the Resolution, with the launch and small cutter, was sent on the same service, to the opposite point of the bay; and the master was despatched in the large cutter, in pursuit of a double canoe, already under sail, making the best of her way out of the harbour. He soon came up with her, and by firing a few muskets, drove her on shore, and the Indians left her: this happened to be the canoe of Omea, a man who bore the title of Orono. He was on board himself, and it would have been fortunate, if our people had secured him, for his person was held as sacred as that of the king. During this time, Captain Cook was preparing to go ashore himself, at the town of Kavaroah, in order to secure the person of Kariopoo, before he should have time to withdraw himself to another part of the island, out of our reach. This appeared the most effectual step that could be taken on the present occasion, for the recovery of the boat. It was the measure he had invariably pursued, in similar cases, at other islands in these seas, and it had always been attended with the desired success: in fact, it would be difficult to point out any other mode of proceeding on these emergencies, likely to attain the object in view: we had reason to suppose, that the king and his attendants had fled when the alarm was first given: in that case, it was Captain Cook's intention to secure the large canoes which were hauled up on the beach. He left the ship about seven o'clock, attended, by the lieutenant of marines, a sergeant, corporal, and seven private men: the pinnace's crew were also armed, and under the command of Mr. Roberts. As they rowed towards the shore, Captain Cook ordered the launch to leave her station at the west point of the bay, in order to assist his own boat. This is a circumstance worthy of notice; for it clearly shows, that he was not unapprehensive of meeting with resistance from the natives, or unmindful of the necessary preparations for the safety of himself and his people. I will venture to say, that, from the appearance of things just at that time, there was not one, beside himself, who judged that such precaution was absolutely requisite; so little did his conduct, on the occasion, bear the marks of rashness, or a precipitate self-confidence! He landed, with the marines, at the upper end of the town of Kavaroah: the Indians immediately flocked round, as usual, and showed him the customary marks of respect, by prostrating themselves before him—there were no signs of hostilities, or much alarm among them. Captain Cook, however, did not seem willing to trust to appearances; but was particularly attentive to the disposition of the marines, and to have them kept clear of the crowd. He first inquired for the king's sons, two youths who were much attached to him, and generally his companions on board. Messengers being sent for them, they soon came to him, and informing him, that their father was asleep, at a house not far from them, he accompanied them thither, and took the marines along with them. As he passed along, the natives every where prostrated themselves before him, and seemed to have lost no part of that respect they had always shown to his person. He was joined by several chiefs, among whom was Kanynah, and his brother Koohowrooah. They kept the crowd in order, according to their usual custom; and, being ignorant of his intention in coming on shore, frequently asked him if he wanted any hogs, or other provisions: he told them that he did not, and that his business was to see the king. When he arrived at the house, he ordered some of the Indians to go in, and inform Kariopoo, that he waited without to speak with him. They came out two or three times, and instead of returning any answers from the king, presented some pieces of red cloth to him, which made Captain Cook suspect that he was not in the house; he therefore desired the lieutenant of marines to go in. The lieutenant found the old man just awakened from sleep, and seemingly alarmed at the message; but he came out without hesitation. Captain Cook took him by the hand, and in a friendly manner asked him to go on board, to which he very readily consented. Thus far matters appeared in a favourable train, and the natives did not seem much alarmed or apprehensive of hostility on our side: at which Captain Cook expressed himself a little surprised, saying, that as the inhabitants of that town appeared innocent of stealing the cutter, he should not molest them, but that he must get the king on board. Kariopoo sat down before his door, and was surrounded by a great crowd: Kanynah and his brother were both very active in keeping order among them. In a little time, however, the Indians were observed arming themselves with long spears, clubs, and daggers and putting on thick mats which they use as armour. This hostile appearance increased, and became more alarming, on the arrival of two men in a canoe from the opposite side of the bay, with the news of a chief called Kareemo having been killed by one of the Discovery's boats. In their passage across they had also delivered this account to each of the ships. Upon that information the women who were sitting upon the beach at their breakfasts, and conversing familiarly with our people in the boats, retired, and a confused murmur spread through the crowd. An old priest came to Captain Cook, with a cocoa-nut in his hand, which he held out to him as a present, at the same time singing very loud. He was often desired to be silent, but in vain ; he continued importunate and troublesome, and there was no such thing as getting rid of him or his noise : it seemed as if he meant to divert our attention from his countrymen, who were growing more tumultuous, and arming themselves in every quarter. Captain Cook, being at the same time surrounded by a great crowd, thought his situation rather hazardous : he therefore ordered the lieutenant of marines to march his small party to the water-side, where the boats lay within a few yards of the shore : the Indians readily made a lane for them to pass, and did not offer to interrupt them. The distance they had to go might be about fifty or sixty yards ; Captain Cook followed, having hold of Kariopoo's hand, who accompanied him very willingly : he was attended by his wife, two sons, and several chiefs. The troublesome old priest followed, making the same savage noise. Keowa, the younger son, went directly into the pinnace, expecting his father to follow; but just as he arrived at the water-side, his wife threw her arms about his neck, and with the assistance of two chiefs, forced him to sit down by the side of a double canoe. Captain Cook expostulated with them, but to no purpose: they would not suffer the king to proceed, telling him, that he would be put to death if he went on board the ship. Kariopoo, whose conduct seemed entirely resigned to the will of others, hung down his head, and appeared much distressed.

"While the king was in this situation, a chief well known to us, of the name Coho, was observed lurking near, with an iron dagger, partly concealed under his cloak, seemingly with the intention of stabbing Captain Cook, or the lieutenant of marines. The latter proposed to fire at him, but Captain Cook would not permit it. Coho closing upon them, obliged the officer to strike him with his piece, which made him retire. Another Indian laid hold of the sergeant's musket and endeavoured to wrench it from him, but was prevented by the lieutenant's making a blow at him. Captain Cook, seeing the tumult increase, and the Indians growing more daring and resolute, observed, that if he were to take the king off by force, he could not do it without sacrificing the lives of many of his people. He then paused a little, and was on the point of giving his orders to re-embark, when a man threw a stone at him; which he returned with a discharge of small shot (with which one barrel of his double piece was loaded). The man having a thick mat before him, received little or no hurt: he brandished his spear, and threatened to dart it at Captai Cook, who being still unwilling to take away his life, instead of firing with ball, knocked him down with his musket. He expostulated strongly with the most forward of the crowd, upon their turbulent behaviour. He had given up all thoughts of getting the king on board, as it appeared impracticable; and his care was then only to act on the defensive, and to secure a safe embarkation for his small party, which was closely pressed by a body of several thousand people. Keowa, the king's son, who was in the pinnace, being alarmed on hearing the first firing, was, at his own entreaty, put on shore again ; for even at that time, Mr. Roberts, who commanded her, did not apprehend that Captain Cook's person was in any danger : otherwise he would have detained the prince, which, no doubt would have been a great check on the Indians. One man was observed, behind a double canoe, in the action of darting his spear at Captain Cook, who was forced to fire at him in his own defence, but happened to kill another close to him, equally forward in the tumult : the sergeant observing that he had missed the man he aimed at, received orders to fire at him, which he did and killed him. By this time, the impetuosity of the Indians was somewhat repressed ; they fell back in a body, and seemed staggered : but being pushed on by those behind, they returned to the charge, and poured a volley of stones among the marines, who, without waiting for orders, returned it with a general discharge of musketry, which was instantly followed by a fire from the boats. At this Captain Cook was heard to express his astonishment : he waved his hand to the boats, called to them to cease firing, and to come nearer in to receive the marines. Mr. Roberts immediately brought the pinnace as close to the shore as he could without grounding, notwithstanding the showers of stones that fell among the people : but ——————, the lieutenant who commanded in the launch, instead of pulling in to the assistance of Captain Cook, withdrew his boat farther off, at the moment that everything seems to have depended upon the timely exertions of those in the boats By his own account, he mistook the signal ; but be that as it may, this circumstance appears to me to have decided the fatal turn of the affair, and to have removed every chance which remained with Captain Cook, of escaping with his life. The busi

DEATH OF CAPT. COOK, IN OWHYHEE, FEB. 14TH, 1779. PAGE 388.

ness of saving the marines out of the water, in consequence of that, fell altogether upon the pinnace; which thereby became so much crowded, that the crew were in a great measure prevented from using their fire-arms, or giving what assistance they otherwise might have done to Captain Cook; so that he seems at the most critical point of time to have wanted the assistance of both boats, owing to the removal of the launch. For, notwithstanding that they kept up a fire on the crowd, from the situation to which they had removed in that boat, the fatal confusion which ensued on her being withdrawn, to say the least of it, must have prevented the full effect, that the prompt coöperation of the two boats, according to Captain Cook's orders, must have had, towards the preservation of himself and his people.* At that time, it was to the boats alone that Captain Cook had to look for his safety; for when the marines had fired, the Indians rushed among them, and forced them into the water, where four of them were killed: their lieutenant was wounded, but fortunately escaped, and was taken up by the pinnace. Captain Cook was then the only one remaining on the rock: he was observed making for the pinnace, holding his left hand against the back of his head, to guard it from the stones, and carrying his musket under the other arm. An Indian was seen following him, but with caution and timidity: for he stopped once or twice, as if undetermined to proceed. At last he advanced upon him unawares, and with a large club, or common stake, gave him a blow on the back of the head, and then precipitately retreated. The stroke seemed to have stunned Captain Cook: he staggered a few paces, then fell on his hand and one knee, and dropped his musket. As he was rising, and

---

* I have been informed, on the best authority, that, in the opinion of Captain Phillips, who commanded the marines, and whose judgment must of the greatest weight, it is extremely doubtful whether any thing could successfully have been done to preserve the life of Captain Cook, even if no mistake had been committed on the part of the launch.

before he could recover his feet, another Indian stabbed him in the back of the neck with an iron dagger. **He** then fell into a bite of water about knee deep, where others crowded upon him, and endeavoured to keep him under: but struggling very strongly with them, he got his head up, and casting his look towards the pinnace, seemed to solicit assistance. Thought the boat **was** not above five or six yards distant from him, yet from the crowded and confused state of the crew, it seems it was not in their power to save him. The Indians got him under again, but in deeper water: **he was however able to get** his head up once more, and being almost spent in the struggle, he naturally turned to the rock, and was endeavouring to support himself by it, when a savage gave him a blow with a club, and he was seen alive no more. They hauled him up lifeless on the rocks, where they seemed to take a savage pleasure in using every barbarity to his dead body, snatching the daggers out of each other's hands, to have the horrid satisfaction of piercing the fallen **victim** of their barbarous rage.

"I need make no reflection on the great loss we suffered on **this** occasion, or attempt to describe what we felt. It is enough **to say,** that no man **was ever** more beloved or admired ; and it is **truly** painful to **reflect, that** he seems to have fallen a sacrifice merely for want of being properly supported ; a fate singularly to be lamented, as having fallen to his lot, who had ever been conspicuous for his care of those under his command, and who seemed, to the last, to pay as much attention to their preservation, as to that of his own life.

"If anything could have added to the **shame** and indignation universally felt on this occasion, it was to find that his remains had been deserted, and left exposed on the beach, although they might have been brought off. It appears from the information of four or five midshipmen, who arrived on the spot at the conclusion of the fatal business, that the beach was then almost entirely deserted by the Indians, who at length had given way to the fire of the boats, and dispersed through the town: so that there seemed no great obstacle to prevent the recovery of Captain Cook's body; but the lieutenant returned on board without making the attempt. It is unnecessary to dwell longer on this painful subject, and to relate the complaints and censures that fell on the conduct of the lieutenant. It will be sufficient to observe, that they were so loud as to oblige Captain Clerke publicly to notice them, and to take the depositions of his accusers down in writing. The captain's bad state of health and approaching dissolution, it is supposed, induced him to destroy these papers a short time before his death.

"It is a painful task, to be obliged to notice circumstances which seem to reflect upon the character of any man. A strict regard to truth, however, compelled me to the insertion of these facts, which I have offered merely as facts, without presuming to connect with them any comment of my own: esteeming it the part of a faithful historian, 'to extenuate nothing, nor set down aught in malice.'

"The fatal accident happened at eight o'clock in the morning, about an hour after Captain Cook landed. It did not seem, that the king or his sons were witnesses to it; but it is supposed that they withdrew in the midst of the tumult. The principal actors were the other chiefs, many of them the king's relations and attendants: the man who stabbed him with the dagger was called Nooah. I happened to be the only one who recollected his **person**, from having on a former occasion mentioned his name in the journal I kept. I was induced to take particular notice of him, more from his personal appearance than any other consideration, though he was of high rank, and a near relation of the king: he was stout and tall, with a fierce look and demeanour, and one who united in his figure the two qualities of strength and agility, in a greater degree than ever I remembered to have seen before in any other **man**. His age might be about thirty, and by the white scurf on his skin, and his sore eyes, he appeared to be a hard drinker of kava. He was a constant companion of the king, with whom I first saw him, when he paid a visit to Captain Clerke. The chief who first struck Captain Cook with the club, **was** called Karimano, eraha, but I did not know him by his name. These circumstances I learned of honest Kaireekea, the priest; who added, that they were both held in great esteem on account of that action: neither of them came near us afterwards. When the boats left the shore, the Indians carried away the dead body of Captain Cook and those of the marines, to the rising ground, at the back of the town, where we could plainly see them with our glasses from the ships.

"This most melancholy accident appears to have been altogether unexpected and unforeseen, as well on the part of the natives as ourselves. I never saw sufficient reason to induce me to believe that there was anything of design, or a preconcerted plan on their side, or that they purposely sought to quarrel with us; thieving, which gave rise to the whole, they were equally guilty of in our first and second visits. It was the cause of every misunderstanding that happened between us: their petty thefts were generally overlooked, but sometimes slightly punished; the boat, which they at last ventured to take away, was an object of no small magnitude to people in our situation, who could not possibly replace her, and therefore not slightly to be given up. We had no other chance of recovering her, but by getting the person of the king into our possession: on our attempting to do that, the natives became alarmed for his safety, and naturally opposed those whom they deemed his enemies. **In** the sudden conflict that ensued, we had the unspeakable misfortune of losing our excellent commander, in the manner already related. It is in this light the affair has always appeared to me as entirely accidental, and not in the least owing to any previous offence received, or jealousy of our second visit entertained by the natives.

"Pareah seems to have been the principal instrument in bringing about this fatal disaster. We learned afterwards, that it was he who had employed some people to steal the boat: the king did not seem to be privy to it, or even apprised of what had happened, till Captain Cook landed.

"It was generally remarked, that, at first, the Indians showed great resolution in facing our fire-arms; but it was entirely owing to ignorance of their effect. They thought that their thick mats would defend them from a ball, as well as from a stone; but being soon convinced of their error, yet still at a loss to account how such execution was done among them, they had recourse to a stratagem, which, though it answered no other purpose, served to show their ingenuity and quickness of invention. Observing the flashes of the muskets, they naturally concluded, that water would counteract their effect, and therefore, very sagaciously, dipped their mats, or armour, in the sea, just as they came on to face our people: but finding this last resource to fail them, they soon dispersed, and left the beach entirely clear. It was an object they never neglected, even at the greatest hazard, to carry off their slain; a custom probably owing to the barbarity with which they treat the dead body of an enemy, and the trophies they make of his bones."

In consequence of this barbarity of disposition, the whole remains of Captain Cook could not be recovered. For, though every exertion was made for that purpose; though negotiations and threatenings were alternately employed, little more than the principal part of his bones (and that with great difficulty) could be procured. By the possession of them, our navigators were enabled to perform the last offices to their eminent and unfortunate commander. The bones, having been put into a coffin, and the service being read over them, were committed to the deep, on the 21st, with the usual military honours. What were the feelings of the companies of both the ships, on this occasion, must be left to the world to conceive ; for those who were present know, that it is not in the power of any pen to express them.

A promotion of officers followed the decease of Captain Cook. Captain Clerke having succeeded of course to the command of the expedition, removed on board the Resolution. By him Mr. Gore was appointed captain of the Discovery, and the rest of the lieutenants obtained an addition of rank, in their proper order. Mr. Harvey, a midshipman, who had been in the last as well as the present voyage, was promoted to the vacant lieutenancy.

Not long after Captain Cook's death, an event occurred in Europe, which had a particular relation to the voyage of our navigator, and which was so honourable to himself, and to the great nation from whom it proceeded, that it is no small pleasure to me to be able to lay the transaction somewhat at large before my readers. What I refer to is, the letter which was issued, on the 19th of March, 1779, by M. Sartine, secretary of the marine department at Paris, and sent to all the commanders of French ships. The rescript was as follows : "Captain Cook, who sailed from Plymouth in July, 1776, on board the Resolution, in company with the Discovery, Captain Clerke, in order to make some discoveries on the coasts, islands, and seas of Japan and California, being on the point of returning to Europe ; and such discoveries being of general utility to all nations, it is the king's pleasure, that Captain Cook shall be treated as a commander of a neutral and allied power, and that all captains of armed vessels, etc. who may meet that famous navigator, shall make him acquainted with the king's orders on this behalf, but, at the same time, let him know, that on his part he must refrain from all hostilities." By the Marquis of Condorcet we are informed, that this measure originated in the liberal and enlightened mind of that excellent citizen and statesman, M. Turgot.

"When war," says the marquis, "was declared between France and England, M. Turgot saw how honourable it would be to the French nation, that the vessel of Captain Cook should be treated with respect at sea. He composed a memorial, in which he proved, that honour, reason, and even interest, dictated this act of respect for humanity ; and it was in consequence of this memorial, the author of which was unknown during his life, that an order was given not to treat as an enemy, the common benefactor of every European nation."

Whilst great praise is due to M. Turgot, for having suggested the adoption of a measure which hath contributed so much to the reputation of the French government, it must not be forgotten, that the first thought of such a plan of conduct was probably owing to Dr. Benjamin Franklin. Thus much, at least, is certain, that this eminent philosopher, when ambassador at Paris from the United States of America, preceded the court of France in issuing a similar requisition ; a copy of which **cannot fail of** being acceptable to the reader.

"*To all Captains and Commanders of armed Ships acting by Commission from the Congress of the United States of America, now in war with Great Britain.*

"GENTLEMEN,

"A ship having been fitted out from England before the commencement of this war, to make discoveries of new countries, in unknown seas, under the conduct of that most celebrated navigator and discoverer, Captain Cook, an undertaking **truly** laudable in itself, as the increase of geographical **knowledge** facilitates the communication between distant nations, in the exchange of useful products and manufactures, and the extension of arts, whereby the common enjoyments of human life are multiplied and augmented, and science of other kinds increased, to the benefit of mankind in general.—This is therefore most earnestly to recommend to every one of you, that in case the said ship, which is now expected to be soon in the European seas on her return, should happen to fall into your hands, you would not consider her as an enemy, nor suffer any plunder to be made of the effects contained in her, nor obstruct her immediate return to England, by detaining her, or sending her into any other part of Europe, or to America ; but that you would treat the said Captain Cook and his people with all civility and kindness, affording them, as common friends to mankind, all the assistance in your power, which they may happen to stand in need of. In so doing, you will not only gratify the generosity of your own dispositions, but there is no doubt of your obtaining the approbation of the Congress, and your other American owners.

"I have the honour to be, Gentlemen,

"Your most obedient, humble servant,

"B. FRANKLIN.

"At Passy, near Paris, this 10th day of March, 1779.

"Minister Plenipotentiary from the Congress of the United States, at the Court of France."

It is observable, that, as Dr. Franklin acted on his own authority, he could only *earnestly recommend* to the commanders of American armed vessels not to consider Captain Cook as an enemy ; and it is somewhat remarkable, that he mentions no more than one ship ; Captain Clerke not being noticed in the requisition. In the confidence which the doctor expressed, with respect to the approbation of Congress, he happened to be mistaken. As the members of that assembly, at least with regard to the greater part of them, were not possessed of minds equally enlightened with that of their ambassador, he was not supported by his masters in this noble act of humanity, of love to science, and of liberal policy. The orders he had given were instantly reversed; and it was directed by Congress, that especial care should be taken to seize Captain Cook, if an opportunity of doing it occurred. All this proceeded from a false notion, that it would be injurious to the United States for the English to obtain a knowledge of the opposite coast of America.

The conduct of the court of Spain was regulated by similiar principles of jealousy. It was apprehended by that court, that there was reason to be cautious of granting, too easily, an indulgence to Captain Cook; since it was not certain what mischiefs might ensue to the Spainards from a northern passage to their American dominions. M. de Belluga a Spanish gentleman and officer, of a liberal and philosophical turn of mind, and who was a member of the Royal Society of London, endeavoured to prevail upon the Count of Florida Blanca, and M. d'Almodavar, to grant an order of protection to the Resolution and Discovery; and he flattered himself, that the ministers of the king of Spain would be prevailed upon to prefer the cause of science to the partial views of interest; but the Spanish government was not capable of rising to so enlarged and magnanimous a plan of policy. To the French nation alone, therefore, was reserved the honour of setting an example of wisdom and humanity, which, I trust, will not, hereafter, be so uncommon in the history of mankind.

The progress of the voyage, after the decease of Captain Cook, doth not fall within the design of the present narrative.*

CHAPTER VII.

CHARACTER OF CAPTAIN COOK—EFFECTS OF HIS VOYAGES—TESTIMONIES OF APPLAUSE—COMMEMORATIONS OF HIS SERVICES—REGARD PAID TO HIS FAMILY—CONCLUSION.

From the relation that has been given of Captain Cook's course of life, and of the important events in which he was engaged, my readers cannot be strangers to his general character. This, therefore, might be left to be collected from his actions, which are the best exhibitions of the great qualities of his mind. But perhaps, were I not to endeavour to afford a summary view of him in these respects, I might be thought to fail in that duty which I owe to the public on the present occasion.

It cannot, I think, be denied, that genius belonged to Captain Cook in an eminent degree. By genius I do not here understand imagination merely, or that power of culling the flowers of fancy which poetry delights in ; but an inventive mind ; a mind full of resources : and which, by its own native vigour, can suggest noble objects of pursuit, and the most effectual methods of attaining them. This faculty was possessed by our navigator in its full energy, as is evident from the uncommon sagacity and penetration which he discovered in a vast variety of critical and difficult situations.

To genius Captain Cook added application, without which nothing very valuable or permanent can be accomplished, even by the brightest capacity. For an unremitting attention to whatever related to his profession, he was distinguished in early life. In every affair that was undertaken by him, his assiduity was without interruption, and without abatement. Wherever he came, he suffered nothing, which was fit for a seaman to know or to practice, to pass unnoticed, or to escape his diligence.

The genius and application of Captain Cook were followed by a large extent of knowledge ; a knowledge which, besides a consummate acquaintance with navigation, comprehended a number of other sciences. In this respect the ardour of his mind rose above the disadvantages of a very confined education. His progress in the different branches of the mathematics, and particularly in astronomy, became so eminent, that, at length, he was able to take the lead in making the necessary observations of this kind, in the course of his voyages. He attained likewise to such a degree of proficiency in general learning, and the art of composition, as to be able to express himself with a manly clearness and propriety, and to become respectable as the narrator, as well as the performer, of great actions.

Another thing, strikingly conspicuous in Captain Cook, was the perseverance with which he pursued the noble objects to which his life was devoted. This, indeed, was a most distinguished feature in his character : in this he scarcely ever had an equal, and never a superior. Nothing could divert him from the points he aimed at ; and he persisted in the prosecution of them through difficulties and obstructions, which would have deterred minds of very considerable strength and firmness.

What enabled him to persevere in all his mighty undertakings, was the invincible fortitude of his spirit.

Of this, instances without number occur in the accounts of his expeditions ; two of which I shall take the liberty of recalling to the attention of my readers. The first is, the undaunted magnanimity with which he prosecuted his discoveries along the whole southeast coast of New Holland. Surrounded as he was with the greatest possible dangers, arising from the perpetual succession of rocks, shoals, and breakers, and having a ship that was almost shaken to pieces by repeated perils, his vigorous mind had a regard to nothing but what he thought was required of him by his duty to the public. It will not be easy to find, in the history of navigation, a parallel example of courageous exertion. The other circumstance I would refer to, is the boldness with which, in his second voyage, after he left the Cape of Good Hope, he pushed forward into unknown seas, and penetrated through innumerable mountains and islands of ice, in the search of a southern continent. It was like launching into chaos: all was obscurity, all was darkness before him; and no event can be compared with it, excepting the sailing of Magelhaens, from the straits which bear his name, into the Pacific Ocean.

The fortitude of Captain Cook, being founded upon reason, and not upon instinct, was not an impetuous valour, but accompanied with complete self-possession. He was master of himself on every trying occasion, and seemed to be the more calm and collected, the greater was the exigence of the case. In the most perilous situations, when our commander had given the proper directions concerning what was to be done while he went to rest, he could sleep, during the hours he had alloted to himself, with perfect composure and soundness. Nothing could be a surer indication of an elevated mind; of a mind that was entirely satisfied with itself, and the measures it had taken.

To all these great qualities, Captain Cook added the most amiable virtues. That it was impossible for any one to excel him in humanity, is apparent from his treatment of his men through all his voyages, and from his behaviour to the natives of the countries which were discovered by him. The health, the convenience, and, as far as it could be admitted, the enjoyment of the seamen, were the constant objects of his attention; and he was anxiously solicitous to meliorate the condition of the inhabitants of the several islands and places which he visited

With regard to their thieveries, he candidly apologized for, and overlooked, many offences which others would have sharply punished: and when he was laid under an indispensable necessity of proceeding to any acts of severity, he never exerted them, without feeling much reluctance and concern.

In the private relations of life, Captain Cook was entitled to high commendations. He was excellent as a husband and a father, and sincere and steady in his friendships : and to this it may be added, that he possessed that general sobriety and virtue of character, which will always be found to constitute the best security and ornament of every other moral qualification.

With the greatest benevolence and humanity of disposition, Captain Cook was occasionally subject to a hastiness of temper. This, which has been exaggerated by the few (and they are indeed few) who are unfavourable to his memory, is acknowledged by his friends. It is mentioned both by Captain King and Mr. Samwell, in their delineations of his character. Mr. Hayley, in one of his poems, calls him the *mild Cook;* but, perhaps, that is not the happiest epithet which could have been applied to him. Mere mildness can scarcely be considered as the most prominent and distinctive feature in the mind of a man, whose powers of understanding and of action were so strong and elevated, who had such immense difficulties to struggle with, and who must frequently have been called to the firmest exertions of authority and command.

Lastly, Captain Cook was distinguished by a property which is almost universally the concomitant of truly great men, and that is, a simplicity of manners. In conversation he was unaffected and unassuming ; rather backward in pushing discourse ; but obliging and communicative in his answers to those who addressed him for the purposes of information. It was not possible, that, in a mind constituted like his, such a paltry quality as vanity could find an existence.

In this imperfect delineation of Captain Cook's character, I have spoken of him in a manner which is fully justified by the whole course of his life and actions, and which is perfectly agreeable to the sentiments of those who were the most nearly connected with him in the habits of intimacy and friendship. The pictures which some of them have drawn of him, though they have already been presented to the public, cannot here with propriety be omitted. Captain King has expressed himself concerning him in the following terms. "The constitution of his body was robust, inured to labour, and capable of undergoing the severest hardships. His stomach bore, without difficulty, the coarsest and most ungrateful food :—Great was the indifference with which he submitted to every kind of self-denial. The qualities of his mind were of the same hardy vigorous kind with those of his body. His understanding was strong and perspicacious. His judgment, in whatever related to the services he was engaged in, quick and sure. His designs were bold and manly ; and both in the conception, and in the mode of execution, bore evident marks of a great original genius. His courage was cool and determined, and accompanied with an admirable presence of mind in the moment of danger. His temper might perhaps have been justly blamed, as subject to hastiness and passion, had not these been disarmed by a disposition the most benevolent and humane.

"Such were the outlines of Captain Cook's character ; but its most distinguishing feature was that unremitting perseverance in the pursuit of his object, which was not only superior to the opposition of dangers, and the pressure of hardships, but even exempt from the want of ordinary relaxation. During the long and tedious voyages in which he was engaged, his eagerness and activity were never in the least abated. No incidental temptation could detain him for a moment : even those intervals of recreation, which sometimes unavoidably occurred, and were looked for by us with a longing, that persons, who have experienced the fatigues of service, will readily excuse, were submitted to by him with a certain impatience, whenever they could not be employed in making a farther provision for the more effectual prosecution of his designs."

"The character of Captain Cook," says Mr. Samwell, "will be best exemplified by the services he has performed, which are universally known, and have ranked his name above that of any navigator of ancient or of modern times. Nature had endowed him with a mind vigorous and comprehensive, which in his riper years he had cultivated with care and industry. His general knowledge was extensive and various: in that of his own profession, he was unequalled. With a clear judgment, strong masculine sense, and the most determined resolution; with a genius peculiarly turned for enterprise, he pursued his object with unshaken perseverance:—vigilant and active in an eminent degree:—cool and intrepid among dangers; patient and firm under difficulties and distress; fertile in expedients; great and original in all his designs; active and resolved in carrying them into execution. These qualities rendered him the animating spirit of the expedition: in every situation, he stood unrivalled and alone; on him all eyes were turned; he was our leading-star, which, at its setting, left us involved in darkness and despair.

"His constitution was strong, his mode of living temperate. He was a modest man, and rather bashful; of an agreeable, lively conversation, sensible and intelligent. In his temper he was somewhat hasty, but of a disposition the most friendly, benevolent, and humane. His person was above six feet high, and, though a good-looking man, he was plain both in address and appearance. His head was small; his hair, which was a dark brown, he wore tied behind. His face was full of expression; his nose exceedingly well shaped; his eyes, which were small and of a brown cast, were quick and piercing; his eye-brows prominent, which gave his countenance altogether an air of austerity.

"He was beloved by his people, who looked up to him as a father, and obeyed his commands with alacrity. The confidence **we placed in him was** unremitting; our admiration of his great **talents,** unbounded; our esteem for his good qualities, affectionate and sincere.

"He was remarkably distinguished for the activity of his mind: it was that which enabled him to pay an unwearied attention to every object of the service. The strict economy he observed in the expenditure of the ship's stores, and the unremitting care he employed for the preservation of the health of his people, were the causes that enabled him to prosecute discoveries in remote parts of the globe, for such a length of time, as had been deemed impracticable by former navigators. The method he discovered for preserving the health of seamen in long voyages, will transmit his name to posterity as the friend and benefactor of mankind. the success which attended it afforded this truly great man more satisfaction than the distinguished fame that attended his discoveries.

"England has been unanimous in her tribute of applause to his virtues, and all Europe has borne testimony to his merit. There is hardly a corner of the earth, however remote and savage, that will not long remember his benevolence and humanity. The grateful Indian, in time to come, pointing to the herds grazing **his** fertile plains, will relate to his children how the first stock of them was introduced into the country; and the name of Cook will be remembered among those benign spirits, whom they worship as the source of every good, and the fountain of every blessing."

At the conclusion of the Introduction to the Voyage to the Pacific Ocean, is an eulogium on Captain Cook, drawn up by **one of** his own profession, of whom it is said, that he is not more distinguished by the elevation of rank, than by the dignity of private virtues. Though this excellent eulogium must be known to many, and perhaps to most, of my readers, they will not be displeased at having the greater part of it brought to their recollection.

Captain James Cook " possessed," say the writer, " in an eminent degree, all the qualifications requisite for his profession and great undertakings ; together with the amiable and worthy qualities of the best men.

" Cool and deliberate in judging : sagacious in determining : active in executing : steady and persevering in enterprising from vigilance and unremitting caution : unsubdued by labour, difficulties, and disappointments : fertile in expedients : never wanting presence of mind : always possessing himself, and the full use of a sound understanding.

" Mild, just, but exact in discipline : he was a father to his people, who were attached to him from affection, and obedient from confidence.

" His knowledge, his experience, his sagacity, rendered him so entirely master of his subject, that the greatest obstacles were surmounted, and the most dangerous navigations became easy, and almost safe, under his direction.

" By his benevolent and unabating attention to the welfare of his ship's company, he discovered and introduced a system for the preservation of the health of seamen in long voyages, which has proved wonderfully efficacious.

" The death of this eminent and valuable man was a loss to mankind in general ; and particularly to be deplored by every nation that respects useful accomplishments, that honours science, and loves the benevolent and amiable affections of the heart. It is still more to be deplored by this country, which may justly boast of having produced a man hitherto unequalled for nautical talents ; and that sorrow is farther aggravated by the reflection, that his country was deprived of this ornament by the enmity of a people, from whom, indeed, it might have been dreaded, but from whom it was not deserved. For, actuated always by the most attentive care and tender compassion for the savages in general, this excellent man was ever assiduously endeavouring, by kind treatment, to dissipate their fears and court their friendship; overlooking their thefts and treacheries, and frequently interposing, at the hazard of his life, to protect them from the sudden resentment of his own injured people.

"Traveller! contemplate, admire, revere, and emulate this great master in his profession; whose skill and labours have enlarged natural philosophy; have extended nautical science: and have disclosed the long-concealed and admirable arrangements of the Almighty in the formation of this globe, and, at the same time, the arrogance of mortals, in presuming to account, by their speculations, for the laws by which he was pleased to create it. It is now discovered, beyond all doubt, that the same great Being who created the universe by his *fiat*, by the same ordained our earth to keep a just poise, without a corresponding southern continent, and it does so. *He stretches out the north over the empty space, and hangeth the earth upon nothing.* Job xxvi. 7.

"If the arduous but exact researches of this extraordinary man have not discovered a new world, they have discovered seas unnavigated and unknown before. They have made us acquainted with islands, people, and productions of which we had no conception. And if he has not been so fortunate as Americus, to give his name to a continent, his pretensions to such a distinction remain unrivalled; and he will be revered while there remains a page of his own modest account of his voyages, and as long as mariners and geographers shall be instructed by his new map of the southern hemisphere, to trace the various courses and discoveries he has made.

"If public services merit public acknowledgments, if the man, who adorned and raised the fame of his country, is deserving of honours, then Captain Cook deserves to have a monument raised to his memory, by a generous and grateful nation.

'Virtutis uberrimum alimentum est honos.'

VAL. MAXIMUS, lib. ii. cap. 6."

The last character I shall here insert of Captain Cook, comes from a learned writer, who, in consequence of some disagreements which are understood to have subsisted between him and our navigator, cannot be suspected of intending to celebrate him in the language of flattery. Dr. Reinhold Forster, having given a short account of the captain's death, adds as follows: "Thus fell this truly glorious and justly admired navigator. If we consider his extreme abilities, both natural and acquired, the firmness and constancy of his mind, his truly paternal care for the crew intrusted to him, the amiable manner with which he knew how to gain the friendship of all the savage and uncultivated nations, and even his conduct towards his friends and acquaintance, we must acknowledge him to have been one of the greatest men of his age, and that reason justifies the tear which friendship pays to his memory." After such an encomium on Captain Cook, less regard may justly be paid to the deductions from it, which are added by Dr. Forster. What he hath said concerning the captain's temper, seems to have received a tincture of exaggeration, from prejudice and personal animosity; and the doctor's insinuation, that our navigator obstructed Lieutenant Pickersgill's promotion, is, I have good reason to believe, wholly groundless. There is another error which must not pass unnoticed. Dr. Forster puts in his caveat against giving the name of Cook's Straits to the straits between Asia and America, discovered by Beering. But if the Doctor had read the Voyage to the Pacific Ocean, published by authority, he would have seen, that there was no design of robbing Beering of the honour to which he was entitled.

From a survey of Captain Cook's character, it is natural to extend our reflections to the effects of the several expeditions in which he was engaged. These, indeed, must have largely appeared in the general history of his life; and they have finely been displayed by Dr. Douglas, in his admirable Introduction to the Voyage to the Pacific Ocean. Under the conduct of so able a guide, I shall subjoin a short view of the subject.

It must, however, be observed, that, with regard to the three principal consequences of our great navigator's transactions, I have nothing farther to offer. These are, his having dispelled the illusion of a *Terra Australis Incognita*; his demonstration of the impracticability of a northern passage from the Pacific to the Atlantic Ocean; and his having established a sure method of preserving the health of seamen in the longest voyages, and through every variety of latitude and climate. Concerning each of these capital objects, I have already so fully spoken, that it is not in my power to add to the impression of their importance, and of Captain Cook's merits in relation to them, which, I trust, is firmly fixed on the minds of every reader.

It is justly remarked, by Dr. Douglas, that one great advantage accruing to the world from our late surveys of the globe, is, that they have confuted fanciful theories, too likely to give birth to impracticable undertakings. The ingenious reveries of speculative philosophers, which have so long amused the learned, and raised the most sanguine expectations, are now obliged to submit, perhaps with reluctance, to the sober dictates of truth and experience. Nor will it be only by discouraging future unprofitable searches, that the late voyages will be of service to mankind, but also by lessening the dangers and distresses formerly experienced in those seas which are within the actual line of commerce and navigation. From the British discoveries, many commercial improvements may be expected to arise in our own times; but, in future ages, such improvements may be extended to a degree, of which, at present, we have no conception. In the long chain of causes and effects, no one can tell how widely and beneficially the mutual intercourse of the various inhabitants of the earth may hereafter be carried on, in consequence of the means of facilitating it, which have been explored and pointed out by Captain Cook.

The interests of science, as well as of commerce, stand highly indebted to this illustrious navigator. That a knowledge of the globe on which we live is a very desirable object, no one can call in question. This is an object which, while it is ardently pursued by the most enlightened philosophers, is sought for with avidity, even by those whose studies do not carry them beyond the lowest rudiments of learning. It need not be said what gratification Captain Cook hath provided for the world in this respect. Before the voyages of the present reign took place, nearly half the surface of the earth was hidden in obscurity and confusion. From the discoveries of our navigator, geography has assumed a new face, and become, in a great measure, a new science; having attained to such a completion, as to leave only some less important parts of the globe to be explored by future voyagers.*

Happily for the advancement of knowledge, acquisitions cannot be obtained in any one branch, without leading to acquisitions in other branches, of equal, and perhaps of superior consequence. New oceans cannot be traversed, or new countries visited, without presenting fresh objects of speculation and inquiry, and carrying the practice, as well as the theory, of philosophy to a higher degree of perfection. *Nautical astronomy*, in particular, was in its infancy, when the late voyages were first undertaken; but, during the prosecution of them, and especially in Captain Cook's last expedition, even many of the petty officers could observe the distance of the moon from the sun, or a star, the most delicate of all observations, with sufficient accuracy

* Lieutenant Roberts's admirable chart will set this matter in the strongest light.

As for the officers of superior rank, they would have felt themselves ashamed to have it thought that they did not know how to observe for and compute the time at sea; though such a thing had, a little time before, scarcely been heard of among seamen. Nay, first-rate philosophers had doubted the possibility of doing it with the exactness that could be wished. It must, however, be remembered, that a large share of praise is due to the Board of Longitude, for the proficiency of the gentlemen of the navy in taking observations at sea. In consequence of the attention of that board to this important object, liberal rewards have been given to mathematicians for perfecting the lunar tables, and facilitating calculations; and artists have been amply encouraged in the construction of instruments and watches, much more accurately and completely adapted to the purposes of navigation than formerly existed.

It is needless to mention what a quantity of additional information has been gained with respect to the rise and times of the flowing of the tides; the direction and force of currents at sea; and the cause and nature of the polarity of the needle, and the theory of its variations. Natural knowledge has been increased by experiments on the effects of gravity in different and very distant places; and from Captain Cook's having penetrated so far into the Southern Ocean, it is now ascertained, that the phenomenon, usually called the *Aurora Borealis*, is not peculiar to high northern latitudes, but belongs equally to all cold climates, whether they be north or south.

Amidst the different branches of science that have been promoted by the late expeditions, there is none, perhaps, that stands so highly indebted to them as the science of botany. At least twelve hundred new plants have been added to the known system; and large accessions of intelligence have accrued with regard to every other part of natural history. This point has already been evinced by the writings of Dr. Sparrman, of the two Forsters, father and son, and of Mr. Pennant; and this point will illustriously be manifested, when the great work of Sir Joseph Banks shall be accomplished, and given to the world.

It is not to the enlargement of natural knowledge only, that the effects arising from Captain Cook's voyages are to be confined. Another important object of study has been opened by them; and that is, the study of human nature, in situations various, interesting, and uncommon. The islands visited in the centre of the South Pacific Ocean, and the principal scenes of the operations of our discoverers, were untrodden ground. As the inhabitants, so far as could be observed, had continued, from their original settlement, unmixed with any different tribe; as they had been left entirely to their own powers for every art of life, and to their own remote traditions for every political or religious custom or institution; as they were uninformed by science, and unimproved by education, they could not but afford many subjects of speculation to an inquisitive and philosophical mind. Hence may be collected a variety of important facts with respect to the state of man: with respect to his attainments and deficiencies, his virtues and vices, his employments and diversions, his feelings, manners, and customs, in a certain period of society. Even the curiosities which have been brought from the discovered islands, and which enrich the British Museum, and the late Sir Ashton Lever's repository, may be considered as a valuable acquisition to this country; as supplying no small fund of information and entertainment.

Few inquiries are more interesting than those which relate to the migrations of the various families or tribes that have peopled the earth. It was known in general, that the Asiatic nation, called Malayans, possessed, in former times, much the greatest trade in the Indies; and that they frequented, with their merchant ships, not only all the coasts of Asia, but ventured over even to the coasts of Africa, and particularly to the great island of Madagascar. But that, from Madagascar to the Marquesas and Easter Island, that is, nearly from the east side of Africa, till we approach towards the west side of America, a space including above half the circumference of the globe, the same nation of the oriental world should have made their settlements, and founded colonies throughout almost every intermediate stage of this immense tract, in islands at amazing distances from the mother continents, and the natives of which were ignorant of each other's existence—is an historical fact, that, before Captain Cook's voyages, could be but very imperfectly known. He it is who hath discovered a vast number of new spots of land lurking in the bosom of the South Pacific Ocean, all the inhabitants of which display striking evidences of their having derived their descent from one common Asiatic original. Nor is this apparent solely from a similarity of customs and institutions, but is established by a proof which conveys irresistible conviction to the mind, and that is, the affinity of language. The collections that have been made of the words which are used in the widely-diffused islands and countries that have lately been visited, cannot fail, in the hands of such men as a Bryant and a Marsden, to throw much light on the origin of nations, and the peopling of the globe. From Mr. Marsden, in particular, who has devoted his attention, time, and study to this curious subject, the literary world may hereafter expect to be highly instructed and entertained.

There is another family of the earth, concerning which new information has been derived from the voyages of our British navigators. That the Esquimaux, who had hitherto only been found seated on the coasts of Labrador and Hudson's Bay, agreed with the Greenlanders in every circumstance of customs, manners, and language, which could demonstrate an original identity of nation, had already been ascertained. But that the same tribe now actually inhabit the islands and coasts on the west side of North America, opposite Kamtschatka, was a discovery, the completion of which was reserved for Captain Cook. From his account, it appears that these people have extended their migrations to Norton Sound, Oonalashka, and Prince William's Sound: that is, to nearly the distance of fifteen hundred leagues from their stations in Greenland, and the coast of Labrador. Nor does this curious fact rest merely on the evidence arising from similitude of manners; for it stands confirmed by a table of words, exhibiting such an affinity of language as will remove every doubt from the mind of the most scrupulous inquirer.

Other questions there are, of a very important nature, the solution of which will now be rendered more easy than hath heretofore been apprehended. From the full confirmation of the vicinity of the two continents of Asia and America, it can no longer be represented as ridiculous to believe, that the former furnished inhabitants to the latter. By the facts recently discovered, a credibility is added to the Mosaic account of the peopling of the earth. That account will, I doubt not, stand the test of the most learned and rigorous investigation. Indeed, I have long been convinced, after the closest meditation of which I am capable, that sound philosophy and genuine revelation never militate against each other. The rational friends of religion are so far from dreading the spirit of inquiry, that they wish for nothing more than a candid, calm, and impartial examination of the subject, according to all the lights which the improved reason and the enlarged science of man can afford.

One great effect of the voyages made under the conduct of Captain Cook, is their having excited a zeal for similar undertakings. Other princes and other nations are engaged in expeditions of navigation and discovery. By order of the French government, Messrs. de la Perouse and de Langle sailed from Brest, in August 1785, in the frigates Boussole and Astrolabe, on an enterprise, the express purpose of which was the improvement of geography, astronomy, natural history, and philosophy, and to collect accounts of customs and manners. For the more effectual prosecution of the design, several gentlemen were appointed to go out upon the voyage, who were known to excel in different departments of science and literature. M. Dagelet went as astronomer; M. de la Martiniere, P. Recevour, and M. de la Fresne, as naturalists; and the Chevalier de Lamanon and M. Monges, junior, as natural philosophers. The officers of the Boussole were men of the best information, and the firmest resolution: and the crew contained a number of artificers, in various kinds of mechanic employments. Marine watches, and other instruments, were provided; and M. Dagelet was particularly directed to make observations with M. Condamine's invariable pendulum, to determine the differences in gravity, and to ascertain the true proportion of the equatorial to the polar diameter of the earth. From some accounts which have already been received of these voyagers, it appears, that they have explored the coast of California; have adjusted the situation of more than fifty places, almost wholly unknown; and have visited Owyhee, and the rest of the Sandwich Islands. When the expedition shall be completed, the whole result of it will doubtless be laid before the public.*

Although Captain Cook has made such vast discoveries in the Northern Ocean, on and between the east of Asia and the west coast of America, Mr. Coxe has well shown that there is still room for a farther investigation of that part of the world. Accordingly, the object has been taken up by the Empress of Russia, who has committed the conduct of the enterprise to Captain Bil-

---

* An account of this voyage during the years 1785, 1786, 1787, 1788, has been published in France, from papers transmitted at different times by La Perouse; but nothing since the year 1788 has been received relative to the progress of the voyage, or the fate of the voyagers, who are all supposed to have perished by shipwreck.

lings, an Englishman in her majesty's service. As Captain Billings was with Captain Cook in his last voyage, he may reasonably be supposed to be properly qualified for the business he has undertaken. The design, with the execution of which he is entrusted, appears to be very extensive and important; and, if it should be crowned with success, cannot fail of making considerable additions to the knowledge of geography and navigation.

There is one event at home, which has evidently resulted from Captain Cook's discoveries, and which, therefore, must not be omitted. What I refer to, is the settlement at Botany Bay. With the general policy of this measure, the present narrative has not any concern. The plan, I doubt not, has been adopted with the best intentions, after the maturest deliberation, and perhaps with consummate wisdom. One evident advantage arising from it is, that it will effectually prevent a number of unhappy wretches from returning to their former scenes of temptation and guilt, and may open to them the means of industrious subsistence and moral reformation. If it be wise and prudently begun and conducted, who can tell what beneficial consequences may spring from it, in future ages? Immortal Rome is said to have risen from the refuse of mankind.

While we are considering the advantages the *discoverers* have derived from the late navigations, a question naturally occurs, which is, What benefits have hence accrued to the *discovered*? It would be a source of the highest pleasure to be able to answer this question to complete satisfaction. But it must be acknowledged, that the subject is not wholly free from doubts and difficulties; and these doubts and difficulties might be enlarged upon and exaggerated, by an imagination which is rather disposed to contemplate and represent the dark than the luminous aspect of human affairs. In one respect, Mr. Samwell has endeavoured to show, that the natives of the lately explored parts of the world, and especially so far as relates to the Sandwich Islands, were not injured by our people, and it was the constant solicitude and care of Captain Cook, that evil might not be communicated in any one place to which he came. If he was universally successful, the good which, in various cases, he was instrumental in producing, will be reflected upon with the more peculiar satisfaction.

There is an essential difference between the voyages that have lately been undertaken, and many which have been carried on in former times. None of my readers can be ignorant of the horrid cruelties that were exercised by the conquerors of Mexico and Peru; cruelties which can never be remembered without blushing for religion and human nature. But to undertake expeditions with a design of civilizing the world, and meliorating its condition, is a noble object. The recesses of the globe were investigated by Captain Cook, not to enlarge private dominion, but to promote general knowledge; the new tribes of the earth were visited as friends, and acquaintance with their existence was sought for, in order to bring them within the pale of the offices of humanity, and to relieve the wants of their imperfect state of society. Such were the benevolent views which our navigator was commissioned by his majesty to carry into execution; and there is reason to hope that they will not be wholly unsuccessful. From the long-continued intercourse with the natives of the Friendly, Society, and Sandwich Islands, some rays of light must have darted on their infant minds. The uncommon objects which have been presented to their observation, and excited surprise, will naturally tend to enlarge their stock of ideas, and to furnish new materials for the exercise of their reasoning faculties. It is no small addition to their comforts of life and their immediate enjoyments, that will be derived from the introduction of our useful animals and vegetables; and if the only benefit they should ever receive from the visits of the English, should be the having obtained fresh means of sustenance, that must be considered as a great acquisition.

But may not our hopes be extended to still nobler objects? The connection which has been opened with those remote inhabitants of the world, is the first step toward their improvement, and consequences may flow from it, which are far beyond our present conceptions. Perhaps our late voyages may be the means appointed by Providence, of spreading, in due time, the blessings of civilization among the numerous tribes of the South Pacific Ocean, and preparing them for holding an honourable rank among the nations of the earth. There cannot be a more laudable attempt, than that of endeavouring to rescue millions of our fellow-creatures from that state of humiliation in which they now exist. Nothing can more essentially contribute to the attainment of this great end, than a wise and rational introduction of the Christian religion; an introduction of it in its genuine simplicity; as holding out the worship of one God, inculcating the purest morality, and promising eternal life as the reward of obedience. These are views of things which are adapted to general comprehension, and calculated to produce the noblest effects.

Considering the eminent abilities displayed by Captain Cook, and the mighty actions performed by him, it is not surprising that his memory should be held in the highest estimation, both at home and abroad. Perhaps, indeed, greater honour is paid to his name abroad than at home. Foreigners, I am informed, look up to him with an admiration which is not equalled in this country. A remarkable proof of it occurs in the eulogy of our navigator by Michael Angelo Gianetti, which was read at the royal Florentine academy, on the 9th of June, 1785, and published at Florence, in the same year. Not having seen it, I am deprived of the power of doing justice to its merit. If I am not mistaken in my recollection, one of the French literary academies has proposed a prize for the best eulogium on Captain Cook; and there can be no doubt but that several candidates will appear upon the occasion, and exert the whole force of their eloquence on so interesting a subject.

To the applauses of our navigator, which have already been inserted, I cannot avoid adding some poetical testimonies concerning him. The first I shall produce is from a foreign poet, M. l'Abbé Lisle. This gentleman has concluded his "Les Jardins" with an encomium on Captain Cook, of which the following lines are a translation.

"Give, give me flowers: with garlands of renown
Those glorious exiles' brows my hands shall crown,
Who nobly sought on distant coasts to find,
Or thither bore those arts that bless mankind:
Thee chief, brave Cook, o'er whom, to nature dear,
With Britain, Gallia drops a pitying tear.
To foreign climes and rude, where naught before
Announced our vessels but their cannon's roar,
Far other gifts thy better mind decreed
The sheep, the heifer, and the stately steed;
The plough and all thy country's arts; the crimes
Atoning thus of earlier savage times.
With peace each land thy bark was wont to hail.
And tears and blessings filled thy parting sail.
Receive a stranger's praise; nor Britain, thou
Forbid these wreaths to grace thy Hero's brow,
Nor scorn the tribute of a foreign song,
For Virtue's sons to every land belong:
And shall the Gallic Muse disdain to pay
The meed of worth, when Lewis leads the way?
But what avail'd, that twice thou dar'dst to try
The frost-bound sea, and twice the burning sky,
That by winds, waves, and every realm rever'd,
Safe, only safe, thy sacred vessel steer'd;
That war for thee forgot its dire commands?
The world's great friend, ah! bleeds by savage hands."

There have not been wanting elegant writers of our own country, who have embraced with pleasure the opportunities that have offered of paying a tribute of praise to Captain Cook. The ingenious and amiable Miss Hannah Moore has lately seized an occasion of celebrating the humane intentions of the captain's discoveries.

> "Had those advent'rous spirits who explore
> Through ocean's trackless wastes, the far-sought shore,
> Whether of wealth insatiate, or of power,
> **Conquerors** who waste, or ruffians who devour:
> **Had these** possess'd, O Cook! thy gentle mind,
> Thy love of arts, thy love of human-kind;
> Had these pursu'd thy mild and lib'ral plan,
> DISCOVERERS had not been a curse to man!
> Then, bless'd Philanthropy! thy social hands
> Had link'd dissever'd worlds in brothers' bands;
> Careless, if colour or if clime divide;
> Then lov'd, and loving man had liv'd and died."

Soon after the account arrived in England of Captain Cook's **decease, two** poems were published in celebration of his memory; **one of** which was an Ode, by a Mr. Fitzgerald, of Gray's Inn. **But** the first, both in order of time and of merit, was an Elegy, **by Miss** Seward, whose poetical talents have been displayed in many beautiful instances to the public. This lady, in **the beginning of** her poem, has admirably represented the principle **of humanity** by which the captain was actuated in his undertakings.

> "Ye, who erewhile for Cook's illustrious brow
> Pluck'd the green laurel, and the oaken bough,
> Hung the gay garlands on the trophied oars,
> And pour'd his fame along a thousand shores,
> Strike the slow death-bell!—weave the sacred **verse,**
> And strew the cypress o'er his honour'd hearse;
> In sad procession wander round the shrine,
> And weep him mortal, whom ye sung divine!

"Say first, what Power inspired his dauntless breast
With scorn of danger and inglorious rest,
To quit imperial London's gorgeous plains;
Where, rob'd in thousand tints, bright Pleasure reigns,
What Pow'r inspir'd his dauntless breast to brave
The scorch'd Equator, and th' Antarctic wave?
Climes, where fierce suns in cloudless ardours shine,
And pour the dazzling deluge round the Line;
The realms of frost where icy mountains rise,
'Mid the pale summer of the polar skies?—
IT WAS HUMANITY!—on coasts unknown,
The shiv'ring natives of the frozen zone,
And the swart Indian as he faintly strays
' Where Cancer reddens in the solar blaze,'
She bade him seek:—on each inclement shore
Plant the rich seeds of her exhaustless store;
Unite the savage hearts, and hostile hands
In the firm compact of her gentle bands;
Strew her soft comforts o'er the barren plain,
Sing her sweet lays, and consecrate her fame.

"IT WAS HUMANITY!—O Nymph divine!
I see thy light step print the burning Line!
There thy bright eye the dubious pilot guides,
The faint oar struggling with the scalding tides—
On as thou lead'st the bold, the glorious prow,
Mild, and more mild, the sloping sunbeams glow;
Now weak and pale the lessen'd lustres play,
As round th' horizon rolls the timid day;
Barb'd with the sleeted snow, the driving hail,
Rush the fierce arrows of the polar gale;
And through the dim, unvaried, ling'ring hours,
Wide o'er the waves incumbent horror low'rs."

Captain Cook's endeavours to serve the inhabitants of New Zealand, by the vegetables and animals he left among them, are thus described:

"To these the hero leads his living store,
And pours new wonders on th' uncultur'd shore,

The silky fleece, fair fruit, and golden grain;
And future herds and harvests bless the plain.
O'er the green soil his kids exulting play,
And sounds his clarion loud the bird of day;
The downy goose her ruffled bosom laves;
Trims her white wing and wantons in the waves;
Stern moves the bull along th' affrighted shores,
And countless nations tremble as he roars."

I shall only add the pathetic and animated conclusion of this fine poem:

"But ah!—aloft on Albion's rocky steep,
That frowns incumbent o'er the boiling deep,
Solicitous and sad a softer form
Eyes the lone flood, and deprecates the storm—
Ill-fated matron!—for, alas! in vain
Thy eager glances wander o'er the main!—
'Tis the vexed billows, that insurgent rave,
Their white foam silvers yonder distant wave.
'Tis not his sails!—thy husband comes no more!
His bones now whiten an accursed shore!—
Retire,—for hark! the sea-gull shrieking soars.
The lurid atmosphere portentous low'rs;
Night's sullen spirit groans in ev'ry gale,
And o'er the waters draws the darkling veil,
Sighs in thy hair, and chills thy throbbing breast—
Go, wretched mourner!—weep thy griefs to rest!

"Yet, though through life is lost each fond delight,
Though set thy earthly sun in dreary night,
Oh! raise thy thoughts to yonder starry plain,
And own thy sorrow selfish, weak and vain;
Since while Britannia, to his virtues just,
Twines the bright wreath, and rears the immortal bust
While on each wind of heav'n his fame shall rise,
In endless incense to the smiling skies;
The ATTENDANT POWER, that bade his sails expand
And waft her blessings to each barren land,

> Now raptur'd bears him to th' immortal plains,
> Where Mercy hails him with congenial strains;
> Where soars, on Joy's white plume, his spirit free,
> And angels choir him, while he waits for THEE."

Captain **Cook's** discoveries, among other effects, have opened **new** scenes for a poetical fancy to range in, and presented new **images to** the selection of genius and taste. The Morais, in particular, of the inhabitants of the South Sea Islands, afford a fine subject for the exercise of a plaintive Muse. Such a Muse hath seized upon the subject; and at the same time, **has** added another wreath to the memory of our navigator. I refer to a lady who hath already, in many passages of her "Peru," in her "Ode on the Peace," and above all, in her "Irregular Fragment," amply proved to the world, that she possesses not only the talent of elegant and harmonious versification, but the spirit of true poetry. It is somewhat remarkable that female poets have hitherto been the chief celebrators of Captain Cook in this country. Perhaps a subject which would furnish materials for as rich a production as Camoens' Lusiad, and which would adorn the pen of a Hayley or a Cooper, may hereafter call forth the genius of some poet of the stronger sex.

The Royal Society of London could not lose such a member of their body as Captain Cook, without being anxious to honour his name and memory by a particular mark of respect. Accordingly, it was resolved to do this by a medal; and a voluntary subscription **was** opened for the purpose. To such of the fellows **of** the society as subscribed twenty guineas, a gold medal was appropriated; silver medals were assigned to those who contributed a smaller sum; and to each of the other members one in bronze was given. The subscribers of twenty guineas were, Sir Joseph Banks, president; the Prince of Anspach, the **Duke of** Montague, Lord Mulgrave, and Mr. Cavendish, Mr. **Peachy, Mr.** Perrin, Mr. Poli, and Mr. Shuttleworth. Many designs, as might be expected, were proposed on the occasion. The medal which was actually struck, contains on one side the head of Captain Cook in profile, and round it JAC. COOK OCEANI INVESTIGATOR ACERRIMUS; and on the exergue, REG. SOC. LOND. SOCIO SUO. On the reverse is a representation of Britannia, holding a globe. Round her is inscribed, NIL INTENTATUM NOSTRI LIQUERE; and on the exergue, AUSPICIIS GEORGII III.

Of the gold medals which were struck on this occasion, one was presented to His Majesty, another to the Queen, and a third to the Prince of Wales. Two were sent abroad: the first to the French king, on account of the protection he had granted to the ships under the command of Captain Cook; and a second to the Empress of Russia, in whose dominions the same ships had been received and treated with every degree of friendship and kindness. Both these presents were highly acceptable to the great personages to whom they were transmitted. The French king expressed his satisfaction in a very handsome letter to the Royal Society, signed by himself, and undersigned by the Marquis de Vergennes; and the Empress of Russia commissioned Count Osterman to signify to Mr. Fitzherbert the sense she entertained of the value of the present, and that she had caused it to be forthwith deposited in the Museum of the Imperial Academy of Sciences. As a further testimony of the pleasure she derived from it, the Empress presented to the Royal Society a large and beautiful gold medal, containing on one side the effigies of herself, and on the reverse a representation of the statue of Peter the Great.

After the general assignment of the medals, (which took place in the spring of the year 1784), there being a surplus of money still remaining, the president and council resolved, that an additional number should be struck off in gold, to be disposed of as presents to Mrs. Cook, the Earl of Sandwich, Dr. Benjamin Franklin, Dr. Cooke, provost of King's College, Cambridge, and Mr. Planta. About the same time, it was agreed that Mr. Aubert should be allowed to have a gold medal of Captain Cook, on his paying for the gold, and the expense of striking it; in consideration of his intention to present it to the King of Poland.

During the two visits of the Resolution and Discovery at Kamtschatka, it was from Colonel Behm, the commandant of that province, that the ships, and the officers and men belonging to them, had received every kind of assistance which it was in his power to bestow. His liberal and hospitable behaviour to the English navigators, is related at large in Captain King's Voyage. Such was the sense entertained of it by the Lords of the Admiralty, that they determined to make a present to the colonel of a magnificent piece of plate, with an inscription expressive of his humane and generous disposition and conduct. The elegant pen of Dr. Cooke was employed in drawing up the inscription; which, after it had been subjected to the opinion and correction of some gentlemen of the first eminence in classical taste, was as follows:

" VIRO EGREGIO MAGNO DE BEHM; qui Imperatricis Augustissimæ Catherinæ auspiciis, summaque animi benignitate, sæva, quibus præerat, Kamtschatkæ littora, navibus nautisque Britannicis, hospita præbut: eosque in terminis, si qui essent Imperio Russico, frustra, explorandis, mala multa perpessos, iterata vice excepit, refecit, recreavit, et commeatu omni cumulate auctos dimisit; REI NAVALIS BRITANNICÆ SEPTEMVIRI in aliquam benevolentiæ tam insignis memoriam, amicissimo, gratissimoque animo, suo, patriæque nomine, D. D. D. M.DCC.LXXXI."

Sir Hugh Palliser, who through life manifested an invariable regard and friendship for Captain Cook, has displayed a signal instance, since the captain's decease, of the affection and esteem in which he holds his memory. At his estate in Buckinghamshire, Sir Hugh hath constructed a small building, on which he has erected a pillar, containing the fine character of our great navigator that is given at the end of the Introduction of the last Voyage, and the principal part of which has been inserted in the present work. This character was drawn up by a most respectable gentleman, who has long been at the head of the naval profession, the honourable admiral Forbes, admiral of the fleet, and general of marines; to whom Captain Cook was only known by his eminent merit and his extraordinary actions.

Amidst the numerous testimonials of regard that have been paid to Captain Cook's merits and memory, the important object of providing for his family hath not been forgotten. Soon after the intelligence arrived of his unfortunate decease, this matter was taken up by the Lords of the Admiralty, with a zeal and an effect, which the following authentic document will fully display.

"(L. S.) "At the Court of St. James, the 2d of February, 1780.

Present: "The KING'S Most Excellent Majesty in Council.

"Whereas there was this day read, at the Board a memorial from the Right Honourable the Lords Commissioners of the Admiralty, dated the 27th of last month, in the words following: viz.

"'Having received an authentic account of the death of that great navigator Captain James Cook, who has had the honour of being employed by Your Majesty, in three different voyages, for the discovery of unknown countries, in the most distant parts of the globe; we think it our duty humbly to represent to your Majesty, that this meritorious officer, after having received from Your Majesty's gracious benevolence, as a reward for his public services in two successive circumnavigations, a comfortable and honourable retreat, where he might have lived many years to benefit his family, he voluntarily relinquished that ease and emolument to undertake another of these voyages of discovery, in which the life of a commander, who does his duty, must always be particularly exposed, and in which, in the execution of that duty, he fell, leaving his family, whom his public spirit had led him to abandon, as a legacy to his country. We do, therefore, humbly propose, that Your Majesty will be graciously pleased to order a pension of two hundred pounds a-year to be settled on the widow, and twenty-five pounds a-year upon each of the three sons of the said Captain James Cook, and that the same be placed on the ordinary estimate of the navy.'

" His Majesty, taking the said memorial into his royal consideration, was pleased with the advice of His Privy Council, to order, as it is hereby ordered, that a pension of two hundred pounds a-year be settled on the widow, and twenty-five pounds a-year upon each of the three sons of the said Captain James Cook, and the same be placed on **the** ordinary **estimate of** His Majesty's navy; and the Lords Commissioners of the Admiralty are to give the necessary directions herein accordingly.

"W. FAWKNER."

The preceding memorial to the king was signed by the Earl of **Sandwich, Mr. Buller,** the Earl of Lisburne, Mr. Penton, Lord Mulgrave, and Mr. Mann; and the several officers of the board of admiralty seconded the ardour of their superiors, by the speed and generosity with which his majesty's royal grant to Captain Cook's widow and children passed through the usual forms.

Another occasion was afterwards seized of conferring a substantial benefit on the Captain's family. The charts and plates, belonging to the Voyage to the Pacific Ocean, were provided at the expense of government; the consequence of which was, that a large profit accrued from the sale of the publication. Of this profit, half was consigned in trust, to Sir Hugh Palliser and Mr. Stephens, to be applied to the use of Mrs. Cook, during her natural life, and afterwards to be divided between her children.

Honour, as well as emolument, hath graciously been conferred by his majesty upon the descendants of Captain Cook. On the 3d of September, 1785, a coat of arms was granted to the family, of which a description will be given below.*

Our navigator had six children; James, Nathaniel, Elizabeth, Joseph, George, and Hugh. Of these, Joseph and George died soon after their birth, and Elizabeth in the fifth year of her age. James, the eldest son, who was born at St. Paul's, Shadwell, on the 13th of October, 1763, is now a lieutenant in his majesty's navy. In a letter, written by Admiral Sir Richard Hughes, in 1785, from Grenada, to Mrs. Cook, he is spoken of in terms of high approbation. Nathaniel, who was born on the 14th of December, 1764, at Mile-End, Old Town, was brought up likewise in the naval service, and was unfortunately lost on board his majesty's ship Thunderer, Commodore Walsingham, in the hurricane which happened at Jamaica, on the 3d of October, 1780. He is said to have been a most promising youth. Hugh, the youngest, was born on the 22d of May, 1776; and was so called after the name of his father's great friend, Sir Hugh Palliser.

It hath often been mentioned, in terms of no small regret, that a monument hath not yet been erected to the memory of Captain Cook, in Westminister Abbey. The wish and the hope of such

* Azure, between the two polar stars Or, a sphere on the plane of the meridian, north pole elevated, circles of latitude for every ten degrees, and of longitude for every fifteen, showing the Pacific Ocean between sixty and two hundred and forty west, bounded on one side by America, on the other side by Asia and New Holland, in memory of the discoveries made by him in that ocean, so very far beyond all former navigators. His track therein is marked with red lines. And for crest, on a wreath of the colours, is an arm imbowed, vested in the uniform of a captain of the royal navy. In the hand is the union jack, on a staff Proper. The arm is encircled by a wreath of palm and laurel.

a monument are hinted at in the close of Dr. Douglas's Introduction to the government edition of the last voyage; and the same sentiment is expressed by the author of the Eulogium at the end of that Introduction. Sir Hugh Palliser has also spoken to the like purpose, in a communication I received from him. It would certainly redound to the honour of the nation, to order a magnificent memorial of the abilities and service, of our illustrious navigator; on which account, a tribute of that kind may be regarded as a desirable thing. But a monument in Westminister Abbey would be of little consequence to the reputation of Captain Cook. His fame stands upon a wider base, and will survive the comparatively perishing materials of brass, or stone, or marble. The name of Cook will be held in honour, and recited with applause, so long as the records of human events shall continue in the earth; nor is it possible to say, what may be the influence and rewards, which, in other worlds, shall be found to attend upon eminent examples of wisdom and of virtue.

THE END.

Derby & Jackson's French Classics.

THE STANDARD FRENCH CLASSICS.
NEW AMERICAN EDITIONS.
(*Uniform with* DERBY & JACKSON'S *Standard British Classics.*)
EDITED BY O. W. WIGHT, A.M.
TRANSLATOR OF M. COUSIN'S PHILOSOPHY, AND EDITOR OF SIR WILLIAM HAMILTON'S PHILOSOPHICAL WORKS.

THERE having long been felt among book-buyers and scholars generally, the need of library editions—convenient in size and reasonable in price—of the greatest and best FRENCH AUTHORS, Derby & Jackson have undertaken to supply this desideratum, by the publication, in uniform style of print, paper and binding, translations of the works of those celebrated French Writers, which have become classic in the History of Literature. Fifteen volumes are now ready, as follows:

MONTAIGNE'S COMPLETE WORKS.
In 4 *vols.,* 12*mo., Cloth,* $5; *Sheep, library style,* $6; *Half calf, gilt or antique,* $9.

FENELON'S ADVENTURES OF TELEMACHUS.
12*mo., Cloth,* $1 25; *Sheep,* $1 50; *Half calf, gilt or antique,* $2 25.

PASCAL'S PROVINCIAL LETTERS.
12*mo., Cloth,* $1 25; *Sheep,* $1 50; *Half calf, gilt or antique,* $2 25.

VOLTAIRE'S CHARLES TWELFTH.
12*mo., Cloth,* $1 25; *Sheep,* $1 50; *Half calf, gilt or antique,* $2 25.

MADAME DE STAËL'S GERMANY.
In 2 *vols., Cloth,* $2 50; *Sheep,* 3 00; *Half calf, gilt or antique,* $4 50.

VOLTAIRE'S LA HENRIADE AND OTHER POEMS.
12*mo., Cloth,* $1 25; *Sheep,* $1 50; *Half calf gilt or* antique, $2 25.

PASCAL'S THOUGHTS.
12*mo., Cloth,* $1 25; *Sheep,* $1 50; *Half calf, gilt or antique,* $2 25.

CHATEAUBRIAND'S MARTYRS.
12*mo., Cloth,* $1 25; *Sheep,* $1 50; *Half calf, gilt or antique,* $2 25.

LA FONTAINE'S FABLES.
Two vols., 12*mo., Cloth,* $2 50; *Sheep,* $3 00; *Half calf, gilt, or antique,* $4 50.

MADAME DE STAËL'S CORINNE.
12*mo., Cloth,* $1 25; *Sheep,* $1 50; *Half calf, gilt, or antique,* $2 25.

THE STANDARD FRENCH CLASSICAL LIBRARY.
Embracing the **preceding** 15 volumes, in a neat case, cloth, $18 75
    Same—Sheep, library **style**, ... 22 50
    Same—Half calf, gilt, ... 33 75
    Same—half calf, antique, ... 33 75

Derby & Jackson's Publications.

THE
STANDARD ANCIENT CLASSICS.

⁎ The following Historical Works are printed in uniform octavo volumes, on fine paper, good type, and bound in a substantial manner. In ordering any of these works, to insure "the genuine edition," it will be well to designate the *octavo* edition.

The Hon. Daniel Webster, in his "Discourses before the New York Historical Society," speaking of the authors of these histories, says:

"Our great teachers and examples in the historical art are, doubtless, the eminent historians of the Greek and Roman ages. In their several ways, they are the masters to whom all succeeding times have looked for instruction and improvement. They are the models which have stood the test of time, and, like the glorious creations in marble of Grecian genius, have been always admired and never surpassed."

MURPHY'S TACITUS. New Edition, with Author's last Corrections. Portrait. 8vo.

Price in Cloth, $2 00; *Sheep, library style,* $2 50; *Half calf, antique,* $3 50.

BELOE'S HERODOTUS, with his Life by Schmitz. 8vo.

Price in Cloth, $2 00; *Sheep, library style,* $2 50; *Half calf, antique,* $3 50.

COOPER'S XENOPHON, the whole Works in one volume. 8vo.

Price in Cloth, $2 00; *Sheep, library style,* $2 50; *Half calf, antique,* $3 50.

SMITH'S THUCYDIDES. 8vo.

Price in Cloth, $2 00; *Sheep, library style,* $2 50; *Half calf, antique,* $3 50.

BAKER'S LIVY. 2 vols., 8vo.

Price in Cloth, $4 00; *Sheep, library style,* $5 00; *Half calf, antique,* $7 00.

DUNCAN'S CÆSAR AND ROSE'S SALLUST. 2 vols. in one.

Price in Cloth, $2 00; *Sheep, library style;* $2 50; *Half calf, antique,* $3 50.

⁎ The above will be sent by mail, post-paid, on receipt of price

W. H. Tinson, Printer and Stereotyper, 43 & 45 Centre St., N. Y.

Derby & Jackson's Publications.

THE
WORKS OF HENRY FIELDING,

WITH A MEMOIR OF HIS LIFE AND WRITINGS,

BY THOMAS ROSCOE.

These volumes contain "Tom Jones," "Joseph Andrews," "Amelia," etc. First complete American Edition. With Portrait on Steel, 4 volumes, 12mo.

Price in Cloth,	. . . .	$5 00
"	Sheep, library style, ...	6 00
"	Half Calf, extra, ...	9 00
"	Half Calf, Antique, ...	9 00

"Of all the works of imagination to which English genius has given origin, the novels of the celebrated Henry Fielding are, perhaps, the most decidedly and exclusively her own; he was the first of the British novelists, and his power of strong and natural humor is unapproached, as yet, even by his successful followers."—*Sir Walter Scott.*

"When we read Fielding's novels, we feel like coming into the fresh air and the common ways of this bright and breathing world. We travel on the highroad of humanity, yet meet in it pleasanter companions and catch more delicious snatches of refreshment, than we can hope elsewhere to enjoy."—*Sergeant Talfourd.*

"Real life and every-day scenes he depicted with a truth and freshness, a buoyancy and vigor, and such an exuberance of practical knowledge, easy satire and lively fancy, that in his own department he stands unrivalled. The perfect skill with which he combined and wrought up his comic powers, seasoning the whole with wit and wisdom, the ripened fruit of all genius and long experience, this great English author is still unapproached."—*Cyclo. English Literature.*

"In 'TOM JONES,' the curiosity of the reader is always kept awake, and, instead of flagging, grows more and more impatient as the story advances, till at last it becomes downright anxiety."—*Dr. Beattie.*

*** The above will be sent by mail, post-paid, on receipt of price.

W. H. TINSON, Printer and Stereotyper, 43 & 45 Centre St., N. Y.

Derby & Jackson's Publications.

THE
WORKS OF LAURENCE STERNE,

Comprising "Tristram Shandy," "Sentimental Journey," "Sermons and Letters." First complete American Edition, with a Life of the Author and Portrait on Steel. 2 vols., 12mo.

Price in Cloth,		$2 50
"	Sheep, library style,	3 00
"	Half Calf, extra,	4 50
"	Half Calf, antique,	4 50

"The writings of Sterne form the best course of morality that ever was written."—*Thomas Jefferson.*

"Inferior to none in conception of rich eccentric comic character, was the witty, pathetic, and sentimental author of 'Tristram Shandy.'"

"Through his whole works shine his little family band of friends and relatives, that immutable group of originals and humorists, which stand out from the canvas with the force and distinctness of reality."—*Cyclo. of Eng. Literature.*

"As to 'Tristram Shandy,' with all its oddities, regarded simply as a work of humor and sentiment, there is no one living who can produce its counterpart, and with the exception of the classic fiction of Cervantes, it stands unparalleled in its peculiar vein."—*Chambers.*

"The author of 'Tristram Shandy' and 'The Sentimental Journey' is immortal. So long as a living language is extant, Sterne will be known as a rare humorist (like all humorists, capable of the deepest pathos), a man of sentiment, a religious man, and a lover. His works are, therefore, a curious collection, including his letters, amatory, condolatory, and business, with some fifty sermons on various topics. Be the man what he might be, his works are among the finest in English literature."—*Newark Advertiser.*

*** The above will be sent by mail, post-paid, on receipt of price.

W. H. Tinson, Printer and Stereotyper, 43 & 45 Centre St., N. Y.

Derby & Jackson's Publications.

THE
WORKS OF SAMUEL JOHNSON,

WITH THE NEW BIOGRAPHY BY LORD MACAULAY.

2 vols. now ready, containing "*The Lives of the Poets,*" etc. 12mo.

Price in Cloth,	$2 50
" Sheep, library style,	3 00
" Half Calf, extra,	4 50
" Half Calf antique,	4 50

"No human being who has been more than seventy years in the grave is so well known to us. * * * * Our conviction is that he was both a great and good man."—*Macaulay.*

"Dr. Johnson's style resembles the rumbling of mimic thunder at one of our theatres, and the light he throws upon a subject is like the dazzling effect of phosphorus, or an *ignis fatuus* of words. * * * What most distinguishes Dr. Johnson from other writers, is the pomp and uniformity of his style."—*William Hazlitt.*

"In massive force of understanding, multifarious knowledge, sagacity, and moral intrepidity, no writer of the 18th century surpassed Dr. Johnson. The 'Lives of the Poets' have a freedom of style, a vigor of thought, and happiness of illustration, rarely attained even by their author."—*Cyclopædia of English Literature.*

"The great characteristic of Dr. Johnson, was uncommon vigor and logical precision of intellect. His reasoning was sound, dexterous and acute; his thoughts striking and original, and his imagination vivid."—*Cleveland.*

"Of all the men distinguished in this or any other age, Dr. Johnson has left upon posterity the strongest and most vivid impression, so far as person, manners, disposition, and conversation are concerned, and when he died, virtue was deprived of a steady supporter, society of a brilliant ornament, and literature of a successful cultivator."—*Sir Walter Scott.*

*** The above will be sent by mail, post-paid, on receipt of price.

W. H. Tinson, Printer and Stereotyper, 43 & 45 Centre St., N. Y.

𝔇erby & 𝔍ackson's 𝔓ublications.

THE
WORKS OF JOSEPH ADDISON,

Including the whole Contents of Bishop Hurd's Edition, with Letters and other Pieces not found in any previous collection, and Macaulay's Essays on his Life and Works. Edited, with Critical and Explanatory Notes, by GEORGE WASHINGTON GREENE. With Portrait and Plates. Complete in 6 vols., 12mo.

Price in Cloth,	. . . .	$7 50
"	Sheep, library style, ...	9 00
"	Half Calf, extra, ...	13 50
"	**Half Calf, Antique,**	13 50

"The uniform tendency of all his writings is his best and highest eulogium. No man can dissemble on paper through years of literary exertion, or on topics calculated to disclose the bias of his taste and feelings, and the qualities of his heart and temper. The display of these by Addison is so fascinating and unaffected, that the impression made by his writings, as has been finely remarked, is 'like being recalled to a sense of something like that original purity from which man has been long estranged.'"—*Cyclopædia of English Literature.*

"It is praise enough to say of a writer, that in a high department of literature, in which many eminent writers have distinguished themselves, he has no equal, and this may with strict justice be said of Addison. We own that the humor of Addison is, in our opinion, of a more delicious flavor than the humor of either Swift or Voltaire. This much, at least, is certain, that both Swift and Voltaire have been successfully mimicked, and that no man has yet been able to mimic Addison. * * * * *

"We have not the least doubt, that if Addison had written a novel on an extensive plan, it would have been superior to any that we possess. As it is, he is entitled to be considered not only as the greatest of English essayists, but as the forerunner of the great English novelists."—*Macaulay.*

₊ The above will be sent by mail, post-paid, on receipt of price.

Derby & Jackson's Publications.

THE
WORKS OF TOBIAS SMOLLETT,

WITH A MEMOIR OF HIS LIFE AND WORKS,

BY THOMAS ROSCOE.

These volumes contain "Roderick Random," "Humphrey Clinker," "Peregrine Pickle," "Count Fathom," etc. First complete American Edition, uniform with Fielding's Works. With a Portrait on Steel. 6 vols., 12mo.

Price in Cloth,	. . . .	$7 50
"	Sheep, library style, ...	9 00
"	Half Calf, extra, ...	13 50
"	Half Calf, antique, ...	13 50

"Of the select few who have consigned fame to posterity by a bold and lively exhibition of national manners, there is, perhaps, no one who enjoys a reputation, or who delineates with traits of broader and more genuine humor, professional peculiarities, habits, and distinctive foibles of different classes, than the author of 'Roderick Random.' It may be said that he fills up a space in prose fiction which Fielding left unoccupied."—*Roscoe's Memoir.*

"The charm of Smollett's Works consists in their broad humor and comic incidents, which, even when most farcical, seldom appear improbable, and are never tiresome. Speaking of 'Peregrine Pickle,' where shall we find a more attractive gallery of portraits, or a series of more laughable incidents?"—*Cyclo. of Eng. Literature.*

"Fielding has no passages which approach in sublimity to the robber scene in 'Count Fathom,' or to the terrible description of a sea engagement, in which 'Roderick Random' sits chained and exposed upon the poop without the power of motion or exertion, during the carnage of a tremendous engagement. Upon many other occasions, Smollett's descriptions ascend to the sublime, and, in general, there is an air of romance in his writings which raises his narratives above the level and easy course of ordinary life."—*Sir Walter Scott.*

*** The above will be sent by mail, post-paid, on receipt of price.

W. H. Tinson, Printer and Stereotyper, 43 & 45 Centre St., N. Y.

Derby & Jackson's Publications.

THE
WORKS OF CHARLES LAMB,

Comprising his Letters, Poems, Essays of Elia, Essays upon Shakspeare, Hogarth, etc., and a Sketch of his life, with the final Memorials. By T. NOON TALFOURD. With a Portrait. 5 vols., 12mo.

Price in Cloth,	$6 25
" Sheep, library style,	7 50
" Half Calf, extra,	11 25
" Half Calf, antique,	11 25

"His curious reading and research, the shrewd observation, fancies, and conceptions of his whole life, were poured into these monthly essays (Elia) with many scenes drawn from his past career—its mirthful and mournful experiences. In some of the essays, topics of humble and domestic life are set off with lively illustrations, fine satire, or graceful description; others are devoted to criticism, and remarks are thrown out at once original and profound. Perhaps nothing so suggestive or striking in this department of literature had appeared since the days of Steele and Addison."—*Encyclopædia Britannica.*

"All these essays (Elia) are carefully elaborated, yet never were works written in a higher defiance to the conventional pomp of style. A sly hit, a happy pun, a humorous combination lets the lights into the intricacies of the subject, and supplies the place of ponderous sentences. Seeking his material for the most part in the common paths of life—often in the humblest—he gives an importance to everything, and sheds a grace over all."—*Sergeant Talfourd.*

"As an essayist, he is entitled to a place beside Rabelais, Montaigne, Sir Thomas Browne, Steele and Addison. * * * * He has refined wit, exquisite humor, a genuine and cordial vein of pleasantry, and heart-touching pathos."—*Cleveland's English Literature.*

*** The above will be sent by mail, post-paid, on receipt of price.

www.ingramcontent.com/pod-product-compliance
Lightning Source LLC
Chambersburg PA
CBHW020533300426
44111CB00008B/649